SUCCESSFUL
SEA TROUT
ANGLING

SUCCESSFUL
SEA TROUT
ANGLING

THE PRACTICAL GUIDE

Graeme Harris and Moc Morgan

COCH-Y-BONDDU BOOKS

To Meirion & Hywel
and to Jane, Fiona & Fraser

With thanks for allowing us
to spend so many days and nights away from home
in pursuit of the sea trout

Series editor: Jonathan Grimwood
First published in the UK 1989 by
Blandford Press,
An imprint of Cassell
Wellington House, 125 Strand
LONDON, WC2R OBB

Copyright ©

Graeme Harris and
Moc Morgan 1989

This 1996 edition
Published & distributed by
COCH-Y-BONDDU BOOKS
MACHYNLLETH, POWYS, SY20 8DJ
TEL: 01654 702837
FAX: 01654 702857

ISBN 0 9528510 1 6

Printed and bound by Creative Print & Design (Wales) Ebbw Vale

CONTENTS

ACKNOWLEDGEMENTS

The authors and the publisher would like to thank the following friends, colleagues and acquaintances who have all assisted in various ways to make this book that much better than it would otherwise have been:

For technical support: We are grateful to Alan Bramley of Patridge Hooks Ltd, Phillip Parkinson of Fly Fishing Technology Ltd, and Ann Parkinson of Sportfish Ltd. We also acknowledge the prodigious efforts by Paul Morgan of Coch-y-Bonddu Books, Penegoes, Machynlleth, Powys, in obtaining the antiquarian and out-of-print publications required for our literature search.

For scientific assistance: Our thanks are due to Dr Andrew Walker (Department of Agriculture & Fisheries for Scotland) for help in locating key reference papers; Bob Williamson (Chief Inspector of Salmon Fisheries for Scotland) for assistance in obtaining Scottish catch statistics; Dr Ken Wheelan (Central Fisheries Board), Dr Gersham Kennedy (Department of Agriculture for Northern Ireland) and Gerry Crawford (Foyle Fisheries Commission) for their invaluable guidance in obtaining – and interpreting – Irish catch statistics; Dr Andrew Ferguson (Queen's University, Belfast) for recent research papers on the taxonomy and systematics of trout; Dr Derek Mills (University of Edinburgh) for pointing us in the right direction on several occasions; and to the Atlantic Salmon Trust Ltd and Welsh Water for their support in the organisation of the first Scientific Workshop on sea trout.

For photographs: While much of the material is our own, we have used certain photographs kindly supplied by others to fill several important gaps. In this respect we are particularly grateful to the following: Dr W.B. Currie, Peter O'Reilly, Chris Mills, John Wilshaw, Dr Derek Mills, Stuart Coy and Dr Andrew Ferguson.

The excellent colour plates used on the front and rear covers were taken by Peter Gathercole – whose pre-eminence as an angling photographer is fully justified.

For general support: Our special thanks are due to Liz and David Gardner who skilfully rendered our pencilled scratchings into comprehensible drawings and to Sue Price and Sue Stokes who typed the manuscript.

We are especially grateful to Sandy Leventon who, as the very busy Editor of the highly regarded and widely read magazine *Trout and Salmon*,

has somehow found time to honour us with the Foreword to this book.
For inspiration, realisation and encouragement: We acknowledge a debt
of gratitude to all those authors who have taken time off from their fishing
to share with us all the benefits of their hard-won experience and, equally,
to those fishery owners and angling associations who provide public access
to our fishing at a reasonable cost. We would also thank those many anglers
who have freely imparted bank-side knowledge on the secrets of their
success and, in so doing, provided much of the inspiration for this book.

The authors fully acknowledge the support, understanding and forbearance
of Jonathan Grimwood, their publisher, and all the staff at Blandford Press
who have helped in our undertaking.

To all the above: Diolch yn Fawr – Thank You.

Swyn Teifi
Pontrhydfendigaid
Ystrad Meurig
Dyfed SY25 6EF

Greenacre
Cathedine
Bwlch
Brecon
Powys LD3 7PZ

May 1987

FOREWORD

If (though Heaven forbid!) it was decreed that I should be allowed to spend the rest of my life in pursuit of only one type of fish, I should immediately plump for the sea trout.

Such magical fish are almost too good for us anglers. Their pursuit demands not only the craft of the hunter but the soul of a romantic — for how many true sea-trout fishers are not in close harmony with their surroundings? The exciting journey down the dusty lanes of summer to one's favourite pool, the sweet scent of honeysuckle hanging in the heavy air; the joys of the bracing moor as one battles against the rain-laden winds to a remote loch where the sea trout have recently arrived. All these delights belong only to the sea trout fisher.

And when the great moment arrives – when there comes a swirl and a heavy pull and a madly screeching reel – the dedicated sea trout fisher knows that this is what *real* fishing is all about. A fish as wild as the wind, untouched by human hand, has taken his lure in the inky blackness of a summer's night; or grabbed his tripping bob-fly in the middle of a storm-tossed loch. Now that's what I call fishing!

Strangely, however, in the rich literature devoted to the sport of angling, comparatively few authors have devoted the pages of their books to this exciting fish. When, as a boy, I first started sea trout fishing, my mentor was R.C. Bridgett, whose *Sea Trout Fishing* was read so often that its pages became dog-eared and grubby and eventually fell out. Therefore I was delighted to see that Graeme Harris and Moc Morgan have given due credit to a man who was years ahead of his angling contemporaries, and whose tactics and theories do not seem old-fashioned – even today. I still have that book, and no amount of money would persuade me to part with it.

But for me, as a novice sea trout fisher, there were many burning questions unanswered in Bridgett's book. I knew he used, as I did then, a silk line; but did he grease it or did he let it sink? How fast did he retrieve his flies, if at all? Were the fly-sizes he mentioned compatible with the so-called Redditch scale with which I was familiar? To a young fisher thirsting for knowledge, it was all very frustrating.

How much less frustrated I should have been had *Successful Sea Trout Angling* been available then! Graeme Harris and Moc Morgan – both dedicated and highly successful sea trout fishers – have left no questions unanswered, nor any stone unturned in their writing of a book that is truly 'complete'.

The authors' combined experience covers some seventy-five years at more than one hundred fisheries throughout the British Isles – from Gwynedd to Galway, Sussex to Sutherland, Cornwall to Caithness and Donegal to Dyfed. Perhaps it would be fair to say that most of their fishing has been done in Wales, land of song and sewin – and where better to gain experience of these enigmatic fish than in the principality that produces more big sea trout than anywhere else in the British Isles?

Judging by the amount of letters I receive each week from readers of *Trout and Salmon*, the popularity of sea trout fishing has increasr d dramatically over the past few years, and to these readers Graeme Harris and Moc Morgan need no introduction. Their practical approach to sea trout fishing, embracing all manner of means to seek the fish's downfall, is truly comprehensive. And even if one is purely a fly-fisher, there is much to be learned from the bait-fisher's approach to these enigmatic fish.

If we had as many books on sea trout fishing as we do on brown trout fishing, anglers might, with a little justification, claim that there was no need for another. But we don't; and there is. With *Successful Sea Trout Angling*, the craft of this magical sport is brought right up to date. It is a necessary book and makes a major contribution to our knowledge of this most sporting of fish.

Sandy Leventon

INTRODUCTION

The original idea for this book was conceived on the banks of the Afon Tywi one evening in late June 1984, when we were whiling away the long hours until twilight and the start of a night's fishing for sea trout. As with all dedicated anglers, the intervening conversation ranged freely over matters appertaining to fish, fisheries and fishing with (quite naturally, in view of our purpose) particular reference to that most sporting but enigmatic of fish – the sea trout.

We both commented on the tremendous upsurge of interest in sea trout angling in recent years as evidenced by the increasing number of anglers now present on the river by day and night, the sudden appearance of various items of tackle specifically 'designed' for sea trout anglers, and the very significant increase in the number of articles about sea trout appearing regularly in the angling press. A decade or so earlier, sea trout angling was considered by many to be a rather esoteric offshoot from the mainstream branches of salmon and brown trout angling which was practised by a small band of fanatics 'clustered' around a few famous venues such as Loch Maree, the Afonydd Dyfi and Tywi and certain waters in Connemara and in the Outer Hebrides. However, the popular view was that sea trout were the poor man's salmon: a rather less worthy alternative to its larger and far more prestigious relative the Atlantic Salmon (*Salmo salar*).

D.G. Ferris Rudd, a famous Scottish angler who published widely under the pseudonym 'Jock Scott' and who wrote *Sea Trout Fishing* in 1969, represented the general attitude of the day to sea trout. His acid test was to ask, 'faced with two invitations for a fishing holiday, one on a good salmon river, and the other on a famous sea trout water, which would you accept?' He then stated that if you chose to fish the famous sea trout water you were a real enthusiast with a soul far above the glamour which surrounds the salmon, and 'made of sterner stuff' than he.

We then noted that while volumes had been written about the brown trout and Atlantic salmon over the last century, very little by comparison had been written about the sea trout; and this lack of historical angling literature was also reflected in the scientific literature. Indeed, it seemed that, with a few notable exceptions, much of what was known about the sea trout had been incidental to work on brown trout or salmon. Thus very little scientific research on sea trout had been undertaken with the result that the fish was surrounded with an aura of myth and mystery based on ignorance; and this was paralleled in the angling literature.

From this point our conversation moved on to ask 'why were anglers so suddenly keen to pursue a resource that had been largely ignored by so many for so long?' We concluded that there were two main reasons for the very obvious upsurge of interest.

First, there was the perceived decline in the general quality of the salmon fishing on many rivers, especially in England and Wales. In many regions of the British Isles there was what could only be termed 'a crisis of confidence' in the future well-being of the traditionally dominant salmon fisheries following a sequence of events over the last 20 years, all of which were believed to spell disaster for the salmon. In the late 1960s to early 1970s we had the ravages of the disease UDN (Ulcerative Dermal Necrosis, the cause of which has never been established).

In the early 1970s we had the depradations of the massive commercial fishery for salmon on its 'newly' discovered sea-feeding grounds off Greenland, which reduced the numbers of returning spring fish. In the late 1970s this was followed by a similar fishery of the Faeroe Islands which also 'decimated' the grilse runs. Then in the early 1980s came the startling discovery that the headwater streams, so crucial for spawning and regeneration, of many rivers in certain regions were no longer able to support fish life because the water had become too acidic as a result of 'acid-rain' and the effects of forestry. If all this was not bad enough, the plight of the salmon was exacerbated further by the dramatic increase in the nature and extent of illegal fishing in coastal waters, in estuaries, within rivers and on spawning grounds, which began in the late 1970s and which continues to increase at a still alarming rate. There seemed to be no future for the salmon. Stocks were declining rapidly, runs were getting later and smaller and individual rod catches had fallen to unacceptable levels. 'Nothing was being done! The 'authorities' were complacent. Government departments were intransigent.' Gloom and doom were everywhere apparent.

It matters not whether the diagnosis was correct or if the prognosis was based on fact. It is what people 'believe' that is important; and many believed so strongly that the salmon was doomed to extinction that various measures to conserve the resource were being widely advocated, ranging from a reduction of the season and a ban on worm fishing to the imposition of quotas on anglers and even a complete moratorium on all salmon fishing for a period of years!

The problem of a perceived decline in the quality of the salmon fishing was general in all regions of the British Isles. It was, perhaps, more pronounced south of the Scottish border; and the famous River Wye serves to illustrate the point.

The River Wye ranks among the 'top ten' salmon rivers in the UK. It is famed for its run of spring fish and also for its crop of 40lb plus 'portmanteux' salmon. Up to 25 per cent of all rod-caught salmon taken in England and

Wales in a typical year are caught in the Wye! The long-term average rod-catch for the Wye up to the late 1970s was about 6,000 fish a year. Over the most recent years this has 'crashed' progressively each year, so that in 1984 the total rod catch was the worst year on record at 1,263 salmon.

The second reason that we identified for the increased demand for sea trout fishing was the general realisation that not only was the still-abundant sea trout the only alternative for the disenchanted salmon angler, but it was also a highly worthy sporting fish *in its own right*. This recent change in the general perception of anglers about the 'image' of sea trout was, we both agreed, due largely to the writings of one man – Hugh Falkus. In 1962 Hugh Falkus wrote what was then only the third book exclusively about sea trout ever published – *Sea Trout Fishing: A Guide to Success*. It was a small book, and, since it appeared at a time when the salmon stocks of the British Isles were possibly larger than at any time during the century, it was somewhat premature and did not achieve the impact that it deserved. However, with what was to be almost impeccable timing, the modest first edition was rewritten, much expanded, and reproduced in 1975. It was immediately acknowledged as a modern classic of the angling literature and very soon became a best-seller – quite rightly so, because it broke new ground in both the very high quality of the publication itself (some 190 photographs) and, more importantly, in the manner of the presentation. Gone was the substantially anecdotal style of writing much beloved by earlier authors, to be replaced by the highly-readable instructive prose of a professional writer who, moreover, clearly knew his stuff. Most authors of fishing books eventually tell you *what* to do. Some may even tell you *how* to do it. Falkus not only told you *what* and *how*, but he also explained *when*, *where* and, more unusually, *why*. So persuasive was his writing, and so impressive the packaging, that many anglers suddenly saw the sea trout (previously regarded almost as 'vermin' in many once-prestigious salmon fisheries) in a completely new light.

At this juncture (we had by now tackled-up and the sun had just set) we both recounted very similar experiences on the different rivers that we each fished regularly and knew 'like the handle of our rod'. The common theme was that each had been assailed by visiting anglers on a weekly or day permit who were clearly recent converts to the chapel of sea trouting. After the initial bankside pleasantries, we were asked the usual questions – where were we fishing, what were we using and how were we fishing it, etc, etc? Our well-intended and helpful replies resulted in our being counselled politely (or not so politely) that we were unlikely to meet with much success because our methodology and philosophy did not follow the Gospel according to Hugh Falkus...Well!

This shared experience then led us to discuss the 'Falkusian' approach to sea trout. Wales, perhaps more than anywhere, is endowed with some of the finest sea trout fishing in the world and, as a consequence, probably has the greatest concentration of dedicated sea trout anglers. It is a small country with even the most remote sea trout fisheries within a 3–4 hour drive. Between us we must be acquainted with several score anglers who are by any standard *very* successful sea trout fishermen. Our conversation focused on these notable, often notorious, individuals in an attempt to identify why they were successful. Was there a pattern to their success that corresponded with the Falkusian approach? After some consideration we had to conclude that there was no apparent common feature associated with these anglers that explained their success, apart from the fact that few if any had read Hugh Falkus, or any other book on sea trout fishing for that matter! Some fished sunk line, others fished floating line; some fished big lures, others fished tiny wee flies; some fished fast, some fished slow; some fished pool tails, others fished pool heads; some fished up, others fished across or down. In fact, each angler was very different, but nonetheless each caught a lot of fish.

As avid sea trout anglers we had, of course, both read the 1962 and 1975 editions of *Sea Trout Fishing: A Guide to Success* (several times) and we had both variously applied the tactics and techniques detailed by Hugh Falkus to the different waters that we fished. However, after some faithful experimentation, we had both reverted to our well-tried-and-tested methods and styles on our particular fisheries, for the simple reason that we each caught more fish 'our way'.

In discussing our brief affair with the Falkusian approach we concluded that we were as a consequence 'wiser' and 'better' anglers because Hugh Falkus, by his own carefully considered and analytical approach, had taught us to *think* about our fishing: to consider *why* we were doing *what* we were doing and to treat every outing as a lesson, i.e. to ask ourselves not only why we had *not* caught fish but also (and equally relevant) why we *had* caught fish on those other occasions.

Thus, it seemed to us that Hugh Falkus had been *so* convincing and *so* successful in his writings that he had created a situation whereby there was a risk that sea trout angling would become stereotyped and ritualised with anglers applying his precepts as if they were written on 'tablets of stone'. In this respect we drew the analogy with the evolution of salmon angling during the 1930s and 1940s when the much-publicised success of A. H. E. Wood, the father of 'greased-line' fishing, effectively stifled original thought for a generation. This, we suggested, was the greatest abnegation of everything that Hugh Falkus was attempting to achieve. Nowhere was Falkus being dogmatic or doctrinaire in his writings. He had developed an approach that suited *his* style and which *he* found successful on those waters that *he* fished. He did not state or imply that other styles would not be successful on different waters. His real message was to *think* about *what* you were doing and *why* you were doing it. Essentially, he provided a basic recipe for success, a standard repertoire of techniques, but he never excluded the opportunity of adding other ingredients to create a different flavour 'according to taste and occasion'.

Thus (and darkness was now fast approaching), we concluded that there was room for another book about sea-trout angling. Nothing is static. Much had changed over the last decade since the second edition of Hugh Falkus' monumental treatise. The technology of fishing tackle had advanced at a rapid rate to open up new opportunities; techniques developed on the English reservoir fisheries during the 1970s and 1980s were being applied successfully to sea trout angling on lakes and rivers; new information about the biology and behaviour of the fish itself provided a different perspective; and there was an obvious change in angler attitudes and ethics. Certainly Falkus did not claim the last word.

We felt that sea trout angling was now passing from infancy to adolescence. Earlier authors, such as Hamish Stuart, R.C. Bridgett, Jeffrey Bluett and F.W. Holiday had set the scene. Hugh Falkus wrote the first act. We could but try to write the second act. Others after us would continue the plot. Thus this book should be regarded as a companion volume to the earlier work by Hugh Falkus. We would stress that our modest contribution is intended to complement rather than contradict what has gone before.

It was now dark enough to start fishing. 'Moc, do you want to fish down first, or shall I? I'm fishing a 2-inch tube on a fast-sink line. You better go first with your sink tip and that cast of wee trout flies. We'll meet up again at midnight for coffee. Give a shout if you want the net.'

'Genwair Blȳg'

PART I
Background and Basics

1 · THE FISH

This is not a scientific text. It is a book about the art of angling for sea trout. Nonetheless it is to be acknowledged that an understanding of certain features concerning the biology, ecology and behaviour of the fish is very relevant to the strategies, tactics and approach to its capture on rod-and-line. Moreover, every *true* angler must, surely, have more than just a passing interest in the life history of the species that has become the focus of attention and endeavour.

In view of the importance of the sea trout to the commercial and sport fisheries of the British Isles in general, and to some regions in particular (Chapter 2), it is surprising how little scientific work on sea trout has been undertaken over the last century. There are still many significant gaps in our knowledge that impose serious limitations on our ability to manage the resource effectively and efficiently.

At the turn of the century, very little was known about sea trout. Indeed, it was to be several years later that there was any agreement on how many different species of 'trout' occurred in the British Isles (see page 24). Any research into sea trout was usually undertaken opportunistically and incidentally to work on its closest and more prestigious relative, the Atlantic salmon (*Salmo salar*). That is not to say that the sea trout was wholly neglected in the scientific literature of the period, because several texts did in fact make reference to 'sea trout'. Of these early writings the most interesting are: *British and Irish Salmonidae* by Francis Day, published in 1887; *British Freshwater Fishes* by Sir Herbert Maxwell, Bart, FRS, published in 1904 (Maxwell was also the author of *Salmon and Sea Trout* which we have taken as the starting point for our review of the angling literature on sea trout; see Chapter 3) and *Life History and Habitats of the Salmon, Sea Trout and Other Freshwater Fish* by P.D. Malloch, published in 1910.

This latter publication is important because Malloch was the first to include information derived from the then recently discovered science of scale reading. Prior to this almost everything that was known about sea trout was derived from limited and local observations that were based largely upon anecdotal and circumstantial evidence rather than what today would be termed 'hard scientific fact'.

Scale reading added a completely new dimension to fisheries science and, among other things, enabled some of the earlier 'scientific' theories about sea trout to be tested (and often refuted!) and allowed detailed characterisation of the structure and composition of the sea-trout 'stocks' of different rivers to be described for the first time. (See page 6.)

Malloch's work heralded the dawn of a new era in our understanding of the biology of the sea trout, at least in descriptive terms. It was followed in 1916 by *The Sea Trout: A Study in Natural History* by Henry Lamond. Although mainly about the sea trout of Loch Lomond (the author was the secretary of the Loch Lomond Improvement Society), it provides a useful synthesis of the state of knowledge (which was not a lot) and speculation (which was extensive) about the life-history of Scottish sea trout at the time.

The next milestone in the scientific literature was in 1930 when *The Life of the Sea Trout: Especially in Scottish Waters* by G. Herbert Nall was published. This presented the results of some eight years' extensive scale-reading studies from numerous regions and rivers of Scotland (and less extensively from other rivers elsewhere) and was supplemented by a modern interpretation of the state of knowledge about the origin, distribution, biology and behaviour of the sea trout: albeit with a strong Scottish flavour. *The Life of the Sea Trout* is a monumental work which is quite remarkable in many respects. Nall was not a qualified scientist and his studies were a labour of devotion which commenced after his professional retirement. His efforts in collecting, preparing and reading scales were, even by modern standards, quite prodigious and his ability to analyse and correctly interpret the limited data available to him was impressive. That is not to say that he was always right in his theories, but subsequent investigations have established that he was often very close to the truth. Nall's contribution to our understanding of, and interest in, the sea trout has been inestimable. Even today, almost 60 years after *The Life of the Sea Trout* was published, Nall's text is still the only definitive scientific book on the sea trout and as such remains the standard reference work for fisheries biologists and managers.

Although Nall did much to identify the many gaps in our knowledge about the sea trout, and as a consequence largely influenced the thrust and focus of subsequent research, interest in the fish by the scientific community waned for almost 30 years other than for the occasional spasmodic publication – usually from abroad. The next significant scientific report on British sea trout did not appear until 1962, when Arthur Went published his paper on 'Irish Sea Trout; A Review of Investigations to Date'. This was essentially a synthesis of the results of scale-reading studies on a large number of rivers in the Republic of Ireland. It helped to broaden our appreciation of the enormous variation that clearly occurred in the composition and characteristics of the sea-trout stocks within and between different regions of the British Isles but it did little to improve our understanding of the many fundamental questions about the biology, ecology and behaviour that had been posed by Day, Malloch, Lamond and Nall. In particular the question 'What is a sea trout?' still remained unanswered!

4

In more recent years there has been a modest increase in interest in the sea trout by the scientific community. Certain significant advances in technology, combined with a heightened perspective of fertile research opportunities and a growing awareness of the socio-economic importance of the resource in several regions, have resulted in several profoundly important studies on sea trout being undertaken over the last decade. The results of these investigations, some of which are essentially long-term and still 'ongoing', have provided much new information on the long neglected topics of migration and movement, population dynamics, reproductive biology, and the taxonomic status of sea trout. However, whereas it is possible to make broad generalisations about the life history of the Atlantic salmon, the brown trout and other more distant relatives of the sea trout with reasonable confidence of stating the 'norm', it is with much less confidence that we attempt to do so for sea trout. It is evident that we still have much to learn and that the sea trout exhibits enormous variation within and between different regions in terms of the structure and composition of local stocks, its migrations in the sea, and its pattern of movement in freshwater.

Thus, with this in mind, we will now attempt to provide a thumb-nail sketch of the life-history of a 'typical' sea trout and then discuss some of the myths that have been promulgated about the biology and behaviour of the fish by various authors over the last century. Our intention here is to present up-to-date information of interest and relevance to the angler. That our scientific knowledge is still far from complete will become obvious. In this endeavour we draw freely on the information presented at the first-ever scientific workshop on sea trout held in October 1984 at Bangor (North Wales) and promoted jointly by the Welsh Water Authority and the Atlantic Salmon Trust Ltd. (This workshop [convened by the first author] brought together for the first time all the scientists and managers in the British Isles with an interest in sea trout. Much new information was presented – some of which has been subsequently published in scientific journals, some of which has yet to be published, and some of which will, sadly, never be published. A summary of the proceedings has, however, been produced (See Reading List, page 35.)

We must now digress slightly from our main theme to explain three separate issues. The first is the complex terminology applied to the various life-history stages of the sea trout. The second is the importance of scale reading to our understanding of the biology of the sea trout. The third, and most important, is the meaning of the term 'sea trout'.

The sea trout has probably been attributed with more local names for its various life-history stages than any other fish. Nall lists nearly one hundred different names used in various parts of the British Isles – and he missed a few! Many of these local terms have long fallen from favour, but some have endured and a few are still quite widely employed. In order to simplify matters we will use the term *smolt* for the seaward migrating juvenile sea trout (the synonyms orange-fin, red-fin, yellow-fin, pink, sprod etc are rarely if ever used today). All post-migrant adult fish we will call *sea trout*, while recognising that the terms 'peal' (Devon and Cornwall), 'white trout' (Ireland), 'bull-trout' (Northumbria) and 'sewin' (Wales) are still used regionally. We will use the term *whitling* for small adult sea trout that return to the river in the same year that they migrated to sea as smolts (i.e. fish that have not spent one winter in the sea) and, in so doing, we embrace the synonyms 'finnock' (Scotland), 'herling' (Solway) and 'school-peal' (West Country). (While the term 'finnock' is very widely used in Scotland – and seems to be gaining popularity in Ireland, our preference for the term whitling is based on its impeccable ancestry: it was the term preferred by earlier scientists [such as Nall] and by pre-eminent angling authors [such as R.C. Bridgett]).

The term 'kelt' refers to a recently spawned adult fish that has not yet returned to the sea. A 'maiden fish' is one that has yet to mature and spawn for the first time. Some authors describe the whitling as the 'grilse' stage of sea trout. This is wrong. The grilse stage of salmon is universally used to define a maiden fish that has spent one winter in the sea after migrating as a smolt (= .1+). The whitling is the pre-grilse (= .0+) stage. It does not normally occur in salmon.

Much of our knowledge about the life history of the sea trout and, particularly, our understanding of the differences in the structure and composition of the stocks of different river systems has been obtained by scale reading. This is not the place to enter into a heavy discourse on the subject but it is necessary to stress that the discovery that the life history of most fish could be determined by a careful examination of their scales was of fundamental importance to fisheries science.

Since the number of scales on a fish is fixed at birth, the scales grow at the same rate as the fish. Examination of the scales reveals a series of concentric

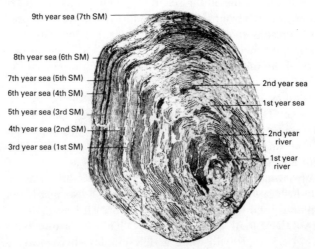

9th year sea (7th SM)

8th year sea (6th SM)

7th year sea (5th SM)
6th year sea (4th SM)

5th year sea (3rd SM)

4th year sea (2nd SM)

3rd year sea (1st SM)

2nd year sea

1st year sea

2nd year river

1st year river

Scale from the largest rod-caught Dyfi sea trout of 20lb 12oz taken in 1958. Scale formula = 2.2 + 7SM+ = 11 years old. An example of a fast-growing long-lived fish. (Photo: G.S. Harris.)

6

rings where new material is deposited at the margin of the scale. When the fish grows quickly the rings are wider apart and when the fish grows slowly they are closer together. The rate of growth is seasonal in trout and salmon. The fish grows faster in summer and slower in winter. This is shown on the scale by the grouping of the growth rings into bands – termed summer and winter bands. Thus the age of the fish can be determined by counting the number of winter bands.

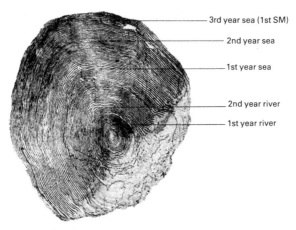

River Tweed sea trout 18lb 14oz taken by the nets in August 1969. Scale formula = 2.2 + SM+ = 5 years old. An example of a fast-growing short-lived fish. (Photo: G. S. Harris.)

Moreover, since the rate of growth of the fish and its scales are (roughly) proportional, it is possible to back-calculate the length of the fish at each year of life if the length of the scale and the length of the fish is known. Fish such as salmon and (as we shall see) sea trout cease feeding on their return to the river to spawn and growth ceases. Certain minerals – such as calcium and zinc – stored in the scales are absorbed and used for the production of eggs and sperm (= milt). This results in the scale margin becoming eroded and the pattern of rings disrupted; but when the fish returns to sea and growth recommences this erosion is replaced by new material which, because it does not replace the growth rings, results in a characteristic 'spawning mark' being recorded on the scales.

In addition to showing the age, growth rate and reproductive history of the fish, the scales can also be used to confirm whether it spent time in the sea by analysis of certain elements – essentially strontium – which are more abundant in the sea than in fresh water. This, however, is not a definitive test for distinguishing between sea trout and brown trout: it merely establishes that a 'trout' has spent some time feeding and growing in the sea. [As we shall discuss later, some sea trout spend their entire life in fresh water and some brown trout may go to sea!]

The age and life-history of a sea trout can be expressed by its 'scale formula'. This adopts a standard convention for describing the age at which the fish went to sea as a smolt (= river life), the number of years (= winters) spent in the sea before returning to the river to spawn for the first time (= sea absence), and the number of spawning marks shown upon the scales. Thus:

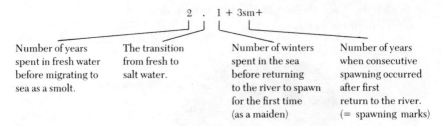

Number of years spent in fresh water before migrating to sea as a smolt.	The transition from fresh to salt water.	Number of winters spent in the sea before returning to the river to spawn for the first time (as a maiden)	Number of years when consecutive spawning occurred after first return to the river. (= spawning marks)

In the above formula, the fish was in its seventh year of life when captured. It went to sea as a two-year-old smolt, spent one complete winter (= year) in the sea before returning to spawn for the first time and then spawned in each of the next three years.

The scale formula 3. + means that the fish is a whitling that went to sea as a three-year-old smolt and returned to the river in the same year. It had not yet spawned. (Had it done so it would have been a 3.sm+ fish.) The scale formula 2.2 + 4sm + relates to an eight-year-old fish in its ninth year of life when captured which had migrated to sea as a two-year-old smolt, spent two years in the sea before returning to spawn for the first time and then spawned in each of the next four consecutive years.

'*What is a sea trout?*' This profoundly important question was first posed by Henry Lamond in 1916. He wrote: 'There is one question – not so simple as it looks – that appears to me to require some investigation before any inquiry into the life history of the sea trout is undertaken and that question is – What is a sea trout?' He adds: 'It is...a question which has not yet been very satisfactorily answered by anybody...' Today, some 70 years later, the question still requires a satisfactory answer!

However, in order to avoid complicating our synthesis of the main points concerning the biology and life history of the fish at this juncture we propose to kick the question to touch for the time being and return to it later (page 23). Thus, for the present purpose we will use the term 'sea trout' in the simplest possible sense to include all trout that spend a part of their life feeding and growing in the sea.

The European trout (*Salmo trutta*) has been introduced by man to many different parts of the world that lie outside its natural range. The list of countries where brown trout now occur in self-sustaining populations is really quite amazing and includes Ecuador, Chile, Peru, Kashmir, South Africa, Papua, Japan, Madagascar, Puerto Rico and Mexico. In some countries, such as New Zealand, Argentina and the Falkland Islands, these importations have resulted in the creation of significant runs of sea trout alongside thriving populations of river trout. However, while the world distribution of the brown trout has been increased dramatically over the last century, this has not applied to sea trout also. There are two possible explanations for this; firstly that only the eggs of brown trout were imported, and secondly that the temperature and other characteristics of the rivers in their lower reaches are such that the environment is hostile to the migration of trout to and from the sea. The latter is the more plausible explanation.

The *natural* distribution of the sea trout is similar to that of the salmon but their geographical range is not identical (Fig. 1). The most important difference is that while the Atlantic salmon is to be found on the Eastern sea board of Canada and the United States of America (from about Ungava Bay [Quebec] in the north to the Hudson River [New York State] in the south) there are no *natural* stocks of brown trout or sea trout on the American continent. (However, *Salmo trutta* has been introduced to North America and sea trout and brown trout now occur over a wide if discontinuous range.)

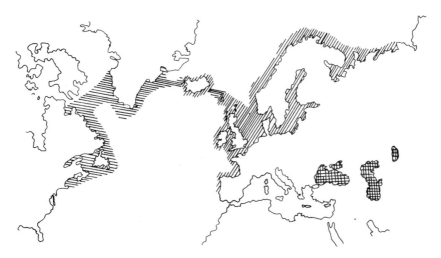

Fig.1. The natural (= native) distribution of sea trout (*Salmo trutta*) and Atlantic salmon (*Salmo salar*) after the last ice age. Marine distributions are very approximate. Sea trout also occur (as sub-species) in the Black Sea (*S. trutta labrax*), the Caspian Sea (*S. trutta caspius*) and in the Aral Sea (*S. trutta aralensis*). The Mediterranean was very much cooler during the ice age and sea trout had a more southerly distribution. Relic populations of brown trout still occur in Algeria, Corsica and Sardinia.

The natural range of sea trout includes Iceland and the Faeroe Islands and it is widespread throughout Scandinavia. It occurs in the White Sea and the Cheshkaya Gulf (Russia) in the North, throughout the Baltic and down the coast of Europe as far south as Northern Portugal. It is likely that the sea trout extended much further south during the last ice-age. Relic populations of non-migratory trout occur in Algeria and in countries bordering the western and north-eastern Mediterranean. While there are no sea trout in the Mediterranean (which is much warmer now than it was then), the rivers

9

entering the Black, Aral and Caspian Seas are still reputed to contain sea trout. (At least one taxonomist has recognised six different subspecies of *Salmo trutta* throughout this range.)

The sea trout is closely related to the Atlantic salmon. Both species have similar life histories but it is to be noted that there are some very significant differences. The similarities are in the main that the salmon and sea trout are both 'anadromous' in that the mature adult fish spawn in fresh water where the juveniles pass through the common stages of egg, alevin, fry and parr before migrating to sea as smolts.

The principal differences between salmon and sea trout in relation to their life-history are that most salmon migrate much further out to sea than sea trout and, as a consequence, are older (and, therefore, larger) on their first return to fresh water as 'maiden' or unspawned fish. By contrast, the sea trout is much better able to survive after spawning. It is unusual (in the British Isles) to find a salmon that has survived to spawn for a second time. Whereas only about 1 per cent of male salmon and 5 per cent of female salmon survive to spawn more than once, a large (but very variable) proportion of the run of sea trout (up to about 50 per cent in some situations) consists of 'multiple' or 'repeat' spawners – some of which may have spawned up to 11 times (page 19). Once maturity is reached the sea trout spawns in each con-secutive year until its death. Some may miss a year – but such fish are very unusual.

Although some salmon may return to the river within a few months after migrating to sea as smolts (as pre-grilse), such fish are rare. The pre-grilse (or whitling) stage is, however, very common in sea trout and the stock may consist of a very high proportion of such fish in some rivers.

There is much variation within and between the sea trout of different regions and so it is difficult to describe the life history of a 'typical' sea trout. We shall take the characteristics of Welsh sea trout as our standard.

Spawning takes place in the autumn and spans the period late October to mid-December. The peak of spawning activity occurs in mid-November and, as a general rule, the spawning season for sea trout is some 2–3 weeks ahead of that for salmon. A few sea trout (known as bluebacks or greybacks in Wales) may enter the river in January-March and spawn in the early spring (The first author has stripped eggs from ripe female sea trout in February which still had the marks of sea lice on their body, indicating that they had only been in fresh water for a few days. He has also caught sea trout in March [by electrofishing – not angling] which were still fairly fresh and within a few days of spawning.) – but these 'late-run' fish are more common with salmon and in some rivers they may be rare or non-existent.

Sea trout, by virtue of their smaller average size, are able to penetrate much smaller spawning streams and deposit their eggs in much finer gravel than salmon. However, large sea trout may utilise the same spawning streams and gravels as the salmon. Where sea trout and salmon both utilise the same areas for spawning some (inter-specific) competition is to be expected. However, since the salmon usually spawns some two weeks after the sea trout, any competition for spawning sites tends to favour the later-spawning salmon and results in the eggs of sea trout being 'overcut' (i.e. dug out of the gravel) and so destroyed.

Spawning activity is largely conditioned by water temperature. It may be delayed in a 'warm year' and is earlier in Scotland than in (say) Devon and Cornwall. The success of spawning – and, hence, the number of sea trout (and salmon) smolts going to sea in subsequent years is largely conditioned by rainfall. In a wet year the adults are able to penetrate well upstream into the tributaries but in a dry year much spawning takes place in the main river and lower reaches of the feeder streams. It is generally accepted that the 'peaks-and-troughs' in the abundance of sea trout (and salmon) are correlated with rainfall – a wet year allowing greater colonisation of the available spawning and nursery catchment by adult fish so that more smolts (and, therefore, returning adults) are produced as a direct consequence.

After hatching sometime in February or March (depending on water temperature) the alevins remain buried in the gravel for about another month and feed on the reserves of food stored in their yolk sacs. They emerge in March or April/May as free swimming fry and soon show the characteristic finger-markings along their sides that characterise the parr stage.

It is at the fry stage that we lose track of their juvenile life history because the parr of the migratory (sea) trout cannot be distinguished on the basis of appearance from the parr of the non-migratory (brown) trout. It is only when the 'trout' parr undergoes the important physiological transformation to become a smolt, with its characteristic silver coat, that descriptive studies on the sea trout can recommence.

The smolt transformation is significant. Conventional wisdom states that this is a pre-adaption to life in the sea which affects its behaviour, camouflage and ability to regulate its salt-balance so that it is better able to survive and thrive in the marine environment. The unconventional view states that the smolt transformation has no particular evolutionary or genetic significance in that it is no more than a fortuitous symptom of stress (possibly caused by overcrowding in the river environment) which results in a seaward movement by the affected parr. Whatever the reason, the important point is that it does *not* occur in those trout destined to spend their entire life in fresh water.

The peak months of the smolt migration in Wales are March and April (some 2–3 weeks in advance of the main migration of the salmon smolts), but sea-trout smolts may occur as early as January and as late as June in some systems. While the main smolt run occurs in the spring, it appears that a second seaward movement of parr, silvery-parr or smolts occurs during the autumn and the unknown contribution of these autumn migrants to subsequent runs of adult sea trout warrants further research.

The age of the smolts on migration varies from region to region (Table 1).

In the British Isles the greater part of the population consists of fish that are two or three years of age but a few one-year and four-year old smolts usually occur also. A typical sea trout smolt is approximately 150 mm (6 inches) in length and is usually larger than a salmon smolt of the same age. Some very large smolts may occur in certain rivers – up to 200 mm (8 inches) or more. On entering the estuary the smolts adapt to a different feeding regime and commence a phase of rapid growth which is readily shown on their scales.

Table 1: Age of sea trout smolts on migration to the sea
(Selected Rivers)

District/River	1	2	% Smolt Age in Years 3	4	5
Scotland: Findhorn	—	10.2	60.2	25.8	3.8
Spey	—	29.2	59.4	10.8	0.6
Tweed	0.6	79.1	19.6	1.2	—
Wales: Tywi	0.3	68.6	31.1	—	—
Dyfi	0.6	62.0	36.8	0.9	—
Ireland: Screebe	—	32.6	58.1	9.3	—
Waterville	—	56.0	37.0	5.9	1.1
Argideen	5.9	74.2	19.9	—	—

Sea trout may spend anything up to three complete years in the sea before returning to fresh water as 'maiden' fish to spawn for the first time. However, fish which have spent two or three post-migration years at sea are unusual and represent a very small part of the total run in any river (if they occur at all). The greater part of the smolt migrations returns to the river either in the same year (as whitling or .0 + seawinter fish) or during the following year (as .1+ seawinter fish). In some rivers a very large proportion of the smolts return as whitling (Table 2).

The size of maiden sea trout on their first return to fresh water can vary enormously, depending on the geographical location of the river, the quality of the feeding in the sea and the length of sea absence. Most British sea trout return to fresh water after less than a year (.0+) or a year (.1+) in the sea. A few may spend two winters in the sea (= .2+) and a very small number may return to spawn for the first time after three winters in the sea (as .3+).

Typically whitling (.+ fish) range in size from ¼ to 1lb in weight over much of the British Isles. Sea trout having spent one year (= winter) in the sea may range in size from 1½ to 5lb in weight, depending on the geographical location. A .2+ fish may weigh up to 10lb, or even more, on the Tweed or Dyfi. In Ireland it may weigh only 2–4lb. A .3+ fish is, as we have said, rare. In Ireland it might weigh 5lb, on the Dyfi or Tweed it may weigh 15–20lb.

One particular myth about sea trout still widely promulgated in the

Table 2: Proportion of adult sea trout in each sea age group
(Selected Rivers)

Region	River	Maiden Fish Sea Age Group (Summers)				Previous Spawners (with SMs)
		.+	.1+	.2+	.3+	
Ireland:	Gowla	83.3	11.6	0.7	0.2	4.2
	Waterville	47.3	26.0	3.6	0.1	23.0
	Foyle	0.7	53.7	8.4	0.4	36.8
Wales:	Dyfi	32.4	25.1	1.9	0.2	40.1
	Tywi	19.9	29.4	3.2	0.6	46.9
Scotland:	Bervie	41.3	51.5	—	—	7.2
	N. Esk	70.1	24.4	0.2	—	5.3
	S. Esk	65.0	29.1	0.1	—	5.8
	Ewe/Maree	52.4	22.3	7.8	0.8	22.3
	Tweed	14.5	34.8	42.0	0.9	7.8

angling literature is that the sea-trout smolts on entering tidal waters remain within the estuary or, otherwise, feed in adjacent coastal waters close to their river origin. This is a gross over-simplification of what is now known to be a complex and very variable pattern of behaviour. In some rivers it may indeed be that on leaving the river a large number of smolts remain in the estuary or adjacent coastal waters for much of the time – and never move any great distance away from the river mouth. In other rivers, however, it is evident that few, if any, of the smolts take up a semi-permanent residence within the estuary and that sea trout can (and do) make long-distance migrations out to sea. This pattern of behaviour may be the norm for much of the smolt run in some rivers where whitling do not constitute a significant component of the stock.

Perhaps the best-researched region in this context is on the south-east coast of Scotland and the north-east of England where, as a result of some 40 years' work by various agencies, smolts and kelts from several rivers have been tagged periodically, and their subsequent movements traced from the tags returned by anglers and various kinds of commercial fishermen. Thus, by way of example, smolts tagged in the lower reaches of the Tweed and Coquet show an extensive cyclic migration in the North Sea. Coquet smolts were recovered off East Anglia in July (some being recaptured only 20 days after tagging). In July and August recaptures were recorded off the coast of Holland, Denmark, and, subsequently, off the Norwegian coast. The fish then recrossed the North Sea and, roughly a year later, adults were recovered in or near to the donor river. While the evidence from the Coquet and Tweed would suggest a general pattern of long-distance migration in the sea, the results from other regions present a rather different picture.

Tagging on the Scottish rivers North and South Esk (some 70 miles North of the Tweed) involving both smolts and kelts, showed that *most* fish restricted their movements to the area south of the Tweed or north to the Spey.

Although three fish were recaptured off Scandinavia, these errant sea trout represented only a small proportion of the fish recaptured. Likewise, information from the diminutive River Axe in Devon shows an eastward migration of smolts as far as the Avon (Hants) and a westward migration as far as the Otter–which in relative terms is not very far!

Several areas of Scotland and the Scottish Islands are noted for producing 'good' sea trout angling in tidal and coastal waters. A very notable example on the east coast of Scotland is famed Ythan fishery; but many other notable examples occur in the Shetlands and Orkneys and on the west coast of Scotland. Large parts of the west of Scotland (and also the western seaboard of Ireland) are characterised by large fjord-like estuaries. The only recent study of sea trout movements in such estuaries was undertaken in the 1970s on Loch Etive. This classic 'sea loch' (near Oban, Argyllshire) receives smolts from several rivers (such as the Awe) and presents a seemingly complex situation in terms of the post-smolt migrations of the sea trout. The typical pattern of smolts in this large, deep 'estuary' was that the smolts remained in the loch following their migration in the spring, moved out (to 'sea') in the summer and returned to the loch in the autumn–when some ran upstream into the various river systems. These fresh water migrants then re-entered the loch in February. The autumn migrants which returned to the sea loch, but which did not enter the rivers, remained in the loch over winter and moved out to sea the following spring.

This study, which is quite fascinating in terms of its detail, complexity and general relevance to large parts of the British Isles, perhaps raises more questions than it sets out to answer! What is evident, however, is that the behaviour of sea trout in fjord-like estuaries which are essentially salt water as opposed to brackish water may be very different to that occurring elsewhere.

During the early 1970s large numbers of sea trout were tagged as either smolts or as adults on the spawning ground in three adjacent rivers in mid-Wales (Dyfi, Dysynni, Mawddach), each of which has a relatively large – but shallow and sandy – estuary. The results are of interest in several respects because they contrast with those obtained from the deep fjord-like estuaries off the Scottish west coast, and suggest that the smolts move well out into the Irish sea. Several smolts were recaptured within a few weeks of tagging off the east and south-east coast of Ireland, and several fish tagged as spawned adults (= kelts) were taken in the vicinity of Arklow (Co. Wicklow). The longest migration recorded by a tagged adult fish in the Welsh studies was from the upper reaches of the Dyfi to Fenit (Co. Kerry) on to *west* coast of Ireland.

These tagging studies indicate that in some parts of the British Isles adult and smolt sea trout can migrate long distances in the sea. In some areas this may be the typical behaviour for a large proportion of the stock but in other regions most fish may remain fairly near to their river of origin and, in some situations, may spend much of their period of residence in the sea in or very close to the estuary.

Another popular myth that can be dismissed is that the sea trout, on returning to fresh water, is prone to stray and enter a river other than that in which it was produced. Some sea trout tagged as either smolts or kelts in one river may be recaptured in another river on returning from the sea, this in itself is not clear evidence of straying. Most examples of this behaviour are from tagged fish captured well down in the lower reaches of the river system – usually by commercial netsmen fishing in the tideway. It is now believed that this phenomenon of apparent straying into the 'wrong' river is part of a pattern of normal searching behaviour by the returning fish. Salmon – and probably sea trout also – are thought to relocate their river of origin by olfaction (= smell). As the smolt drops downstream during the spring some characteristic chemical component of its smell becomes imprinted into its memory and it is this 'imprint' that enables the returning adult to seek out and then penetrate its parent stream. Several rivers may enter the sea close to each other, some may even have common estuaries. The recapture of a tagged fish in the lower reaches of a river other than the one in which it was originally tagged is now recognised as 'searching' as distinct from straying. The fish was literally 'testing the water' and, as now shown in several tracking studies, will go back to sea if it has selected the *wrong* river.

The scientific community now accepts that the homing behaviour of adult sea trout, like that of salmon, is remarkably accurate on returning from the sea to spawn and that the incidence of straying is not significant in any practical sense. Indeed, examples of what must be accepted as true straying are scarce. One such example concerns a 3lb sea trout tagged as a spawning fish in the headwaters of the Dyfi which was recaptured by an angler the following year in the headwaters of the Tywi. This was very much the 'wrong' choice. The Tywi is some 150 miles to the south and east of the Dyfi and the recapture point was roughly 60 miles up-river from the estuary!

The increasing number of tagging studies undertaken in recent years have shown that the popular assumption that sea trout may wander from one river to another in order to spawn is a fiction. Moreover, these studies have shown that not only is migration specific to the river of origin, but it may also be specific to the tributary of origin and, even more specifically, to the pool or glide of origin within a tributary. Several workers (the first author included) have tagged sea trout as either smolts or kelts in one particular area of a tributary and recovered the *same* fish from the *same* location in the *same* tributary in two or three or even four consecutive years. Moreover, sea-trout adults, after having migrated to one tributary, have demonstrated a clear tendency to return to that same tributary when physically removed up-river to another location.

In recent years a great deal of important information about the movements of sea trout from the sea into estuaries and then from estuaries into, and through, river systems has been obtained by fitting adult fish with radio or acoustic tags and tracking their subsequent movements past fixed receiving stations, or by using portable, hand-held, receivers or hydrophones to ascer-

15

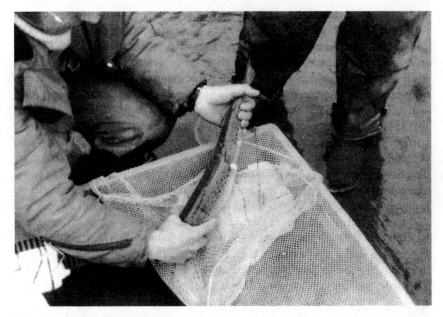

Tagging and radio-tracking have provided much new information about the movements and migratory behaviour of the sea trout. (If you catch a tagged fish please make sure that you report it to the appropriate agency.) (Photo: Nigel Milner.)

tain their position within the river. In this way the discrete movements of individual fish can be traced for up to several months.

Although such studies, which are very onerous and extremely costly to undertake in terms of manpower, are still in their infancy, they have produced much useful and relevant information. But, before summarising some of the main points, we must caution that one of the significant features of this work has been to suggest that every fish is an individual with its own peculiar behavioural characteristics. While certain general trends and tendencies become apparent as the body of scientific data grows, there is much variation about the norm. The following appreciation is a synthesis of pooled data obtained from the Fowey (Cornwall) and the Tywi and Glaslyn (Wales).

Once in the river, most upstream movement occurs at night on normal (= clear) to low flows. This occurs shortly after dusk and ceases around dawn. River flow (or discharge rate) appears to be relatively unimportant, although sea trout tend to move further upstream on higher flows – possibly because physical movement is easier when the depth is greater. After heavy rain, when river flows and water colour are elevated, movement also takes place by day. Upstream movement at night usually ceased after 10–14 days and was resumed only in response to a further increase in river flows. (The threshold for response may decrease nearer to spawning time when increased hormonal levels 'trigger' movement at much lower flows than earlier in the season.)

Larger sea trout (2½–10lb weight) tracked in May generally penetrated well into the river system within *7–10 days*. In fact, these early sea trout covered the majority of their ultimate migration distance to their spawning grounds within this very short period. Smaller sea trout (whitling) tracked later in the year (July) moved upstream at a slower rate but, nevertheless, penetrated much of the accessible river system within *7–10 days*.

Sea trout netted and tagged in the sea outside their (assumed) river of origin remained at sea for up to 24 days before entering the estuary. Once within the estuary, movement was usually directed by tidal flow. Whereas some fish moved directly from the estuary into the river on the rising (= flood) tide, others moved up with the flood and back again with the falling (=ebb) tide. There was, however, usually a nett upstream movement through the tidal section into the river. Within the estuary some fish adopted a fixed position for a period of time for no apparent reason. This was more frequent on ebb than on flood flows. In the lower freshwater reaches of the river the adult sea trout may spend long periods (up to three months) holding in deep water and in pools near to the confluence of tributaries known to be important spawning streams (see page 210).

Information on the upstream movement of fish can be obtained also from electronic fish counters. Fish-counter data from the Lune, Kent and Derwent (north-west England) provides a further insight into the migration of sea trout of up to 4lb weight within the river. (Practical difficulties in distinguisting electronically between sea trout and salmon are such that an upper limit of 4lb had to be set as the threshold for discriminating between the two species. Few salmon weigh less than 4lb.) These studies have reinforced much of what has been adduced from tracking studies and established that sea trout will move upstream under a very wide range of flow conditions. On the Kent, 80 per cent of the sea trout present below the counter moved upstream during discharges of 20–30 per cent of the average daily flow (= ADF). This accords with parallel data from other English rivers. An increase in flow elicited a greater response to upstream migration – especially during the later part of the season. Most movement took place at night, but fish also moved upstream during the day when river levels were high or the water was coloured. Other studies have suggested that (in the upper reaches of a river) while sea trout are more likely to move when the river level increases, the most likely period for movement is as the flood begins to recede. In fact, in one study, it was shown that the recession has more effect on movement than has the actual height of the flood.

Before leaving the topic of migration, homing and movement, we would comment on the sad fact that a good fishkill caused by pollution or poaching does much to advance our knowledge about the composition and abundance of local stocks. In August 1984 the Afon Mawddach in mid Wales was affected by a massive pollution from a gold mine located in the middle reaches of the river. 1984 was a serious drought year throughout Wales with next to no significant rain falling from spring until autumn. River levels in the Mawddach had been so low from May onwards that the river had virtually ceased to flow to sea and some of the tributaries had dried out. The tragic pollution (caused by the illegal crushing of ore) resulted in a slug of highly toxic water moving downstream over a period of several days until it reached the estuary and was diluted. Despite a major fish rescue operation as the pollutant moved inexorably downriver, some 2,000 adult salmon and sea trout were killed over the eight-mile-section of river affected.

The point of this narrative is to reinforce the scientific evidence that sea trout, unlike salmon, will move into and through the lower reaches of a river on very low flows. Nobody – until faced with the disastrous proof of some 2,000 dead carcases of fish up to 12lb weight – would have believed for one moment that so many fish could have penetrated so far upstream in so little water.

One curious feature of sea trout is the marked preponderance of female fish in the smolt and adult populations. In theoretical (Mendelian) terms the ratio of males to females should be approximately 1:1. In situations where sea trout are absent (such as above impassable waterfalls) the ratio of males to females does in fact approximate 1:1. But all the past studies on sea trout *smolts* have shown the occurrence of many more females than males; and this curious imbalance has also been widely reported among spawning adults.

It is now accepted that this strange phenomenon is explained by some of the male fish becoming sexually mature as parr. The phenomenon of precocious sexual maturity (termed 'neoteny' or 'paedogenesis') in the male parr is well known in Atlantic salmon and it has been shown that the mature *dwarf* salmon males can take part in spawning and successfully fertilise the eggs of the much larger females. The important difference in this respect between salmon and sea trout is that while the precocious male salmon parr may subsequently smolt and migrate to sea, none of the mature male sea trout parr undergo the smolt transformation. (Certainly, no sexually mature male sea-trout smolt has ever been reported.)

Several workers have examined the sex ratios of resident 'trout' in various regions and found a total, or near-total, absence of females in some rivers. Since no population can reproduce without mature females it was to be concluded that all the females had migrated to sea and, by an extension of logic, that the population consisted solely of sea trout.

Mature female smolts have never been recorded for sea trout (or salmon). It is interesting to speculate that *if* the precocious sexual maturity and non-migration of the males had been paralleled in the females during the evolutionary history of the sea trout, it would provide a provocative explanation for the occurrence of the non-migratory 'brown' trout.

The behaviour of whitling in relation to their pattern of return from the sea is complex and not fully understood. In some rivers a very large proportion of the stock may consist of sea trout that have spent less than a year in the sea; while in other rivers the whitling run may be small and represent an insignificant proportion of the total stock. Thus whitling are rare in the Coquet, represent 20 per cent of the rod catch in the Tywi, 45 per cent in the Teifi and more than 50 per cent of the rod catch in many Irish and some Scottish rivers. (See also Table 3.)

Nall (and others) suggest that very few whitling that enter fresh water do so for the purposes of spawning. However, research in Ireland and Wales has established that a significant proportion of the whitling run does mature and spawn during the year of entry. Irish studies have established that up to 25 per cent of the whitling run matures and investigations in Wales suggest that these mature whitling – which are predominantly males – may make an important contribution to spawning success.

The peak of the whitling run in many rivers occurs in July/August, but some whitling may occur prior to and after this period. In some rivers large shoals of 'whitling' enter the river over winter.

That a variable (but usually large) proportion of the whitling run does not enter the river for the purposes of spawning must now be accepted. Why whitling should forsake the richer feeding of tidal waters to re-enter the river for no apparent purpose is difficult to explain in terms of life-cycle strategy. It has been suggested that it is no more than an accidental 'overshoot' of their normal coastal and estuarial feeding range: or that they 'followed' runs of larger spawning fish into the river. None of the speculations seem particularly plausible.

It is convenient here to mention some sea-trout superlatives: namely the largest, oldest, most-spawned and fastest-growing sea trout.

For many years the British record rod-caught sea trout was a 22½lb fish taken in the River Frome (Dorset) in 1946. This fish was recently deleted from the British Record list because there was good reason to believe that it was a previously spawned salmon. The record is currently held by a fish of 20lb taken on the River Esk in November 1983. Larger fish have been taken by commercial fishermen from a number of rivers in the British Isles. The largest authenticated sea trout known to us is a 27lb fish recovered from the River Luce in Kirkudbrightshire (Scotland). The oldest British sea trout is still the 12½lb fish taken in the Kinlochewe river in Sutherland in October 1928. It was in its nineteenth year and had previously spawned 11 times (scale formula = 4.3 + 11 sm+). This same fish is also the most-spawned British sea trout on record.

From the limited data available from past scale-reading studies it seems that the River Ewe/Loch Maree system is unusual for the longevity and multiple-spawning characteristics of its sea trout (Table 3). Nall records from his scale collection three fish in their fifteenth year, two in their fourteenth year, nine in their thirteenth year and 27 in their twelfth year after hatching. Few other rivers can match this. The Ailort (Inverness) comes close but the oldest fish was only in its fourteenth year and the maximum number of spawning marks was eight.

South of the Scottish border the record for longevity is shared by two fish: a sea trout of 20¾lb from the Dyfi and a 14lb fish from the Irt

The largest authenticated British sea trout to date. A beautifully proportioned female of 27lb from the River Luce in South West Scotland. Larger sea trout have been reported from several Welsh and Scottish rivers but never authenticated. This fish, found in 'mysterious' circumstances, was 11 years old (scale formula = 2.2 + 7SM+). (Photo: Stuart Coy.)

(Cumberland). The Irt fish had spawned eight times and, along with a 15lb fish from the Avon (Devon) and a 16¼lb fish from the Dyfi, this appears to be the greatest number of repeat spawnings recorded for English and Welsh sea trout. The maximum number of spawning marks reported for Irish sea trout is five and there have only been a very few fish of more than ten years of age in the Irish Scale collections.

It is impossible to find any scientific basis for the belief so widely held by many anglers that adult sea trout continue to feed extensively on their return to fresh water. The simple fact of the matter is that only *two* proper investigations into the nature and extent of feeding have been undertaken, and both indicate that the sea trout is more closely related to the salmon than to the brown trout in terms of its feeding behaviour on its return from the sea.

The first study was carried out in 1926 by Nall on sea trout from Loch Maree in Scotland, while the second study was carried out in 1971 (by the first author) on sea trout from the Afon Dyfi in Wales. Both studies were based upon analyses of 150 stomachs, but it is proper to note that there were

Table 3: Frequency of spawning: percentage of previously spawned fish showing one or more spawning marks on scales

District/River	No. of Spawning Marks								
	1	2	3	4	5	6	7	8	9
Ireland: Waterville	64.9	19.1	9.1	5.0	1.9	—	—	—	—
Inny	59.0	31.0	10.0	—	—	—	—	—	—
Foyle	77.0	22.0	1.0	—	—	—	—	—	—
Gowla	83.3	16.7	—	—	—	—	—	—	—
Wales: Dyfi	58.9	19.0	9.5	4.8	3.0	3.0	0.8	0.8	—
Tywi	53.3	32.0	8.5	3.7	2.5	—	—	—	—
Scotland: Ewe/Maree	38.7	30.0	14.6	7.8	4.4	2.2	0.9	0.9	0.9
Ailort	48.5	27.4	12.0	6.7	3.1	1.3	0.7	0.3	—
Spey	63.2	29.2	6.0	1.6	—	—	—	—	—
N. Esk	81.0	14.2	2.7	—	—	—	—	—	—

certain differences between the two samples. The first consisted exclusively of fish obtained *on the fly during the day in stillwater* and contained mostly whitling; the second consisted of fish obtained by various means, including angling and electro-fishing, of which 66 per cent were taken on the fly at night in running water and only about 50 per cent were whitling.

Notwithstanding these differences the results are revealing. The Scottish sample showed that 62 per cent of fish contained 'little or no' food in the stomach compared with 93 per cent in the Welsh sample. It may be that sea trout in lakes are more prone to feed than in rivers and/or that whitling are more likely to continue feeding than larger, older, fish. (This is a view held by many angling authorities and one to which we also subscribe.) It seems logical that those whitling that have returned to fresh water for some inexplicable reason other than to spawn should, in survival terms, continue to ingest whatever food they can find.

Nall lists the range of food organisms found in his Scottish sample as 'a bumble bee, wasps, water beetles, small land beetles, various insects and small crustaceans, but not fish'. A summary of the food organisms found in Welsh sea trout is shown in Table 4. Of the three stomachs which were either 'full' or 'distended' with food in this study:

— one male whitling *kelt* of ½lb weight contained 87 salmonid eggs;
— one female whitling of ½lb weight contained one trout parr (2½ inches length) and one chironomid adult;
— one female sea trout (c. 2lb weight) contained two trout parr (2 inches and 3 inches length), one salmon parr (4 inches length), three stonefly larvae, one caddis larvae and four chironomid adults.

It is to be noted that the feeding of brown trout was also compared in each of the above studies. In the Dyfi study the stomachs of all brown trout examined were more than half full, and in the Scottish study those brown-trout stomachs examined were 'gorged' with food while sea trout taken in the 'same place at the same time' had much less food in their stomachs.

As a result of his Loch Maree work and 'perfunctory investigations of stomach contents in other districts', Nall draws several tentative conclusions and felt confident enough to make certain general statements about the fresh water feeding of adult sea trout. Thus he states 'Though sea trout, taken in the sea or in brackish tidal waters, are at times gorged with food, in fresh water they feed more intermittently and with a less robust appetite than freshwater trout.'

The Welsh study (Table 4) certainly supports this view and, on the basis of the obvious differences in the extent of feeding, could qualify it to read '... *much* more intermittently and with a *far* less robust appetite...'.

Table 4: Freshwater diet of adult sea trout: Afon Dyfi
The occurrence and numbers of different food organisms in 150 stomachs (112 stomachs were empty. The table is based on 38 stomachs containing some food)

Type of Food	Frequency of Occurrence in Stomachs	Total No. of Animals
Lubricidae		
Lumbricus terrestris	1	1
Crustacea		
Gammarus pulex		
Plecoptera — larvae		
Leuctridae	10	10
Nemoridae	2	2
Perlodidae	4	4
Perlidae	1	3
Ephemoptera — larvae		
Ecdyonuridae	2	2
Unidentified	3	3
Trichoptera — larvae		
Unidentified (cased)	5	7
Diptera		
Unidentified — adults	3	3
Simulidae — larvae	1	1
— adults	1	1
Chironomidae — larvae	5	6
— adults	10	30
Tabanidae — adults	1	1
Coleoptera — adult		
Unidentified	1	1
Helminthidae	1	1
Corixidae	1	1
Dermaptera		
Forficulina sp	1	1

Hymenoptera		
Formicidae — F. rufa	2	3
Diplopoda		
Unidentified	1	4
Araneidae		
Unidentified — terrestrial	1	1
Lepidoptera		
Heterocera — unidentified	1	1
Pisces		
S. trutta (parr)	2	3
S. salar (parr)	1	1
Salmonid ova	3	92
Unidentified material		
Vegetable	2	2
Freshwater animal	5	5
Marine animal	4	4

Bearing in mind that if all the food items from the stomachs of the 150 sea trout in the Welsh study had been contained in a single sea trout of 3–4lb weight the stomach would be nowhere near full, we have little hesitation in stating that whereas whitling, especially that proportion of the run not destined to spawn on their return to fresh water (page 19), *may* continue actively to seek out and take whatever food may be available, those sea trout that have entered the river for the sole purpose of spawning do not 'feed' in the normal sense of the word. They may occasionally ingest items of food if they become readily available, but this behaviour does not constitute feeding in the accepted sense of obtaining nourishment in order to sustain life and to grow in size. It is now universally accepted that the salmon does not feed in fresh water; even though the odd food item may be found in the stomach of the occasional fish. Instead it sustains life by utilising the accumulated reserves of food ('fat') stored in its body during its period of feeding and growth in the sea. In many rivers the sea trout may be as large as and numerically equivalent to salmon. If suppressed feeding in the adult is accepted as a mechanism to avoid depleting the limited food resources required to sustain the offspring in salmon, why should this same survival mechanism not also apply to sea trout? Nall, writing in the context of his Scottish study, stated the matter simply. 'A moment's reflection should convince us that if they did feed regularly, the food in our rivers and lochs would be quite inadequate to supply the needs of the shoals of sea trout which run up during summer and autumn, to say nothing of the permanent stocks of fresh water trout and other fish.'

We must now return to the question that we deliberately avoided at the start of this chapter: WHAT IS A SEA TROUT? The question is not wholly academic. The answer is of paramount importance to the future well-being of the resource because, quite simply, how can we properly manage and

23

regulate the fisheries if we do not know what it is that we are managing? For example, what is the point of restocking with sea trout to maintain or increase stocks when we do not know if they will migrate to sea and return as 'sea trout' or stay behind in the river and become 'brown trout'?

The question can be rephrased in several ways which serve to highlight the nature of the problem and encapsulate some of the more popular theories about the origins and relationships of sea trout and brown trout. Thus:–

1. Are *sea trout* merely sea-run brown trout which have dropped down-river to enter the estuary and moved out to sea?
2. Are *brown trout* merely non-migratory sea trout which spend their entire life in the river without migrating to sea?
3. Are *sea trout* and *brown trout* two separate and distinct species that breed true to type?
4. Are *all forms of trout* (see trout, brown trout, river trout, lake trout, Ferox, Gillaroo, slob trout, etc) merely products of the environment with no genetic basis for their occurrence?
5. Is there a genetic basis to explain the many forms of trout that can occur?
6. Is the sea trout best regarded as a 'compound' or 'composite species' consisting of two different genetically based components: true-breeding sea trout and a proportion of sea-run brown trout?

Each of the above has its proponents and opponents, but the scientific community is still seeking to come up with an answer to the seemingly simple question first posed by Henry Lamond in 1916. Much new information has become available over the latter part of the intervening period but the situation is very complex and a plausible explanation, while probably just around the corner, is not yet available.

In order to understand the complexity of the problem, we must go back to 1758 when the Swedish scientist Carl von Linné (Linnaes) published his 'Systema Naturae'. This established the binomial system of scientific nomenclature and made him the father of modern taxonomy.

Taxonomy is the science of classifying plants and animals into groups (taxonomic units) on the basis of their similarities and differences. The basic unit is the species. This always has two names which are in Latin. The first (written with a capital letter) identifies the genus. The second (written without a capital letter) identifies the species. Thus within the genus *Salmo* we have *Salmo salar*, the Atlantic salmon, *Salmo trutta*, the European trout, and *Salmo gairdneri*, the Rainbow trout.

During the Victorian era, taxonomy was a fashionable science. The only problem was that each taxonomist working on trout described various 'new' species so that it became all very confusing. Indeed, there were almost as many species of trout as taxonomists describing them! New species were described on the basis of almost any difference in appearance (morphology) or construction (anatomy). Characteristics such as colour and size, and the number of spots, teeth, vertebrae and caecal appendages to the gut, were variously used to describe new species along with almost anything else that could be qualified and characterised as 'different' – such as the thickness of the stomach wall.

Francis Day, writing in 1867, recognised three different species of trout in Europe: *Salmo eriox* – the sea trout; *Salmo trutta* – the river trout; *Salmo fario* – the brook trout. However, at about the same time, another taxonomist recognised *ten* different species within the British Isles, of which five were migratory and five were non-migratory. Thus for migratory or sea-run species:–

Salmo trutta – the sea trout or salmon trout
Salmo cambricus – the sewin or western sea trout
Salmo brachypoma – the finnock or eastern sea trout
Salmo gallivensis – the Galway sea trout
Salmo Orcadensis – the Orkney sea trout

And for non-migratory or freshwater species:–

Salmo fario – the river trout
Salmo stomachicus – the gillaroo trout
Salmo ferox – the great lake trout
Salmo levensis – the Loch Leven trout
Salmo nigripinnus – the Welsh black-finned trout

Other taxonomists variously described other different trout species, either in addition to or instead of the above, such as *Salmo lacustris* – the lake trout; *Salmo esturias* – the estuary or slob trout, and it all got very confusing and biologically inexact. The heated scientific debate about the taxonomy of trout that ensued in the latter part of the nineteenth century has been described as the war between the 'Lumpers' and the 'Splitters'. The Splitters were those who described anything that looked different as a new species. The Lumpers argued that the trout was a very flexible and plastic species and claimed that the many forms described as species by the Splitters were merely the result of differences in the local environment rather than genetic differences. In their view, a trout that fed on snails had a thick stomach wall as a direct consequence of its diet and so the gillaroo (*Salmo stomachicus*) was no different from any trout that did not feed on snails. Likewise *Salmo ferox* only became the great lake trout because it fed on fish instead of insects, and so grew to a large size.

By the early part of the twentieth century the war was over. The Lumpers had won. Thus for the last fifty years conventional scientific wisdom has accepted that there is but one species of trout in the British Isles – *Salmo trutta*. It was, however, accepted that it was a very plastic species that could exist in a variety of different forms depending upon the local environment.

That is the accepted conventional wisdom. But, as we shall see, conventional wisdom can change as new information becomes available.

One of the most pervasive themes in the angling literature is that sea trout are merely brown trout which drop down to the estuary and then go to sea and which then return to the river to spawn as sea-run trout. It is conjectured that over-crowding in the river environment causes some fish to be displaced down-river and, also, that they can be washed out to sea during severe flooding.

The occurrence of estuary-feeding brown trout (often called 'slob trout') is well documented from several river estuaries in the British Isles. Such fish are usually well marked and often heavily spotted. They are more common in certain types of estuary than in others. (They are rare in England and Wales.)

Support for the brown trout displacement theory was once based on the appearance of impressive runs of sea trout in parts of New Zealand, notwithstanding the 'fact' that only brown trout were imported from Europe in the 1860s. Thus, 'sea trout are brown trout that go to sea'! *However*, careful scrutiny of the meticulous records of the 'Acclimatisation Societies' has shown that eggs from sea trout *were* imported on at least six separate occasions during the first decade of introductions.

Further support for the view that brown trout gave rise to sea trout is based on the argument that if sea trout are prevented from migrating to sea they can complete their entire life history in fresh water. This, combined with the fact that brown trout can adapt to, and thrive in, salt water quite readily was thought to be telling proof. However, the fact that sea trout can complete their entire life cycle in fresh water if prevented from migrating may not be significant. So can the Atlantic salmon!

The theory that sea trout and brown trout are distinct and true-breeding species leans heavily on the occurrence of the smolt transformation in juvenile sea trout and its absence in the brown trout. Stripping eggs and milt from non-migratory brown trout parents and rearing the offspring in a hatchery yields mature adults that fail to undergo the smolt transformation, whereas repeating the experiment with eggs and milt from migratory (sea trout) parents yields offspring that produce smolts.

The smolt transformation is a traumatic and complex physiological change that seemingly pre-adapts the young fish for life in the sea so that it is better able to survive. It affects its behaviour, osmo-regulatory mechanism, and camouflage. It would be a disastrous change for a fish remaining in fresh water and which is under genetic control. Moreover, it has been established that even when sea trout were prevented from migrating to sea as smolts and were reared through to sexual maturity in fresh water, the offspring of the second and third generations showed no reduction in the innate tendency to become smolts.

The composite or compound theory has some appeal; but only because it offers a simple way out of what is clearly a very complex situation. There is little doubt that some brown trout can, and do, drop down to the sea and re-turn to the river to spawn as sea-run trout indistinguishable in appearance from those returning sea trout that went to sea as smolts. In some localities a large proportion of the returning fish may be of brown-trout origin while elsewhere they may be few and far between.

The question 'What is a sea trout?' was discussed at great length by the assembled experts at the 1984 'Sea Trout Workshop' (page 5). Much new information was presented, but the only area of broad agreement was that the question was wrong in the first place! Let us now ask 'What is a brown trout?' Why do some sea trout remain behind in fresh water as brown trout instead of migrating to the sea?

It is now held that (in the recent evolutionary history of the species at least) the sea trout is the ancestor of all other forms of trout. The popular expla-nation is that during the ice age, which spanned a period of some 900,000 years and ended only some 10,000 years ago, virtually all of the British Isles was at some time covered in ice so that any fish living in our rivers or lakes would have been eradicated or forced to migrate into the sea and move south in order to survive. The ice age had several periods (stadials) when the ice front receded and advanced but eventually our river systems were *recolonised from the sea* to give the present native range of *Salmo trutta*. Ultimately some sea trout lost the urge to migrate back to sea and remained behind to complete their entire life-cycle in fresh water, so giving rise. to the non-migratory brown trout.

One of the most exciting advances over the last decade has been the deployment of a technique called 'electrophoresis' to the confused taxonomy of the trout. Electrophoresis entails separating proteins derived from blood, muscle tissue, liver etc which have slight differences in their chemical construction by their different rates of migration (or mobility) in an electric field. Enzymes and other proteins are the primary products of the gene and so by examining different kinds of protein and their frequency of occurrence it is possible to obtain a biochemical 'fingerprint' of the fish. The technique has wide application. It can be used to distinguish between different species, identify hybrids (page 31), isolate geographical races and even recognise different populations of fish within the same river or lake.

Virtually all of the relevant electrophoretic studies on trout undertaken to date have been in Ireland where some 40 river systems have been examined. From these investigations it has been postulated that our rivers were colonised from the sea by two successive invasions of trout – the 'Ancestral' and the 'Modern'. The former is characterised by the LDH-5 (105) allele (LDH is the enzyme lactic dehydrogenase; an allele is an alternative form), while the latter, which is possibly of a more southerly origin, is characterised by the LDH-5 (100) allele and is more common.

Both invasions of sea trout gave rise to resident brown-trout populations. The ice age wrought momentous changes to the geomorphology of the British Isles. As the ice receded the landmass, freed from the vast weight

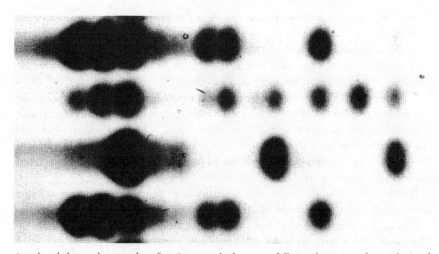

Starch-gel electrophoresis identifies proteins which exist in different forms (= polymorphic) and so provides a genetic 'fingerprint' for the recognition of different 'strains', 'races' and sub-species of trout. The zymogram shown here is stained to identify the enzyme phosphoglucose isomerase. The two similar outer bands are for two separate brown trout. They are different from the Atlantic salmon (inner bottom). A natural hybrid between trout and salmon is shown also (inner top). (Photo: Dr A. Ferguson.)

of ice that had covered it, rose upwards and resulted in the creation of impassable barriers (waterfalls) to upstream migration. Since any trout above such falls which migrated to sea could no longer return upstream to spawn and perpetuate their genes, there would have been a very strong selection pressure for non-migration and a loss of the sea-going habit if the upstream population was to survive.

The results from the Irish studies are interesting, if somewhat confusing. In some rivers genetic differences between brown trout and sea trout were apparent; in others the 'trout' population was heterogenous with no apparent distinction between migrants and non-migrants. Elsewhere there were distinct differences between the sea trout of neighbouring rivers (reinforcing the evidence from tagging studies [page 15] that sea trout do not stray between different rivers) and in most situations there were distinct differences in the resident trout of different rivers and, often, between the resident trout in different tributaries of the same river.

So what is a sea trout/brown trout? Electrophoresis has told us much but it still has not provided the answer. The technique is relatively crude and of limited value in the detection of genetic differences which may have evolved in only the last 10,000 years. Our answer may, therefore, have to await the development of even newer advances in gene technology which allow *direct* examination of mitochondrial and nuclear DNA. However, it is now widely accepted that there is a genetic basis for the existence of sea trout and brown trout and that the two forms do *not* owe their existence solely to the chance effects of the local environment.

Staying with the general theme of genetics, we will move on to consider the occurrence of local races and of hybrids.

Several eminent icthyologists have recognised the existence of different races of sea trout within the British Isles: but opinion as to where these occur and as to what constitutes a 'race' varies. It is evident that we still have a great deal more to learn about this topic which has important implications for the way we manage our fisheries in the future. More is known about the genetic composition of local stocks of salmon than sea trout but, since both have a similar anadromous life history and both return to their natal (= donor) river to spawn with a high degree of specificity, there may be important parallels between the two species.

Three different forms of trout from Lough Melvin in the north-west of Ireland: Sonaghen or Welsh Black-finned Trout, *Salmo nigripinnis* (top); the Great Lake Trout, *Salmo ferox* (centre); Gillaroo, *Salmo stomachicus* (bottom). These three forms were originally described as separate species, but for the last 70 years 'conventional wisdom' has held that they were no more than environmentally-produced variants (ecophenotypes) within the single 'plastic' species *Salmo trutta*. But some scientists now argue that these three forms at least qualify as distinct species because they are reproductively isolated within Lough Melvin, and individual fish can be correctly identified on the basis of their morphological, biochemical-genetic and meristic data. (Photo: Dr A. Ferguson.)

Modern scientific opinion, based mainly on electrophoresis, now holds that genetically different local stocks of salmon occur in many different river systems. Indeed in some larger systems genetic differences may occur within the salmon populations of certain tributaries of the same river. The simple explanation for these differences in that the local river environment creates a selection pressure that favours a particular 'type' of fish which is better able to survive in that particular environment. Thus in fast flowing streams parr with large pectoral fins may be at an advantage because the fish are better able to 'hold bottom' and do not have to expend energy in swimming against the current. Likewise, in rivers where the geology and hydrology of the catchment is such that the stream bed is rocky with large spawning gravels, the selection pressure may favour large fish that can utilise large gravel for spawning and so fish that spent longer at sea and grew larger before returning to spawn for the first time would be at an advantage.

Conventional wisdom now stresses the importance of maintaining the genetic integrity of these local stocks by avoiding the importation of 'alien' genes from different river systems when restocking with eggs, fry, parr and smolts. The arguments against the traditional practice of introducing 'new blood' – so favoured in the past in order to 'improve the stocks' – are quite simple:

1. The stock of fish in a particular river has been selected by the particular local environment to best survive under the prevailing conditions.
2. The introduction of stocks from different rivers may be detrimental because the introduced fish may not be well suited to survive in the new environment and any that do survive may breed with native fish and so dilute the 'fitness' of the local stock.

Herbert Nall recognised two 'races' of sea trout in the British Isles on the basis of differences in the structure and composition of the stocks of various rivers as shown from his scale reading investigations. There were a fast-growing but short-lived race on the east coast of Britain, which extended in range from the Kyle of Sutherland in the north to Sussex in the south, and a slower-growing but longer-living race in the west that extended over the remainder of the British Isles and encompassed Wales. Nall stated that both types occur in Ireland, 'the east coast type in rivers that have important estuaries'. Some seventy years earlier, another icthyologist recognised a 'northern' race and a 'southern' race – which included the sea trout of Wales and Ireland – but he freely admitted that 'the two races pass from one to another by insensible gradation' and that 'individuals of the southern type were found in the northern part of the British Isles; and vice versa'.

Recent work on salmon has led to the proposition that there are two distinct types of fish in the North Atlantic which may, arguably, be recognised as the sub-species: *Salmo salar europaeus* and *Salmo salar americanus*. Furthermore, it has been propounded that *S. salar europaeus* is further sub-divided into two distinct races in the British Isles – the 'Celtic' and 'Boreal' forms. It is a matter for speculation to suggest that what applies to S. *salar* also, by the same logic, applies to S. *trutta*. It is likely that this is so, in our view. Perhaps, bearing in mind the occurrence of short-lived sea trout in the Tweed region and in southern England and the occurrence of long-lived sea trout in Wales and on the west coast of Scotland (which may reflect their proximity to ancestral areas of origin), this explains the geographical distribution of Nall's 'eastern' and 'western' races of sea trout – the Boreal race being short-lived and the Celtic race being long-lived. But how you explain the situation that *appears* to exist in Ireland, we do not know!

As yet our knowledge is limited as far as sea trout are concerned. However, it is likely that many of the recognised differences between the sea trout stocks of different rivers, districts and regions in terms of such characteristics as, for example, smolt age, length of time spent in the sea, extent of seaward migration, longevity and spawning frequency are, directly or indirectly, the result of genetic differences. In this respect we draw attention to the curious situation that exists between the sea trout stocks of Wales when compared with the east coast of Ireland. Both fish have access to the same feeding grounds in the Irish sea but there are very obvious differences in the age composition and growth rate of the fish: the Irish fish being smaller and having a shorter life span. Very few Irish fish attain a weight in excess of 10lb but such fish are relatively common in Wales. Another anomaly is the very different nature of the sea-trout stock of the Waterville/Currance system in the south west of Ireland. This is a long-lived stock which has yielded more sea trout with 'official' specimen-status (= 6lb plus) than all the many other Irish sea-trout fisheries combined.

Several early writers accepted that the sea trout was a natural hybrid between the migratory salmon and the non-migratory brown trout. Indeed the term salmon-trout was widely popular until the turn of the century – and is still used occasionally even today.

It has been known for a long time that artificial hybrids between salmon and trout can be produced in hatcheries, but whether such hybrids occurred in nature was a matter for speculation. However, recent research (based on the electrophoretic mobility of blood proteins) has shown that natural hybrids can indeed occur. Up to 1 per cent of all fish identified by their captors as *salmon* on the basis of external appearance contained trout characteristics in their blood and were, therefore, hybrids. However, even though hybrids are more common in some rivers than in others, they are relatively rare and nobody would now accept that the sea trout owes its existence to a breakdown of the barriers that exist to prevent breeding between the members of different species.

Finally we return to the question 'What is a sea trout?' – but we do so in a rather different sense than before. We discuss here how to tell the difference between sea trout and salmon.

31

There is little doubt that it is sometimes very difficult to distinguish between the two species, even for the expert. The best single test is from reading the scales to determine the life-history of the fish. But even then this may not prove with certainty whether the fish was a salmon or sea trout. 'Difficult fish' occur from time to time and the problem is usually greatest

Top: The heavier spotting above and below the lateral line is characteristic of sea trout (bottom). The shape of the salmon (top) is more streamlined than that of the sea trout which has a 'larger' head. *Bottom left*: The maxilla of the sea trout (bottom) extends beyond a line drawn vertically behind the eye. In salmon (top) it rarely does so. Size for size, the sea trout has a larger mouth than the salmon. *Bottom right*: The tail fin of the salmon (top) is more V-shaped than the sea trout (bottom) and it has a narrower wrist. In larger sea trout the tail is slightly convex, straight, or slightly concave. Note the difference in the shape of the anal fins. (Photo: Dr M. Berg.)

with fast-growing maiden sea trout of 'grilse' size (4–8lb weight). Problems also occur with previously spawned salmon, as these can be quite heavily spotted and are often identified as sea trout by their captors. In this instance, however, scale reading usually discovers the error.

The misidentification of salmon and sea trout by anglers and commercial fishermen is quite extensive in some areas with large sea trout. It is not unusual for up to 10 per cent of the scales submitted by netsmen in scale-reading studies, and stated to be 'sea trout' or 'salmon', to have been wrongly identified. This is particularly prevalent with small grilse salmon. Anything less than about 4lb in weight is frequently assumed to be a sea trout.

However, 'difficult fish' are the exception rather than the rule and, provided you know what to look for, it is usually quite easy to distinguish between the two species. We should stress that there is no single, wholly reliable, diagnostic feature. Sometimes several characteristics may have to be checked before the diagnosis can be confirmed with confidence. We include below a list of some of the more useful external characteristics which can be used to distinguish between sea trout and salmon. Each paragraph refers to a specific point.

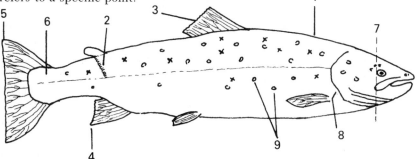

Fig. 2. Diagnostic features of sea trout.

1. *General shape*. Allowing for much variation both within and between the two species and different local stocks, the sea trout is generally broader, heavier and stockier, whereas the salmon is more slender and streamlined in shape.
2. *Adipose Scale Count*. The number of scales in a line drawn obliquely downwards and forwards to the lateral line from the *hind* edge of the adipose fin is 13–16 (usually 14) in sea trout and 10–13 (usually 11) in salmon. (Size for size of fish the scales of sea trout are smaller, and so more numerous, than salmon.)
3. *Dorsal Fin Ray Count*. The number of branched rays in the dorsal fin is 8–10 for sea trout and 10–12 in salmon.
4. *Anal Fin Shape*. The anal fin of sea trout is more 'pointed' in shape than the salmon. The outer fin ray of sea trout extends beyond the inner ray when the fin is pushed against the body. In salmon the outer fin ray does not extend beyond the inner ray.

33

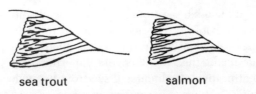

sea trout   salmon

Fig. 3. Anal fin shape.

5. *Tail Shape.* This is, perhaps the first test used when any doubt arises. By and large it is very useful. The rays of the caudal fin (= tail fin) of the sea trout are more equal in length than with salmon. In sea trout the tail shape is straight, slightly curved inwards (concave) or, less common, slightly curved outwards (= convex or 'rounded'). In salmon it is usually concave and distinctly V-shaped.

6. *Caudal Peduncle.* The caudal peduncle (= wrist) of the sea trout is thicker than in salmon. This makes it easier to pick up a salmon by the tail as it is less likely to slip from the grasp than a sea trout of the same size.

7. *Maxillary Extension.* The maxillary bone forms the upper jaw or lip of the fish. In adult sea trout this extends beyond a line drawn vertically behind the rear of the eye. In salmon it may fall short or extend to the rear of the eye – but not beyond. This is a 'key character' – but varies with the size of the fish. In juveniles (parr and smolts) it is different in that in parr the maxilla extends to the middle of the eye pupil in salmon and to the posterior edge of the pupil in sea trout. Size for size the maxillary extension is greater in sea trout. In salmon, regardless of size, the maxilla does not extend beyond the rear of the eye.

8. *Gill maggots.* The gill maggot (*Salmonicola salmonea*) does *not* infest sea trout; it is found on salmon that have spent a long time in fresh water. The sea louse, *Lepeophtheirus salmonis*, occurs on both species and its presence on a fish is a sure indication that it is recently 'fresh-run' from the sea. Any fish with gill maggots, as distinct from sea lice, is undeniably a salmon!

9. *Spots.* To quote Nall, this is 'a very untrustworthy test', but it can help to make the diagnosis when considered alongside other features of the fish. In general terms, the sea trout has more spots than the salmon. However, some sea trout are 'lightly' spotted while some salmon are 'heavily spotted', in species-specific, relative, terms. In maiden (= unspawned) fish, the spots on salmon rarely extend *below* the lateral line. The sea trout usually, but not always, has more spots below the lateral line.

These nine 'tests' are enough for practical purposes. All are based on morphology (= external appearance). There are other tests, based on the number of gill filaments (16–18 in sea trout and 18–22 in salmon) or caecal appendages to the intestine (33–61 in sea trout and 53–77 in salmon) but they require some skill in dissection and anatomy and have little relevance to the angler 'on the bank'.

For practical purposes, the best 'key' characteristics are, in order of utility: a) an 'impression' based on shape and spotting; b) tail shape; c) maxillary extension distance; d) adipose scale count; e) anal-fin ray length. If you need to go any further then you have a 'problem' fish, for which scale reading is most likely to provide the answer.

Reading List and Key References

Day, Francis, *British and Irish Salmonidae*. 1887. Williams & Norgate, London.

Lamond, Henry, *The Sea Trout: A Study in Natural History*. 1916. Sherrat & Hughes, Manchester.

Le Cren, E.D. (*ed*), *The Biology of the Sea Trout*. [Summary of symposium held at Plas Menai 24–26 October 1984] 1985. Atlantic Salmon Trust Ltd, Moulin, Pitlochry, Perthshire, Scotland.

Malloch, P. D., *The Life History and Habitats of the Salmon, Sea Trout and Other Freshwater Fish*. 1910. Adam & Charles Black, London.

Maxwell (Bart), Sir Herbert, *British Freshwater Fish*. 1904. Hutchinson & Co., London.

Nall, G. Herbert, *The Life of the Sea Trout*. 1930. Seeley, Service & Co. Ltd, London.

2 · THE FISHERIES

The British Isles are endowed with a wealth of sea-trout fisheries. With the notable exception of the east coast of England, within the area bounded by the Yorkshire Esk in the north and the Kentish Stour in the south where the slow-flowing and eutrophic rivers are naturally devoid of self-sustaining stocks of sea trout, the species is very widely distributed and occurs at varying levels of abundance throughout the remainder of England, Wales, Scotland and Ireland.

Within this extensive range there are still a few black spots where once prolific salmon and sea-trout fisheries have been eradicated or seriously depleted as a result of man's activities during and after the Industrial Revolution. The several rivers of the South Wales coalfield are a classic example of the deleterious effects of gross pollution by industrial and domestic effluents and of the construction of impassable weirs to divert or abstract water which have denied migratory fish access to their ancestral spawning and nursery areas upstream. Sadly, the destruction and depletion of our migratory fisheries was not just restricted to Wales, and similar, localised examples exist in Scotland (the Clyde and the Forth), in England (the Tyne) and in Ireland (the Spidal River – Co. Galway).

All is not gloom, however. The rehabilitation of the Afon Rheidol (mid-Wales) during the mid-1960s, following a diminution in the residual pollution from the aftermath of the lead and zinc mines, shows what can be achieved. The Rheidol now produces some excellent fishing, and some *very* large sea trout. Salmon and sea trout have returned to the adjacent Afon Ystwyth and, following a dramatic improvement in the water quality of the Afon Taff in South Wales prodigious efforts are being made to restore its sea-trout and salmon stocks as quickly as possible. A small 'founder' stock of sea trout has appeared in the nearby Rhymney and in the neighbouring Llwyd and Ebbw; so that there is good reason to believe that by the turn of the century the sea trout will occupy all of its former range throughout Wales. Hopefully, this will be paralleled elsewhere.

While the sea trout is very widely distributed throughout the British Isles with self-sustaining stocks occurring in countless watercourses ranging in size from the very largest rivers to the smallest coastal streams, it is to be noted that not all rivers provide good sea-trout angling. Some rivers may contain very few sea trout and in other rivers the bulk of the stock may enter after the end of the fishing season and, while plentiful in biological terms, is unavailable to the angler in practical terms.

It is a curious and, as yet, unexplained phenomenon that the rivers Severn, Wye and Usk which flow into the Bristol Channel are among the most productive salmon fisheries in England and Wales, but contain virtually no stocks of sea trout even though they are close to other notable sea-trout rivers. In a good season the Wye has produced over 6,000 salmon to the rods but the recorded rod catch of sea trout has rarely exceeded an annual total of 40 fish. The Usk has produced over 1,500 salmon to the rods in a good year but the sea trout rod catch is seldom more than about 80 fish. A parallel situation occurs in the Welsh Dee which enters the sea at Chester (but see page 39).

Similar examples of productive salmon rivers with, apparently, few sea trout occur also in other regions. The Grimersta system in the Hebridean Isle of Lewis still provides some wondrous salmon fishing; but catches of sea trout are insignificant by comparison. The Tay salmon fishings are legendary; but sea trout appear to be relatively few and far between within the main river – although certain tributaries, such as the Almond, have fairly substantial sea trout runs, and the nearby River Earn, which shares a common estuary with the Tay, provides good sea trout fishing. In Devon, the Exe contains both salmon and brown trout in respectable numbers, but is practically empty of sea trout. In Northern Ireland the Bush, a notable salmon fishery, has no sea trout to speak of.

Rivers with good or even abundant stocks of sea trout but which are unproductive to angling either because the bulk of the sea trout run late in the year (often after the close of the angling season) or because they are, by reputation, dour and unresponsive to the inducements of anglers are the Tweed in south-east Scotland and the Coquet in north-east England. Both contain large stocks of sea trout, many of which attain gargantuan proportions – especially in the Tweed where sea trout in excess of 20lb weight regularly feature in the commercial net catch. The Till (an English tributary of the lower river) is famed for its large but uncatchable sea trout. Data from the fish trap at Warkworth on the Coquet has shown that vast numbers of sea trout enter the river after the end of the fishing season, with many attaining specimen size. A quite staggering statistic is that the average run of sea trout into the Coquet over the last 25 years has been over 10,000 fish a year (with an average weight of about 5lb) compared with a total rod catch of only about 250! – that is until it is realised that most of the run enters just before the end of the fishing season and continues in strength to late December.

The quality of our sea-trout fisheries is inevitably judged on what is caught, and each fish must be reported and recorded if it is to become a catch statistic. We have shown the official catch statistics for the rod and commercial fisheries of each region over recent years (Table 5). We must caution that interpretation of the record is fraught with difficulties and at best it merely indicates the minimum level of catch. Whether that minimum catch repre-

Table 5: Declared national catch statistics for sea trout for both rods and commercial instruments[1]. (Based on official statistics).

Region	Method	Number of Sea Trout Caught			
		1982	1983	1984	1985
Scotland	Rods	33695	40159	42141	51538
	Commercial	122312	80686	114477	71757
England	Rods	17120	15596	12174	11511
	Commercial	25552	75945	84762	83094
Wales	Rods	21421	23561	18386	20868
	Commercial	7788	8566	10937	5097
Irish Republic	Rods	20491	25257	18878	N/A[3]
	Commercial	37853	48486	N/A[3]	N/A
Northern Ireland	Rods	N/A[3]	N/A	N/A	N/A
	Commercial	N/A[3]	905	946	526
Foyle F.C.[2]	Rods	276	1103	1106	494
	Commercial	4999	6573	3588	4834

[1] Commercial Instruments include nets, traps and fixed engines.
[2] The Foyle Fisheries Commission is an independent management agency. The Foyle flows through both the Republic of Ireland and Northern Ireland.
[3] N/A denotes that data is either not available or not yet published.

sents the true catch, approximates the true catch, or is nowhere near the true catch, is a matter for speculation (and grave concern, page 367).

The above comment applies to the national catch records generally. At a regional and local level the historical or the contemporary catch record *may* be quite good. Much depends on how it is collected and the effort put into collecting it. In some areas catch data for sea trout is not collected at all! Where it is collected it may be compiled in different ways: 1) by catch returns submitted by the individual angler or commercial fisherman directly to the statutory management agency (as in Wales); 2) by records maintained by the owner or occupier of the fishery and then compiled centrally (as in Scotland); and c) by diary-records of fish 'known' to have been caught maintained by enforcement staff (some parts of England). The Irish catch record has historically been collected by 'any manner of means'!

The point we would make is that while the catch record may give an indication of the strength and pattern of the runs of fish, and of the average size of the fish, within a fishery, the information may in itself be misleading and not give a true feel for the quality of the angling. Catch records should be treated with circumspection and interpreted carefully! One fundamentally important piece of further information required is the amount of angling effort that generated the catch. Another is the constraints imposed on when, where and how the angler may fish. A section of water controlled by an angling association with 100 members may yield a catch of (say) 500 sea trout whereas a similar stretch of water fished by a syndicate of 20 rods may yield only 200 fish. The former is undoubtedly the more productive *fishery*, but the latter

38

yields twice as many fish to each rod and clearly provides superior *fishing* for the individual angler. Similarly, fisheries where the methods of fishing are restricted to fly-only, or which allow spinning and worming on floodwater only, will be less productive in terms of the numbers of fish caught than a fishery where unrestricted 'multi-method' fishing is permitted. However, the fact that the catch is higher on the multi-method fishery does not mean that it is better; it merely reflects a higher rate of exploitation on the available stock. (See also Chapter 19.)

Do not be misled by statistics! Some of the best sea-trout fishing is to be had in small coastal streams and small lochs that very few people have ever heard of and which never appear in the angling guides.

The official catch statistics produced by the ten Regional Water Authorities in England and Wales are very detailed. They are presented on a river-by-river basis (unlike Scotland – see below) and state the total number, weight, and month of capture of salmon and sea trout for the rods and nets. All this is very helpful for the angler as it allows each river system to be compared in useful terms. (Some Water Authorities provide even more detailed information in their annual fisheries reports than can be found in the statistics produced centrally by the Ministry of Agriculture, Fisheries and Food.)

Sadly, the law in Scotland does not allow the details of fish catches on any one fishery to be disclosed for a period of ten years. Thus the catch statistics for Scotland are published by the Department of Agriculture and Fisheries on a regional and district basis in such a way that it is impossible to discover how many sea trout were caught by the rods or nets on (say) the Nith, Tweed, Spey, Deveron or Ailort in the seasons immediately prior to an intended visit. This grouping of catch data on a regional basis also applies in the Republic of Ireland; although the 'confidentiality rule' does not apply there.

We understand the history behind this statutory provision for ten-year confidentiality, but wonder if it is necessary or justifiable any longer. A great deal can change in terms of the abundance and composition of the runs over ten years! However, many estates and fishing hotels keep meticulous records for their fisheries and, in order to attract your custom, will reveal details of the catch in recent seasons.

By way of final comment on the relative merits of the sea-trout fisheries in different regions we would make the point that many fisheries may be undervalued in relation to their sea-trout potential because, quite simply, *they are not being fished properly in terms of how, where and when they are fished.*

We mentioned above that the Welsh Dee is not regarded as a sea trout river. Yet research carried out in the 1960s showed that there was a substantial run of sea trout into that river *during the angling season*. This observation has been reconfirmed recently by the occurrence of large numbers of sea trout in the observation chamber associated with the electronic fish counter at Chester weir. We have mentioned above the surprising number of sea trout that ran the Mawddach during the drought of

A tragic sight! The results of a deliberate poisoning by poachers using cyanide in one small pool on the Afon Clwyd in 1984. Many of the fish weighed upwards of 5lb. The largest weighed 12lb. A good fishkill can reveal much! There are many more larger sea trout in our rivers than shown by the anglers' catches. Do we fish for them properly? (Photo: Bob Hewitt.)

1984 as shown by the tragic fish kill incident in August – many of which were of double figure weight (page 18). Other fishkills on the Afon Tâf, Glaslyn, Clwyd and Dyfi in recent years have established that the incidence of very large sea trout is far higher than generally recognised by anglers on the basis of the numbers caught. Ireland is not noted for producing large sea trout: a 6lb fish has 'official specimen status' (see page 52). Within the list of Irish 'specimen' sea trout, the Erriff has achieved some minor claim to fame but a recent investigation which entailed trapping the run of spawned (= kelt) sea trout leaving Lough Tawnyard has shown that there are many more 'specimen' sea trout entering the Erriff than anyone would have accepted based on their occurrence in the rod catch. Why then does a particular river not produce more sea trout or more specimen sea trout? There are three possible explanations:

1. If no-one bothers to fish for sea trout then none will be caught! Only a few anglers fish seriously for sea trout on the Welsh Dee and so only a small proportion of the run is captured.
2. In order to catch sea trout successfully you must fish for sea trout – and you must do it properly! The fact that few sea trout are caught on a particular river does not necessarily mean that they are scarce. We suggest that one of the reasons why more large sea trout are not caught (especially on Irish and some Scottish rivers) is that very few anglers fish for them properly.
3. The traditional 'best' period for sea trout is June to September. Most anglers concentrate their efforts to within this limited period. We admit that come September, when the nights lengthen and the air temperature cools, the appeal of night fishing wanes quickly; and we can understand why so many sea-trout anglers switch their attention to daylight fishing for the run of autumn salmon that occurs in many rivers. Nevertheless, we suspect that many more sea trout (especially 'large' sea trout) would be caught in April and May (depending on the river) and also in September and October if more anglers started their sea-trout fishing earlier and finished it later. Large sea trout run the Tywi and Dyfi in April and May but hardly anyone fishes for them at that time. Substantial 'autumn' runs of large sea trout occur in many rivers (especially on the east coast) but, again, very few anglers fish for them at night.

The pattern of runs of sea trout into different rivers can be very variable in terms of the sizes of the fish and their relative abundance over the season. Some have a run of very large fish in the spring or in the autumn – or in both periods. Some have vast runs of whitling in the summer while others appear to have virtually no whitling run at all (e.g. the Coquet).

The run may, thus, consist of different groups of fish – whitling, maidens, previous spawners – which vary locally in abundance and which enter the river in variable proportions at different times of the year. It is the occurrence and strength of each of these components which characterises each

41

fishery and creates its appeal to the angler.

In Wales – using the Tywi, Teifi, Dyfi and Conwy as examples – the first sea trout appear in April and May, and these are large fish in the 7lb to 10+lb weight class. The main run starts in early June and builds to a peak in mid-July, and consists of fish in the 2–5lb weight class; but some much larger fish continue to enter the river in this period. The run of 2–5lb fish begins to decline in July, but is reasonably abundant in August and tails off in September and October. The run of whitling appears in late June, peaks in late July/August and tails off noticeably in mid-September. Large sea trout reappear again in increased numbers in late August and some very large fish of 6lb plus are present in the rivers in September and early October. (The sea trout angling season finishes on October 17th in Wales.) Table 6 gives the monthly distribution of the rod catch in the four main sea-trout districts of England and Wales.

Table 6: Monthly pattern of rod catches of sea trout in 1984 for main regional water authority areas. (Comparable data not published for Scotland or Ireland)

Region	Mar.	Apr.	May	June	July	Aug.	Sept.	Oct.	Nov.	Dec.
			Proportion of Total Rod Catch of Sea Trout in Each Month							
Welsh	0.5	1.0	2.2	10.2	22.2	22.0	30.4	11.5[1]	NIL	NIL
South West	0.4	0.7	5.1	13.9	31.4	23.3	21.5	2.5	0.1[2]	0.1[2]
North West	NIL	NIL	4.9	19.1	23.5	21.7	24.5	6.2[1]	NIL	NIL
North East	NIL	0.8	0.3	0.8	1.2	3.3	21.2	72.4[1]	NIL	NIL

[1] season ends during October
[2] late season fishing during these months on some rivers in Cornwall
Nil = close season or no catch declared

The *best* period for catching 'large' sea trout in Wales is June to early July and then in early September. The *best* period for taking sea trout in quantity is July and August when the stock of fish of all sizes is at its maximum and this is a good chance of taking fish from ½lb to 20lb. (Very few of the larger [10lb weight plus] sea trout taken in Wales are caught after August.) However, September can be 'good' on many stillwater fisheries in Scotland and Ireland. The *best* period for big sea trout is late spring and early autumn, depending on the region. Generally, late July and August is the *best* period for whitling.

Apart from a lightning tour of the sea-trout fisheries of the British Isles by geographical region (page 43), we have avoided any detailed guidance on 'where to fish'. We recognise the value of the information to the angler; but we also acknowledge the impossibility of providing it here. Quite simply the problem is that there is so much sea-trout fishing available in terms of the number of rivers and still waters where sea trout can be caught, and so many interests (estates, hotels, associations, farmers) making fishing available on a day, week, season, rod-day/season, accommodation plus, or some other basis, which when combined with the fact that club secretaries change frequently, fishing rights change hands occasionally, and prices and access conditions change regularly, all serve to make the information rapidly outdated.

The best that we can hope to do here is to 'point' the angler in the right direction. In the following sections we attempt to characterise the main features of the sea-trout fisheries within each region of the British Isles. We include (where available) statistical data on catches in an attempt to provide a 'feel' for the fisheries of each region. We start 'at the top' with Scotland, and here include the Orkneys and the Shetland Isles merely as a matter of geographical convenience.

Scotland

As far as Scottish sea trout are concerned it is difficult to know where to start. It is a land of plenty and of contrast and extremes. Like Ireland it has so much to offer; but we would stress that sea-trout fishing in Scotland is very different to Ireland in several respects.

The problem with Scottish sea trout fishing is that it is grossly under-rated and largely overshadowed by the abundance and wealth of the more prestigious salmon – of which Scotland has more than its fair share (the Scottish salmon fishery represents about 20 per cent of the declared world catch). The importance attached to the salmon in many regions of Scotland tends to deny the sea-trout angler access to some potentially superlative sea-trout fishing unless willing to pay salmon prices, and even then night fishing may be 'discouraged' (to put it mildly) on those salmon fisheries where the beats rotate. daily. (Until we were disabused of the notion we thought – ingenuously it would seem – that Scottish fishery owners could maximise their income by letting salmon fishing by day and sea trout fishing by night, at a discounted price for a less worthy quarry of course! This would also have the advantage of keeping poachers off the water between dusk and dawn, we mooted. The counter-argument was that no salmon angler would wish to pay good money for fishing to have his beat for the next day disturbed overnight by sea trout anglers. Nevertheless, and we understand this view, the point is worth 'leaving on the table').

Scottish sea-trout fishing appears to suffer from several problems of perception. 'Myth often repeated very soon becomes fact', and it is a fact that the popular perception of Scottish sea trout by anglers 'south of the border' is that it is a) unobtainable, b) expensive, and c) of moderate quality with fish of modest size. This is a nonsense and the perception does not accord with reality. It is true that there is much fishing in Scotland which is a) unobtainable, and b) expensive, *but* Scotland is a big country with many rivers and there is much superlative fishing available to the visiting angler at a reasonable price. Moreover the quality of the sea trout is certainly not to be denigrated. They may have a smaller average weight than in some regions, but then many more are caught; and there is every chance of encountering your 'fish of a lifetime' on almost any Scottish water. Double-figure sea trout are *not* uncommon in Scotland despite popular opinion. Several fisheries, such as the Eachaig, Ailort, Maree/Ewe system, Loch Lomond and the Tweed, produce double-figure sea trout in almost every year, and such fish are less frequently recorded from many less notable fisheries, such as the Earn and the Ruel (Argyllshire). Let there be no doubt that Scotland has much to offer to the visiting sea trout angler (see Table 7).

Scottish sea-trout fishing is a wonderful blend of hotel, estate and association fishing; of rivers, still waters and tidal fishings; of exclusive and prohibitively costly fishing; and of surprisingly cheap water available by the day or week to the visitor.

Our problem here is to do it justice. The task is so daunting that we have every sympathy with F.W. Holiday (see Chapter 3) who described the English and Welsh sea-trout fisheries in detail but drew a line at the Scottish border with the comment, 'In this brief survey of sea trout rivers I don't propose to journey north and over the Tweed. Scottish sea trout fishing is still the best in Britain...'. Clearly he was overwhelmed – and so are we. All we can do is to mention some of the more notable sea-trout waters, while stressing that there is very much more with many fisheries just awaiting to be discovered by the angler. Perhaps the best-known waters are Loch

The 'Stepping Stones'. The River Shiel in Wester Ross (Scotland) is a relatively small west-coast river producing some good sea trout. (Photo: R.O.M. Williams.)

Table 7: Scottish sea trout catches – rod fishing (1981–1985) by regions*
(Source DAFS — statistical bulletins)

Region	Districts Embraced by 'Region'	1982 No.	1982 Wt*	1983 No.	1983 Wt*	1984 No.	1984 Wt*	1985 No.	1985 Wt*
East	Tweed, Forth and Tay	3335	7877	3824	9007	2081	4970	2596	6909
North East	South Esk to Ugie	5734	9690	6899	12866	5838	11649	8355	17299
Moray Firth	Deveron to Conon and Alness	6854	14113	883	18807	13005	26459	11580	26656
North	Kyle of Sutherland to Hope and Grudie	1774	2818	1659	2474	1628	2539	2198	3663
North West	Inchard to Kirkaig and Skye + small Isles	3190	6024	3781	6435	4346	7848	5649	9609
West Coast	Sunart and Aline to Mull/Jura	1474	2155	1913	2797	1754	2695	2484	3502
Clyde Coast	Carrodale/Iorsa to Stinchar	2096	4007	3319	6180	4328	9400	7059	15528
Solway	Luce to Annan[2]	7887	15211	7868	14602	5845	11639	6702	14793
Outer Hebrides	Lewis, Harris and the Uists	1351	3430	1234	2065	3318	4052	3176	4333
Orkney/Shetland	– sic –			NOT RECORDED				1739[1]	3350[1]
ALL SCOTLAND									
— RODS	All Districts	33695	65325	40159	75799	42141	81251	51338	105041
— COMMERCIAL GEARS		122312	299087	80686	210621	114477	278809	71757	188175
— ALL METHODS		156007	364412	120845	286420	156618	360060	123295	293216

* = weight in pounds imperial
1 = Shetland only
2 = Border Esk included with English (= Northwest data)

45

Loch Ba on the Isle of Mull, Inner Hebrides. An excellent long NW/SE loch with good dapping winds. (Photo: W.M. Currie.)

Maree, Loch Lomond, the Spey and the Ythan. Then there is Loch Shiel, Loch Stack and Loch Hope followed by the Conon and Beauly estuaries, the Dee, Deveron and Don, the Brora and Ness, the Almond and Earn, the Findhorn and, of course, the Tweed. There is good fishing on the islands also – such as Lochmaddy and Lochboisdale in the Uists and Loch Stenness in the Orkneys. One area of particular interest for us is the Solway where there are many good sea trout fisheries such as the Nith, Annan, and Border Esk.

England

Sea trout fishing is geographically patchy on the east coast. Sea trout occur in Northumbria, principally the Tyne, Wear and Coquet, and in the Yorkshire Esk but there is then a great void all the way south to the County of Kent. They have recently reappeared in the Kentish Stour but there are further gaps as we move around the coast until we reach the Sussex Ouse, noted for its large sea trout. While several rivers in Sussex and Hampshire contain the odd sea trout (such as the Beaulieu) it is not until we reach Wessex that the sea trout stocks begin to become abundant. The Stour, Piddle and Frome all yield a few fish, but the Avon produces a respectable catch to the rods. English sea trout fishing proper starts in Devon with the Teign and while most rivers in Devon and Cornwall (both north and south) contain sea trout, the principal rivers are the Dart, Plym, Tavy, Lynher, Camel, Fowey and Taw.

Table 8: Declared catches of sea trout by rods and commercial instruments for regional water authority areas in England and Wales: 1983 season (Weight in lbs)

Water Authority[1]	Commercial Instruments			Rods		
	Number Declared	Total Weight	Average Weight	Number Declared	Total Weight	Average Weight
Northumbrian[3]	34012	141751	4.2	692	2852	4.1
Yorkshire[3]	26057	116303	4.5	146	452	3.1
Southern	159	750	4.7	247	832	3.4
Wessex	651	3612	5.6	2151	3605	1.7
South West	7356	17881	2.4	8548	11967	1.4
North West	7710	20055	2.6	3812	6986	1.8
Welsh	8566	30939	3.6	23561	42458	1.8
TOTAL[2]	84511	337087	3.9	39157	69152	1.8

[1] Sea trout fisheries do not occur in the Severn Trent or Thames Water Authority areas.
[2] There is no rod fishery for sea trout in Anglia but the various licensed coastal nets catch 5796 lbs of sea trout.
[3] The sea trout caught by the 330 licensed nets fishing in the sea off Anglia, Yorkshire and Northumbria are predominantly of Scottish origin.

The north-west region has some good sea-trout fishing in Lancashire and the Lake District. The two main fisheries are the Eden and the Lune with the Border Esk, Derwent, Ehen, Leven and Ribble being in the second order.

While the sea trout of the north-east and south have a high average weight and often attain specimen status (Table 9), much of the fishing in the south is unobtainable or expensive in practical terms. Access to English sea-trout angling is focused essentially on the south-west and north-west.

Fishing hotels are few and far between but there are several in Devon and Cornwall and a few in the north-west. There is still much private water held by owners or syndicates, and the visiting angler must gain access to the fishing principally through clubs and associations. Many good clubs exist in Cornwall and in the north-west and the situation is improving in Devon.

If you are interested in stillwater fishing for sea trout then you must look elsewhere. Sea trout enter a few lakes in the Lake District area (such as Coniston and Windermere) but they are rarely caught by anglers.

Wales

Wales is a favoured country as far as its share of rod caught sea trout is concerned in terms of their general abundance and large average size and, also, in respect of the widespread availability and relatively low cost of the fishing (Table 10). The sea trout is to Wales what the salmon is to Scotland and the brown trout is to Ireland.

The Usk and Wye are virtually devoid of sea trout. There are several once-polluted rivers in the South Wales coalfield where the sea-trout stocks are showing exciting signs of recovery. The Tawe is much improved and there is reasonable fishing in the Ogmore, Neath, Loughour. But Welsh sea trout fishing proper starts with the Tywi, a superlative river, and continues with a

Table 9: Declared rod catches of sea trout in English water authority areas for principal rivers: 1983–1985 seasons. (Weight in lbs)

		1983		1984		1985	
		Number	Weight	Number	Weight	Number	Weight
Northumbria	Coquet	178	783	151	678	130	563
	Tyne	259	1131	598	2352	315	1494
	Wear	156	593	197	433	179	702
	Total[1]	692	2882	1010	3958	675	2922
Yorkshire	Esk	146	452	256	1058	209	711
	Total[1]	146	452	256	1058	209	711
Southern	Ouse	63	336	17	103	124	726[2]
	Total[1]	247	832	156	867	124	726[2]
Wessex	Avon	1631	2867	903	1987	1387	2444
	Frome	87	279	96	211	70	211
	Total[1]	2151	3605	1265	2783	1668	2944
South West	Teign	1359	N/A[3]	944	1399	1056	15923
	Dart	545	N/A	437	814	283	647
	Yealm	44	N/A	39	520	316	482
	Tavy	558	N/A	295	418	362	495
	Fowey	1512	N/A	782	1080	804	1019
	Camel	1189	N/A	687	948	451	605
	Taw	838	N/A	592	858	458	8668
	Torridge	329	N/A	60	902	108	211
	Total[1]	8548	N/A	5041	7537	4838	7478
North West	Ribble	526	1085	433	862	201	431
	Lune	1080	1986	1220	2365	1069	2517
	Derwent	397	557	352	627	279	609
	Eden	757	1501	1216	2105	698	1536
	Border Esk	398	686	632	1181	619	1043
	Total[1]	3812	6986	4446	8268	3993	8492
	English Total	15596	*	12174	24471	11507	23343

[1] The 'total' catch includes other data for minor rivers
[2] Data for other rivers obviously missing!
[3] Not available
Source = MAFF statistics

host of other notable waters such as the Cleddau (East and West), Tâf, Teifi, Rheidol, Dyfi, Mawddach, Seiont and Clwyd (Table 11).[13] In addition to these major rivers many of the smaller streams, such as the Aeron, Glaslyn, Gwyrfai, Llyfni and Ystwyth, are attractive and available venues for the visiting angler. Welsh sea-trout fishing is predominantly river-based. Sea trout enter a few lakes, such as Talyllyn (River Dysynni), Dinas and Gwynant (Glaslyn), Padarn (Seiont) and Coron (Anglesey) where a few are

Table 10: Declared sea trout and salmon catches for Wales by rods and commercial instruments for the 10-year period 1976–1985 (Weight in lbs. Data from Wye, Usk and Dee excluded)

| | SEA TROUT | | | | SALMON[1] | | | |
| | RODS | | COMMERCIAL | | RODS | | COMMERCIAL | |
Year	Number	Weight	Number	Weight	Number	Weight	Number	Weight
1976[2]	9506	17676	8993	31993	2435	19208	4019	32197
1977	14628	28891	6907	24680	4310	33494	3441	27615
1978	14549	24482	6499	21631	3770	32844	4579	38473
1979	22345	40200	10394	35284	3540	25862	3541	25179
1980	20642	38551	12223	40607	4041	34201	4756	41069
1981	22174	45036	9761	36255	3455	30348	6510	57571
1982	21308	39165	7682	28582	3024	23606	3271	28561
1983	22288	41951	8433	30377	3907	30449	3477	29723
1984[2]	18265	33570	10754	43369	2122	15119	2533	21352
1985	20549	42538	4990	16574	3946	34784	2758	25388

[1] The term salmon includes grilse
[2] 1976 and 1984 were severe drought years. The data is based on a fairly constant return of catch of about 100% from the 140 licensed commercial fishermen and about 60% from the 16–20,000 licensed anglers over the period. The data clearly shows the importance of sea trout in Wales. In terms of total weight of fish taken, the rod catch of sea trout exceeded that of salmon in 7 of the 10 years while the net catch of salmon was less than for sea trout in 4 of the 10 years.
(Source = Welsh Water)

Table 11: Rod catches of Welsh sea trout in principal rivers 1983–1985. (Weight in lbs)

| | 1983 | | 1984[2] | | 1985 | |
	Number	Weight	Number	Weight	Number	Weight
Wye	16	46	17	40	68	176
Usk	43	98	89	145	95	290
Dee	161	266	92	167	137	251
Tawe	490	1132	719	1280	658	1412
Tywi	6312	13829	5909	12494	5078	14021
Tâf	491	881	198	352	323	713
Cleddau	849	1012	1238	1406	866	1109
Nevern	487	592	380	497	245	343
Teifi	2786	3712	2649	3546	2558	1366
Dyfi	1434	3429	966	2044	1186	3377
Dysynni	201	279	101	130	147	255
Mawddach	1018	2498	620	1582	281	475
Glaslyn	435	660	403	552	307	486
Dwyfawr	1698	2337	491	807	964	1529
Seiont	862	987	186	257	337	438
Ogwen	306	444	178	290	194	257
Conwy	422	836	230	592	344	1067
Clwyd	1514	2121	1447	2528	1744	2706
Others[2]	4036	7299	2473	4083	5334	10984
TOTAL	23561	42458	18386	37293	20868	43622

[1] 1984 was a severe drought year in Wales
[2] Includes minor rivers – and shows their cumulative importance in terms of their contribution to the total catch!

The famous Gwydyr Hotel water on the Afon Conwy (North Wales). The Conwy is noted for its
very large sea trout. It still holds the record for the largest rod-caught British sea trout. This is a
fish of 21lb 8oz taken in July 1955. Another rod-caught fish of 21lb was also taken in the same
year. (Photo: M.J. Morgan.)

occasionally caught in the latter half of the season. Nevertheless, stillwater
sea-trout fishing is not part of the Welsh scene. Alas!

Unlike Scotland there is very little hotel fishing in Wales. Perhaps the
best known are the Gwydyr Hotel at Betws-y-Coed on the Conwy and the
Brigans Inn at Mallwyd on the Dyfi. Short but productive sections of hotel
water are available on a few other rivers such as the Teifi and Cothi (a major
tributary of the Tywi with some excellent sea trout).

The main characteristic of salmon and sea-trout angling in Wales is that
outside the Dee, Wye and Usk catchments large stretches of first-class fishing
are owned or controlled by local angling associations who make permits avail-

able to the visiting or non-resident angler at a reasonable cost on a season, week or day basis. For example, the Llandysul Angling Association has some 20 miles of single- and double-bank fishing on the Teifi and the New Dovey Fishery Association (1929) Ltd owns the fishing rights on 19 miles of continuous double-bank fishing from the estuary up to the middle reaches, with a further 7 miles of single-bank fishing continuing upstream! Likewise, virtually all of the worthwhile fishing on the Seiont, Gwyrfai and Llyfni, Dwyfawr, Rheidol and Ystwyth, and the Western Cleddau is controlled by local clubs. There are several Associations on the Tywi and Teifi with large

The semi-tidal Limekiln Pool on the Dyfi in late spring. (Photo: G.S. Harris.)

sections of water and there is also good club fishing on the Clwyd/Elwy, Aeron, Tawe and Conwy.

From any point in Wales it is usually no more than an hour's drive to available club fishing on one of the principal sea-trout rivers and the problem facing the visitor is generally one of too much opportunity rather than too little!

Ireland

Sea trout are traditionally called 'White trout' (Breac geal) in Ireland, but the Scottish term 'finnock' has recently become widely used for the smaller fish of up to 1lb weight.

There is a fantastic wealth of sea-trout fishing available in Ireland (Table 12) but much of it has yet to be properly explored and promoted. Certain fisheries such as the Waterville/Currane system in Kerry, the Cashla system in Connemara (much loved by Kingsmill Moore), the Ballynahinch fishery in county Galway and the Delphi fishery in county Mayo are well known from the all-too-limited literature on Irish fisheries, but there is very much more sea-trout fishing available than generally realised.

Irish sea trout are of the short-lived, slow-growing type and do not normally attain any great size. A 'good' rod-caught sea trout by Irish standards would weigh about 2lbs and the official qualifying weight for 'specimen' status set by the Irish Record Fish Committee is a modest 6lbs. The occasional double-figure sea trout is taken but such fish are rare by Scottish and Welsh standards.

While the sea trout of the western (Atlantic) coast are generally smaller

Lough Tawnyard. A lovely sea trout water on the Erriff System in Co. Mayo. (Photo: Peter O'Reilly.)

Table 12: Declared sea trout catches for rods and commercial instruments in the republic of Ireland[1] for 1982–1984 (Weight in lbs)

REGION/DISTRICT	Method	1982 Number	1982 Weight	1983 Number	1983 Weight	1984 Number	1984 Weight
EASTERN: Dundalk, Drogheda Dublin, Wexford	Rods	3793	3355	5585	5133	4688	4649
	Nets	*2	4683	*	13042	*	*
SOUTHERN: Waterford, Lismore	Rods	*	*	*	*	102	101
	Nets	*	717	*	3837	*	*
SOUTH WESTERN: Cork Kerry	Rods	4859	7251	3086	4415	399	546
	Nets	*	2699	*	3216	*	*
WESTERN: Ballinakill, Galway, Connemara	Rods	9367	7720	12199	10875	9598	10547
	Nets	*	1793	*	231	*	*
NORTH WESTERN: Bangor, Ballina, Sligo	Rods	1256	1085	1483	1514	2045	2112
	Nets	*	1080	*	21	*	*
NORTHERN: Ballyshannon Letterkenny	Rods	1268	1137	2275	1650	1726	1803
	Nets	*	5590	*	4041	*	*
ALL DISTRICTS: TOTAL TOTAL	Rods	20491	20550	25257	23929	18878	19457
	Nets	*	37853	*	48486	*	*
GRAND TOTAL	COMBINED	?	58403	?	72415	?	?

[1] Irish catch statistics are a mystery. They are probably the least accurate in the British Isles.
[2] not collected or not available or not published!
(Source = Central Fisheries Board)

53

than those of the rivers of the southern and eastern coast which drain into the more productive waters of the Irish and Celtic seas, it is curious that the sea trout of the east coast do not attain the same large size of Welsh fish since the both utilise the same sea feeding grounds. Or do they?

It is often stated that sea trout larger than 2lbs weight are relatively scarce in Irish waters. Certainly on many fisheries over 80 per cent of the sea trout taken are whitling – and often unusually small whitling at that. While Irish sea trout may be generally smaller on average than elsewhere, it is likely that there are many more large fish waiting to be caught if they were fished for properly. That they do exist is known from the large numbers taken by the commercial fishery. (A sample of 2,000 sea trout taken from drift nets in 1977 had an impressive average weight of 4.4lbs; and similar sampling in the Galway, Dingle, and Castletownbere areas in 1981 also gave an average weight of about 4lbs.) We have mentioned that partial trapping of the kelts moving out of Lough Tawnyard on the Erriff showed that there were many more large sea trout entering the fishery than shown by the angling catch and we would add here that the delightful Ballynahinch fishery is one of the few fisheries in Ireland where there is any tradition of fishing for sea trout at night. It is perhaps of singular significance that quite large numbers of sea trout of 2–5lbs are taken each year from this fishery.

Irish sea-trout fishing has much to offer. The lake fisheries of the west are still only lightly fished and the river fishing has, we suggest, great potential for exploration by the enterprising angler who is prepared to experiment. As one fisheries manager despairingly stated '. . . the vast majority of larger Irish sea trout die of old age'.

Lough Currane, near Waterville, is a unique system which deserves special mention as almost 50 per cent of all the Irish sea trout weighing 6lbs or more (Table 13) have been caught here. This is the only system in Ireland containing the long-lived 'race' of sea trout and so, in contrast, its stock contains a much higher proportion of multiple-spawning fish than elsewhere.

The main sea-trout fisheries are located in the west – in Donegal, Mayo, Connemara, Kerry and West Cork. They are typically a series of small lakes located in blanket-bog and joined by short canal-like rivers. In this area by far the greater proportion of the rod catch of sea trout is taken in stillwater and river fishing is the exception rather than the rule. This is magnificent, wild, country and there are over 30 first-class fisheries to choose from. Our recommended 'top ten' would include Screeb, Inver, Gowla, Ballynahinch, Erriff, Delphi, Newport, Burrishoole, Drumcliffe and, of course, Cashla. The fishing in these lakes can be quite exceptional at times and catches of 20 or more sea trout between two anglers sharing a boat during a day's fishing are not unusual; an anglers typical 10-trout bag would include 5 or 6 whitling and 4 or 5 fish ranging from 1–3lbs weight.

One area of Ireland ripe for development is Donegal. Little has been written about the sea-trout fishing of this remote and beautiful region but

Table 13: Irish rod caught 'specimen' sea trout (since 1955) as accepted by the Irish Specimen Fish Committee (Qualifying Weight = 6lb 0oz)

Region/Water	No. of Specimen Fish	Best Weight lb oz
WESTERN REGION		
Waterville Fishery	54	11−1
Delphi Fishery	10	9−12
Eriff Fishery	8	8−2
Inver Fishery	6	6−14
Ballinahinch Fishery	3	8−7
Burrishoole Fishery	2	7−4
Achill Island	2	14−3[1]
Bell Harbour	2	10−8
Palmerstown River	2	8−4
Doohola Lough	2	6−4
Lough Gowla	1	7−1
Glengariff River	1	6−12
Whitewater (Kilkee)	1	6−7
Sneem River	1	6−6
River Dowros	1	6−0
EASTERN REGION		
River Boyne	4	10−8
River Shimna (Co. Down)	3	16−6[2]
River Margy	2	6−2
River Dargle	1	12−0
River Dodder	1	11−0
West Pier (Dun Laoghaire)	1	7−2[1]
Bangor (Co. Down)	1	7−0·
River Colligan (Dungarvan)	1	6−6
	(110)	

[1] = taken in the sea
[2] = Current Irish Record

some of its fisheries may come to rival and even surpass the better known venues in Connemara and Mayo. Systems worth investigating are Owenea, Glen, Gweebarra, Lagha and Glenvagh.

By comparison with the west, there are relatively few lake fisheries on the south and east coast of Ireland. Here river fishing dominates but there are surprisingly few notable sea-trout rivers. The best are, perhaps, the Mattock (Co. Meath), the Bride and Argideen (Co. Cork) and the Dargle (Co. Wexford). But this vast area is, again, ripe for investigation and since the sea trout are of the faster-growing (Irish sea) type, a fish of 5lb or more is always a possibility.

Access to Irish sea-trout angling is relatively easy to obtain and remarkably cheap when compared with England and Scotland. It is a varied blend of private, hotel, club and free fishing. In some parts private or hotel fishing predominates, in other parts large sections of water are controlled by angling clubs. One unusual feature about Irish game fishing is the unbelievable amount of 'free fishing' available. 'Free' means that no charge is levied for access to the fishing but the permission of the landowner must be sought – always. Do not abuse a rare privilege.

Ireland is a land of contrasts and extremes and is mecca to many anglers (game, coarse and sea) from the United Kingdom and other parts of Europe. The Irish Government has long since recognised that angling is important to the national economy and one highly creditable initiative taken by the State has been, through the aegis of the Central Fisheries Board, to buy the fishing rights on the Erriff and the famous Galway fisheries in order to promote angling tourism. We have fished the Erriff and have nothing but the highest praise for what has been achieved there.

As the demand for sea-trout angling continues to increase we predict that Ireland will be the land of the future. Good ferry connections exist from several ports and for many anglers in England and Wales, Ireland is a good deal nearer than the many parts of Scotland. In this we are much encouraged by a recent strategy report issued by the Central Fisheries Board concerning the future management and development of Irish sea trout fisheries. Among many other things this suggests that the sea trout should be defined as a sport fish which is not subjected to specific exploitation by commercial fishing methods. Since the commercial fishery takes the larger sea trout of 1½–2lbs and more in weight, any significant reduction in the level of commercial exploitation would doubtless result in a dramatic improvement in the quality and appeal of the angling on many sea trout fisheries.

Legislation

In concluding this quick tour of the British Isles we must make a few general comments about important differences in the legislation of the various regions. In addition to obtaining a permit to fish from the owner or controller of the fishing, anglers must also obtain a rod licence to fish for salmon and sea trout in England, Wales and Ireland. The income from rod licences is used to finance fisheries management work, such as anti-poaching patrols, fish-pass construction, habitat improvement and restocking. Rod licences are not required in Scotland (where the local fisheries service is funded differently).

It is illegal to fish for salmon and sea trout on a Sunday in Scotland – but not elsewhere. (In Wales Sunday fishing is prohibited by the New Dovey Fishery Association (1929) Ltd; but this is a club rule not statutory law. We know of no other examples outside Scotland.)

Fishing in tidal waters is a noted attraction in several parts of the British Isles. It may or may not be free of any permit charge depending on the region and locality. The law relating to fishing in tidal waters is very different in England and Wales when compared with Scotland and the situation is complex. As a general rule there is a public right of fishing in tidal waters in England and Wales because, as a consequence of Magna Carta (1215), the fishing rights are not the subject of private ownership. However, the fishing rights may be privately owned if they had been granted to individuals by the Crown before 1215 and a permit may be required in some estuaries such as the Dyfi, Dysynni and Conwy. In Scotland, which did not unite with England and Wales until 1707 and where in any event Scottish 'Feudal Law' continued to apply, fishing rights in tidal waters are the property of the 'Crown' or, where granted to an individual, are in private ownership. Hence, a permit to fish will be needed. Scottish 'Feudal' law does not, however, apply to the Orkneys or to Shetland (once Norwegian territory) where 'Udal' law applies – and where the right of fishing in the sea is the property of the landowner. A permit may not be required in practice to fish certain tidal waters in Scotland: but our advice is to assume that it is until you have established to the contrary. While fishing in tidal waters may be free south of the border, the right to cross private land to get to the water may be subject to a 'fee' in many parts of England and Wales (such as the Dwyfor estuary).

All fishing rights in fresh water (= non-tidal water) are the subject of ownership. The right of fishing may be attached to the ownership of the land or separated from it (i.e. the owner of the land may or may not own the fishing). In theory there is no such thing as 'free' fishing for salmon and sea trout in England and Wales, Scotland and Northern Ireland. In practice, certain fisheries are free of any permit charge, especially in the Republic of Ireland. Free fishing exists in Loch Lomond in central Scotland. While there is none that we know of in England and Wales, there seems to be a great deal in Ireland. The best-known example for sea trout is Lough Currane in the south west (Co. Kerry). There is, however, much more 'free' fishing in Ireland than most people realise. (The prospect of 'free' fishing is superficially attractive. *BUT* since it is 'free' there is no control, other than voluntary control, within the statutory legislation. Free fishing is often abused and may be something to avoid!)

Fisheries are regulated in three ways: 1) by statutory law; 2) by byelaws and orders made under statutory law; and 3) by the 'rules and regulations' imposed by the owner or controller of the fishing. Essentially, byelaws and orders are local fine-tuning of statutory law. Rules and Regulations have no status in fisheries law, but non-compliance may get you banned from the fishery or, in England and Wales, result in a prosecution under the Theft Act 1968.

Do not assume that what is lawful and permissible in one region/area/fishery is the same in another region/area/fishery. Some fisheries may be fly-only. Others may allow spinning and worming on flood water, or it may be restricted to certain parts of the fishery. Some may allow spinning on low water; others may ban it altogether. Worm fishing may be banned by local byelaw (Devon) or be subjected to a shortened season (Wales). Maggot fishing may be banned by byelaw or regulation and this may also apply to float fishing. Under statutory (= primary) legislation there is enormous variation in the length of the fishing season. It may end in September (= Tywi), or

October (= Seiont), or November (= Tweed) or December (= Fowey) depending on the region/district/fishery.

Always check on the constraints imposed on the fishing as to *where, when* and *what* you may fish. Maggots, prawns, shrimps and floats are banned in many districts.

Our final comment is this: irrespective of where, when and what you may fish, DO NOT NEGLECT TO SUBMIT YOUR CATCH RETURN.

Finally we deal with two questions that we are often asked. The first is how to describe the 'typical' sea-trout fishery. The second is how to describe the 'ideal' sea-trout fishery.

Is anything typical with sea trout? There are many positive statements in the literature about what constitutes a sea-trout river. We broadly agree with the body of opinion that declares the 'typical' sea-trout river to be a short spate stream where the waters are acidic (= barren) rather than alkaline (= productive). It is a fact that most alkaline waters (having a pH of 7) or more are not good sea-trout fisheries (e.g. the English chalk streams, namely the Itchen, Lough Corrib and the delightful River Suir (Co. Waterford) even though they provide excellent fishing for brown trout. But some chalk streams do produce sea trout (e.g. the Test) and some notable brown-trout fisheries (such as the Teifi) provide excellent fishing for sea trout, salmon and brown trout alike. Neither are sea-trout rivers necessarily short. The Tywi is not a short river, neither is the Tweed or the Spey, nor is the Vistula (Poland). However, the Wye, Usk and Severn are longish rivers with few sea trout – and would seem to support the generalisation. In the West Country, the Exe (Devon) is both a good salmon and brown trout river which, like the Usk, is insignificant as a sea-trout fishery. Nevertheless it is a fact that the best sea-trout rivers are: a) relatively short; b) not good brown-trout fisheries; c) at best only moderate to mediocre salmon fisheries, and d) mainly spate streams with an unproductive freshwater environment. While 'the exception proves the rule', the enigmatic sea trout would seem to tolerate many exceptions!

Sadly, there is no such thing as the 'ideal' sea-trout fishery, and anyway our ideal may not be yours. It all depends on what you want from your sea-trout fishing. We are both essentially river anglers when it comes to sea trout; but we look forward with anticipation to our periodic, and all too in-frequent, visits to the lochs of Scotland and the loughs of Ireland. All we can say is that we have fished more than a few hallowed and prestigious sea-trout fisheries over the years, but some of the most enjoyable and memorable days (and nights) have been spent on insignificant waters of little consequence in terms of their size and reputation for the number and average weight of sea trout caught.

We have mentioned large sea trout briefly in Chapter 1. Many areas of the British Isles are noted for their large fish but 'large' is a relative term and some rivers and regions produce larger sea trout than others. In Wales and certain parts of Scotland the chances of catching a 'specimen' sea trout of 15–20lb weight are greater than elsewhere. In England a sea trout of 10–15lb would be a very good fish, and in Ireland anything weighing more than 6lb is accorded 'specimen' status.

The Irish Specimen Fish Committee has kept a record of all sea trout in excess of 6lb weight reported since 1952. (Their list of specimen sea trout is shown in Table 13.) The current record is held by a fish of 16lb 6oz taken in the River Shimna in 1983. It can be seen that very few fish attain a weight of more than 10lb and that few rivers produce more than just the odd specimen. The number of 'specimen' fish produced by the Waterville/Currane system is really quite remarkable!

Unfortunately similar 'lists' are not available for England, Wales or Scotland and it is difficult to give any feel for notable big fish waters other than in very non-specific terms.

Several fish larger than the 1983 20lb sea trout from the Esk (see page 19) have been taken on rod-and-line in past years, but for one reason or another they have not been accepted by the British Record Fish Committee; even though scale reading established that they were sea trout and not salmon. It is curious that the 'official' Welsh record sea trout – a fish of 21½lb taken on the Conwy in 1955 and accepted by the Welsh Record Fish Committee – is larger than the record accepted by the British Record Fish Committee! The largest sea trout taken by an angler on the Afon Dyfi was caught in 1958 and weighed 20¾lb. Another fish of 21lb was taken on the Conwy in 1955, and in 1980 the Welsh record nearly fell to a fish of 21¾lb from a tributary of the Afon Tâf in South Wales.

Until recently the largest authenticated sea trout taken by *legal* means (rods or nets) was a fish of 24½lb taken by the Dyfi nets in 1959. A 24lb fish was taken by netsmen in the same river in 1985 and another fish of 27lb was reportedly taken by the same netsman in 1977, but was never authenticated. Scotland also produces some very large fish and some in excess of 15lb weight are usually reported each year from the west coast. The largest authenticated British sea trout to date is the fish of 26lb in weight found dead

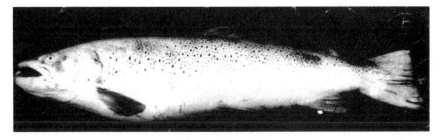

The largest authenticated rod-caught sea trout from the Afon Dyfi in Mid-Wales. Caught on a fly in 1958 by Arthur Humphreys of Machynlleth, it weighed 20lb 12oz. The heavy diffuse spotting is characteristic of old fish that have spawned several times. This one was 11 years old and had spawned 7 times. (Photo: A. Humphreys.)

in the River Luce in Wigtownshire. (We have been unable to verify the reported capture in 1985 of a larger fish of 26½lb taken in nets from an unnamed river in Argyllshire.)

There is little doubt that the disease Ulcerative Dermal Necrosis (=UDN) that ravaged the salmon and sea trout fisheries of the entire British Isles from about 1967/8 until the mid-1970s resulted in the disappearance of large sea trout from many fisheries for many years. 'Double-figure' fish were very few and far between for almost a decade or more in those fisheries where the attainment of large size depended upon reaching an old age.

Anyone who was fishing from 1967 will remember the carnage, with rivers littered with countless infected fish – usually heavily fungussed – that were dead or dying. Fortunately the disease waned steadily during the 1970s and, although still with us, is no longer a serious problem. As we have seen in Chapter 2, it usually takes *at least* four or five sea-years for a sea trout to attain a double-figure weight after migrating as a smolt and during that period it may have returned to the river to spawn in three or four successive years. Any fish which survived the disease on its first return to the river as a maiden fish was equally susceptible to infection on each successive return and so the probability of reaching an old age and a large size was much diminished. Thankfully, large sea trout appear to have steadily increased in numbers in recent years.

3 · THE ANGLING LITERATURE

Even allowing for the fact that there was considerable confusion about the relationship and taxonomic status of the various forms of migratory or sea-going trout until about 60 or 70 years ago (so that many Victorian and Edwardian anglers little understood that the different techniques employed for taking 'bull trout', 'salmon trout', 'sea trout' and 'whitling' were in fact all means of taking the same species of fish) it is surprising that so little has been written about sea-trout angling in view of the widespread abundance and distribution of the fish and its superlative sporting qualities. Even today, there are less than half a dozen major works dedicated *solely* to sea-trout angling and the minor status of the fish in the sporting literature parallels closely its minor status in the scientific literature. Thus, much of what has been written about sea trout angling has been incidental to either brown trout or salmon (usually the latter). Several authors have in fact written about sea trout but this has frequently been only a chapter or two included (more for completeness and almost as an afterthought) in some broader treatise on its more esteemed relatives.

In this review we attempt to do no more than introduce you to those experts and authorities who, in our view, have contributed materially to the development of the sport as we know it today. We confine ourselves largely to those books which deal primarily with sea trout or which refer to sea trout in some way relevant to our theme.

In order to set the scene we will use as our starting point *Salmon and Sea Trout* by Sir Herbert Maxwell published in 1898. This is not a random choice. Sir Herbert Maxwell, Bart, MP, FRS, was an eminent scientist and highly-respected authority on British fisheries and fishing who published widely on a range of technical and sporting topics. It is, therefore, a convenient place to start, as it links the old with the new and provides us with a feel for the status and regard for sea-trout angling at the turn of the last century. If we give Maxwell undue emphasis it is for this reason. *Salmon and Sea Trout* is about 'how to propagate, preserve and catch them in British waters'. The use of the collective pronoun overstates the emphasis given to sea trout, since the book deals almost exclusively with salmon. There is, however, one short chapter on 'Salmon Trout Fishing'. Although the title of the book refers to 'sea trout', Maxwell carefully avoids the term in the Chapter heading since, as he states, it embraces the bull trout (*Salmo eriox*),

61

'a coarse, bad rising fish' which he suggests could usefully be extirpated from Great Britain and whose presence was inimical to salmon. Thus we see the confusion that existed in both the angling literature and the scientific literature about what constituted the fish which we today know as sea trout.

After promptly dismissing the bull trout as worthless, Maxwell admits that he is willing to concede superior fighting qualities to the fish generally known as *Salmo trutta* – the white trout, whitling, sewin, finnock herling, peel (*sic*). At this point we lose him. Bull trout, as we now know, are in fact previously spawned sea trout of usually largish size. Yet, Maxwell talks of *salmon-trout* of 6–7lb being 'commonly met' in the British Isles. It seems that if large sea trout were catchable they were salmon trout. If they could not be caught then they were 'extirpable' bull trout!

Maxwell was familiar with sea trout (sorry, salmon trout) fishing in both Ireland and Scotland. He suggested using a built cane rod of 10–12ft rather than a 16–17ft rod of greenheart, and stated that the leader should be scaled down in strength from that used for salmon 'to gut of 14/1000–17½/1000 of an inch' (?).

He believed that 'the sea trout [*sic*] is an active, predacious creature, prone to seize any small object with a life-like motion which may pass near it. . .'.

He discusses (briefly) both lake fishing from a boat – when it was 'seldom prudent to go out with less than a pair of stout rowers' – and, interestingly, from the bank, 'to enjoy the utmost excitement'. For lake fishing he suggests that anything more than two or three flies on the leader would be 'sure to land you in untimely entanglement'. He says little more on the subject other than to suggest that the bob-flies on the leader should have permanent loops to allow for easy detachment (he would have been using gut-mounted flies) 'for there is no occasion for scrupulously fine tackle'.

On rivers he is a little more helpful – but not much. He deprecates bait fishing as a pursuit 'so simple and uninviting' and adds that there is more to be said for minnow fishing 'but it must be said by someone else for I have never put it in practice'. The best river conditions in his view were after a period of flood. He cast down-and-across and stated that the flies (note the plural) 'must be worked at a moderate rate, not too fast, if it be desired to get the heaviest fish, for large fish are not so nimble on the rise as half pounders'. Apart from the inherent truth of the statement, the point worth noting is that he advocated 'working' the flies. His views on striking are noteworthy also. He recommended that sea trout must be struck 'very quick' on the rise. If you wait till you feel the fish, you will be too late. . .'. As we shall see later, this is sound advice. But he also recommends striking from the reel 'without the aid of a finger on the line' to avoid being smashed by the take. This, he notes, is contrary to the practice of most sea-trout fishers. He emphasises the importance of avoiding a belly developing in the line as it fishes round in the current and recommends keeping a straight line between the rod and the fly. He states that, unlike salmon or brown trout, a 'salmon trout generally

...refuses a second offer at a fly that he has missed'. He adds that this 'constant characteristic' is made up for by the fact that 'it is not a rare thing for a single rod to take fifty to one hundred sea trout in a day in July or August on the West Coast of Scotland, when the water was in good order'.

Maxwell has little to say about how to fish when the river was not in 'good order', apart from using a 'tinselled fly' when there was a breeze during the day, or by fishing at night – preferably below an obstruction where 'sea trout collect in great numbers and take the fly greedily'. He notes that 'some people affect a white fly for night fishing; others reckon black a great medicine' [see pages 73 and 77 for the recurrent use of this term, now immortalised by Hugh Falkus], but that it did not seem to matter what colour was used so long as the flies were 'stout and serviceable'.

He notes that sea-trout flies were mainly of two classes, all the standard salmon flies – such as Dusty Miller and Silver Doctor – on sizes 8–4 on the Limerick scale (equivalent to about 6–12 on the modern scale) and the large trout flies consisting of either 'the English imitations of *March Browns*, *Red Spinners* and *Yellow Duns*...or Scottish loch flies, such as the *Red-and-Teal*, the *Woodcock and Yellow*...'. He then makes the first reference to the use of the tandem-mounted fly for sea trout, stating that 'there is nothing that has more attraction for sea trout than a large red palmer; if tied on two hooks, one behind the other, so much the better'.

In setting the scene, Maxwell establishes that sea trout were regularly taken in both river and loch, that the equipment was scaled down salmon tackle with small salmon or large trout flies being used. Night fishing was something to be done when the river was 'out of order' for daylight fishing and was not highly regarded (at least in Scotland). The impression given was that sea-trout fishing was fun but little more than an interesting diversion from the more serious business of salmon fishing. The view that sea trout fed in fresh water was unquestioned and confusion clearly existed about the various 'types' of sea trout.

Almost 20 years were to elapse before anyone had anything much more to say about sea trout. The next major work, and one which did much to promote the sporting image of the fish in its own right, was the grossly mistitled '*Book of the Sea Trout*' by Hamish Stuart, published in 1917. The book was in fact published posthumously from an almost complete draft manuscript and notes assembled after his death at sea from the illness that occasioned the voyage by his friend and editor Rafael Sabatini. The introduction by R.B. Marston is superlative.

The book is largely about sea trout, but only in lakes. It is a great pity that the intended section on fishing for sea trout in rivers was never completed by the author. It also contains several chapters about salmon fishing which, while wholly out of context, are interesting none the less in supplementing the unique Hebridean flavour of this book. It has been said, correctly, that 'this is where it all started'.

Stuart was regarded as a 'radical' by his peers. He advocated using a single-handed rod, the use of smaller than usual flies of the 'trout' type in preference to small salmon flies, and generally used a team of 3 – consisting of a *Mallard and Claret* on the tail, a *Woodcock and Green* on the middle dropper and a *Zulu* on the top dropper (= bob-fly). Hook sizes were from 8–12. It almost goes without saying that he fished from a boat without a companion but with a gillie to attend to his needs.

His view that sea trout should not be struck until the fish was felt caused him to be widely abused by his critics – and there were many! His views on the biology of the sea trout show an acceptance and understanding of conventional theory in that he held that the various migratory forms of trout are all the one 'sea trout' and that sea trout are more of an estuary fish than salmon. His main 'mistake' in terms of his credibility and the ready acceptance of his views was his refusal to accept the enormous contribution to our subsequent understanding of the life of the sea trout made by scale reading (see page 6).

Stuart was without doubt an expert on lake fishing for sea trout. His comments on river fishing are relevant also. Anyone fortunate enough to gain fishing in the islands that form the Scottish Hebrides would be wise to read '*The Book of the Sea Trout*'. Dated it may be, but it contains much interesting background information and is still relevant today.

The next authoritative work appeared in 1927 when Major R.H. Chrystal published *Angling Theories and Methods*. Chrystal was a loch-fishing expert and a great authority on the Western Isles – where in many respects he was a successor, if not a disciple, of Hamish Stuart. Much of the content of *Angling Theories and Methods* relates to salmon, and the relevance of Chrystal's writing is that he largely agrees with Stuart. This again is a good read for anyone with access to fishing in the Islands. (Chrystal also wrote *Angling at Lochboisdale*, published in 1939. This is an angling journal covering the period 1882–1937, relating to his experiences in South Uist and makes fascinating reading.)

Sea-trout fishing in its formative years had an exclusive Scottish flavour and, moreover, was focused on loch fishing rather than river fishing.

The first major text on river fishing appeared in or about 1920, when J.C. Mottram published *Sea Trout and Other Fishing Studies*. This slender work was largely responsible for popularising the short vogue for dry-fly fishing that endured through the 1930s and 1940s and whose only strong convert was, as we shall see, Major Kenneth Dawson. It is not very clear where Mottram actually practised his art. His knowledge of the English Chalk streams is evident. It is likely that he developed his preference for the dry fly in Southern England and practised on sea trout elsewhere. Any geographical reference in the book relates, curiously, to the Shetland Isles where much sea-trout fishing occurs in tidal waters and where it is unlikely that much opportunity to use the dry fly would have arisen. It is likely that Mottram fished fairly widely, possibly in Wales. He mentions that the largest sea trout to his rod weighed 16¾lb and we note that a fish of this weight is recorded by Alfieri and Menzies in their 1937 publication *Where to fish for Salmon and Sea Trout* as being taken from the River Dyfi by one J.C. Mottram. The record does not state whether it was caught on the dry fly.

Much of the book concerns the author's views and theories about river ecology, the preservation of water flies, the effects of water temperature, the taxonomic status of sea trout – combined with digressions on the sex of brown trout, scale reading and a discourse on 'Fisherman's Flowers'. The last third of the book gets to the point. He makes no mention of spinning, and wet-fly fishing is very much subordinate to the main theme of dry-fly fishing by day *and at night*.

Mottram was well schooled in the imitative style of dry-fly fishing and his basic approach was that of the classic 'English School'. He was perhaps the first to note that dry fly killed well in moonlight when the wet fly was 'practically useless'.

Mottram was credited with being the first to advocate the dry fly for sea trout. He did much to popularise it but, while Hamish Stuart made passing mention to the fact that the 'floating fly' can be used with success, it was quite popular in many areas of Scotland in the preceding period. One of the most authoritative articles on the subject by A. Buxton was published in 1913. He took fish of between 11lb and 17lb on the dry fly; so perhaps 'one J.C. Mottram' did take his 16¾lb Dyfi sea trout on the dry fly after all!

Historically speaking, Mottram's delightful contribution to the sparse literature on sea-trout angling has made little impact on the evolution of the sport. Although we sense that there could be an upsurge of interest in dry-fly fishing 'around-the-corner', it is still the wet fly that continues to rule supreme, and credit for this fact must go to one particular author.

There have been few really great books on sea trout angling. The first was *Sea Trout Fishing* by R.C. Bridgett, MAB, BSc, published in 1929. This is a wonderful book in many ways. It is, in the over-used words of critics, 'one of the best angling books ever written'. Yes, it is dated – but only in terms of the tackle technology. In many other respects, notably his philosophy and approach to the sport, the author was way ahead of his time.

Bridgett fished widely for sea trout from the Solway to Wester Ross and from the Hebrides to Connemara. He was, quite evidently, equally at ease on river and lake but stated a clear preference for fishing rivers and then for daylight fishing with the wet fly. He was, in fact, rather apologetic about night fishing and, like Maxwell, regarded it as justifiable only when the river was too low for anything else. He regarded worm fishing as poor sport, but felt that spinning was acceptable and an art worth learning, and notes that the dry fly could be applied usefully under certain circumstances.

Bridgett's views on tackle are now fairly conventional. Not for him the long double-handed rods of the day but a rod of 10-ft length 'which I can still wield with one hand for an 8 hour stretch'. His style of fishing was akin to fishing for salmon with the cast made down-and-across and the flies swung across the current without being worked back. He was more than helpful on the selection of suitable flies for different waters but declined to state any strong preferences of his own. For night fishing he was possibly the first to note that the slender, thin-bodied flies so favoured today were preferable to the generously hackled and bushy flies of his period. He usually fished 2, sometimes 3, flies on his leader and was strongly committed to the sunk line. He states that in his experience the surface/subsurface or 'bob' fly exercised no great fascination at night – something that no modern angler could accept – and that a fly deeply sunk seemed to be most effective. He is, perhaps, the first to advocate the deep-sunk fly for night fishing!

Bridgett was also an adept lake fisherman. Indeed, in addition to *Sea Trout Fishing* and his highly original 1922 work on *Dry Fly Fishing*, which was significant because it dealt with typical Scottish rivers rather than the English chalk streams, Bridgett is perhaps even more widely acclaimed for his highly innovative *Loch Fishing in Theory and Practice* published in 1924, and his highly readable books *By Loch and Stream* and *Tight Lines* published in 1922 and 1924 respectively. He was the first to advocate the 'round-the-corner' technique of using the forward movement of the drifting boat to fish the flies 'on the swing'. His style of boat fishing was the traditional team of flies with the 'bob-fly' worked across the surface but, contrary to the views of many – both then and now – stated that the point fly on the leader was the most deadly. Bridgett also fished at night on lakes when he would use a size 4 fly (*Black Doctor*). He thus achieves the distinction of being among the first to recommend fishing a large fly at night.

From a background of literature with a distinctly Scottish flavour, the next generation of books moves to the South West of England, and concerns angling on heavily-fished club waters as opposed to the 'limited-access' delights of private fishing. Since there are no lakes containing sea trout in Devon and Cornwall the emphasis is, naturally, on river fishing; and essentially on night fishing at that.

Sea Trout and Occasional Salmon, by Jeffrey Bluett, was published in 1948 and is based on some 30 years' experience on West Country moorland rivers: principally the Tavy in Cornwall. By all accounts Bluett was a remarkably successful sea-trout angler – something that he attributes mainly to the simple fact that he concentrated his efforts on one particular river which he got to know well. (This is the soundest advice possible!)

He set great store by his belief that sea trout became suspicious and educated, and advanced the theory that the reason why sea trout were harder to catch on English and Welsh rivers by day compared with Scotland and Ireland (something noted by other writers) was that these rivers were fished much more heavily. This largely conditioned his approach to sea-trout fishing and explains his advocacy of extreme caution and 'finer tackle and smaller flies than in the days of our ancestors'. He was essentially a fly fisherman and then largely a night fisherman. He makes no reference to worming (something now prohibited by byelaw in Devon for many years) and discusses spinning briefly; but in so doing was among the first to make the point that it was necessary to spin faster for sea trout than for salmon.

His views on flies were unconventional in that he, like Bridgett, preferred slender rather than bushy flies and often fished large flies (size 4–7) at night. He stressed the need to fish a fine leader even at night, and in this was at variance with the views of Maxwell, Stuart, Chrystal and Dawson. He disagreed also with the view that an angler should stick to just 2 or 3 patterns, stating that 'conditions of light, environment, height, colour, temperature and rate of flow of water and condition of fish vary so greatly that it must, I think, be necessary to have some half-a-dozen patterns in varying sizes to meet all eventualities'. He advocated 'a selection of a number of patterns which are as different from one another as possible and which cover various colours and types'. Among the various patterns suggested by Bluett as suitable for sea trout we see mentioned for the first time the large tandem and streamer-type lures so popular today for sunk lure fishing.

He mentions daylight fly fishing but briefly, stating 'I would sooner catch sea trout by night than by day', and clearly does not feel the need to apologise or excuse hmself for his view as did some earlier authors.

Bluett advanced the theory, based upon his personal catch records, that 'better sport is obtained during the growing of the moon than during the waning'. No one has ever expressed an opinion to refute or support this observation. His style is fairly typical by today's standards but he was one of the first to clearly recommend working the flies with a figure-of-eight re-trieve and to advocate the fast-moving surface/subsurface fly (when the night was warm and the fish active) and the slow-moving, deeply sunk fly (when the night was cold and the fish not moving). He rarely fished all through the night but noted that dawn often gave 'a crowded hour of glorious life'.

Bluett, who wrote many articles on sea trout in the angling press under the pen-name 'Sou'wester', was widely regarded as a sea-trout expert and he is to be credited with introducing many of the ideas developed by later authors on the approach to and techniques of night fishing. He, perhaps more than anyone, did much to popularise and make night fishing 'acceptable'.

Major Kenneth Dawson was another highly regarded angler author of his day who wrote widely about West Country fishing. He wrote *Salmon and Sea Trout in Moorland Streams* first published in 1928 and revised in 1947, *Successful Fishing for Salmon and Sea Trout* published in 1951 and *Modern Salmon and Sea Trout Fishing* first published in 1938 and revised in 1948. He, like Bluett, also fished the Tavy.

Dawson, who wrote widely under the pen-name 'West Country' was primarily a salmon angler. His most up-to-date work was the 1948 revision of *Modern Salmon and Sea Trout Fishing*; this contains three chapters on sea trout, of which two are relevant here as they encapsulate more or less all that he has to say.

He was among the first to promulgate the generalisation that it was harder to catch sea trout in daylight on southern rivers and, probably, for this reason, both he and Bluett agree that sea trout fishing requires a delicate approach and extreme finesse.

Although he fished the wet fly, he is generally regarded as one of the few skilled dry-fly anglers, and was the first to advocate its use at night. In this context, Dawson is also the first to mention the use of the 'wake fly' – a lure fished to cause disturbance on the surface and later rediscovered in the 1960s by Hugh Falkus. Dawson, who was quite conventional in his approach to salmon, was surprisingly radical when it came to sea trout in that he was not averse to spinning with a large phantom minnow kept 'near to the surface' *at night*.

It is interesting how Bluett and Dawson – both West Country anglers and both fishing the same river – agreed and disagreed on approach, tactics and techniques. Dawson did not fish the sunk fly and generally thought the flies for night fishing unimportant – 'one light, one dark'. Both fished a dropper for surface fishing at night, both recovered line by working the fly with a figure-of-eight retrieve. However, Dawson believed it unwise to fish a fine leader, rarely fished larger than size 8, and in strong contrast liked a bright moon, 'the brighter the better'. Whereas Dawson, who had a somewhat limited repertoire of techniques, suggested packing up if the fish were not taking, Bluett suggested perseverance by moving elsewhere, fishing finer or fishing differently.

Although breaking the chronological sequence of published works, it is convenient to remain in the West Country and to consider here *The Torridge Fishery* by L. R. N. Gray, published in 1957. 'Lemon Gray' spent his formative years on the banks of the River Usk and eventually, after a career spent mostly 'away', became the proprietor of the Devon Lodge Hotel fishery on the River Torridge. Anyone who has ever stayed at a fishing hotel will appreciate this book!

He writes in a provocative, no-nonsense style and clearly did not tolerate fools gladly. As Maurice Wiggin states in the preface, had he been born in an earlier age, his chances of survival would have depended on his skill in the duel! Sadly, *The Torridge Fishery* is largely about salmon, riverbank politics and the psychology of running a fishing hotel; but there is one memorable chapter on sea trout – would that there were more!

Gray continues the theme developed by Bluett and Dawson, and stresses that a stealthy approach and delicacy in fishing is required. He deals largely with night fishing, says little of relevance on spinning, and (to say the least!) was not in favour of worming. Gray was clearly an angler who 'knew his water'. That his water was a small part of one large West Country river is neither here nor there. On *his* water, he states that fish tend to 'go down' after the initial dusk rise and then the main rise continues usually until 01.00 hours or 02.00 hours. It is interesting to note that he, like so many 'local' anglers who live close to the water, tended to pack up and try again another day if fish did not respond after 15 minutes or so. However, although he states that he rarely fished through the night, he notes that the pre-dawn rise (Bluett's 'crowded hour of glorious life') was often the most productive and

68

certain – especially for the larger sea trout. We wonder how many would agree with that view?

It is really with Gray that we see the surface/subsurface fly clearly defined as a standard technique. He fished a floating line with the last two yards left ungreased so that it sank and fished a bushy, well hackled fly on the top dropper (a *Badger and Yellow* or a dry sedge) and a slender fly on the point. He, like Bridgett and others before, observed that a black fly was good on a dark night. He also stresses the importance of working the flies and keeping in close contact at all times if many takes are not to be missed.

Few authors have much to say in favour of worm fishing. Alexander Mackie, MA, published *The Art of Worm-Fishing* in 1912, and is probably to be credited with the first book wholly on the subject of clear-water worming. Mackie was in fact a keen fly fisherman who was 'driven by circumstances' to develop his skill as a fisher of the worm. Interestingly – because it is a subject that looms large today – he discusses the question of cruelty in sport. He takes the view that it is no more cruel to catch a fish on a worm than on a fly, and suggests that the 3-hook Stewart mount or the 2-hook Pennell mount minimises any cruelty to the worm and has practical advantages in fishing.

Much of what Mackie, who fished Scottish waters, has to say about tackle has been overtaken by modern technology; but his approach and techniques are still relevant. He declared a preference for lob worms as opposed to any other type and advocated mounting them 'head downmost' so that they floated downstream just as if they had 'slipped from dry land' (the head 'being the heaviest part' sinks deepest). Mackie fished his worms upstream using no weight and advocates a stealthy approach with a long rod (he used a two-handed greenheart salmon rod of 16 feet in length!), and preferred to use a line of 'substantial thickness' to give 'much greater command' of the situation. Mottram also observed that a thicker line caused greater resistance to the current and so allowed the worm to be worked in slow moving water, and it is curious to note that whereas Mackie adopted the 'upstream' approach of the dry-fly fisherman when fishing the worm, Mottram, who was very much a dry-fly angler, employed the downstream-and-across style commonly employed when wet-fly fishing.

Books on worm fishing are indeed scarce and those applying the technique to sea trout are even rarer still. Mackie wrote primarily about brown-trout fishing – but mentions sea trout. Mottram deals solely with sea trout: as does Stirling whose *Fishing for Trout and Sea Trout with Worm and Wet Fly* is notably readable on both topics. Sidney Spencer's *Clear Water Trout Fishing with Worm* was first published in 1935 (and variously reprinted and reissued in 1972 and 1977) and makes several references to sea trout in the general context of upstream worming.

Although Gray used a partly greased line for his sea-trout fishing, the first reference to the use of the greased line for sea trout appears to be by Anthony Crossley, who published *The Floating Line for Salmon and Sea Trout* in 1939. He was a disciple of A.H. Wood, who developed the technique of fishing the subsurface fly for salmon and, not unnaturally, adapted it for sea trout. *The Floating Line for Salmon and Sea Trout* is very largely about salmon. All reference to sea trout is contained in one chapter: but what a fascinating chapter it is!

The River Em in Sweden is famed for its large sea trout. Crossley had the good fortune to fish the water in 1928 and from 1932 to 1938. The details of his personal catch must, surely, inspire envy in most anglers in the British Isles. In 1928 he records that in the 29 days of his vacation he took 47 sea trout ('Nothing special about that'!) – *with an average weight of 17lb*!! His best fish weighed 28lb and his most notable bag was four fish of 20½, 20½, 26 and 26½lb – *in one hour's fishing*!

Crossley fished the sunk line occasionally, but most of his sea trout were taken by day and by night on the floating line using standard salmon flies of about size 5 by day and up to size 5/0 at night – but dressed with more 'hackle than for salmon'. His technique was identical to that employed in greased-line fishing for salmon – the fly fishing round with the current and not being 'worked' by recovering line – and, as with salmon, he did not strike a taking fish but gave line and allowed the fish to hook itself.

His approach to sea trout was rather radical by the standards of both then and now; but it must be remembered that conditions are very different in Sweden and that large sea trout tend to behave like salmon in their movement to the fly. Nevertheless, Crossley illustrates that the modern technique of using very large flies on a floating line at night is not new.

From Scandinavia, our review of the literature takes us back to Scotland and to *Fishing for Trout and Salmon* by Terence Horsley, published in 1944. This is yet another book about salmon and brown trout which contains only one chapter referring to sea trout in small Scottish rivers.

Horsley was another advocate of the greased line for sea trout – although he fished the sunk line for whitling. He fished small single-hook flies (sizes 10–12) using either small trout flies (*Butcher, Peter Ross* etc) or small salmon flies (*Jock Scott, Silver Charm* etc) but, like so many writers, he states the belief that size was more important than the pattern of fly. However, when standard methods failed he was not averse to fishing a 1¾-inch tandem lure. He reckoned that night fishing was more productive than daylight fishing (catching two or three at night to every one by day). Horsley's preference for the greased line/subsurface fly seems to have been conditioned by his belief that sea trout lay in shallow water on a warm night and that those in deeper water remained near enough to the surface to see a fly within 1–2 inches of the top. Of spinning and worming he says little, other than to recommend fishing a worm 'under the bank', or using a natural minnow or blue and silver Devon minnow on a flood.

Still remaining in Scotland we come to *Fishing for Sea Trout* by H.P. Henzell published in 1949. Henzell also wrote *The Art and Craft of Loch Fishing*, published in 1937, and it is with sea-trout fishing in lakes that he seems to be more familiar, since this is where his emphasis lies.

Henzell covers river fishing with the fly and worm – briefly. For him river fishing had the 'great disadvantage' that it was 'almost entirely confined to the hours of darkness', and he hints that night fishing is slightly unsporting in that 'luck enters too much into the whole affair'. He then goes on to question why sea trout can be caught much more readily by day on a lake compared with a river. This, he suggests, is because in a lake 'they realise that they can move about in such an expanse of water without encountering the same danger' as in the narrow, shallow river. He notes, contrary to the view of some preceding and later Scottish authors, that Scottish sea trout can be equally as difficult to catch in daylight as an some rivers in England, Wales and South Scotland.

Henzell's discourse on lake fishing for sea trout is interesting because it provides a 'feel' for developments over the period since Stuart and Chrystal. Much of his fishing was done on Loch Maree and in the Outer Hebrides at Harris and South Uist. He covers both lake fishing with the wet fly and by dapping, and is the first to deal with stillwater dry-fly fishing in any detail.

Henzell is a supporter of the evidently increasingly popular school of anglers who believed that the sea trout was 'disinclined' to feed in fresh water. His favoured fly, dry or wet – and sometimes with two of them on his cast (up to size 6) – was a *Black Pennell*; of which he states 'some writers admit that it is a good fly, while others leave it out altogether; whereas I have found it so outstandingly the best of all sea trout flies for the loch that nothing would induce me to make up a cast without it, and I would cheerfully admit to being robbed of all other patterns if I were allowed an unlimited supply of it'. Many anglers – on river or lake – would agree that a black pattern is a good pattern by day or night.

Henzell's treatment of dry-fly fishing pioneers new ground, as indeed does his coverage of dapping. He is also first to mention trolling a spinner or natural dead-bait in stillwater (albeit in passing and with clear disapproval) and he is the first to show any real enthusiasm for spinning, which he practised with a multiplier, expressing the view that the 'modern' fixed-spool reel was an abomination that removed all the skill and joy from playing a fish.

From the 1940s we now move into the next decade when the impact of the tremendous post-war improvements in tackle technology made themselves apparent, and when the advent of the motor car as a means of general trans-portation for the individual angler brought about a whole new dimension to the sport of angling. This is perhaps when game fishing lost its elitist 'class' image and when, as a result of a redistribution of wealth, greater access to more remote waters, and the acquisition of large sections of 'good' water by local angling clubs, many new anglers were recruited to the sport from very different social backgrounds. The result of this was that 'traditional' attitudes and ethics that had dominated for well over 100 years in the literature on game fishing were subject to a sudden 'liberalisation' and the adoption of a new approach. Spinning, and to a lesser extent worm fishing, now became 'acceptable', and, indeed, many anglers came into the sport via this route rather than by graduating directly from the traditional 'fly-or-nothing' school.

The Fisherman's Handbook by George Brennand was published in 1951 and covered 'Trout, Salmon and Sea Trout with Notes on Coarse Fishing'. This is fairly typical of a new genre of 'fishing books'. Gone is the censorious attitude to fishing ethics so typical of the last century and the traditional anecdotal style adopted by many authors ('a day on Loch Maree, the Border Esk or Loch Lomond', etc) is replaced by a straightforward, instructional approach. The Fisherman's Handbook is the sort of present that angling fathers gave to young sons, and even today it is still a good 'primer'. The style is essentially encyclopaedic but it gives a good feel for the general attitude to sea-trout fishing some 30 years ago, albeit with a strong 'Scottish' flavour.

Brennand summarises the then modern knowledge on the biology of the fish, and gives a list of fishing venues (both aspects very dated now), and it is evident that there had been little improvement in scientific knowledge of the species over the period since Nall's classic text published in 1930 (Chapter 2). Included also are details of suitable tackle, wet-fly fishing by day and night on rivers, dry-fly fishing and lake fishing. Spinning and worm fishing are discussed in some detail and much other general information is presented. It is here we see development of the debate on the merits of gut leaders versus nylon monofilament. Brennand recommends the use of real gut 'as the antics of hooked sea trout may (and often do) find out the obscure weakness of Monofil lines...'. Sea trout angling has evidently become recognised as a sport in its own right but is still 'intermediate' between brown-trout and salmon fishing in terms of technique and style. Daylight fishing, according to Brennand, required small flies fished salmon-style, while night fishing has evidently become established as an acceptable means of taking sea trout: although the techniques of so doing seem to be no more than an extension of daylight fishing into the hours of darkness using larger flies. Brennand's views on flies are that you need 'plenty of different sorts', and he is one of many to note the appeal of the 'Teal, Silver and Blue' for sea trout. This he describes as 'the consistently best night fly I have ever used...'. His treatment of spinning is interesting in that it is here that we see the first signs of the 'spinning revolution' occasioned by the combination of the fixed-spool reel and fine nylon 'monofil' spinning lines. However, the technique is little more than an adaptation of the standard down-and-across approach of Devon minnow fishing for salmon and it is evident that little progress has been made in developing spinning for sea trout as a separate branch of the art. This also applies to worm fishing which is presented by Brennand as the traditional 'upstream' style which, because of its similarity to dry fly fishing in the classic mode of the English chalk streams, has made it an (almost) acceptable method of presenting a baited hook to game fish.

Brennand also touches briefly on sea-trout fishing in estuaries. However, credit for being the first to cover this much-neglected aspect of sea-trout fishing in any detail (in fact he devoted a whole book to the subject) must go to Richard Clapham, whose Fishing for Sea Trout in Tidal Water was published in 1950 and covers 50 years' experience of fishing in estuaries, principally in the River Leven which flows out of Lake Windermere in the English Lake District.

Clapham, who was regularly partnered by his wife, covers spinning, fly fishing and worming; but it is with spinning, which he describes as the 'most sporting' and most 'effective means' of fishing estuaries, that he is most comfortable. His technique for both spinning and fly fishing was down-and-across, allowing the current to swing the lure round in heavy water before recovering line or working the lure in slower water. He fished a sunk-line with one fly and is another to use the term 'medicine' to describe the attributes of a fly – in this instance it is the tandem mounted worm fly that is 'good medicine' – along with '*Terrors, Demons, Alexandras, Rubber Tubes* and *Dandies...*'.

He is rather scathing about greased-line fishing, and it is interesting to note how different authors can have diametrically opposed prejudices. Crossley, Horsley and Holiday were all devoted greased-liners but Clapham likens fishing a fly on a floating line to using a worm or prawn with a float (and clearly regards each method as unsporting).

Modern nylon lines were not for Clapham who was still wedded to gut substitute and he, like many before him, had a marked preference for spinning with the natural minnow (mounted in a 'scarab' lined with silver paper) as opposed to the artificial (Devon) minnow.

In historical terms *Sea Trout Fishing in Tidal Waters* is an interesting book. It is, however, dated and there is little similarity between the long, well defined, sandy or muddy estuaries fished by Clapham and those short, rocky and weeded estuaries more common in the north and west of Scotland where most of the fishing for sea trout in tidal waters is practised today.

Two books which are required reading for stillwater sea-trout anglers appeared at about the same time. The first was *Catching Salmon and Sea Trout* by G.P.R. Balfour-Kinnear, published in 1958; the second was that masterpiece of angling literature *A Man May Fish* by T.C. Kingsmill Moore, published in 1960 (revised and enlarged edition published in 1979).

Balfour-Kinnear had a long and distinguished career as an angler and angling author. He also wrote *Flying Salmon* and *Spinning Salmon* (published in 1937 and 1938 respectively). *Catching Salmon and Sea Trout* is very largely about catching salmon; but there are five good chapters on sea trout and much of the rest of the book is very relevant in a general sense – especially his discussion of how changes in water and weather conditions affect fishing methods.

He was a strong proponent of greased-line fishing for sea trout but, in complete contrast to convention, he manipulated his cast and line to fish the fly quickly, as opposed to drifting it down and across at the same speed as the current. He also advocated using nymph-like flies for sea trout. These were conventionally dressed like low-water salmon flies but with the wing lying *along* the hook shank (size 10).

Balfour-Kinnear's chapter on dapping is interesting in that he is among the first to give the subject any detailed treatment. He notes the differences between dapping for brown trout and for sea trout, and advances the theory that the floatant used to treat the larger artificial flies used in dapping for sea trout is the cause of so many missed fish, because they are repelled by the taste or smell and eject the fly immediately after taking it. His discussion on the different forms of rise to the dap fly and on striking is relevant.

Generally speaking much of the literature on fishing tends to be repetitive and to some extent derivative. Occasionally, however, we come across an author who declines to accept the standard method of doing things without question and who develops his own particular style, methodology and approach. In this way the sport is enriched and advanced. Balfour-Kinnear had over 60 years' practical experience of fishing a wide variety of waters and had cause to question repeatedly the orthodox methods. He states: 'It is because I have persistently tried new lures and new methods of presentation when the fish were taking – thereby often catching less fish than I would otherwise have done – that I have been able to find out conclusively what lures and methods are the most productive in different conditions.' Sadly he fished mostly for salmon. Had he fished for sea trout more often it is likely that his inquiring, innovative mind would have made a major contribution to the development of our sport.

T.C. Kingsmill Moore was another 'thinking' angler, not content blithely to accept the orthodox without proper question. He was a distinguished judge of the Irish High Court and of the Supreme Court and contributed to Irish political life as a member of the Senate. He was also an ardent angler with more than 50 years' experience, and his delightful book *A Man May Fish* is rightly acknowledged as a modern classic. In his own words, 'No one but a master or a fool is dogmatic about fishing....'.

Kingsmill Moore writes largely about lake fishing and his relevance is two-fold. Firstly this is one of the very few books about fishing in Ireland, and secondly his lengthy and very relevant treatment of fish vision, weather and water conditions and the importance of form and pattern in the choice of flies is significant. Not for him is the oft-repeated view that 'the pattern of the fly is unimportant', and as a consequence he bequeathed to posterity such classic trout flies as the *Kingsmill* and the beautiful 'Bumble' series of carefully conceived and painstakingly evolved lake flies (pages 333–5). Although only one chapter is dedicated to 'White Trout in River and Lake', much of the discursive and anecdotal sections of the book are relevant to sea trout and are, in any event, highly readable. His section on fish vision in relation to how it moves to the fly is a masterful presentation of a complex topic by a layman.

From stillwaters we eventually return to rivers and to F.W. Holiday, whose *River Fishing for Sea Trout* published in 1960 is important because it is the first book to deal with Welsh waters. Holiday lived in Pembrokeshire, where he had access to a number of excellent sea-trout rivers, notably the

Teifi. He was a regular contributor to the angling press, and in 1956 published a slim volume on *Sea Trout* in the comprehensive 'How to Catch Them' series. *River Fishing for Sea Trout* is a much-needed expansion of his earlier work.

Holiday is true to his title and says nothing about stillwater fishing for sea trout. The author was essentially a wet-fly angler with much experience of Welsh rivers, and wisely sticks to what he knows best. He is at his best when dealing with night fishing (and at his worst during his extensive lapses into river bank politics). He has much to offer the reader, despite the polemics.

Holiday was a 'greased-liner' of the old school. He believed that the cast should fish round as slowly as possible with a belly in the line so that the fly was presented broad-side on to the fish and that the strike should be delayed until 'the fish takes line'. He stressed that 'the fly at all times must never be in direct tensional contact with the rod tip'. He states that 'almost all fishing for sea trout is now done with the greased or floating line'. In this respect he was wrong. The floating line was not as popular as all that in the early 1960s as far as sea trout fishing in Wales was concerned; and his style of fishing it was certainly far from typical.

It is with Holiday that we see the subsurface technique of fishing the fly at night evolved to its modern form, although he used somewhat smaller flies (size 9) than those later recommended by Falkus and generally accepted as the norm today. He is, we believe, among the first to recommend the tube-fly and Waddington Shank for sea-trout fishing and the first to mention the use of the maggot attached to the fly when night fishing.

Holiday disliked worming but was more favourably disposed towards spinning. He is among the first to recommend spinning 'upstream-and-back' for sea trout, and to recommend a fast retrieve when working the lure. He is also among the first to discuss light spinning on low-water in any detail, and his coverage of the whole subject of spinning is, perhaps, of more relevance than his treatment of fly fishing. He notes the greater appeal of the natural minnow over the artificial minnow, and is the first to recommend the use of the Quill Minnow for sea trout.

Holiday is an interesting author. He had his own very personal style of fishing and his own peculiar preferences and prejudices. He talks much sense. In certain respects he was ahead of his time, and in other respects he was wedded to the past. Not for him the modern advances in tackle. He preferred gut leaders to nylon, silk lines to plastic coated, and described forward-tapers as 'expensive trifles'. Many anglers today would disagree with his views on fishing the fly by day and on striking (which he did from the reel – as did Maxwell and Hamish Stuart). Nevertheless *River Fishing for Sea Trout* is a significant text. If Stuart and Gray can be forgiven for their dogma in stating their preferences and prejudices then so too can Holiday!

Our historical review of the sparse literature over the preceding 65 years has shown that sea-trout angling was regarded as either scaled-down salmon fishing or as scaled-up brown-trout fishing. This is seen in the 'intermediate' nature of the tackle used, typically the length of rod, weight of line and strength of leader. It is also seen in the general size of fly and in the various tactics and techniques employed – 'not quite salmon or not quite brown trout'. A few notable authors, principally Jeffrey Bluett on rivers and Kingsmill Moore on lakes, developed an approach to sea-trout fishing which was styled neither on salmon nor on brown trout but was instead specific to the sea trout itself. However, their teachings were not widely acknowledged at the time, and sea-trout angling continued to be practised as something in between salmon and brown-trout and, with a few notable exceptions, continued to be less popular than either. Although it was to be almost twenty years before sea-trout angling was to enjoy its present widespread increase in popularity, the initial stages of the modern sea-trout revolution began as far back as 1962 with the publication of *Sea Trout Fishing: A Guide to Success* by Hugh Falkus. Falkus was one of those very lucky anglers who not only live very close to their fishing but also happen to own it. The fishing in this instance is one of the best sections of the Cumberland Esk, a small river in the English Lake District which flows into the Solway at Ravenglass.

In his slim 1962 volume, Falkus deals almost exclusively with night fishing. He makes some reference to daylight fishing with a spinner on heavy water and refers to low-water fishing with the upstream worm with obvious enthusiasm, but only in passing. No mention is made of stillwater fishing for sea trout, low-water spinning, worm fishing on heavy water, daylight fly fishing or estuary fishing, and, while generally well received, *Sea Trout Fishing* did not have the impact that it deserved. In 1975 a second edition was produced. The title was the same but there was no comparison with the earlier 1962 edition. This had been virtually re-written and very much expanded to encompass heavy spinning and worm fishing on both spate and low-water conditions in greater detail. Included also was a brief section covering stillwater fishing with the wet-fly and by trolling, along with another section of fishing for sea trout in salt water. However, the emphasis was still on night fishing, but next to nothing was said about sea-trout fishing in daylight with the wet fly, dry fly or dapping.

Falkus has done more than anyone to popularise the sport of sea-trout angling. He was both a naturalist and professional writer and, therefore, able to present his observations and experiences in a highly readable way. In this he was aided by his publishers, who produced a second edition lavishly endowed with some 186 photographs and numerous line drawings: something unprecedented in a book of this type. This second edition rapidly became a best-seller and is still in print. It has been repeatedly described as a 'classic' and indeed it is, both in terms of the literature on sea trout and in terms of fishing books in general. We note with interest that the formula has been repeated with his equally 'monumental' *Salmon Fishing: A Practical Guide* published in 1984.

While the entire text of *Sea Trout Fishing* is compulsory reading for all aspiring sea-trout anglers, it is for his dissertation on night fishing that Falkus will forever be remembered. Most previous authors (if not all) developed one particular style and, generally, applied it to the exclusion of any other method. Thus Dawson principally fished the dry fly at night, while Bluett mainly fished the wet fly on a sinking line and Holiday stuck with the 'greased' line. Falkus, however, developed a repertoire of different techniques which included the surface (wake) lure, the subsurface lure fished on a floating line and the sunk lure fished on a sinking line. He also developed a 'routine' which entailed fishing the subsurface fly until 'half-time' and the sunk lure during the 'second-half' when the fish often 'went down' and failed to respond to a lure fished in the upper levels of the water. Falkus has also done much to popularise the use of larger than traditional flies and lures. His 'Medicine' flies consisting of minimal body dressing and sparse hackle with a slender wing are now widely used on most sea-trout rivers in England and Wales (although they do not seem to be so widely used in Ireland or Scotland). His 'secret weapon' with its short flying-treble is now widely popular as a means of fishing the maggot in conjunction with the fly and as a device for dealing with fish which come short to the fly.

While we may disagree with certain aspects of Hugh Falkus's approach to night fishing, we are in general agreement with his general philosophy, and readily acknowledge the enormous and unprecedented contribution that he has made to the art and science of night fishing for sea trout. His analytical and carefully rationalised approach to angling is an example to all.

The *Art of Sea Trout Fishing* by Charles C. McLaren is a delightful little book of only 120 pages published in 1963 as Number 3 in the series 'Angling Paperbacks'. It is exclusively Scottish in flavour and perspective – and remarkably comprehensive for its size. Worm fishing and spinning are dealt with fairly superficially and very little is said about river fishing at night. Its main interest is in the inclusion of a chapter on sea-trout fishing in sea pools, estuaries and the open sea and in its coverage of loch fishing.

The author was brought up on the banks of Loch Maree, and his treatment of stillwater fishing with the wet fly and by dapping is excellent. He is among the first to mention night fishing for sea trout on lakes and another to recommend large flies (size 1 or 1/0) for sea trout under certain conditions. It is interesting to note that McLaren recommended fishing a team of three flies when river fishing in daylight with the bob-fly worked across the stream to make a steady wave against the current, as when lake fishing. Many earlier authors, such as Bridgett, noted that a fly which drags across the surface of the river in daylight sometimes produced a response from sea trout. McLaren puts it more strongly, stating, 'The use of the top dropper on the surface will yield sea trout when no other method of fishing will'. In order to work the bob-fly effectively, he recommends using a rod of 12 ft in length, and a light level line.

In 1928, when only 13 years old, Charles McLaren caught a 12½lb sea trout from the Kinlochewe River entering Loch Maree. Scale readings showed this fish to be 18 years old and to have spawned 11 times. This fish holds the record to this day as being the oldest and most spawned sea trout recorded from British waters (see p. 19).

Sea Trout Fishing by Jock Scott was published in 1969 as Volume 35 in the remarkable 'Lonsdale Library' series of sporting books which covered everything from Horsemanship and Boxing through to Wildfowling and Cricket. Jock Scott was the pen-name of D.G. Ferris Rudd. He also wrote *Salmon and Trout Fishing up to Date* (1960), *Greased Line Fishing for Salmon* (1935), *Fine and Far Off* (1952) and *Spinning up to Date* (1937).

His *Sea Trout Fishing* was to be the third book bearing that title and was written towards the end of a long and distinguished career as an angler and author. Arguably, it is as significant as the book of the same title published seven years earlier by Falkus, in that it focuses largely on stillwater fishing with the wet fly, dry fly and by dapping, and deals with daylight fishing with the wet fly in addition to discussing night fishing and saltwater fishing. It is more complete in some respects than even the 1975 much-revised edition of Falkus, but it is also very dated. It is perhaps this latter feature that provides its interest and value, since it provides an important link between the old and the new in terms of style, tackle, tactics and attitudes towards sea trout. It is noteworthy that the chapter on sea-trout angling literature stops short at F.W. Holiday (1960) and makes no mention of the 1962 publication by Falkus. We find this rather curious as Jock Scott was evidently widely read, and this omission seems to emphasise our earlier point about the lack of impact of Hugh Falkus' modest first edition.

Jock Scott writes essentially in a Scottish context and almost everything he says indicates a salmon-like approach to his sea-trout fishing. This is seen in his preference for double-handed spinning rods, multiplier reels, double hooks and in his choice of flies and manner of fishing them. He fished mainly 'greased-line' on rivers and preferred to fish the sunk line in lakes.

It is fascinating to encounter an author writing in the late 1960s still debating the relative merits of gut versus nylon leaders (and declaring a preference for the latter!), still opting for wire spinning traces and plaited spinning lines and deploring the advent of the modern forward taper fly-line as 'spinning with a fly rod'. Notwithstanding these anachronistic foibles, Jock Scott has much to offer and gives us a feel for Scottish sea-trout angling in the late 1960s. We include him in our list of essential reading; along with Bridgett, Bluett, Kingsmill Moore and Falkus. Traditional he may be, but there is nothing wrong with that. He was by all accounts as successful on the many waters that he fished as other more radical and innovative writers were on their waters. It is always worth remembering that the sea trout is a widely diffuse species in its distribution and in the composition of the different stocks. It is evident that the same approach to angling may not be wholly applicable in different rivers and different regions of the British Isles. Certainly, the contrast between the styles advocated by Falkus and Scott is marked *but* both anglers caught a lot of fish nonetheless.

From Scotland we move briefly back to Wales and to *Sea Trout*, by Clive

Gammon, published in 1974 as part of the Osprey series of books covering game, coarse and sea fishing for various British fishes. The author is a well-known angling personality and writer who fished the Tywi, one of the premier sea-trout rivers in Europe, for many years and who is perhaps better known for his writing and broadcasting on sea angling.

Sea Trout is written in a crisp instructive style. He is anti-worm and states that lake fishing for sea trout is 'repetitive and somewhat boring'! He makes passing reference to fishing with spinner, fly and bait in the sea and deals chiefly with spinning and fly fishing in rivers.

Gammon fished both the floating and sinking lines and generally agreed with Falkus that sea-trout flies should be larger than those employed by most anglers. His basic approach was to fish a sink-tip line by casting down and across and letting the fly fish round, keeping an upstream belly in the line so that the fish could turn with the fly and hook itself. In slow water he recommended stripping the line back to increase the speed of movement of the fly. His style of night fishing was a blend of surface, subsurface and deep sunk fly, more or less as suggested by Falkus (except that he only 'worked' the fly in a slow current). His tactics for dealing with short-rising fish which 'plucked' the fly without taking it were either to fish a sinking line slow and deep or to change to a floater and strip line 'fast to create a surface wake'.

His section on spinning is short but comprehensive. He covers the different tactics and styles suitable for high, medium and low water in relation to the distribution and behaviour of the fish. He is the first to note that the 'Toby' lures are bad hookers, and to state clearly that the 'throbbing swing' of spinner swung across the current without rewinding, as in salmon spinning, is inappropriate for sea trout. He also states that it is impossible to fish too fast for sea trout, and recommends the upstream cast into deep water alongside a near bank as being particularly effective for sea trout. *Sea Trout* is a book crammed with much good advice. Although we disagree with Gammon's deprecatory comments on lake fishing and worming, we are in almost total agreement with everything that he says about spinning for sea trout.

Dr William B. Currie is another Scottish writer, perhaps better known as a salmon angler than as a sea-trout angler. He has, however, written much about sea-trout angling in Scottish waters and is an author who inspires confidence. His *Game Fishing* was published in 1962, to be followed by *A Game Fisher's Year* in 1969. His latest and most impressive publication, which contains an update of his sea-trout writings, is *The Guinness Guide to Game Fishing* published in 1980. This is a lavishly-illustrated book covering salmon, brown trout, rainbow trout, brook charr and grayling in Scottish waters, and includes a quite superlative section headed 'The Quest for Sea Trout' which is a minor classic in its own right.

Currie writes in great detail about fly fishing on rivers and lakes and makes no mention of either spinning or worming. He discusses where sea trout lie in relation to river flows and covers both daylight and night fishing.

He states that the basic art of sea-trout fly fishing is similar to that of trout downstream wet-fly fishing, declares that he likes to fish a long line (20 yards) and work the flies from the moment that they touch the water, and he generally fished the floating line with two flies on the leader. He makes the interesting observation, which accords with our own experiences, that the floating line usually takes the fresher (more active fish) but is not as productive as the sunk line for the larger fish.

His approach to night fishing is based upon the thesis that sea trout, unlike salmon, tend to rove about the pool by day and night – moving up to the head and back to the tail. He describes sea trout fishing as a 'sandwich'... 'we fish the floating line in the gloom of the evening, concentrating on the tails of the pools and on the known turning places in the head. When the evening rise wears off, and these places become more or less unproductive, we can sink the flies, or fish a sunk lure, searching for sea trout in the deeper lies.' Although there are several differences in the approach to river fishing for sea trout at night as advocated by Falkus and Currie, they also have much in common. We can see in the above statement by Currie that there has been a gradual merging of the 'Scottish' and 'English' styles over the twenty-year period since Falkus first published his views, such that there is now general uniformity north and south of the border in the adoption of a standard repertoire of techniques evolved specifically for sea trout entailing variously the surface (wake) fly, the subsurface fly and the sunk lure.

Anyone wishing to obtain an up-to-date perspective on lake fishing for sea trout in Scotland could do no better than to read Currie's sub-section on sea trout in lochs. He covers both wet fly fishing and dapping and is another to mention fishing at night for sea trout in stillwaters. Although he deals mainly with the larger lochs, such as Hope, Stack, Maree, Moidart and Eilt, almost everything he says accords with our own observations and experiences on smaller and less prestigious waters in Ireland and Scotland.

For our final contribution in this review of the literature we move to Loch Lomond, Scotland's most southerly sea trout lake. Anyone contemplating fishing Loch Lomond or any other large lake for that matter would be wise to read *Angling on Lomond* by Bill McEwan, published in 1980. This is a fascinating book written in a highly readable and amusing style by an author who clearly knows his water like the back of his hand. Although he makes no particular distinction between salmon and sea trout in his various chapter headings his messages are no less clear or valuable. He covers wet-fly fishing and dapping, and his sections on boat handling and how to fish various drifts in different conditions of wind and weather have general application. The chapter on trolling is excellent and yet to be bettered in the literature. Apart from being packed full of information about Loch Lomond it is widely interspersed with amusing anecdotes, several of which are quite hilarious. The book is specific to Loch Lomond, *but* do not make the mistake of thinking that it is relevant only to that one lake. Much of what McEwan has to say is widely relevant elsewhere.

References & Reading List

We have (as far as we are aware) included all the authors who wrote solely or substantially about sea trout. As a general rule we have quoted their most up-to-date publication on the subject (e.g. Currie, Falkus, Henzell, Holiday, Jock Scott) even though reference may have been made to their earlier writings. Many authors include a chapter (or two) on sea trout in numerous publications on game fishing. Those included here were chosen because, in our view, they either had something original to say or they adequately portray general attitudes to the sport at the time or in a particular area.

Adamson, W.A. (1961). *Lake and Loch Fishing for Salmon and Sea Trout*. A & C Black, London.

Balfour-Kinnear, G.P.R. (1958). *Catching Salmon and Sea Trout*. Thomas Nelson & Sons Ltd, London.

Bluett, J. (1948). *Sea Trout and Occasional Salmon*. Cassell & Co. Ltd, London.

Brennand, G. (1951). *The Fisherman's Handbook: Trout, Salmon and Sea Trout, with Notes on Coarse Fishing*. Ward Lock & Co. Ltd, London.

Bridgett, R.C. (1929). *Sea Trout Fishing*. Herbert Jenkins Ltd, London.

Cass, A.R.H. (N/D – c.1946). *Catching the Wily Sea Trout*. Herbert Jenkins Ltd, London.

Clapham, R. (1950). *Fishing for Sea Trout in Tidal Waters*. Oliver & Boyd, London.

Chrystal, R.A. (1927). *Angling Theories and Methods*. Herbert Jenkins Ltd, London.

Crossley, A. (1939). *The Floating Line for Salmon and Sea Trout*. Methuen Publishers, London.

Currie, W.B. (1980). *The Guinness Guide to Game Fishing*. Guinness Superlatives Ltd, Middlesex.

Dawson, K. (Revised edition = N/D probably c.1948: 1st Edition 1938) *Modern Salmon and Sea Trout Fishing*. Herbert Jenkins Ltd, London.

Falkus, H. (1975) (Revised edition). *Sea Trout Fishing: A Guide to Success*. H.F. & G. Witherby Ltd, London.

Gammon, C. (1974). *Sea Trout*. Osprey Publishing Ltd, Reading.

Gray, L.R.N. (1957). *The Torridge Fishery*. Nicholas Kaye Ltd, London.

Horsley, T. (1944). *Fishing for Trout and Salmon*. H.F. & G. Witherby Ltd, London.

Henzell, H.P. (1949). *Fishing for Sea Trout*. Adam & Charles Black, London.

Holiday, F.W. (1960). *River Fishing for Sea Trout*. Herbert Jenkins, London.

Kingsmill Moore, T.C. (1983). *A Man May Fish*. Colin Smythe, Gerrards Cross.

Mackie, A. (1912). *The Art of Worm Fishing*. Adam & Charles Black, London.

Maxwell, Sir H. (1898). *Salmon and Sea Trout: How to Propagate, Preserve and Catch Them in British Waters*. George Routledge & Sons Ltd, London.

McClaren, C.C. (1963). *The Art of Sea Trout Fishing*. Oliver and Boyd Ltd, London.

McEwan, Bill. (1980). *Angling on Lomond*. Albyn Press Ltd, Edinburgh.

Mottram, J.C. (N/D = c. 1923). *Sea Trout and Other Fishing Studies*. The Field Press Ltd, London.

Scott, Jock. (1969). *Sea Trout Fishing*. Seeley, Service & Co. Ltd, London.

Spencer, S. (1986). *Clear Water Trout-Fishing With Worm*. H.F. & G. Witherby Ltd, London.

Stirling, J. (1931). *Fishing for Trout and Sea Trout with Worm and Wet Fly*. Philip Allan University Press, Glasgow.

Stuart, H. (1917). *The Book of the Sea Trout: with some Chapters on Salmon*. Martin Secker, London.

4 · TACKLE TECHNOLOGY

Every true angler takes great pride in his tackle and, if like us, will acquire numerous ancillary bits-and-pieces which are not essential to the main purpose of catching sea trout but which, nevertheless, makes the task that much simpler or that much more enjoyable, Space does not permit us to consider all the paraphernalia of angling – such as fly boxes, hook-snoods, line-minders, wading staffs, nipper knives, hook hones, clip-on extension reels, leader dispensers, blood-knot tyers, fish carriers; and the hundred and one other gadgets and items of gear that are produced to benefit the angler. We reluctantly restrict ourselves here to a consideration of only those items of tackle that are absolute essentials; such as rods, reels and lines.

Within this constraint, we discuss our personal choice of tackle generally under the appropriate sections and chapters. However, it is relevant that we should consider here a number of salient and common points together so as to avoid unnecessary repetition later on.

There have been enormous advances in the technology of fishing tackle over the last few decades with many new materials and processes being developed that provided the angler with enormous benefits in terms of the quality, durability, reliability amd versatility of the tackle now available. Nonetheless, the modern angler is in some respects less well served by the tackle-trade than his predecessors. Browsing through the pages of the lavishly produced catalogues of the 1920s, 1930s and 1940s published by firms, such as Hardy Bros, Mallochs of Perth, Cummins and Westley Richards it is impossible not to be impressed by the range and choice of products then available. Where today, for example, would the modern angler go to find the amazing variety of minnows, spinners, spoons and mounts available 40 years ago?

We will follow the conventional approach of discussing rods and reels first and then lines and terminal tackle. This is convenient although, as others correctly point out, it is more logical to start with the terminal tackle and work back to the rod, since *what* you fish and *how* you fish it materially affects the choice of line and, therefore, the type of rod selected for a particular purpose.

Rods

The introduction of glass-fibre rods in the 1950s presaged the decline of the split-cane rod which had been universally popular for well over half a century. Steel rods had appeared a few years earlier but they enjoyed only a brief existence, Cane was technically never one of the best materials for a fly rod, and hollow glass fibre had many obvious advantages. It was stronger, lighter, more durable and, above all, much cheaper than cane. Within a few years glass-fibre rods had captured the greater part of the market. Cane rods continued to be produced, but had become very expensive by comparison. This, coupled with the fact that good-quality bamboo was becoming harder to obtain in quantity, resulted in many once-famous firms ultimately dropping cane rods from their ranges over the next decade or so.

The advent of carbon-fibre rods in the early 1970s as a spin-off from space-age technology soon saw the rapid decline in the popularity of glass fibre. At first carbon-fibre (or graphite) rods were expensive and suffered from a number of defects. These teething problems were very soon remedied, however, and the carbon-fibre rod now reigns supreme. Glass-fibre and split-cane rods are still manufactured, but total sales of both now represent only a very small part of the market.

The popularity of carbon-fibre rods is wholly justified, since they have many advantages over cane and glass. They are very much lighter (a typical 10-feet-long fly rod in cane, glass and carbon would weigh about 8½, 6½ and 3½ ounces respectively). They are also thinner in section; and therefore present less air resistance when casting. There is less tip vibration ('wobble') when flexed; so that the cast is longer and more accurate. There is a high resistance to bending; so that the rod moves the line faster, giving a longer cast for the same effort. They transmit vibration better; so that the strike can be timed more precisely and the fish played with more 'feel'. We could go on extolling the merits of carbon fibre; but suffice it to say that we gave our glass-fibre rods away many years ago and relegated our better cane rods to the collectors' cabinet and we now use carbon-fibre rods for all forms of spinning, worming and fly fishing.

In recent years the basic carbon-fibre rod has been 'improved' in various ways. Instead of having the carbon fibre running along the vertical (butt to tip) axis of the rod, some are wound in a double-helix around the axis. This improves the strength of the rod and resists torsional (twisting) stress when casting – especially when roll-casting. Other rods have been 'improved' by the incorporation of 'boron' (particles of boron gas deposited in filaments of tungsten to produce 'boron fibre'). While it is argued that this gives the rod great strength and a faster, smoother action, plus more sensitivity, carbon/boron rods are more expensive and we are not convinced that there is really any significant, *tangible* benefit over good carbon fibre.

Yet another 'modern miracle' is Kevlar. This is a shock-resistant, flexible, man-made fibre reported to be some 20 per cent lighter than carbon. Rods which combine Kevlar with carbon are claimed to be 'better'. A more recent 'major advance' in the technology of the modern fishing rod is 'Kevlar-Whisker'. The 'whisker' is made of silicon carbide, which is reputed to have a tensile elasticity and strength *twice* that of boron and *thrice* that of carbon, while being 20 per cent lighter than carbon. So it will undoubtedly continue, with 'newer' and 'better' and 'improved' products continually being launched on the market. However, we doubt that the quantum-leap from cane to carbon will ever be experienced again. Instead we can expect to see a steady, and largely imperceptible, evolution in the technology of rods, as one man-made product is superseded by another.

There is no such thing as an 'all-purpose' rod. Each style and method of fishing requires a different 'ideal'. Inevitably the angler must compromise in order to reduce costs and the vast amount of tackle that he would otherwise have to transport about the country. However, given no such practical constraints we would probably select at least nine different lengths and types of rod:

1. low-water spinning: 7-ft length rated for lines 4–8lb strength;
2. heavy-water spinning: 10-ft length rated for lines 8–12lb strength;
3. heavy-water worming: 10-ft length rated for lines 8–12lb strength;
4. low-water worming: 13-ft length rated for lines 4–8lb strength;
5. fly-fishing sunk lure: 10-ft length rated for lines AFTM 7–9;
6. fly-fishing subsurface lure: 11-ft length rated for lines AFTM 7–9;
7. dry-fly fishing: 9-ft length rated for lines AFTM 5–8;
8. dapping: 17-ft length;
9. wet-fly fishing: 12-ft length rated for lines 5–7.

Each of these rods has a special purpose, and each has a different action best suited for that particular style of fishing for which it is to be used. Thus a dry-fly rod has a stiffer, more positive action than a wet-fly rod; a spinning rod has more action in the tip than a worming rod; and a rod for fishing the sunk fly is more powerful than a rod for fishing the surface fly, etc.

Rationalisation is necessary, and some rods can be used for more than one style of fishing without undue penalty. Thus we tend to use our 10-ft length spinning rods for heavy-water worming; and we often use our 11-ft sub-surface fly rod for low-water worming, for dapping (with an 18-inch screw-in extension handle) and (minus the extension handle) for all other forms of wet-fly fishing. Our 10-ft length sunk-fly rod is used also for dry-fly fishing and, very occasionally, for low-water spinning. Thus, the 'complete' sea-trout angler could manage with a minimum of three rods;

1. 10 feet length sunk-fly/dry-fly/low water spinning
2. 11 feet length subsurface fly/low water worming/wet-fly
3. 10 feet length heavy spinning/worming.

However, this would be very much a compromise and, like most compromises, is not perfect. In practice, it would be difficult to exclude the addition of a 7–8-ft length spinning rod for use on low water.

Reels

It is frequently stated that the reel used for fly fishing is the least important item of tackle and that if you want to save money you should start with the reel.

The fly reel has two main functions: 1) to hold the required length of fly line and backing line in a convenient manner; 2) to allow the line to be unwound and rewound as and when required.

There is a wide choice of fly reels on the market and the basic centre-pin design has been with us for a very long time. However, the 'perfect' fly reel for sea-trout fishing has yet to be developed. Some have come close but none as yet have managed to incorporate *all* the basic requirements. The ideal reel for sea-trout fishing would have the following features:

1. an exposed spool to allow the fish to be played by finger pressure on the rim;
2. a cageless design with a quick release spool, to allow lines to be changed over simply and quickly without risk of damaging the line by pinching it between the spool and the cage;
3. a rapid (geared) rewind to allow line to be recovered quickly when playing a fish;
4. a silent brake or check for night fishing;
5. a left or right-hand rewind facility;
6. an adequate spool capacity to contain fly lines rated AFTM 5–9 *plus* about 100–150 yards length of 20lb strength backing line;
7. a weight of no more than about 6oz;
8. durability combined with a sensible price.

There are some beautiful reels on the market, but some of the more prestigious (and expensive) are engineered with such fine tolerances that it requires only a few grains of sand to enter the works and the reel almost grinds to a halt. We can see no good reason why all but a few reels are built with a cage surrounding the spool. The cage may add strength to the reel but it also adds weight, makes it difficult to change a spool quickly without the risk of pinching and damaging the fly line, and unless the spool is designed to have an exposed rim (another added complication) it makes it difficult, if not impossible, to play a fish by applying finger pressure to the spool rim.

A rapid rewind facility is often very necessary when playing sea trout at night or when boat fishing. We do not like playing a fish with coils of loose line lying about all over the place. A geared rewind that recovers line quickly is very useful and most of our reels have this very desirable attribute. Automatic reels which give and recover line against a spring have many advantages in that line can be recovered 'at the speed of light' if so required. They are, however, rather heavy, and sadly lack the spool capacity to take a fairly thick fly line *plus* a sensible and safe length of backing.

We find it curious that many fly reels are made with noisy checks or ratchets that can be adjusted to control the ease at which the spool turns on its spindle. How many anglers actually 'strike' from the reel these days? If you are recovering line to work your flies – as you should be when practising most forms of fly fishing for sea trout – you *cannot* strike from the reel! *And* a 'strong sturdy ratchet' is not necessary when playing a fish *if* you can adjust the pressure on the spool by finger control. Finger pressure when playing a fish is always preferable as it allows the angler to keep in close touch with the fish and to adjust the rate at which line is given with immediate response and sensitivity. It should be the angler that plays the fish, not the reel. Checks make a noise, and noise is something to be avoided at night when fishing club waters. Not because it disturbs fish, but because the intermittent 'scream' of a ratchet attracts other anglers like moths swarming to a light. We enjoy the companionship of others – but within reason!

By and large the weight of a reel is not a particularly important consideration with the length of rod usually employed in sea-trout angling. The need to counter-balance the weight of the rod is hardly a consideration with the modern, light, materials used in their manufacture, and anything up to about 7oz is perfectly acceptable for the rods of about 11-ft length or shorter as widely used in sea-trout fishing.

While the modern multiplier reel is a wonderful example of highly sophisticated engineering, we much prefer the cheaper and simpler fixed-spool reels for spinning and bait fishing. As far as sea trout are concerned, the fixed-spool reel does eveything that a multiplier would be required to do and it also does some things that it cannot – such as cast a *very light bait on an ultra-fine line.*

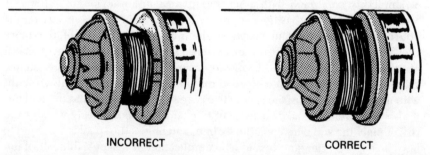

INCORRECT   CORRECT

Fig.4. Always ensure that the spool of the reel is loaded to full capacity. The fuller the spool, the more line recovered with each turn of the handle. Proper loading is very important with fixed-spool reels. Underloading results in reduced casting distances caused by increased friction on the line as it passes over the edge of the spool. Avoid overloading too, as this results in coils of line springing off the spool when the bale arm is opened.

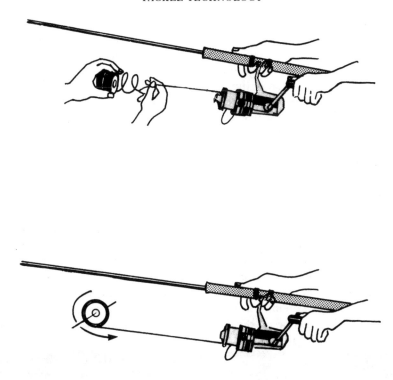

Fig. 5. Care should be taken to avoid twisting the line when loading a fixed-spool reel. The correct way is to feed the line off the storage spool so that the twist of the coils is cancelled out by the direction of the movement of the bale arm as it lays the line onto the spool of the reel.

There are several very good fixed-spool reels currently available. We use the same model for both spinning and worming on high and low water and carry interchangeable spare spools loaded with 4lb, 6lb, 8lb, 10lb and 12lb nylon. The spools are each capable of carrying a minimum length of 100–150 yards of nylon which has been properly loaded to optimum capacity on the spool without any twist in the line (Figs 4 & 5).

A good spinning reel with a fast line recovery is always a wise investment. It is likely to do a great deal of work over a season. Proper servicing is important, and remember if you fish in tidal waters that, since salt water is a corrosive, the reel should be carefully cleaned afterwards.

Fly Lines

We propose to deal with the subject of fly lines in some detail because, in our view, they are fundamentally important to successful sea-trout fishing on both rivers and lakes (but more so on rivers). We use the plural 'lines' deliberately because we consider it very necessary to use several different types of lines in our fishing; each of which has been specially chosen for a particular purpose related to the style of fishing and the prevailing conditions of river and weather.

The big breakthrough in the technology of fly lines occurred in the early 1950s with the introduction of the plastic-coated line. Over the last 30 years the advances in fly-line concepts have been so extensive that it is easy to become overwhelmed by the multiplicity of specifications and range of choice. Indeed the seemingly simple matter of buying a fly line is now so complicated that few anglers can be expected to understand the advanced technology of the modern product.

Prior to the 1950s the angler had to make only a few basic decisions apart from the cost of the line. The standard colour of lines was green, they were manufactured from silk and all of them sank unless 'greased' after purchase to make them float. The decision was thus to choose a line of the correct 'balance' for the rod – and whether or not to be rather radical and choose a forward taper instead of a double taper. Today the choice seems infinite. One manufacturer claims a product range of 315 different types of fly line! The only thing common to modern fly lines is basically that they consist of a plastic coating around a braided level core. However there are many

The modern plastic-coated fly line was introduced in the 1950s and did much to revolutionise sea trout angling. We usually carry 5 different lines at any time – a floater, neutral density, slow-sink, medium-sink, and fast-sink. Careful planning and the use of spare spools much reduces the number of reels stored in the tackle bag. (Photo: M.J. Morgan.)

different 'plastics' with widely different properties which confer different characteristics to the line. Thus, the modern fly line comes in a wide range of colours (white, straw, grey, black, blue, brown, mahogany, several shades of green, fluorescent orange, etc). It is manufactured in a variety of tapers (double, forward, long-belly, rocket, shooting, level, etc) and it may float either *on* the surface or *in* the surface or, for a neutral density line, *just below it*. If it sinks, it may do so at a rate which can be subjectively termed as 'slow', 'medium', 'fast' or 'very fast'. We could go on, but to do so would be confusing. In fact, having made the point, the matter can be simplified to a few basics: namely 1) line weight, 2) line taper, 3) sinking rates, 4) colour.

Fly lines are today manufactured in a range of weights based upon a standard developed by the American Fishing Tackle Manufacturers Association. This standard, now known as the AFTM standard, is widely employed and, while far from perfect, it has done much to simplify what was before a hit-and-miss decision in correctly balancing the weight of a line with a particular rod.

The AFTM scale goes from 1 to 12, but few dealers stock lines below 5 or above 10. For sea trout the most popular line weights are AFTM 6–9. The single most popular weight is AFTM 7 and we use lines so rated for most boat work and for daylight fishing on low water. Much of our river fishing on normal to high flows by day, and virtually all of our night fishing, however, is done with AFTM 8/9 lines.

Irrespective of your choice of taper and sinking rate, the most important consideration when choosing a fly line is that it should balance (or 'work') the rod properly during casting. This is an important point as each and every rod will 'work' best with a certain weight of line. Almost all rods manufactured today state the line rating for the rod somewhere just above the handle, e.g. AFTM 8/9 or AFTM 5/6. The first number is the recommended rating for a double-taper line, and the last number is the rating for a forward taper line. *However*, some manufacturers rate their rods over quite a wide range of AFTM numbers. (The first author regularly uses one rated 4–10.) This seemingly wide tolerance of line weights is not a manufacturers' ploy to sell more rods but a feature of the widely recognised inadequacies of the AFTM standard. The AFTM standard was based on the premise that most (American) anglers tended to aerialise (= extend) about 30 feet of line when casting before making the forward delivery. It is the weight of this first 30 feet of line (measured in grains) that is used as the basis of the AFTM standard for describing lines and rating fly rods.

The general rule is that 'stiff' rods require heavier lines and 'soft' rods require lighter lines to work them properly. Length is immaterial – a 9-ft length 'reservior' rod for fishing deep sunk lures may be rated AFTM 9 while a 12-ft length 'loch' rod for boat fishing with a team of three small subsurface flies may be rated AFTM 5/6. The weakness of the AFTM system is that it ignores the speed at which the line travels through the air in casting. The speed at which any line of a given weight moves through the air in casting can affect the distance achieved with a particular rod. A light line moved fast has more 'weight' and may have the same effect on the rod as a heavy line moved slowly. Thus two different anglers using the *same* rod and line may achieve very different casting distances dependent on their casting action. But the same two anglers using the same rod may achieve the same casting distance when the slower caster fishes a heavier (AFTM 9) line and the faster caster fishes a lighter (AFTM 7) line. Thus the length of line aerialised in casting affects its weight and, hence, its action on the rod. Many British anglers tend to aerialise more than the 30 feet of line that is the basis for the AFTM system. If, for example, an angler aerialises 40 feet of AFTM 7 line, the effective weight on the rod increases by about 30 per cent and may be equivalent to an AFTM 10 rating. Thus, *balance* depends on matching the rod to the line rating *plus* the casting action of the angler. This fact explains the seemingly wide tolerances in terms of AFTM range given by some rod manufacturers.

North American anglers have a wider choice of line tapers than British anglers. In Britain, the choice is limited to four basic tapers – of which only the last three are readily available from tackle dealers. These are shown (Fig. 6) as:

a) level or standard taper;   c) forward taper;
b) double taper;   d) shooting head taper.

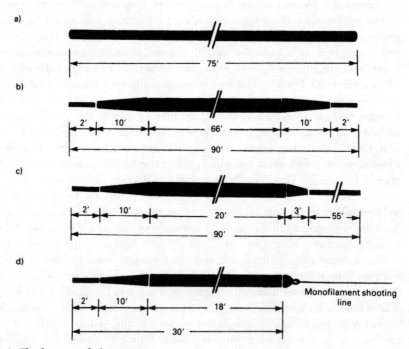

Fig. 6. The four main fly line tapers.

The level taper is hard to obtain because it is not popular. Only McClaren advocates its use for sea trout. We have never met an angler who used a level taper line.

The double taper line is probably still the most popular of all tapers used in fly fishing. We can see practical advantages of the double taper line in salmon fishing and in some contexts for brown-trout fishing, but cannot accept why this should be so for sea trout. The double taper line has a very long history and we suspect that its continued popularity is based largely on tradition and the promulgation of several myths. The most common selling point (repeatedly trotted out in angling catalogues) is that with a double taper you are buying 'two lines for the price of one'. This is on the basis that when one half wears out you can turn the line round and use the other half. This was, perhaps, a valid point with the old silk lines – not because one end wore out particularly quickly but because the line could be reversed when one half became waterlogged when fishing the 'greased' (= floating) line and began to sink after several treatments of 'floatant' during the course of the day. We have turned double taper lines when the plastic coating of the 'front-half' has been damaged by a snag or, most commonly, by treading on it in studded waders, but we have *never* yet had cause to reverse a double taper line because one half had worn out – even after several years' continuous use. Modern plastic coated fly lines are very durable, provided that they are looked after properly, and the ability to reverse a double taper is not a consideration that should particularly influence the choice of a fly line.

Three myths still promulgated by some writers are that double taper lines are better than forward taper lines because: a) they allow a more delicate presentation; b) it is easier to change the direction of a cast with a double taper; and c) it is impossible to mend line or to roll-cast with a forward taper. These statements may be correct or incorrect, *depending on the length of line being cast*. The important point to remember is that the standard forward taper line and the double taper line are practically identical up to a distance of about 15 yards, and should therefore be no different in their casting characteristics up to this length. Only when the length of line is extended beyond 15 yards will they behave differently. The following points should be remembered, however.

a) While delicacy is important when fishing for sea trout, 15 yards is in fact a fairly long cast and only a few master-casters can place a fly delicately and with precision at greater distances. Rarely will it be necessary to cast much more than 18 yards when night fishing or boat fishing.
b) Mending line is a technique of slowing down the speed at which the fly swings across the current (Fig. 47). It is important when fishing the subsurface fly 'greased-line' style (page 177), but it is not a technique that we recommend when fishing for sea trout by day or by night.
c) The roll-cast is useful in certain situations (page 276) but it would not usually be done with a long line when sea-trout fishing.

Thus, we see no good reason for using double taper lines. The forward taper line is a far better choice and almost all of our fly lines are of this type. It has, in our view, three distinct advantages not provided by the double taper. Firstly, it sinks with a straighter profile than the double taper when a long cast is employed and so provides for more direct contact when striking (Fig. 7). Secondly, 'shooting line' on the forward cast in order to achieve distance is much easier. This is important when fishing in confined situations where it is not possible to aerialise a long line on the back-cast. Third, it casts better into a wind because the weight is in the forward section of the line.

Some anglers seem to think that the forward taper line is a radical new concept. It is not. J. J. Hardy introduced the 'Filip' series of lines as long ago as 1901 and it is possible that forward taper lines were manufactured even earlier. They have never been popular for sea-trout fishing.

The shooting head taper is popular among reservoir trout anglers as a means of casting very long distances. The short length of fly line is usually attached to a strong nylon monofilament backing line which, since it offers very little resistance, is more readily 'shot' on the forward presentation than is possible with conventional backing line. Special monofilament is manufactured for use with shooting heads. The best backing line is 'memory-free' so that it does not retain the shape of the coils created by being wound on the reel.

While we have several types of shooting head which we use for stillwater trout fishing when very long casts are necessary, we do not recommend their general use for sea-trout fishing. They might have some useful application when fishing a large river or when bank fishing for sea trout on a lake (Chapter 15) when very long casts may, at times, be required, however, they are fairly crude in terms of achieving delicacy and accuracy and the 'bump' of the splice that joins the line to the backing as it enters the top ring is very disconcerting when night fishing!

While the traditional silk lines which dominated the market until the mid-1960s all sank if they were left ungreased, none could achieve anything like the depths that can be achieved with the range of sinking lines now available. The introduction of the modern fast-sinking line that cuts through water like a knife through butter and enabled a fly to be presented to fish lying in deep water has provided unprecedented opportunities for sea-trout anglers which many have yet to appreciate fully.

Fishing the sunk fly during the later stages of the night when the sea trout 'go down' as recommended by Cass and subsequent authors was not really sunk-fly fishing in the modern sense because it was not possible to achieve any great depth with the ungreased silk lines then available. In anything more than a slow current the line did not have time to sink to any depth before it was swept round and had to be recast. Today, however, it is possible to select a sinking line which enables the fly to fish near the bottom in most situations other than in very deep or very fast water (Fig. 8).

The rapid evolution and development of the modern fly line has not been

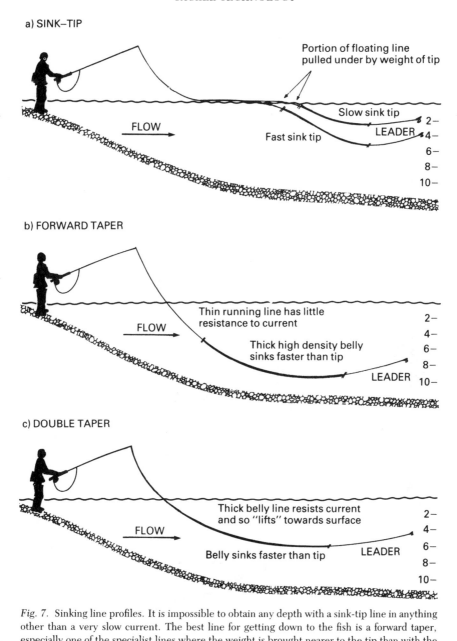

a) SINK–TIP

Portion of floating line
pulled under by weight of tip

FLOW

Slow sink tip

2–

LEADER

4–

Fast sink tip

6–

8–

10–

b) FORWARD TAPER

FLOW

Thin running line has little
resistance to current

2–

4–

Thick high density belly
sinks faster than tip

6–

8–

LEADER

10–

c) DOUBLE TAPER

FLOW

Thick belly line resists current
and so "lifts" towards surface

2–

4–

Belly sinks faster than tip

LEADER

6–

8–

10–

Fig. 7. Sinking line profiles. It is impossible to obtain any depth with a sink-tip line in anything other than a very slow current. The best line for getting down to the fish is a forward taper, especially one of the specialist lines where the weight is brought nearer to the tip than with the standard forward taper. There is, however, little difference in the sinking profiles of most forward and double taper lines over the 'normal' casting distance of about 15 yards as employed in most sea trout fishing.

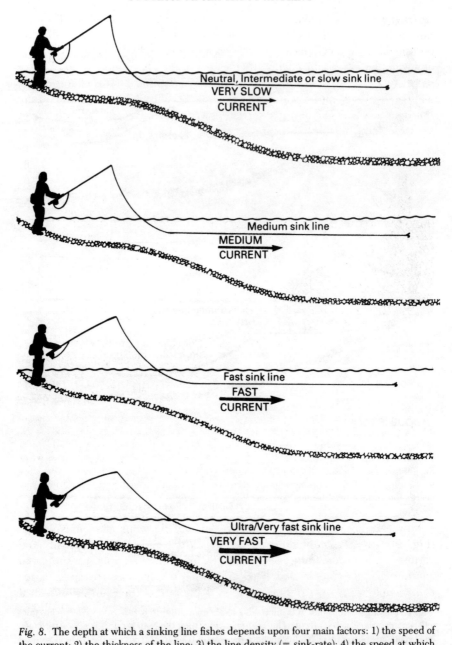

Fig. 8. The depth at which a sinking line fishes depends upon four main factors: 1) the speed of the current; 2) the thickness of the line; 3) the line density (= sink-rate); 4) the speed at which line is recovered during the retrieve. By way of illustration we show how four very different current speeds can result in lines of very different sink-rates fishing at about the same depth. It is impossible to fish a fly at any significant depth in a *very* fast current; even with the fastest of sinking lines.

restricted simply to sinking lines. Floating lines have also evolved. They are now guaranteed to float without any form of further treatment (apart from an occasional wipe down once or twice a season to remove any dirt and grime) and some have a plastic coating that is chemically formulated to repel water so that they actually sit *on* the surface rather than *in* it. This characteristic allows a very soft lift-off when recasting on, as there is little resistance from the water surface. We now use such lines as a matter of preference whenever we have occasion to use a floater.

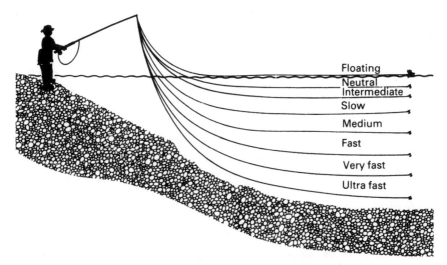

Fig. 9. Modern fly line technology now provides the sea trout angler with a range of lines of different densities that fish on, in and below the surface. Great advances have been made in the development and production of sinking lines and it is now possible to obtain lines that will fish at virtually any depth from just below the surface to very deep indeed. Of course, in running water the depth to which a line will sink depends on the speed of the current and the rate at which the line is retrieved when 'working' the flies. The faster the current or the rate of retrieve, the nearer the surface that the line fishes.

Most manufacturers market a range of lines that sink at various speeds (Fig. 9). Unfortunately there is no standard terminology to classify the various sinking rates: one manufacturer's 'medium sink' may be similar to another manufacturer's 'slow sink' or another's 'fast sink'. However, some firms helpfully express the density or sinking rate of their lines in practical terms and the following table is provided to show the variety of choice available. Table 14 is important to note that the sinking rates quoted by manufacturers are for still water, and not what would be expected in running water. The speed of the current can have a dramatic effect on the rate at which a line sinks (Fig. 8). In running water the resistance of the line will cause it to be lifted up towards the surface to an extent dependent upon the thickness of the line, its density, the speed of the current, and whether or not it is being 'worked'. Thus in a very fast current (say in the rush of water

Table 14: Line sink rates

Description[1]	Sinking speed (inches/second
Neutral[2]	0.5–0.75
Intermediate	1.25–1.75
Slow	1.75–2.50
Medium	2.00–3.00
Fast	3.75–6.00
Very Fast	7.00–9.00
Ultra Fast	>9.00

[1] Authors' classification.

[2] Can be treated to float as and when required.

entering the neck of the pool) the flow may be so fast that it is necessary to use a 'very fast' sinker in order to fish the fly just beneath the surface. By contrast, in the slow-moving belly section it may be necessary to use a slow or intermediate sinker in order to fish just beneath the surface.

Sink-tip lines combine a short front section of 10 to 15 feet of sinking line with a long rear section of roughly 70 feet of floating line, and are widely popular with many anglers who believe that they provide the best of both worlds. Gammon recommends their use for subsurface fly fishing. So does Falkus.

The sink-tip concept is nothing new. Many of our earlier authors who used silk lines – such as Gray and Holiday – recommended leaving the front few yards of line 'ungreased' so that it sank. Nowadays it is possible to obtain lines where the front section is manufactured to sink 'slow', 'fast' or 'extra fast' so that a fly can be fished at a range of different depths – at least in theory.

However, buying a sink tip line is rather a hit-and-miss business, as few, if any, manufacturers describe the sinking rates of their tips in useful terms. This problem resulted in the second author fabricating his own by equipping a standard floating line with a range of detachable sinking tip sections of various lengths and sinking rates. This had many advantages but it could not overcome the problem inherent with all sink tip lines in that the change in density from the heavy forward sinking section to the floating rear section makes them difficult to cast.

We still have our sink tip lines and use them from time to time. While the floating rear section does make it far easier to lift off a long line prior to recasting, this one principal advantage is far outweighed by the problems of variable line densities when casting and the fact that, even with a 15-ft section of 'extra fast' sinking tip, it is impossible to fish a fly deeply with such lines, as the speed of the current combined with the rate at which the line is recovered tend to work the fly towards the surface. Thus we much prefer to use normal sinking lines for all our subsurface and sunk line fishing. There is a wide range of sinking rates available, and by careful choice of the correct sinking rate it is possible to fish the fly at the required depth for much longer than is possible with a sink tip line.

The much-loved (but not lamented) silk lines of yesteryear were invariably green; and so line colour was not the issue that it is today. The first white plastic coated fly lines appeared on the market some 15 years ago to be followed in quick succession by lines of many different colours and hues. The highly-visible line colours were introduced originally to help the stillwater trout fishermen detect the very gentle takes often experienced when nymph fishing in calm water by the movement of the line. The debate about whether they were more visible to the fish than the traditional dark lines has raged intermittently in the angling press ever since. The argument was largely settled by some amazing underwater photography by Brian Clarke and John Goddard as illustrated in their fascinating book *The Trout and the Fly: A New Approach* published in 1980. This deals largely with trout vision and what the trout sees on the surface and above the surface. Among other things they compared the visibility of three differently coloured lines (brown, green and white) when viewed from underwater and discovered the following:–

1. During casting, when the lines were in the air, the white line was *less* visible against the sky above. However, unlike the dark lines, it tended to give off an occasional flash in bright sunlight that was clearly visible below water.
2. With the three lines on the water surface each cut off the light to the same extent *within the window* of vision, but reflected light from the bottom illuminated the underneath of the white line slightly to make it more visible (but not appreciably so).
3. The most startling result was achieved when the three lines were tested on the surface of the water *in the mirror* that surrounds the window. They found that the white line was 'vastly more visible' than either the green or brown lines. 'It lay like a great bright crack in the face of the mirror; and when cast onto the mirror, it fell like a great flash of lightning across the whole field of vision.'

The floating line is widely used for salmon and sea-trout fishing on rivers and lakes. The researches of Clarke and Goddard show quite clearly that light-coloured lines (white, yellow, peach) may be a serious handicap on rivers and stillwaters when fishing the floating line as the flash of light in the face of the mirror may scare many fish. We now prefer to use darker and apparently less obvious lines when fishing a floating line for sea trout although we still use the paler, more visible floating lines when nymph fishing for brown and rainbow trout.

Most sinking lines are manufactured in the darker, more subdued colours. For much of our daylight fishing in rivers we use grey or dark green lines (colour is not, of course, a significant consideration when night fishing) but on peaty lakes we prefer to use brown lines whenever possible.

Before leaving the subject of fly lines we wish to make a few general comments about line selection, casting and line care.

Do not restrict your sea trout fishing to the use of just one or two lines. While more recent authors, such as Currie, suggest that only two lines are really necessary for sea-trout fishing (usually a floater and a sink-tip or slow sinker), Gammon and Falkus recommend the use of three different lines a floater, a sink tip and a 'high density' (fast sinking) line. Although both preferred double taper lines, Gammon opted for lines rated AFTM 6, while Falkus recommended AFTM 7.

We regularly use *five* different lines for our river fishing (all AFTM 8/9 forward tapers). These are a floater (for dry-fly work), a neutral density (for sub-surface work), a slow sink, a medium sink and a fast/very fast sink. For much of our fishing we use the neutral density and medium sink lines, but the inclusion of the other three lines enables us to fish our flies and lures effectively over a far greater range of depths and river conditions than would otherwise be possible. For lake fishing we mainly use just two types of line (Fig. 10), a floater and a neutral density (both AFTM 7 forward taper). Occasionally we will also use a slow or medium sink line to 'get down' to fish in adverse conditions.

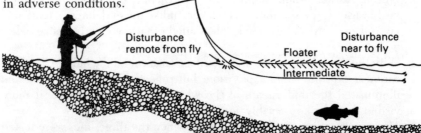

Fig. 10. A neutral density line avoids the problem of line wake (veeing) when working the subsurface fly on a floating line. The only surface disturbance is where the line enters the water.

As far as we are aware, no previous authors have advocated forward taper lines for sea-trout fishing. All were solidly in favour of the traditional double taper. One of the problems experienced by many anglers when casting forward taper lines is the tendency to aerialise too much line when casting. This is a bad fault because extending too much line so that the thinner running line is aerialised prevents a smooth transfer of energy from rod to line and militates against the formation of a proper loop – the essence of good casting. Shock waves forming in the line dissipate the energy of the cast, resulting in a shorter, sloppy, presentation and there is increased wear on the line as a result of casting stress. The quickest way to wear out a forward taper (apart from treading on it) is to extend line as if it was a double taper. Thus when casting a forward taper line it is important to aerialise only the thicker forward section and to 'shoot' the thinner rear section of running line on the delivery. Many British anglers brought up on the traditional double taper have yet to learn that the two different lines require very different casting styles. Over-aerialising line when casting a forward taper is the cause of most of the casting problems experienced with such lines by many anglers and is, perhaps, the explanation why they are still much less popular than double tapers.

It is often difficult to judge the correct length of line outside the rod tip before lifting off to recast a double taper. Not so long ago one American company produced its forward taper lines with a special marker molded into the line exactly 10 feet behind the forward 'head' section. Line was recovered prior to recasting until this specially thickened short section was 'felt' to strike the crook of the finger. When this occurred the angler knew that the correct length of line for achieving the best distance with the least difficulty was extended outside the rod tip. We understand that no manufacturer now produces forward taper lines with this very useful built-in marker. This is a pity, and it is an idea that should be revived.

Virtually all manufacturers have now adopted a standard code for describing the characteristics of their fly lines in terms of taper, weight and density. In order to select the correct line it is necessary to understand the coding system. Thus, a line may be described as WF8S or DT7F. The coding is in fact quite simple.

Table 15: Standard coding description for fly lines

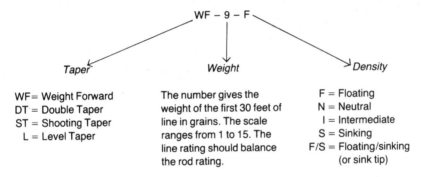

Taper	Weight	Density
WF= Weight Forward DT = Double Taper ST = Shooting Taper L = Level Taper	The number gives the weight of the first 30 feet of line in grains. The scale ranges from 1 to 15. The line rating should balance the rod rating.	F = Floating N = Neutral I = Intermediate S = Sinking F/S = Floating/sinking (or sink tip)

The standard cast is the basic overhead cast. Virtually all boat fishing and the greater part of most bank fishing in lakes and on stillwaters will utilise the overhead cast. However, it is often very useful to be able to employ other less conventional casts to accommodate situations where it is impossible to extend the line behind the angler on the back-cast. There are three main casts that can be employed to overcome the problems of restricted back-casting space such as may occur when fishing with a high or overgrown bank behind the angler. These are the roll-cast, the spey-cast and the steeple-cast. We would advise every angler to obtain some acceptable degree of proficiency in at least one, preferably two, of the alternatives to the overhead cast. To do so will open up opportunities to fish water which is otherwise unfishable. It will also save a great deal on lost time, temper and tackle.

Holiday states that the sea trout angler 'need learn but two casts...the overhead and roll-cast'. While the roll-cast is quite useful at times when boat fishing or when fishing small rivers it is not a good cast for achieving distance with the relatively short rods used in sea-trout fishing. In any event the roll-cast is the basis of the far more useful Spey or switch cast, and we would recommend that efforts should be directed in this direction.

The steeple-cast is in essence an overhead cast where the back cast is directed vertically upwards as opposed to horizontally backwards. It requires some mastery in order to obtain a delicate presentation, but it is useful for extending a long cast with a forward taper line. As we have noted above, the mechanics of roll-casting or switch casting a line of more than about 15 yards in length require the use of a double-taper.

Whether fly fishing, spinning or worming, the ability to cast a line a reasonable distance with accuracy and delicacy is the first requirement. There are many good publications on the theory of casting but reading about it and doing it are two very different things. Practice makes perfect. However, it is very easy for the self-taught angler to develop bad casting habits which, once identified, are difficult to rectify. The best advice that we can give on casting is to consult a professional instructor recognised by the Association of Professional Game Angling Instructors (look for the advertisements in angling journals).

Casting lessons will cost money but, in terms of the typical angler's total expenditure over a year in pursuit of his sport, it is likely to be money very well spent.

We will discuss later the importance of recovering line in order to 'work' the flies when sea-trout fishing. While Stuart and Bridgett suggested 'waggling' the rod tip to impart movement and action to the flies, this is not, as we shall see, the correct way to work a fly. There are basically two methods of recovering line: the 'figure-of-eight' retrieve where the line is collected in the palm of the 'spare' hand by manipulation of the fingers, or the 'strip-and-coil' technique where the line is pulled back with the spare hand and either coiled in loops held by the rod hand or, less desirably, dropped onto the bank, into the water or into the boat. The former technique is suitable for working the fly back slowly, but stripping is essential if the fly is to be worked fast.

A point to note when using the strip-and-coil technique is that the first coil should be larger than the second coil which, in turn, should be larger than the third coil etc. If the earlier coils are smaller than the latter coils the line tends to become tangled when recasting.

Finally on the subject of fly lines here are a few words about line care. Nothing lasts forever, and while the modern fly line is indeed very durable it is no exception. Fly lines are not cheap (we recommend buying the best that you can afford) and we are always mystified by the fact that very few anglers seem to make any effort to prolong the active life of these lines by treating them with proper care. The old silk lines required much care and attention

100

between trips and the discipline of looking after a line became an accepted ritual. While plastic-coated lines can be forgotten about over the season it is good practice to strip them off the reel at the end of the season, wipe them down with mild detergent to remove grit and grime, treat them with 'replasticiser' and hang them in loose coils in a cool dry place. This simple routine can extend their life and action by several seasons. Once the plastic coating begins to crack and peel the line is finished. Do not leave lines in heat or bright sunlight and avoid contact with solvents, oil and petrol. Never over-extend into the running line of a forward taper when false casting. The running line is for shooting and it will not support the weight of the head in false casting. Aerialising the running line in casting is the biggest single cause of failure with weight forward (= forward taper) lines. So don't do it!

By way of a final word on the important subject of fly lines, we must mention the very recent introduction of the 'new generation' of 'Airflo' lines (manufactured by Fly Fishing Technology Ltd). Launched in 1987, these lines replace the PVC coating on all 'plastic' fly lines with a high-energy polymer. Perhaps their most significant features are that the polymer coat will not crack and that they have virtually no stretch or 'memory'. This lack of stretch yields several potential benefits to the angler in that less power is absorbed by the line in casting, the take of a fish is more readily 'felt' and the strike is transmitted with greater speed and power.

Our experience with these new lines has been limited to just a few outings before we 'go to press' and so we must reserve judgement on the various claims by the manufacturers. The claim that 'takes' are transmitted to the angler more positively appears valid (at least with Rainbows) and we are attracted by the prospect of experimenting with line tapers previously denied by other manufacturers to the British angler. So . . . 'watch this space'!

Leaders

The introduction of reliable nylon monofilament lines in the mid-1950s brought about a major revolution in both spinning (Chapter 7) and worm fishing (Chapter 6). It also took much of the hassle out of preparing leaders for fly fishing. ('Leader' is an excellent North American term for the length of fine line used to connect the fly or flies to the thick fly line. It is preferable to the ambiguous term 'cast' used traditionally by British anglers and so we will use it throughout.)

If there is a problem with modern nylon it is that it is manufacturered primarily to meet the requirements of coarse and sea anglers; whose numbers vastly exceed game anglers. In commercial marketing terms the very special requirements of game fishermen represent a small and inconsequential part of the total market. There is a very big difference in the characteristics of nylon required for leaders when compared with that for spinning and worming. The characteristics of a leader (apart from the obvious fact that it should be invisible to fish) are that it should transmit the energy of the cast from the fly line to the fly as smoothly as possible so that the leader is fully extended and the fly presented as delicately as possible. It should, thus, have a good turn-over and a straight lay. The best nylon for leaders is one that has no memory and which is fairly stiff while being as thin (= invisible) as possible. While level (untapered) leaders can be used for the larger and therefore heavier lures since the weight of the lure itself facilitates the extension of the leader, a tapered leader is desirable when fishing small flies and/or when presentation is important. While it is still quite difficult to obtain thin, stiff, memory-free nylon in spool lengths of 25 yards (or more) so that you can tie your own, it is possible to buy good knotless tapered leaders – provided you are prepared to shop around.

One of the advantages claimed for gut was that it absorbed water so that it sank better than nylon. The demand from coarse fishermen for specialist nylon lines suitable for different styles of fishing has provided the game fisherman with incidental benefits. For example, it is now possible to obtain top-quality monofilament that is formulated either to float or to sink. Whenever possible we try to obtain all our nylon lines from stockists who cater for the specialist coarse angler for the simple reason that the range of choice is far better.

Unless fishing with heavy lures on strong leaders, we prefer a tapered leader as the presentation of the fly is always important – even at night. The tapered leader transmits the energy from the cast to the fly far better than a level leader and so improves distance and accuracy while also conferring a more delicate presentation. As we write, yet another technological break-through is launched. This is the 'braided-taper leader'. These have been around for some time in France and America but, for some reason, British anglers seemed unaware of their existence – until now. The basic leader is in fact a braid of ultra-fine nylon filaments with a carefully formulated compound taper that transmits the energy of the cast progressively and smoothly down to the tip. Traditional nylon leaders are much stiffer than the fly line to which they are attached, and are therefore relatively bad transmitters of casting energy. We have used braided-taper leaders (which come in a range of lengths, strengths and tapers and can be treated to float or to sink at various speeds) only briefly. They certainly *do* present a fly beautifully (notably with a side wind) and we must accept much of the advertising 'blurb' associated with the continuing sales drive. Problems are evident in attaching droppers to the braid and we are doubtful if they are quite as 'invisible' to fish as claimed by their manufacturers. (The same claim was (and still is) made for white floating fly lines – but Clarke and Goddard have shown that this can sometimes be far from the truth; see page 97.) We reserve our judgement on the general benefit of braided leaders for the time being in the general context of wet-fly fishing for sea trout.

Nylon monofilament is also available in a range of colours and hues. We are not too concerned about the colour-tint of the nylon used in river fishing but, as any stillwater trout angler knows, the shade or hue of nylon used in lake fishing can be very important. We prefer the brown tinted nylon to the green but, for most purposes, the colourless (clear or transparent) nylon has more general application. Whatever nylon you choose, and almost every angler eventually develops a liking for a particular brand, be sure to pick one that is as non-reflective and 'glint-free' as possible. Clarke and Goddard have shown that the 'flash' of the sun reflected from a fly line is highly visible from underwater in the window-of-vision of the fish. *This applies also to nylon monofilament.* Some brands are very highly polished. We avoid these like the plague and are careful to select a brand of nylon with a dull or matt finish to minimise the risks of leader flash.

The leader can be treated to sink with a variety of proprietary compounds. We make our own from a mixture of Fuller's earth (a very fine clay sold at most chemists), glycerine and washing-up liquid. This is simply mixed to a paste in arbitrary proportions, rolled into balls and carried in a small tin or plastic pot until required. It lasts indefinitely and is cheaper and just as good as the branded product. Far better, however, to use a dull nylon that sinks naturally.

Spinning lines and to a lesser extent nylon lines used in worming are subject to a great deal of wear over a season. Some lines are made specially for spinning that are more resistant to abrasion and, latterly, highly visible, fluorescent, nylon lines have appeared which are gold or clear blue. The greater visibility of the fluorescent nylon in daylight enables the angler to pin-point the position of the bait or lure in the water more readily. This allows better control over the movement of the bait or lure and facilitates bite detection when bait fishing. Since fluorescent materials work only in the presence of ultra-violet light and the water surface effectively screens out the ultra-violet rays in daylight, the line below the water does not fluoresce and is, hence, no more visible than non-fluorescent nylon. We have used both colours. The gold is excellent when spinning on coloured water and the pale blue has advantages when worming on low water when, as sometimes occurs, it is necessary to watch the movement of the line and strike on the 'lift'.

Line care is just as important with nylon as it is with fly lines. Never leave your nylon line in excessive heat or direct sunlight. We make a point of checking carefully all our nylon line before the start of the season (both on our reels or on the spare spools carried for making up leaders) and reject any if we have the slightest doubt about its reliability and strength. Do not save pennies by using line that may have perished. It is cheap enough to replace regularly.

In parallel with advances in the technology of fly lines, recent months have seen what may be a significant breakthrough in the technology of lines for spinning and bait-fishing. In 1988 the giant American Du Pont Company launched its new 'Prime Plus' cofilament line as an alternative to the nylon

monofilament lines that have held sway for about forty years. These combine
the properties of a low stretch polyester core with a shock-absorbing
coplymer outer sheath. Such lines would appear to have many advantages,
especially for low water worming, because reduced stretch implies better
bite detection and better transmission of speed and power on striking. So,
again . . . 'watch this space'.

Shock Leaders

Before leaving the subject of lines, here is a word about shock leaders and
line strengths. A shock leader is a link of intentionally elastic line between
the fly line and the leader. Its purpose is to absorb much of the impact of
really savage takes which might otherwise result in the leader breaking
under the strain – particularly if the strike is over-powerful in relation to the
strength of the leader and the weight of the fish. A 'smash-take' can be a sorry
experience! Fishing for sea trout in daylight requires no less finesse than
when fishing for brown trout. Indeed we would argue that it actually
requires more finesse in terms of using the finest leaders that are sensible for
the size of fish likely to be encountered. The problem is that sea trout invariably come in a larger range of sizes than brown trout and, in relative terms,
than even salmon; and, weight for weight, they fight harder than both!

When fishing the falling flood in daylight, when large fish (5lb weight) are
travelling and just as likely to be encountered as small whitling of 1½–1lb
weight (and when savage takes are often the norm), we occasionally err on
the side of caution if we are fishing small flies (and, as a consequence using
finer leaders) by attaching about 12 inches of 'shock gum' between our leader
and fly line. This is an elastic material similar in appearance to nylon that
stretches up to a certain point and then gradually stops doing so until it will
stretch no further. Its purpose is to absorb any sudden shock-stress on the
leader caused by a leaping, plunging fish. It comes in two sizes (strengths),
one for trout and the other for salmon. The breaking strain of the trout size is
about 7lb weight, more than sufficient for most situations. In theory the
length of shockgum will reduce the effect of the strike, since it 'gives' to the
fish. In practice we have found that we hook just as many fish (and we may
possibly land more by way of compensation).

Hooks

Having dealt with the major items of tackle we now come to the most
important – the hooks. Although the basic design of the fish hook has not
changed over the centuries, there are many different types. Although the
choice of different patterns is perhaps not as great as it was 40 or 50 years
ago, it is still fairly extensive, and some of the old hook shapes such as the

'Limerick', 'Sproat' or the 'Captain Hamilton' bend are still popular today.

Anglers will indulge themselves by investing in expensive rods and reels and all the other paraphernalia of their sport, but far too many baulk at the miniscule extra cost of buying good-quality hooks. A good hook is inevitably expensive because it must be made individually by hand and cannot be churned out by the thousand by a machine. Machines can produce many hooks very quickly and cheaply but in order to do so they must use a 'soft' wire with a low carbon content. They can be hardened and tempered but can never be as strong as a hook made from wire with a high carbon content. Such wire cannot be processed into a hook by machine and so each hook must be hand-made by a craftsman if it is to be really strong.

Apart from the quality of the wire, there are other features that distinguish a good hook from a bad one. A long point requires too much penetration to grip properly, it bends too easily and is inadequate to deal with large fish or a tough surface. A long barb inhibits penetration and weakens the hook. The barb should be set at the best angle to provide easiest penetration while giving the firmest possible hold. The shape of the bend of the hook should be such that there are no stress points while providing an obvious locus where the hold is greatest. This will be the point of maximum strain during the strike/play and it should be forged to increase strength. The gape should be wide enough relative to the shank to assure a good hold while minimising leverage.

Singles, doubles or trebles – which is best? This is a common question and one to which there is no simple answer. To some extent it depends on how you are fishing and to some extent on how the fish are responding. The treble hook is almost universally used for spinning on the basis that it is the best 'hooker'. Why then is it not more widely used in fly fishing? The argument that the hook is rotating may or may not be valid when discussing the apparently reduced hookability of spoons and wobblers (page 158) when the hook turns with the lure. But what about spinners where the hook does not rotate? How many anglers who fish with single hooks on a fly would even contemplate using a single hook on a spinner. (A single hook is unavoidable when bait fishing if the worm is to envelop the hook properly; see page 139.)

Jock Scott preferred doubles when fishing for sea trout (he admits he was unusual in this respect), but most of our other authors fished singles from preference. Some (like Bridgett) indicated that a few 'wee doubles' could usefully be added to the fly box; but the double-hook has never been very popular. The argument that they hold better has not held sway over the counter-argument that they require a harder strike to set the hooks and that the leverage caused when playing a fish of one hook on the other may weaken the hold, so single hooks are the norm, at least when fishing conventionally with standard flies.

One problem with the larger sizes of double and treble hooks is that they assume unattractive proportions in relation to the 'bulk' of the hook. We use them quite happily down to size 8 but a size 6 double is a disproportionate hook for sea trout: and a size 4 treble is even worse! We would however strongly dispute the 'big fish, big hook' school of thought. We have both caught many 8lb plus sea trout on small hooks. Not one of the double-figure sea trout that we have taken over the last few seasons was caught on a hook larger than size 8. The 14lb fish taken by the first author in 1982 was hooked, played and landed on a size 12 outpoint treble (fished on a 2½-inch Marchog). He has also taken four other fish over 10lb on hooks no larger than size 10.

We are convinced that while large flies or lures may often be necessary to catch sea trout, it is *not* mandatory to use large hooks. The current vogue popularised by Falkus for large flies and lures tied single or in tandem on size 4 singles is fine, but remember that a big hook requires a lot of power in the strike and this in turn requires a quick response and a strong leader. As we have stated above, unnecessarily strong leaders are to be avoided under most circumstances.

Finally a word about hook sizes. A size 8 hook is not always a size 8 hook. Different manufacturers use different scales, and while most correspond to the Old Redditch Scale or ORS (at one time Redditch, south of Birmingham, England, was the centre of the world's hook-making industry – alas, no more!) there are minor variations, and some use other scales.

All the hook sizes referred to (in Chapter 3) have been converted where necessary to the ORS as a standard for comparison. Maxwell (our earliest author) refers to the 'Limerick Rational Scale', but there have been several others used over the last century. Great confusion resulted from the introduction of the 'New Scale' in the 1930s. Prior to this most anglers had got used to a system whereby the largest hooks had the smallest numbers (e.g. size 6 was bigger than size 10). The New Scale reversed this and (logically) gave the smaller hooks the smaller numbers. The New Scale was introduced originally for dry-fly hooks but operated alongside the 'Old' scale in respect of other hooks for several years before it was dropped. Ostensibly it would seem simple to introduce an 'International Scale' so that a size 8 in New Zealand or Canada was the same as a size 8 in Sweden or Scotland. But, we are told, that the problem of standardising hook sizes in a simple and easily understood system is 'exceedingly complex' and it is likely to be many years before anything like the AFTM system of rating fly lines can be introduced for the fish hook.

Falkus, in a singularly provocative statement, said 'I believe that a fly hook can be too sharp', and he suggested that the carborundum stone (carried as an item of ancillary equipment) should be used to take some of the sharpness *off* the hook point instead of for improving sharpness. We cannot disagree too strongly!

His view was that the hook should slide across the bony part of the mouth until it comes to softer gristle before it takes hold. If the hook is too sharp it may take a shallow hold in the bone and then give way when the fish is played. He may be right on a few occasions – when a blunt hook may slide off the bone into gristle. But it is the majority of occasions that should concern us most! We believe that there can be no compromise. Hooks should *always* be as sharp as possible. Win some, lose some; that is angling. However, we are convinced that you lose many more fish with a blunt hook.

Weights

Weight is often attached to the line when spinning or worming in order to achieve greater casting distance and so that the lure or bait can be fished on or near to the bottom. It is also used to reduce the speed at which the bait moves downstream with the current when worm fishing.

We discuss the various types of fishing weight used when worming and spinning later (Chapters 6 and 7). The purpose of mentioning the subject here is to note that the weights used in fishing contain a high proportion of lead and that it is very likely, by the time we go to press, that the UK Government will have introduced legislation requiring anglers in England and Wales to use 'lead-free' alternatives for all weights between the commonly used sizes of 0.6 grams and 1oz. This is because it has been estimated that about 3,000 swans die each year from lead poisoning, as a result of ingesting discarded or lost fishing weights. This issue has generated much debate, but most responsible bodies now accept the scientific proof that anglers are indeed to blame for the agonising death of some swans and that, while the problem is more prevalent in coarse fishing areas, no practical exemption from the prohibition can be made for game fishermen.

Swivels

Despite all the cautions and admonitions of preceding authors, we do not proposed to mention swivels as used in spinning and worming other than to say that the modern swivel is both very efficient and very reliable. We have rarely had a swivel let us down either by jamming or by pulling apart. Gone are the days when the problem of line-twist caused by the uni-directional spin of the lure necessitated periodically alternating between clockwise and anti-clockwise spinners in order to untwist the line or when it was necessary to attach celluloid or plastic anti-kink vanes to the line above the spinner to resist twisting.

The swivel is an essential item of tackle when spinning; any angler who tries to spin without one will soon discover just how important it is to have one to counteract the problem of line-twist. We often use a swivel when worming, not to remove line twist because the bait does not spin, but to act as a stopper for the weight and to form a break-point should the bait become snagged. There are, however, other ways of forming a 'stopper' to keep the weight at the required distance above the hook (such as split shot, stopper knots or plastic ledger stops) but the swivel is a convenient means of creating a step-down from a stronger mainline to a weaker trace so that if a break occurs when worming (or spinning) it takes place *below* the swivel and so results in the minimum loss of nylon line.

We should add here a word of caution about using split shot as ledger-stops with fine nylon lines. In order to keep the heavy ledger weight at the required distance above the bait it is usually necessary to pinch the shot tightly onto the line. In so doing there is a serious risk of damaging the line so that it breaks at well below its test strength. Thus when using finer nylon lines for low water worm fishing it is advisable to use either a plastic ledger-stop, a swivel or, otherwise, to mount the weight(s) on a separate rig.

5 · KNOTS AND WRINKLES

'And always tie good knots.' We forget who said these immortal words, but they represent the best advice given to any angler. There are scores of different knots that may be used by the angler. There are special knots for tying the line to the reel, the leader to the fly line, the fly to the leader, for making droppers, for making sure that the lure fishes in line with the leader – and for ensuring that it doesn't! There are special knots used in spinning, and even splices, devices and glues to use instead of knots. We find that in practice we use very few different means of attaching A to B, and suggest that the two main criteria for any knot are that it should be as strong as possible and as simple as possible: and if it can be tied in the dark so much the better. Whole books have been written on the subject of the infinite variety of knots, joints and splices used in angling for attaching A to B. Here is a selection of those that we have found dependable for a specific purpose, starting at the reel and working out towards the hook.

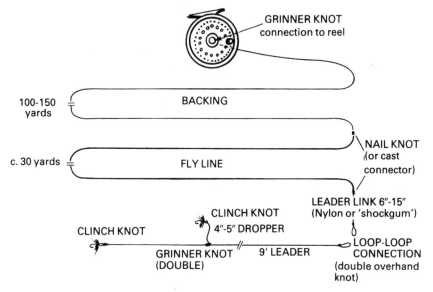

Fig. 11. 'Ready for Action'
The fully mounted fly line with a typical selection of knots and connections.

109

Attaching the fly line backing or nylon mainline to the Reel Spool

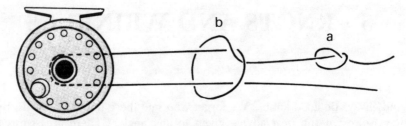

Fig 12. The Reel Knot
This is a simple but secure means of joining thick backing or strong nylon to the spool of the reel. Pass free end round the spindle or arbour of the spool and tie an overhand knot at tip (a). Pass knotted free end around mainline and tie second overhand knot (b). Pull firmly to slip loop (b) tight onto spool. Trim free end close *before* tightening.

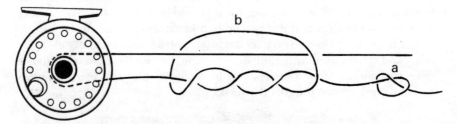

Fig. 13. The Mono Reel Knot
This is better for finer lines which are inclined to slip. It is important to have confidence in the reel knot. This is essentially a development of the standard Reel Knot (above) except that the knotted free end is passed through loop (a) four times instead of just once.

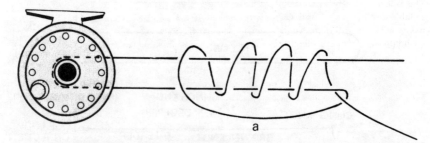

Fig. 14. The Grinner Knot (or Duncan Loop Knot)
We always use this very secure knot whenever we can. It is more simple than it looks. Lay free end parallel to mainline and then fold back to form loop (a). Pass free end over the two main strands to form four loops and pull knot tight. Trim free end and pull firmly on mainline to slip knot down tightly onto the spool. *Learn this knot.* It has many applications.

Attaching backing line to Fly Line

The junction between the fly line and the backing line should be small enough to pass through the rod rings without jamming and as smooth as possible so as not to cause false striking as it 'hits' the top ring when using a shooting head. Nylon and Dacron backing lines require different knots to the junction used for braided nylon backing. The feathered and whipped splice was popular for silk lines but this was very fiddly and has now been superseded by much simpler and more reliable alternatives.

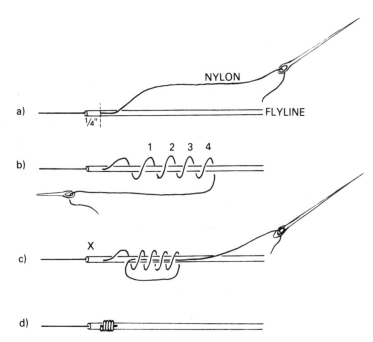

Fig. 15. *The Needle Knot*
This is a reliable knot, also useful for joining the leader or leader-link to the fly line. It is not suitable for thin fly lines or thick backing (in which event use the Nail Knot). Thread free end of nylon or backing through eye of a suitable needle. Insert needle into free end of fly line and push into core to emerge about ¼ inch from end (a). Wrap backing around fly line to form four loose coils (b). Loop back (c) and pass needle along line *beneath* coils. Grasp fly line firmly close to free end at x and pull firmly and steadily on free end of backing to ease coils neatly down onto line near to tip. Trim close (d). The backing joint can be whip-finished and coated to provide a very smooth junction. In practical terms this is not necessary if the joint is well made.

Fig. 16. *The Nail Knot*
This is our standard knot under this heading. Simpler than the Needle Knot and suitable for all lines (other than braided nylon). Lay 'Nail' or something similar (a matchstick even) along fly line and backing (or leader-link) as shown (a). Form four coils (b). Pull gently on free end to ease coils neatly down onto nail. Grasp tip of fly line and main length of backing firmly near tip. Remove nail and pass free end of backing under coils using gap created by removal of nail (c). Pull firmly on free end to bed coils tightly and neatly into position near to tip of fly line. Trim free ends to form neat junction (d).

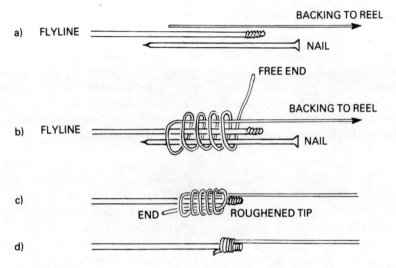

As an added safety measure to ensure that the backing line (or link) bites down into fly line without risk of slipping, it is worth roughening the plastic coating with a pair of fine scissors. The resulting knot is equally as neat as the Needle Knot except that the backing does not emerge from the centre of the fly line. Provided the two free ends are trimmed close this is no practical disadvantage.

Fig. 17. The Cast Connector

This is simple, effective and very neat, but slightly bulky. Always check that the connector will pass through the rod ring freely before using (it should do so). Connectors are made in two sizes. The larger (salmon) size is suitable for joining thicker lines. The smaller (trout) size is suitable for joining finer lines. The standard connector has two holes of different sizes. Ensure that the larger hole is used for the thicker of the two lines. This cannot be used with thick braided backing line.

Push fly line through one end of connector and tie a simple overhand or figure of eight knot as appropriate. (The latter is more bulky.) Pull tight and trim close. Push free end of backing (or leader link) through other end of connector and tie bulkier figure of eight or clinch knot. Pull tight and trim close (a).

Pull both knots firmly into connector and exert strong pressure to ensure that neither slips out. If this occurs re-thread using a bulkier knot (b).

We use cast connectors mainly for joining backing line to fly lines or for attaching a leader link of shock gum to the other end of a fly line. They can be used for attaching leaders directly to the fly line but a change of leader requires cutting and retying the stop knot (which is unduly complicated in the dark).

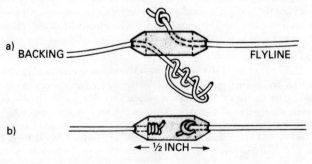

Backing Attachment

Braided monofilament backing is too bulky for joining to fly lines by conventional means. (We use braided monofilament occasionally for shooting-head lines as it is less coil-prone than most monofilament backing lines.) Modern adhesives are marvellous. Braided mono can be glued to the fly line to provide a strong connection suitable for most purposes. Until recently the glued knot was usually whip-finished and coated with 'Vycote' to provide a neat, smooth joint. A 'cast sleeve' can now be used where the diameter of the backing braid is suitable.

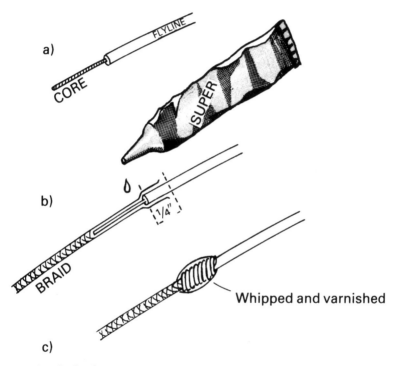

Fig. 18. The Glued Splice
Carefully strip the plastic dressing from about 1 inch of fly line to escape the braided level core (a). Tease open the free end of the hollow braided backing and manipulate core of fly line down into backing until it overlaps fly line by at least ⅛ inch (b). Apply one drop of 'super glue' to the overlap and allow it to penetrate the joint thoroughly. AVOID DIRECT FINGER CONTACT. (The alternative is an embarrassing trip to hospital and a painful excision of finger and line.) Using rubber gloves or a strip of polythene, apply pressure to the joint by rolling it between thumb and forefinger. Neatly whip over joint after trimming ends of braid close to provide a smooth joint by coating with 'Vycote' (c).

Fig. 19. The Sleeve Joint
This dispenses with the glue and whipping to form a very neat joint. It is best suited for braided taper leaders but can be used for fly line provided the fly line and lever braid fit tightly. Our experience of this link – which is a new concept – is so far limited to reservoir trout fishing. It is fine for fish up to 3lb. We have yet to test it on a 20lb fish; but our confidence is growing.

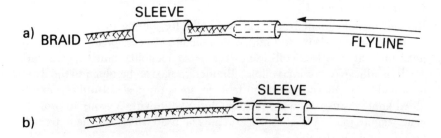

Cut off a ½-inch piece of plastic sleeve and thread it onto braid. (Heat end of braid to form a congealed point and then trim off after threading if braid is difficult to insert) Insert about 1 inch of the fly line into the braid (a). Slide the sleeve up and over the end of the joint (b).

The sleeve can be pushed back down the braid to allow a quick change of fly line – nice in theory, but unlikely to be required in practice.

Attaching Leader or Leader-link to fly line

This is where a neat connection is important. A bulky or poorly-formed knot or join is to be avoided. The means of connection should pass through the rod rings without jamming or causing a 'bump' (which results in false-striking) and it should not cause a 'wake' when fishing a fly on or just beneath the surface. Some anglers, who do not know better, attach the line to the leader with a figure-of-eight knot (Fig. 22). Others, who know better, use a leader-link consisting of about 6–15 inches of either stiff (20lb strength) nylon or 'shock gum'. The advantage of a leader-link is that it permits the 'Loop-to-Loop' connection to be made. This is still the quickest method of changing a leader yet devised. It is slightly more bulky than other forms of joining leader to fly line but is widely applicable to most situations.

The leader-link is attached to the fly line with a nail knot (Fig. 16) or a cast connector (Fig. 17). A leader loop knot is then tied at the free end.

Fig. 20. The Leader Loop Knot
Fold 3–4 inches of line back on itself (a) to form a tight loop x. Wrap end of loop back twice around double strand of nylon (b). Pass first loop back through newly-formed second loop (c) and pull through easing knot up or back to form loop of the required size. Trim free end. The correctly formed loop knot (d) should *not* slip back along the nylon.

It is far easier to wrap the double line back inside loop x in the form of an overhand loop made with a double wrap (e and f) instead of the standard textbook method shown opposite.

a)

END

b) END

X

c)

d)

e)

f)

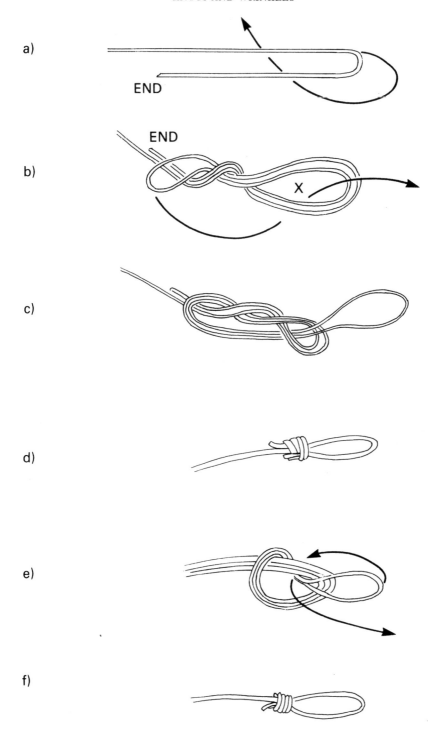

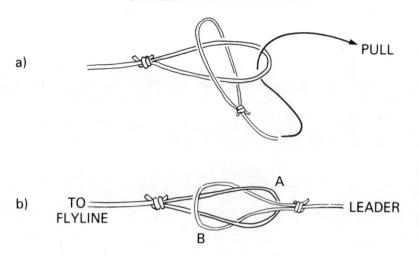

Fig. 21. *The Loop-to-Loop Knot*
Slip the loop of the leader over the loop of the link a). Pass free end of the leader up through the loop of the link b) and pull loops tight. The completed connection b) is readily undone by pushing the two loops together. Always ensure that the link loop is large enough to allow the size of fly or lure being used to pass through it otherwise it will have to be removed and the practical advantage of the connection will be lost by having to retie the fly.

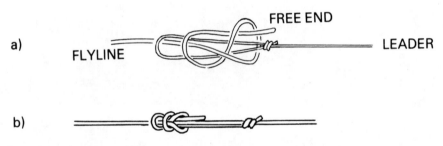

Fig. 22. *The Figure-of-Eight Knot*
We use this occasionally when, for some reason, we are without a leader link. It is simple and quick, but untidy. The fly line is passed through the loop and then turned back and over the loop to form a classic figure-of-eight. The free end is tucked under the first coil and the knot pulled tight a). The free end of the fly line lies along the leader so that it does not snag weeds b).

For Attaching Fly to Leader or Swivel, Hook or Spinner to Main Line

Many anglers still persist in using knots originally developed for the particular characteristics of gut. Fortunately, nylon has now replaced gut and new and better knots have been devised which are far more suitable. Some traditional knots are still very useful, such as the tucked half-blood knot. How-

116

ever, the Grinner, as recommended by the late (great) Richard Walker, is becoming increasingly popular and is now our favourite knot for most purposes.

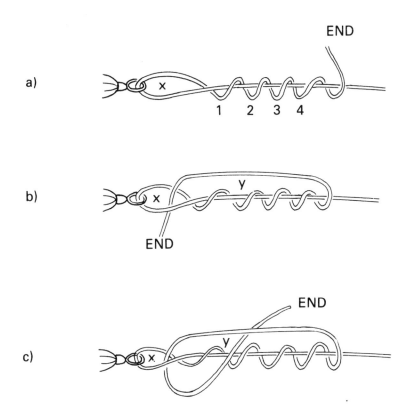

Fig. 23. The Tucked Half-Blood Knot (or Clinch Knot)
Pass free end of nylon through the eye of the hook, spinner or swivel. (If using very fine nylon the line can be looped through the eye a second time for greater security.) Wrap free end over line to form four coils a).

Pass free end through loop formed at eye x and then 'tuck' it back through loop formed after making the coils y). Pull firmly on free end to ease coils down on to the line so that they slip back tight against the eye c).

This is a very reliable knot. When using strong lines (6lb or more) the 'tuck' c) can be omitted to form a conventional half-blood knot. This has the advantage that it can be undone quickly by pinching the coils between the thumb and index finger and slipping them back up the line (see also Grinner Knot). The tuck makes this impossible.

Fig. 24. The Grinner Knot (or Duncan Loop Knot or Uni-Knot)
This is our basic knot. Reputed to be 15 per cent stronger than the half-blood knot although it is somewhat more complicated. Learn this knot; you will not regret it. Pass free end of nylon through eye and lay back along main line. Fold free end back to form loop x a). Wrap free end around doubled length of line inside loop x four times and pass end out through loop b). Pull firmly to ease coils down onto line and slide knot back to eye. Trim free end close c).

Strong leaders are often necessary when fishing for sea trout at night with small flies. A small

117

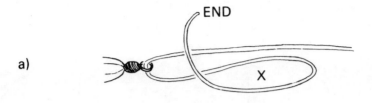

a)

b)

c)

END

Knot eased back to form a loop

d)

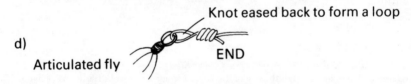

Articulated fly

END

fly fished on a strong leader lacks 'action'. Several knots have been devised to overcome this problem and allow the fly to articulate on a strong leader. We achieve this with the Grinner Knot by easing the coils back up the line after tightening to form a small loop behind the knot. It will tighten up when a fish takes but can be easily slipped open again afterwards d).

Hook manufacturers still persist in making hooks with an up-eye or a down-eye. Up-eye hooks are traditional for dry-fly fishing while down-eye hooks are traditional for wet-fly fishing. A straight eye is preferable for all forms of wet-fly fishing as it allows the fly to fish in line with the leader using modern knots. For dry-fly fishing the up-eye may have an advantage in throwing the leader up off the surface so that the fly fishes without the leader causing disturbance close to the fly. For dry-fly fishing we recommend the traditional Turle Knot (devised by R.B. Marston) or the Wood Knot (devised by A.H.E. Wood).

118

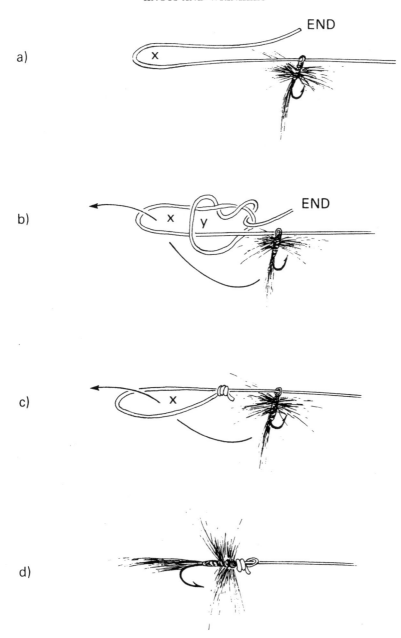

Fig. 25. The Turle Knot

Pass the free end of the leader up through the eye and slip the (dry) fly up the leader out of the way. Fold the line back to create loop x (a). Wrap free end over doubled line to form loop y and form two turns before passing free end out of loop y (b). Pull free end gently to bed down knot but leave loop x open c). Slide fly back down line and pass up through loop x. Pull tight and trim free end d).

119

a)

Leader point

b)

c)

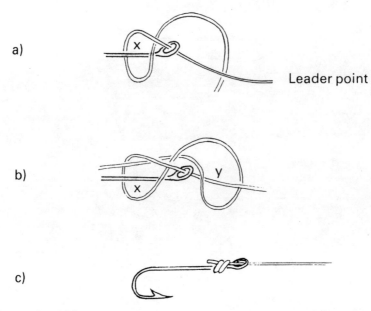

Fig. 26. The Wood Knot
Pass free end up through hook eye and wrap over the shank to form loop x (a). Pass free end back over line to form loop y and feed back into and out of loop x (b). Ease loop y back over eye of hook and pull free end to bed the two coils down neatly behind eye. Trim free end (c).

This is basically a figure-of-eight knot with a difference. It is simpler and neater than the Turle Knot since the free end lies back along the hook shank. However, the Turle Knot is simpler to use with very small flies.

Making Droppers in Leaders

In order to make your own leaders with one or two droppers you will need to know three basic knots.

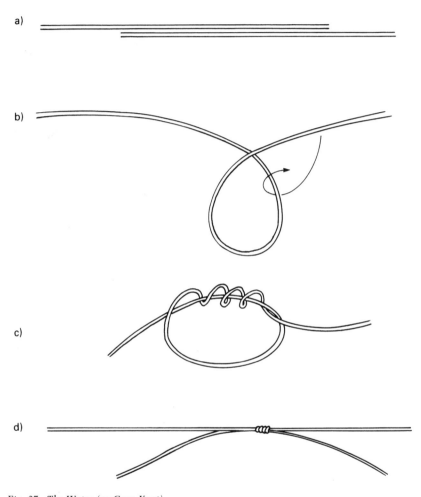

Fig. 27. The Water (or Cove Knot)

This is a very old knot originally recommended for joining two lengths of horse hair. It is best suited for joining short lengths of line and is a quick knot for making tapered leaders.

Lay two lengths of nylon together so that they overlap by about 6 inches when merely joining the strands, or by about 12 inches when making a dropper a). Turn the paired line back to form a loop b). Wrap the free ends of the paired line around the doubled loop of line to form three or four coils c). Lubricate and draw together tightly. The finished knot d) will have two free ends emerging from either end of the knot. One of these will form the dropper. Most anglers select the dropper that protrudes towards the rod (up the line) as this sticks out better. Other anglers choose the dropper that protrudes downwards (towards the point of the leader) on the basis that it is stronger as it is formed from the mainline rather than the knotted link. Never use less than four turns for fine nylon.

a)

FREE END A

B

FREE END B

END A

b)

A

END B

B

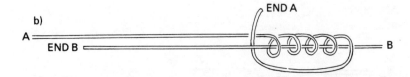

END A

c)

A

B

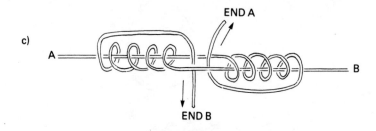

END B

Trim free end A close

d)

A

B

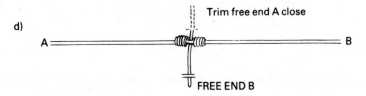

FREE END B

Fig. 28. The Blood Knot

This is another old knot with impeccable credentials. It is very reliable, but fiddly and requires practice.

Lay the two lengths of nylon in parallel so that they overlap by about 8 inches a). Wrap free end of line A over line B to form four close coils, and then fold back to form a loop and pass free end *up* between lines A and B. Pull free end gently to ease coils back so that they can be pinched together between thumb and finger. Do not pull too tight b).

Now repeat on other side by forming four coils by wrapping B over A in the opposite direction to those formed previously, so that free end B is passed *down* between lines A and B. *This is very important* c).

Now comes the difficult bit as you really need two pairs of hands to tie this knot. Using the mouth, a colleague, or ingenuity, draw the knot tightly by pulling firmly on all four ends with equal and simultaneous pressure (!). Moisten to prevent slipping before pulling tight. The two free ends should stick out on opposite sides from the centre of the knot. Choose one as the dropper and trim other end close to the knot d).

122

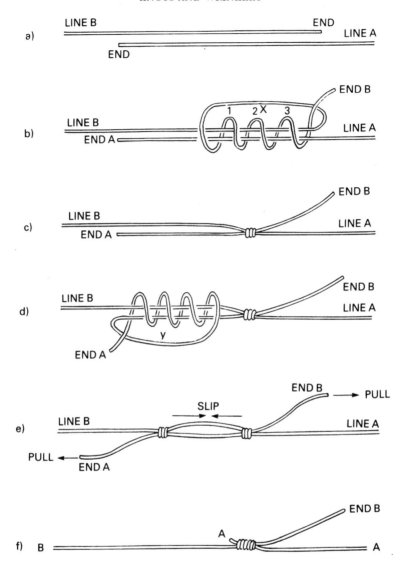

Fig. 29. The Double Grinner Knot

Reported to be some 15 per cent stronger than the blood knot, the double grinner knot is much favoured by those who have bothered to learn it. It looks complicated, but with a little practice is much simpler to tie than the blood knot (since it requires only one pair of hands). We now use nothing else for making droppers.

As with the blood knot, overlap the free ends of lines A and B by about 10 inches a). Bring free end B back to centre for form loop x, and then wrap end B around lines A and B to form 3 coils and pass free end B out through loop x (b) and then pull tight (c). Repeat with free end A to form loop y etc (d) and pull tight (e). Pull on free ends A and B to slide the two parts of the knot together e).

As with the Water Knot, the two droppers emerge at either end of the knot f). The downward-pointing dropper is the more secure. We have the utmost faith in this dropper knot.

PART II
River Angling

6 · WORM FISHING

Wales, with its numerous sea-trout rivers and preponderance of club fishing, is arguably the 'Headquarters' of worm fishing in the British Isles. The official catch records for the Principality show that roughly 40 per cent of all rod-caught sea trout declared each year are taken on the worm (the proportion for salmon is about 45 per cent).

The demand for salmon and sea trout fishing today is such that almost every yard of fishable water is utilised. Many sections of water on the 'minor rivers' and on the tributary streams are unfishable with the fly and spinner. They are often no more than a few yards wide, strewn with rocks, set within steep banks and heavily overgrown with bankside vegetation. Frequently, they are only fishable for a few weeks at the end of the season because of the lateness of the runs of fish: and then only during, or just after, a flood. Without the worm, many important fisheries would cease to exist and many anglers would be denied the few opportunities to catch salmon and sea trout that they now enjoy.

In our view, worm fishing is a perfectly legitimate and acceptable method of taking sea trout and salmon. It is, moreover, a skilful and challenging method of so doing which should be incorporated into the repertoire of the complete sea-trout angler. It is not, as variously stated by its critics 'dirty' and 'cruel'. Neither is it 'murderous' or more 'deadly' than spinning or fly fishing. True, large catches of fish are taken on the worm under ideal conditions. But the same applies to both fly fishing and spinning at times. More sea trout are taken each year on the fly than by any other method. Nothing, in our view, is more 'murderous' and 'deadly' than fly fishing at night when the river is in perfect order, the weather right and the pools well stocked with fresh fish. Many anglers have taken spectacular catches of sea trout on the fly at night and yet no-one has advocated banning night fishing on the grounds of conservation – yet! The one thing that worm fishing is not is 'unskilled'. Try it and see! Fishing the *running worm* effectively on dead low water is, perhaps, more skilful than any other form of angling.

There is, however, one facet of worm fishing that is cause for concern. This relates to the behaviour of the worm fishermen rather than to anything else.

There is nothing more depressing than to arrive at the waterside to find worm fishermen staked out on each pool (usually at the head) and hunched

The disreputable face of low-water worm fishing. The once notorious Llanelltyd Pool on the lower Mawddach (Mid-Wales) at the tidal confluence. A relatively 'quiet' day in August. This is static ledgering at its worst! It is both anti-social and unproductive. Had it been raining the green umbrellas would have sprouted alongside each of the six chair-bound anglers. (Photo G.S. Harris.)

in a characteristic posture over a rod firmly set in a rod rest and the line leading to a static worm anchored to the bottom with a lump of lead in the vicinity of where it is hoped the fish will be. The worm and the angler in perpetual immotion! Sadly, this problem – and it is a real problem – is becoming increasingly prevalent on many club waters. Quite apart from the fact that a static worm attached to a grounded rod probably represents the most ineffective form of sea-trout angling yet devised, the technique, if it can be so described, is selfish in that it denies other, more peripatetic anglers, access to the pool.

Several clubs in Wales have attempted to deal with the problem of static ledgering within their 'Rules and Regulations' in various ways. Some have stipulated that the running worm only may be used. Others require that the rod should be held at all times while worm fishing, while some clubs have banned worming on clear water altogether or allocated certain sections of water to worming. On other waters a time limit is specified for the occupancy of a pool if another angler expresses the wish to fish through the water. This is encouraging. Those clubs and proprietors who have responded thus are to be congratulated. It is to be hoped that others will do likewise!

Few authors have much to say in favour of worm fishing for sea trout. The literature, such as is readily available, falls into three general categories: 1) those against it; 2) those mentioning it, more for completeness rather than any real desire or ability to instruct; and 3) those in favour.

The three 'Bs' (Bridgett, Bluett and Balfour-Kinnear), who are otherwise recommended as worthwhile reading, make no mention of worm fishing and were presumably against it: either from preference or prejudice. Dawson gives the subject nine lines, while Henzell has slightly more to say, describing it as 'profitable, but not fishing' and then 'murder, and unskilled murder at that'. Clapham, who deals with sea-trout fishing in tidal waters, covers the entire topic in one half page concluding that 'it is a tedious business'. Gammon employs about the same number of lines to say that 'there is a case to be argued for the time-hallowed practice of fishing the worm in low, clear water', but gives no instruction, adding only that worm fishing as commonly practised (i.e. ledgering) is the 'least sporting', 'most boring' method, 'with very many, much better ways to catch the most noble fish we have in Britain'. Cass is more generous. He states that it is not his duty to moralise but to advise. This he does in some 21 lines to conclude with the admonition to those who feel tempted to put the method into operation – 'Don't'.

The second category of authors is more liberal towards worming. Jock Scott opens encouragingly to opine that 'Where migratory fish are concerned, the use of the worm is legitimate', but he then dispenses with the subject in no more than 1½ pages of very basic guidance. Holiday in one of the few and therefore precious texts about Welsh sea-trout angling, raises our expectations by offering the view that worming is 'an ancient art calling for persistence and shrewd knowledge of fish lies in high water'. He then promptly abandons the subject.

Various other authors, who have included sections on sea trout in general books on game fishing may make reference to worm fishing, but it is left to our third group of authors before there is any notable enthusiasm for the subject. Mackie was one of the very few early authors who preferred worm fishing to fly fishing:

> Let other anglers laud the fly
> Be it wet, or be it dry;
> I sing a lure of meaner guise,
> A bait that every rod should prize –
> The humble worm.

Although he wrote principally about brown trout and his views on suitable tackle have now been overtaken by many modern advances, he refers to sea trout intermittently and his comments are instructive and relevant. He stresses the importance of concealment, a delicate touch, nice discernment and a quick decision in casting and striking and notes that sea trout are generally more dainty and delicate in their manoeuvres with the worm than brown trout or parr. He stated a clear preference for blue-nose lob worms, adding that 'dew' worms were too large and soft and that brandlings were 'eschewed' by trout. As for weather conditions he favoured low water, a bright sky and a steady barometer.

Mackie was imbued with an uncommon pragmatism for his era. He evidently fished predominantly on small burns and brooks in Scotland and had no time for the duplicity of some critics of the method.

'The thing's amiss' some critics sneer;
'Tis dirty work' and 'Fortune sheer'
Yet empty baskets change their tune,
And they discard, in leafy June,
The fly, for worm.

Somewhat surprisingly for an advocate of dry-fly fishing for sea trout, Mottram also wrote in favour of worm fishing, that is low-water worming rather than spate worming – which he described as simple and deadly, requiring little knowledge and practice for success. By contrast he states that low-water worming requires much skill and long experience for proficiency and, for him, was much more difficult than fly fishing.

He stressed the importance of long casting (20 to 30 yards) and to keep the worm trickling along the bottom by carefully adjusting the weight of lead attached to the depth and strength of the water. He recommended casting downstream and across, with the cast being made above and beyond where the fish lie, employing every skill to ensure that the worm does not pass over and across the fish before it has reached the bottom. He suggested that the angler should move downstream some two yards if the cast elicits no response, and stresses that the size of worm, which he fished on a single hook, size 8, was important. The clearer and lower the river, the smaller the worm. His preference, unlike Mackie's, was for brandlings.

Mottram rejected the 'new' Illingworth reels for worm fishing because they required fine lines which did not offer sufficient resistance to the water to 'sweep' the bait round with the current. (Stirling, however, stressed that any drag should be avoided.) In order to overcome the problem of having enough weight to cast long distances while making sure that the worm did not remain anchored to the bottom when current was lacking or in wind, Mottram suggested embedding a lead bullet in enough cork to make it less heavy in water.

The modern clear plastic 'bubble-floats' which can be filled with water to the required weight would have the same benefits. They are, however, horribly cumbersome things for low-water fishing.

Stirling is one of the few authors whose discussion of worm fishing inspires confidence in the reader. This is simply because he clearly fished the worm himself and had given thought to developing his own style on the basis of experience.

He was one of the first to describe where and how to fish in relation to different river levels. In coloured water with no rise in height, he recommends fishing the deep holes since the fish stay put; whereas on flows above normal level when the fish are travelling he would fish the worm in the shallower, faster water (after trying the fly first). On a flood he would fish near the side where the current bounced off the bank 'creating an eddy inside the main flow' by casting into the current and leading the worm gently into the eddy. He firmly believed that 'travelling' sea trout 'hug' the river bank.

In low water he believed that the best place to fish was in the neck of a pool or the rough white water at its head, with the tail of the pool being productive if the fish were travelling after a flood. He advocated longer rather than shorter rods and, again, emphasised the importance of the weight of lead used. For sea trout he believed that the worm should travel deeper and slower than for brown trout or salmon. He preferred to distribute his weights along the leader as he felt that a single, larger lead caused the worm to double back on the line. In streamy water he used two split-shot and in pools six split-shot in order to get nearer the bottom. He also noted that several small shot were less likely to snag the bottom than a single, larger, lead.

As for the direction of the cast, his usual practice was to fish the runs from the bottom to the top, casting upstream, while the pools were fished downstream from top to bottom. However, he felt it was not too important a matter in most situations. What he did stress as being important was that the worm should travel with the current *as if it were not attached to the line*. He firmly stated that any drag across the current was hostile to success. For this reason he preferred to fish down (or up) on the near bank, crossing over to fish the other side when appropriate. Sea trout, he observed, were at all times shy takers of worm. He always fished with a yard or so of loose line in his hand which, unless he felt a sharp tug, he released as the fish moved off with the worm in its lips in order to give time for the bait to be swallowed (!) In Stirling's view, worm fishing for sea trout required an intimate knowledge of the river and the different holding properties of the various pools.

According to Brennand, the use of the upstream worm for sea trout in dead, low water 'is one of the most pleasant and most interesting methods of all the various ways of defeating these eccentric fish', and like Mackie, he believed that the lower the water, the brighter the sun, then the better the conditions.

Brennand, who occasionally fished the Conwy, brings us into the modern era of tackle technology by his use of the thread-line reel. This he fished with 2lb monofilament line on a dry-fly rod with a 'medium' open bend hook and, contrary to most earlier authors, a 'really large and hearty' lobworm. His recommended technique was to locate a shoal of fish and go below to cast upstream and across to the head of the shoal 'exactly as when dry fly fishing on a chalk stream'. In that he suggested a cast of about 20 yards distance. Brennand, who used no weight, must have been a master-class caster! Possibly this explains his somewhat unusual recommendation for a 'really large' (= heavy) lobworm.

Brennand observed that most sea trout picked up the worm, dropped it, then circled before returning to take it firmly. If he could not see the actual take he struck lightly (he was using 2lb line, remember). He stresses a stealthy approach, concealment, and the importance of playing fish below the shoal to avoid disturbance.

Falkus, our most recent author on the subject of worming, describes ledgering in pools as a 'pernicious evil' but enthuses over the use of the upstream worm. This, in his view, transcends all other methods for sheer skill and enjoyment and demands concentration and practice.

His favourite water for upstream worming was fast, rocky and shallow with 'exciting runs where salmon and sea trout choose to lie in low water'. He advocates a fly rod of about 10 feet in length with a fixed-spool reel and some 200 yards of 16–20lb nylon main line with a leader of 6–10lb nylon attached to a swivel. He preferred a 'Stewart' hook mount with a single worm for rough water but used a single hook with two worms in quieter water. He liked to use redworms or brandlings in low water, a blue-headed lob in medium water and a larger lobworm in heavy water.

The basic technique described by Falkus was the conventional method of working the run upriver casting upstream-and-across and recovering line with the free hand until the worm is opposite the angler; then slowly feeding it out again as the worm passes downstream with the current. Little or no weight was to be recommended. He stresses the need to concentrate on the passage of the worm and to avoid slack line and drag with, at all times, the worm proceeding in front of the line.

It is interesting to note that Falkus employs heavy (thick) monofilament lines for worm fishing on low water. Several earlier authors observed that the finer lines required by the, then, 'new' threadline reels did not present enough resistance to the current to overcome the drag of the casting weight on the bottom: with the result that their bait did not fish downstream effectively. To combat this deficiency they chose to use either fly lines or braided nylon lines, which were thicker, with a finer leader to the hook.

The tactics and techniques to be employed when worm fishing will depend on many considerations such as the length and width of the river available, whether it is overgrown or open, rocky or gravelly, fast or slow flowing, its distance from the sea, the presence of pools and the wind and weather. However, the two most important factors are whether the river level is above or below normal and its variation in levels in the preceeding period.

You can, of course, fish the worm *everywhere* and *everywhen* (subject to statute, bye-laws and local regulations) if you so wish, but it is well worth remembering that other methods may be more productive and challenging under certain conditions. Use the worm by all means, but don't overuse or abuse it.

If it has not become obvious before now, we will declare our preference for fly fishing at most times whenever conditions are right. The one time we would not advocate worm fishing on waters where it is possible to fish the fly is when the river is still flowing high but clear after a flood. Fish the worm if you must under such conditions. You will certainly catch fish. You will also forgo some of the most superlative, exciting and productive daytime fly fishing possible.

For us, worm fishing is reserved for special occasions of (in a word) adversity. The worm is most useful when the river is in flood and when it is affected by drought. At these two extremes of water level it may well be the only method of catching fish. On intermediate flows other methods can be employed and should be considered.

When the summer sun has baked the earth for weeks and the lowly, moisture-loving, earthworm has retreated to the bottom of its 6-feet deep burrows in the garden, it comes as no comfort whatsoever to learn that one acre of pastureland can contain up to 3 million (yes, 3,000,000!) worms or that there are 27 different species of earthworm in the British Isles. When you are desperate 20 will do; no matter the species!

Really dedicated wormers (and there are many in Wales) set great store by the size, colour and 'pattern' of their worms. In this they are really no different from fly fishermen or spinners. A different 'lure' is used for different circumstances. The worm fishermen will generally be concerned with just four of the 27 species of earthworm. (When circumstances are desperate and the wormer is wormless, the blue-grey 'stoneworm' [*Octoclassium cyaneum*] found under stones, or the short squat 'paleworm' [*Dendrobaena subrubicunda*] found in leafmould and under old logs are equally acceptable. A worm is a worm, when you are without.) Fortunately, these four are the most common species encountered. They are:

1. *Allolobophora longa*, the 'blue-head';
2. *Lumbricus terrestris*, the 'lawn' or 'lob' worm;
3. *Lumbricus rubellus*, the 'redworm';
4. *Eisenia foetida*, the 'brandling' or 'dungworm'.

A tough worm is better than a soft one. A big worm is best on heavy, coloured, water. A small worm is best on low water. A lively worm is, in our view, better than a limp, lifeless one.

(Falkus, in his monumental work *Salmon Fishing*, advances the theory that a moribund worm may be better than a live one at times (page 385). With respect to sea trout (and to Hugh Falkus), we disagree. A properly fished worm 'moves', irrespective or whether it is dead or alive. A prawn or shrimp is (very) moribund when mounted on the hook but it is 'moving' when it is being fished. Salmon and sea trout by the nature of their feeding strategies are predators, not scavengers.)

The best all-purpose worm is the 'blue-head'. For some reason these are tougher than lawnworms. Lawnworms are larger than the other species. The 'brandling' (*E. foetida*) with its obvious red and cream striations is loved by some and hated by others (and does smell pretty 'foetid' when you come to eat your sandwiches!). Its pungent aroma does not seem to worry the fish.

This species, along with the 'redworm' (*L. rubellus*) comes in much smaller sizes and is very suitable for low-water fishing.

It is a wise angler who makes provision to guarantee a supply of worms over the season by laying down a stock in advance. This can be done in 4 ways: 1) by maintaining a good compost heap in a shaded part of the garden (for redworms and brandlings); 2) by having ½ tonne of manure (cow, horse, pig – *but not chicken*) deposited in some convenient position and letting it rot down over the year (for brandlings and redworms); 3) by picking worms up off the lawn at night after rain or a good soaking with the hose pipe (for lobworms); and 4) by assiduously digging the garden each spring (for blue-heads).

Worms collected by digging, or picked off the lawn by torch-light, can be stored for months in an old china sink, tea chest or dustbin tucked behind the garage or in some other shaded part of the garden. The container, which must be worm proof, can be filled with garden soil (for lobs and redworms) or leafmould or compost for (redworms and brandlings). Keep them moist but not wet and cover them over against the elements. Forget about feeding them with milk or oatmeal (or anything else). You require tough worms, not fat ones.

Toughening worms requires forethought and planning. Do not bother adding brick dust, sharp sand or other 'additives' to the soil. The best material is fairly dry moss. It takes about two weeks to really toughen up a worm in moss. We keep a secondary container packed with moss and enough worms for a couple of days on permanent standby. By turning this upside down every day the worms are forced to migrate back down through the moss and do not form a 'knot-of-worms' at the bottom. The worms get progressively tougher and, since they are not feeding, progressively cleaner as they continue to void the muddy contents of their digestive tract. They are then carefully sorted to reject any dead or moribund worms and placed in fresh, clean moss the night before use. They can also be stored in damp, shredded newspaper.

Worms are cold-blooded, moisture-loving, light-avoiding creatures. They do not like the sun, heat and very dry conditions. They can survive without feeding for several weeks if kept moist, cool, and in the dark.

Having got your worms to the river bank, look after them. Do not leave them in the sun while fishing and above all do not – whatever you do – leave them locked up in a parked car. A parked car is like a greenhouse. If left in the sun for a few hours (even in the spring and autumn) the temperature inside a car can reach 120°C or more. Under such conditions your worms may 'cook', even if they are in the boot, and rapidly change to a gelatinous mass which soon becomes evil-smelling in the extreme! If you are a 'visiting angler' who has imported enough worms for the duration of your holiday always take the container out of the car and leave it carefully concealed in the shade (a matt of brambles or a large bed of stinging nettles is likely to provide sufficient protection from intruders). Your car may be in the shade when it was first parked alongside the river, but the sun has a habit of moving during the course of the day!

Flood Worming

There are big spates and little spates, dirty spates and clean spates. In a wet summer, when spate has followed spate (such as 1985 in Wales), the river can rise several feet overnight without any appreciable increase in the colour of the water. In a dry year (such as 1976 and 1984) when rivers have been below average summer flow for month after month, a rise of only a foot or so after rainfall can create a really thick and filthy river.

By flood worming, we mean here fishing the worm on coloured water. Under such conditions fly fishing and spinning are impossible because the river is too fast and too dirty for either lure to be visible or fishable and because, in any event, the fish are behaving in such a way that either method would not be effective. In these circumstances worm fishing comes into its own. Indeed, it may be the only method of fishing possible.

Fishing a fly, worm, or spinner successfully on any water, river or loch, fresh or salt, requires an appreciation and insight on what fish do, how they behave and respond, to a particular environment and set of local conditions. The prime considerations in fresh water are, relative to the size of the fish, the depth and velocity of the current and the presence or absence of shelter: either from in-stream (rocks and boulders) or on-bank (trees and shrubs) cover. Thus, for a given height (= depth and velocity) a fish will choose to lie in certain, predictable, positions within the river.

On low clear water, the angler has the distinct advantage that the position of the fish in their chosen lies can often be seen – at least in the shallower, unbroken, water of the pools and glides. On coloured water this is not possible and the real skill in flood-water fishing, whether with the spinner or the worm, is in appreciating how fish respond in terms of their movements and where they choose to lie as the river begins to colour up, reaches its flood peak, and then begins to recede to normal levels and so loses its colour in the process.

Stirling has expressed his views on this important aspect which we have presented above. We would not disagree with much of what he opined. Falkus has more recently reinforced the view that, as the river increases in height, colour and velocity, fish tend to forsake their low water lies and move to new positions, often nearer to the bank and sometimes to positions which would be above water level at normal flows. Then, as the river recedes, they tend to move away from the bank back towards their original positions – which may be above, below or across from where they stationed themselves during the flood. We would, however, add that evidence from fish counters (which record both upstream and downstream movement), from tagging fish with radio transmitters, and from the occurrence of stale fish in the netsmen's

135

catches following a flood, that there is some evidence to show that a particularly 'dirty' flood may cause fish to be repelled by the high level of suspended solids carried by the stream so that they 'turn-on-their tails' and move off downstream towards the cleaner waters of the estuary. We would also add that evidence from fish counters and tagging has also reinforced what every angler 'knew from experience', that sea trout (and salmon) tend to run over a relatively narrow range of river heights (= depths and/or velocities) after the flood peak has passed and the flows are receding. It seems that few fish run as the river is increasing in colour and depth.

Flood worming tackle is not particularly refined. However, it must fulfil certain basic requirements.

Spinning rods are frequently used for flood worming. Many are rather too short and too stiff to be good worming rods. The ideal worming rod for flood worming on larger rivers is about 10–11 feet long with a nice through action to the handle. It should be strong enough to cast about 1oz and sensitive enough in the tip to transmit the feel of a bite without too much bend caused by the resistance of the current to the weight, worm and line. It should also be light enough to be held all day without becoming a burden. A carbon-fibre carp rod with a test curve of about 1½lb is a great rod for flood worming. A nice long handle that can be tucked under the arm and moveable reel fittings are important considerations. A shorter rod (8 feet) has advantages when casting is difficult on heavily overgrown banks.

The reel is of secondary importance. The same fixed spool or close-faced reel used for spinning will be perfectly adequate provided the spool is loaded with at least 100 yards of 10–12lb strength nylon monofilament line. It is rarely necessary to cast long distances when worming in flood water. Most times you will be fishing under the near bank, but plenty of spare line may be necessary when playing a fish; especially one which gets into the main current and drops downstream.

There are five main types of weight suitable for worming (Fig. 30). The

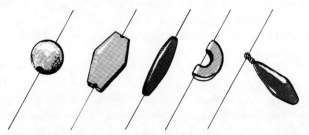

Fig. 30. The five main types of lead used in worm fishing: *a*) **pierced bullet** – the oldest and still most popular ledger weight, *b*) **coffin weight** – reputed to hold bottom better than others, *c*) **barrelweight** – a variation on the bullet, *d*) **fold-over lead** – allows a very quick change and holds the bottom well, *e*) **Arseley bomb** – an oval bullet fitted with a swivel and originally designed for rolling down the steeply shelving banks of Arseley lake. The swivel increases costs to little effect. Does any lead ever roll along the bottom? The smallest sizes of pierced bullet overlap with the largest sizes of split-shot: we much prefer the latter on low water.

amount of weight attached to the line is of crucial importance. The secret of successful worm fishing is to keep the bait moving across or along the bottom at a controlled and contrived speed. A worm which whips through the flood water at the same speed as the current and is suspended in mid-water is worse than useless. Various writers have expressed views on the speed at which the bait should travel. Some suggest the 'best' rate is about one-quarter to one-half that of the speed of the current. Others like the worm to hold bottom and lift and lower the rod to move the weight downstream at whatever rate required. The latter approach has advantages since it allows the water to be searched carefully and systematically. The former approach allows the water to be covered quickly and repeatedly. Each can be right under the same or different conditions.

As the river rises and falls, the speed of the current will change and the amount of weight used may have to be adjusted several times for a given fishing station to achieve the right speed of downstream travel for the worm. A rig which allows weight to be added or removed readily without undoing and retying knots has obvious merits.

The use of a swivel is optional. The worm is not spinning so line-twist is not a problem, but swivels have several coincidental advantages when incorporated into the terminal rig.

There are two basic terminal rigs: the conventional in-line rig with the weight mounted on the line above the hook and the dropper rig with the hook and weight on separate nylon links (Fig. 31). The dropper rig is useful

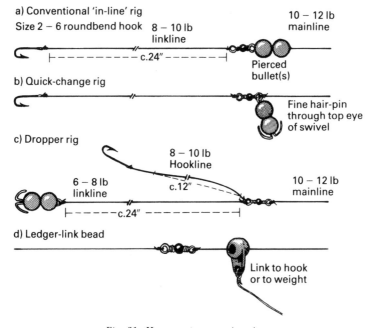

Fig. 31. Heavy water worming rigs.

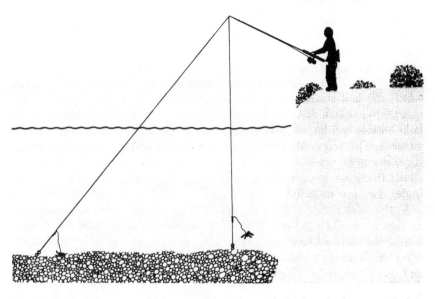

Fig. 32. The dropper rig is useful for worm fishing close to the bank on flood water, as the bait can be fished clear of the bottom so that it dances about in the current and's more 'visible' to the fish. Lengthening the cast has the effect of fishing the worm closer to the bottom and – at a certain distance, depending on the length of the rig – the worm will fish on the bottom just like a conventional in-line rig.

when fishing under the rod tip close to the bank as it enables the worm to be fished clear of the bottom so that it flutters about in the current. As the casting distance lengthens the worm fishes nearer the bottom as the angle of the line to the rod increases and there comes a point when the worm is no longer clear of the bottom. We use the dropper rig for close-in fishing and the standard rig for long-distance worming (Fig. 32).

The bottom fisherman must expect to lose tackle on snags. The cost and frustration of broken line and lost hooks, weights and worms can be mitigated partly by using a slightly weaker length of nylon to join the hook to mainline or, in a dropper rig, to connect the hook and weight links to the mainline. This is where a swivel is useful.

It is often the weight rather than the hook that becomes snagged. A useful rig for fishing a snaggy swim is to mount the weight on to a fine wire hairpin which has been threaded through to top-eye of the swivel. The ends of the hairpin are bent upwards 'anchor-fashion' to hold the weight in position. When the weight snags, a steady pull on the line causes the pin to straighten and liberate the line from the weights. This form of rig has another distinct advantage in that it enables weight to be added or removed very quickly. The pin can also be used to mount lead on the dropper rig (Fig. 31).

There are all sorts of sizes and shapes of weight manufactured. The best weight for flood worming is the cheapest and most common. We use nothing other than pierced bullets for flood worming.

138

Big water equals big worms equals big hooks. For most flood fishing we use size 6 or even size 4. The best worming hooks have a wide gape and round bend to allow the worm to be threaded easily up the shank. On heavy water it may be necessary to mount two or three largish worms on to the hook but for most purposes one good-sized 'blue-head' or 'lob' will suffice.

Forget about hooks with specially barbed shanks to hold the worm in position. Forget also about whipping little nylon bristles onto the shank. They don't work! A short shank of nylon can always be left if required by using a nail knot to tie the hook to the line and leaving the end 'trimmed long'.

There is great skill in mounting a worm on a hook so that it looks natural and keeps lively for hours. Worms should be threaded, rather than 'folded' onto the hook, with as few breaks in the skin as possible.

The typical cast is made up and across so that the weight hits bottom slightly upstream or opposite the angler. The worm is then fished downstream. It is necessary to keep in contact with the 'tap-tap-tap' of the weight as it bumps

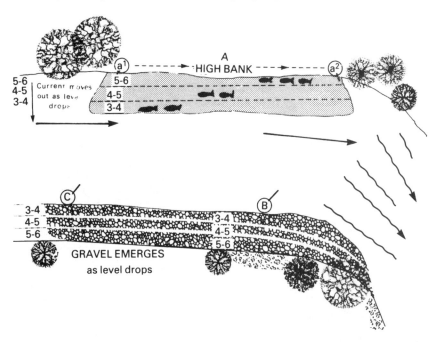

Fig. 33. Fishing the worm on heavy, coloured water requires an understanding of where fish lie in relation to the changing speed of the current and depth of the water as the flood recedes. The section of water beneath the high bank at **A** is too fast, with the river level above 6 feet, to be fished properly: at 6–5 feet depth sea trout lie close to the bank; while at 5–4 feet they lie further out and further up towards the centre of the section, and at 4–3 feet they lie well out on the edge of the main current near the top of the section. The angler would fish **A** by 'walking the worm' down from a¹–a², casting further out (and using less weight) as the level dropped. At 5–4 feet, spinning at position **B** is usually productive, and at 4–3 feet the section is best fished down with a spinner from position **C**.

139

along the bottom at all times in order to feel the take of a fish. It is, therefore, unwise to give line as the weight fishes below you. Fishing from a fixed position means that the bait will swing round in an arc towards the bank and that the worm fishes across the current from the faster to slower water and, since the amount of weight is constant, it travels at different speeds. An area of water may be searched by increasing the length of the cast to the point where the worm fishes too far out and too far downstream. This being so, you can then repeat the process or move to another station. On an open bank it is possible to 'walk' the worm along the length of the lie as it moves downstream parallel to the bank. The worm fishes along the current, not across it. By casting slightly farther out each time (perhaps adding a little more weight to compensate for the increased current) it is possible to search a large area of water quickly and effectively (Fig. 33).

Projections and indentations in the bank create interesting lies. Croys and groynes are attractive to fish (and to anglers) but they must be fished properly. Avoid fishing for too long in the back eddy. Fish will lie in the quieter water at times but they are more likely to hold just on the edge of the current where the flow is linear rather than where it tends to surge, boil and reverse. Do not be afraid to fish in a strong current. Large fish can hold station in surprisingly fast water.

It is a wise move to place a stick or stone along the bank at some convenient spot to indicate the speed at which the river is rising or falling. Many high-water lies only hold fish over a narrow range of flows and depths

Heavy-water worming on the Upper Glaslyn. Note the long rod and the centre-pin reel. (Photo: M.J. Morgan.)

Heavy water at Cenarth Falls on the Lower Teifi. A notable section of bait fishing water which is impossible to fish properly with the spinner or fly. Fishing is prohibited by bye-law between the falls and the notice board to prevent snatching (deliberate foul-hooking). (Photo: M.J. Morgan.)

and you should be aware of what the river is doing at all times. Very often the difference between success and failure may be no more than to cast a yard further out into the current or to move two or three yards further up or down the bank (Fig. 34). Time after time we have seen an angler walk into pool or glide just above or just below another wormer who has been fishing the same station for hours, and immediately catch fish. It has been done to each of us and we each have done it to others.

Some of the most successful worm anglers that we know travel miles up and down the bank during a day's flood fishing. They are as mobile as any daylight fly angler or spinner. A few casts here, a few casts there, a little less weight and try again. A quick flick under that bush. A little more weight and a long cast over to the edge of the current on the inside of the bend. Then back upstream to repeat the process. Go and look for the fish. Do not wait for them to come looking for you.

Flood fishing is essentially a tactile art. The take of the sea trout is 'felt' rather than seen. It is important to keep in touch with the worm by avoiding any unnecessary 'belly' in the line. It is important also that the rod should be sensitive enough to transmit the tap-tap-tap of the weight as it bumps across the bottom. Many bites are sensed initially by the pattern and rhythm of movement of the weight being interrupted or altered.

We hesitate to attribute a characteristic bite to a sea trout as much depends on the size of the fish relative to the size of the bait – a small whitling may have some difficulty in taking a large knot of worms moving at 2 or 3 miles an hour. The bite may be no more than a strong steady pull, or no

141

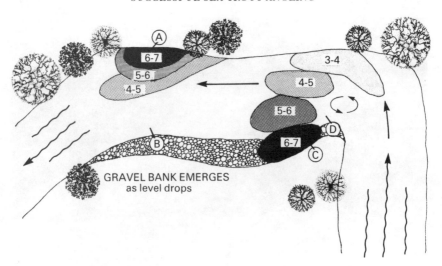

Fig. 34. This pool is fishable on a big flood at two positions. The section at **A** is only productive when the river is between 7–5 feet. At 5–4 feet, when the fish have moved across and up, it is best fished from **B**. The belly of the pool is badly affected by a turbulent swirl that diminishes in severity and extent as the flood recedes. At 7–6 feet the fish lie on the flooded gravel under the bank and are fished for from **C**. At 6–5 feet the gravel begins to emerge and the angler moves to **D** and fishes further across and up as the level drops to 3 feet. The angler who fishes the wrong zone will not catch fish!

Flood worming on the middle reaches of the Afon Dyfi (Llyn-y-Forss). The current cuts into the wooded bank on the left. The two anglers on the right bank are fishing the running worm along the edge of the current down the length of the pool. Very soon, as the river level drops off another foot or so, the best chance of a fish will be with the fly. At this stage of the receding flood the anglers shown would be better employed fishing a spinner in the more distant water down to Llyn Cerrig-Cochion (= the pool of the red stones). (Photo: G.S. Harris.)

pull at all, with the worm stopping dead and the line going solid. It may be a continued series of barely detectable tugs or a series of distinct and intermittent pulls. In our experience it is the latter form of bite that we would describe as characteristic of the sea trout: a couple of short sharp pulls, followed by a pause of (say) two or three seconds, then two or three more sharp pulls and another pause; then, if you are lucky, a good long pull as the fish moves off with the worm.

Generally speaking, it does not pay to wait too long before striking a sea trout. Certainly do not delay as long as with salmon, when it is a mistake to strike too soon. The timing of the strike for sea trout is very much a matter to be decided at the time. No hard and fast rule applies. We would suggest that it is good policy to strike the 'stop' and the 'pull' bites immediately and to strike the intermittent bite after the second or third 'tug'.

Low Water Worming

As the flood recedes and the river becomes progressively clearer and lower, the sea trout are to be found widely distributed in the pools, glides and runs and daytime fly fishing is at its best. As the river level continues to fall the fish move into the shelter of the pools and glides and begin to occupy their normal low-water lies. Daylight fly fishing becomes increasingly less productive but the lower flows and the concentrations of fish now create ideal conditions for night fishing. As the river level shrinks further, the resident fish become staler and even night fishing becomes unrewarding. At this stage, in what has now become a drought, worm fishing comes into its own again as the 'best' method for the conditions prevailing.

As we have said above, the low-water wormer has the distinct advantage over the flood wormer in that the fish are usually visible within the shallower waters of the glides and towards the tails of the pools and their position will not vary much until the next increase in the water level. Careful reconnaissance allows their precise position to be noted. Thus, the low water wormer *knows* precisely where fish are lying. The flood wormer cannot see the fish and *hopes* he knows where they are lying. Low-water worming will usually be practised under adverse conditions of low, clear water and bright sun with clear skies. In such circumstances delicacy of approach and concealment are mandatory. Slow, leisurely movements along the bank and when wading and the lightest possible tackle. A wind to ripple the surface (preferably from the south or west) to afford some cover for the angler on open water is an advantage provided it is not too strong. Casting with light tackle and detecting bites becomes harder as the wind strengthens. A gusting wind is tiresome in the extreme.

A spinning rod may be adapted for use when flood worming with heavy tackle. It will, however, be far from ideal for delicate low water work with fine lines. The ideal low-water worming rod gets progressively thinner in

143

The quieter water downstream of croys and groynes may appear attractive on flood water. But resist the temptation to let the worm settle on the bottom to avoid repeated casting, unless you want to catch brown trout and eels. Such places may be worth fishing at the height of the flood but as the river drops the sea trout move back into the mainstream. The best position to fish at this stage of the flood is along the line of the current to the right of the rod tip. (Another 12 inches off the level and spinning down this entire section would be more productive than continuing with the worm.) (Photo: G.S. Harris.)

The skill in heavy-water worming is knowing where the fish lie on different stages of the flood. This angler fished in the quieter water on the inside of a bend, and got it right, as seen from the airborne fish. A foot higher and this position would have been too turbulent to be productive. A foot lower and fish will be running straight through the faster water. (Photo: G.S. Harris.)

144

taper from the tip to the butt and has an action described variously as 'even', 'slow' or 'parabolic'. The action of a fast-taper (tip action) rod is sharp and positive with the lower section providing the backbone. As the point of taper moves down to the upper third of the rod it acquires a 'standard-taper'. Such rods are less able to force a bait long distances, but their softer action makes them less likely to flick off a soft bait. Even-taper rods impart a slower build-up of power on the cast and tend to 'lob' rather than thrust the worm forward. They are also more gentle when striking and playing the fish but their ability to set the hook at long range is less than with faster taper rods. Therefore, some form of compromise is required and we would opt for a medium taper which combines smoothness of action with power to set the hook firmly at a distance.

It is quite amazing how many anglers ensure that their fly-fishing tackle is properly 'balanced' in terms of the weight of line and reel relative to the action and weight of the rod but completely ignore the same important considerations when spinning and worming. It is impossible to cast a worm and a small weight of perhaps no more than 5g any great distance with a 14lb line and a spinning rod designed to work with 1½oz of weight! Even when a finer line is used the action of the rod is wrong.

A long rod of 12–14 feet has many advantages when worming on low water. In provides better control in playing a fish, allows a longer cast, a bettter strike and more control over the movement of the worm. One of the best low-water worming rods we have used was a 13 feet, carbon-fibre rod produced for barbel fishing. It has proved itself powerful enough to deal with salmon up to 14lb with no difficulty while being gentle enough to allow the fight from a 12oz fish to be enjoyed. It has a good long handle so that it can be tucked under the arm when fishing and the moveable reel fittings allow the reel to be located at any position on the handle as required for balance and convenience. A somewhat shorter rod may be required on smaller rivers or when the banks are overgrown. A good compromise is to adapt your fly rod by acquiring a 12-inch extension handle. This will be light enough, sensitive enough and powerful enough to cope with most situations.

The same fixed-spool reel or closed-face reel used when spinning or flood worming is perfectly suitable for low water work. However you will definitely require a spare spool *fully* loaded with about 100 yards of 5–6lb strength nylon (and another spool loaded with 8lb strength nylon if you wish to fish clear water on higher flows). The spool must be fully loaded to the lip. The length of cast will be reduced by the friction of the line over the lip of the spool if it is not filled to capacity. Remember that very little weight will be used to pull the line off the reel when casting.

Many anglers worm on low water with ultra-fine lines of only 3–4lb strength. While low-water work requires fine line, there is a common-sense limit. The finer the line, the greater the likelihood of it being broken on the strike or when playing the fish. Modern lines are extremely thin and camouflaged to be as invisible as possible and we see little merit in using anything much less than a 6lb strength line, especially where large sea trout are to be encountered or when there is a chance of salmon. The only thing worse than leaving the river bed festooned with lengths of nylon is to have a fish trailing 10 or 15 yards of the stuff from its mouth.

There are various shapes and sizes of weights available (Fig. 30). Some, such as the 'Arlsey Bomb' were designed for a very particular purpose. The 'coffin' weight is supposed to hold bottom better than a round or oval lead. The pierced bullet, however, is universally popular and, in a range of different sizes, wholly suitable for most purposes. A terminal rig that allows weight to be added and removed readily is, as in flood worming, an advantage. We find that much of our low-water worming is done using the larger sizes of split shot clipped onto, or removed as required from, a short nylon dropper some 18–24 inches above the hook (Fig. 35). Avoid, if you can, clipping split shot onto the main line as a means of keeping the weight

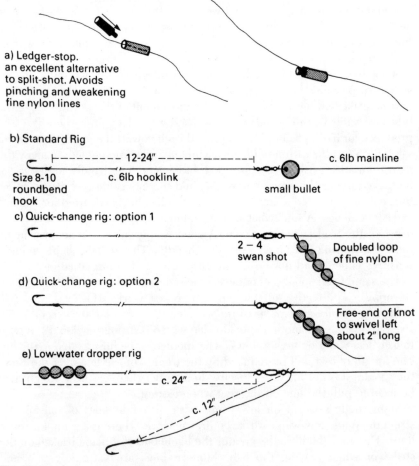

a) Ledger-stop. an excellent alternative to split-shot. Avoids pinching and weakening fine nylon lines

b) Standard Rig

├─────── 12-24″ ──────────┤   c. 6lb mainline

Size 8-10 roundbend hook   c. 6lb hooklink   small bullet

c) Quick-change rig: option 1

2 – 4 swan shot   Doubled loop of fine nylon

d) Quick-change rig: option 2

Free-end of knot to swivel left about 2″ long

e) Low-water dropper rig

└─────────────── c. 24″ ────────┤

c. 12″

Fig. 35. Low-water worming rigs.

the required distance from the hook. It is too easy to weaken the line by pinching it within the shot. A plastic ledger-stop has advantages in overcoming this common problem. A linking swivel also achieves the same function.

The hook size should be sufficient to give a good hold in a large fish while being not too big for the size of worm used. Unless fishing with just a hint of worm on the hook, we suggest that sizes 8–10 are generally applicable. For some reason the two-hooked 'Pennell' and three-hooked 'Stewart' mounts are always referred to as being suitable for clear-water worming. We have never found them necessary; nor, it seems, have many other dedicated 'single-hook' wormers. In our view, a well-mounted worm on a single hook looks more attractive and behaves more naturally than anything on a multi-hook mount. Use them if you wish; but check the strength of the connecting nylon link on shop-bought mounts first. They may not be that reliable.

Smaller worms are generally to be recommended for low water: either redworms or brandlings or a small blue head. The worm should be carefully threaded on to the hook. It is standard practice not to leave too much of head and tail ends trailing on low water. This is not important on flood water – quite the opposite in fact – but on low water sea trout sometimes develop the frustrating habit of nipping at the loose ends close to the hook. In such circumstances the Pennell or Stewart multi-hook tackles do not seem to increase the chances of hooking fish one iota. It may pay to fish a smaller hook and worm or to work the worm faster.

There are basically three techniques of fishing the worm on low water:

1. downstream worming;
2. upstream worming;
3. static water worming.

The downstream worm is by far the most widely practised method of fishing on low water. The cast is made either across or downstream-and-across, depending upon local circumstances, and the worm allowed to work *across* the stream bed as it is carried downstream by the current. In certain situations, it may be possible and productive to fish the worm along the bottom by walking it downstream parallel to the bank. Both techniques have been discussed under flood worming (page 140) but, whereas stealth and concealment are not vital considerations when fishing heavy, coloured water, they are of critical importance when worming on low clear water. Consequently, it is often necessary to fish 'far-off' in addition to fishing 'fine'.

The rate at which the worm moves over the bottom is as important on low water as it is on heavy water. Since sea trout may lie in several different locations within a pool, it may be necessary to increase and decrease the amount of weight several times as the angler works downstream in order that the worm is fished at a suitable speed. A rig which allows this to be done quickly has obvious advantages.

Low-water worming under testing conditions. Llyn-y-Bwtri on the tidal reaches of the Dyfi. The tide has long since ebbed leaving behind a large motionless pool. The angler is fishing an unweighted worm on a 4lb line in the barely discernible current flowing in at the neck where the gentlest of breezes just ripples the surface to conceal his presence from the fish. (Photo: G.S. Harris.)

He got it right! A nice fish of just under 4lb weight taken by the angler in the previous photograph. The rod is an 11-foot length fly rod fitted with a 15-inch extension handle. Perfect in action, sensitivity, and strength for low-water worming with ultra-fine lines.) (Photo: G.S. Harris.)

148

Many critics of the worm admit that the upstream worm fished in the classic style may require a high degree of skill. The technique is similar to traditional dry-fly fishing in that the angler works upstream, gently casting an unweighted worm into the likely lies, and recovers line as the bait drifts back downstream in the current.

This style of worm fishing is, essentially, a technique for the shallower, faster-flowing, runs and streams, where the presence of rocks and boulders and the occurrence of rough, broken water provide the angler with some means of concealment. This is important because, with little or no weight on the line, only short casts are possible. It is not a technique for flat, unbroken, water unless there is a good upstream breeze to ripple the surface and so provide the angler with some cover. Nor is it a method for deep water since the unweighted worm will drift back in the current well above the fish.

Up-stream worming in the classic style is, indeed skilful. It is also very popular – with authors. It is not popular with the vast majority of worm fishermen of our acquaintance.

A long rod allows greater distance to be achieved when casting and provides better control in working the worm along a predetermined path in a rock-strewn swim. The sort of water where the upstream worm may best be used is not, in our view, the sort of water in which sea trout would normally reside on low-flows. Salmon maybe, but given a choice sea trout tend to prefer the quieter deeper, far less turbulent water found in pools and glides. They may lie *temporarily* in broken water after a spate or when moving upstream on low flows but they do not remain there for longer than necessary. Clearly, the sea trout in rivers with different characteristics will distribute themselves and behave differently. The result is that the upstream worm may be more or less effective depending upon the type of river in question.

Apart from the fact that upstream worming tests the angler's ability to 'read the water' in terms of where fish lie and how to cover them with the worm, the main relevance of the technique is that it allows rocky, turbulent water to be fished more effectively than possible by other methods. Most times, however, it is possible to fish the downstream worm on similar water. The advantage of the downstream worm over the upstream worm is that it is possible to fish a longer line. The movement and direction of the worm is more readily controlled and a tighter line results. Its disadvantage is that the fish, which face upstream, are approached from in front so that they are more likely to see the approaching angler. This is much less of problem on fast broken water.

Many anglers often fish a combination of the upstream and downstream worm by casting up-and-across, recovering line as the worm approaches to a position opposite the angler and then releasing line as the worm moves downstream below the angler. The rod is swung round in an arc to follow the movement of the worm during its passage downstream.

Static-water worming does not mean fishing a static worm in the normal sense of ledgering. Sea trout often lie in deep water and in some pools the current may be insufficient to work the worm effectively. This can be a particular problem if the need to achieve casting distance and to get the worm down quickly to the lie necessitates using more weight than appropriate for the speed of the current.

Many anglers are content to leave the worm resting where it landed, on the assumption that, since it is somewhere among the fish, one will take it eventually so that the longer it is left the better. This is when the rod rests appear and the angler settles down to make himself as comfortable as possible. After a while, his attention begins to wander so that the bite – a savage 'jag' that almost pulls the rod from the rest or a very gentle 'tap-tap-tap' that barely moves the line – is either missed or passes undetected.

Under such conditions, it is often more productive to work the worm by moving it a few inches every minute or so by either rewinding a half-turn or pulling back a little line with the spare hand. The sudden movement of the worm along the bottom as it moves from A to B in front of the fish often induces an immediate response which is usually a positive bite as opposed to a tentative nibble. Moving the worm intermittently in this way also ensures that it does not work itself down among the stones or embed itself beneath the silt covering the stream bed in response to its natural instinctive behaviour.

It is a matter for conjecture whether or not it is best to fish a pool or glide from the bottom up or from the top down. It is commonly stated that the angler should approach from behind the shoal and fish for the tail-enders first. Apart from the fact that in this position the angler is less obvious to the fish, it is held that by carefully leading a hooked tail-end fish away from the shoal the remainder will be undisturbed; whereas hooking one of the front-end fish creates disturbance and causes the shoal to break up. That may be so in theory, but we have never found that it works that way in practice. A tail-end fish is just as likely to run up through the shoal as a front-end fish is likely to run down through its companions. All fish should be played carefully to minimise disturbance on low water, but sea trout, unlike salmon, are reluctant to be 'led' and tend to swim about unpredictably immediately following a successful strike. A lot depends on the topography of the water, the pattern of the current, the distribution of the fish and the nature of the banks.

The bite of a sea trout on low water can frequently be so subtle or so sudden that it is missed. The perfect bite is one consisting of a regular series of taps, which allow the angler to calculate his reaction, to pull back slightly to tighten the line and 'know' that the fish is still there. More often that not the bite occurs as no more than a sudden sharp pull and the worm 'comes back gone' or somewhat shorter than when mounted. A characteristic bite in deep, slow water, where the worm is moving very slowly, if at all, is for the inevitable curve of line that develops between the rod tip and the water surface slowly to straighten and then either drop back as the worm is rejected or the bite develops into a slow steady pull on the rod tip which bends accordingly. Touch and (to a lesser extent) vision both play an important part in detecting and connecting with these sudden or gentle bites. It is, therefore, an unwise practice to ground the rod. The rod should be held in the hand and should be swung round to follow the worm as it moves across the stream so that there is the smallest possible curve in the line at all times. Some anglers hold a short length of line between the thumb and forefinger of the free hand to allow the bite to be felt more readily through the line rather than through the rod.

As far as striking on low water is concerned, the best advice we can give is keep in direct contact with the worm, keep alert at all times, and strike the instant you become aware of a bite. Do not wait for a bite to develop as when salmon fishing. Strike immediately and firmly but remember that fine tackle is being used. Too much power in the strike will result in a break.

Having hooked and played your fish you are ultimately faced with the problem of landing it. We much prefer to beach our fish whenever we can but there are situations when a landing net is essential – when boat fishing or when fishing from a high bank, for example.

If you must use a net, then choose the best you can afford, Jock Scott says, 'I do not like nets where the frame collapses. I like to have a rigid frame.' The all-collapsible net where the frame breaks down and then folds back along the handle is indeed very convenient to carry about your person; either clipped onto a belt or attached to a D-ring on a jacket or a waistcoat. However, this type of net has caused many anglers, ourselves included, grief when it has failed to flip-up-and-out into the ready-for-use position, because the bag has somehow become tangled with the arms. This problem can be minimised by using a fold-over net with a rigid frame. While this type of net is suitable in the smaller sizes for trout fishing, the large-diameter frame required for dealing with double-figure salmon and sea trout becomes very cumbersome when folded over and clipped onto a belt.

The best net for sea trout (and salmon) is one with a rigid frame that slides up the handle. This is mounted on a quick-release 'peel-sling' and carried on the back. A large net carried in this position is far less awkward than the clip-on type. It does not get caught up on bankside vegetation and it does not drop off and get lost like the clip-on net. The net that we both favour has a 22-inch frame. It is about 48 inches long when demounted and 72 inches long when the net is extended. This size, while a little large for most sea trout, provides a sensible safety margin for that fish of a lifetime and makes an excellent net for boat fishing when a large net has many advantages.

151

7 · SPINNING

The obvious liberalisation of angling attitudes over the last 30 years or so as shown by the increasing use of the worm at all river-water levels also applies to spinning. Jock Scott, writing as recently as 1969 after a long fishing career spanning the generations of our parents and grandparents, stated, 'In these days of threadline technique, so called spinners are legion; in fact I would say that there are more good performers with a spinning rod than with a fly. I am bound to say that sea trout are susceptible to a minnow or a spoon, but I would like to see my readers give the fly a chance.' While agreeing whole-heartedly with the pious hope expressed by Jock Scott, we nevertheless embark on the subject of spinning!

Early authors such as Maxwell, Mottram, Bridgett and Bluett made little or no mention of spinning. Not until we come to Dawson is there any real enthusiasm for the subject. The reason for this is that early anglers had a rigid code of practice which recognised the fly as the only really 'respectable and sporting' method of taking sea trout and salmon. Nevertheless, a few anglers included spinning in their limited repertoire of techniques for use when the river was too high and too coloured for fly fishing. But even they baulked at spinning on low water and stopped fishing altogether when the fly became unproductive.

Spinning in general, and low-water spinning in particular, was then a great deal more difficult and skilful than it is today! Spinners of the Victorian era used enormous, heavy rods with a dressed line that was cast from coils held in the hand or laid in a basket strapped to the waist. The reels of the day were, like the rods, heavy and cumbersome affairs that were little more than 'winches' for storing the line. Then came the improved centre-pin reels of the free-running Nottingham-type which culminated in terms of technical excellence in the superlative 'Aerial' and 'Silex' reels of the 1920s and 1930s.

But even while the centre-pin reel was steadily being perfected, the first great advances in the evolution of the modern 'casting reel' had begun. In 1884 P.D. Malloch took out a patent for the 'Malloch Casting Reel', and so pioneered the development of the 'cross-wind', 'threadline' or (as it is now generally termed) the 'fixed-spool' reel. The original Malloch reel was essentially a conventional fixed-spool that could be swivelled through 90° for casting so that the line ran off the spool with the minimum of friction. The reel was turned back to the standard position for rewinding and so, inevitably, caused the line to be twisted as it was respooled. The problem of line-twist was overcome in 1905 when Alfred Holden Illingworth patented his 'Illingworth No. 1' reel. This was a complete break with tradition since instead of working on the orthodox (= centre-pin) reel, he went back to the drawing board and started from scratch. As a direct result of Illingworth's innovative and inspirational design there evolved a new type of reel that was eventually to revolutionise light spinning and bait fishing.

We say 'eventually' because, although the improved reels of the era made spinning far easier than hitherto, the thick lines of the day restricted the technique to coloured or heavy water. It was not until the introduction of reliable nylon monofilament lines in the 1950s that light spinning on low clear water became a really practical proposition. The only problem was that the tremendous advances in the technology of lines and reels meant that almost anyone could now cast a lure to the far bank after just a few practice casts. The result was that the appeal of spinning increased dramatically, although many fisheries remained faithful to tradition and prohibited spinning on low water – something that continues to this day in many places.

Spinning, like other techniques, has its moments, and like other techniques it can be abused or over-used. In our experience it is not profitable on the rising flood, when the water is usually at its thickest and dirtiest, and when the sea trout are moving out of the rapidly increasing current at their normal low water lies to take up different positions in the quieter, less turbulent water on either side of the main current and often very close to the river bank. In such conditions they seem to respond best to a bait placed under their noses and are, in any event, virtually impossible to cover effectively with a spinner.

The art of spinning has advanced enormously over the last few decades, so it is only the more recent authors who have anything useful to say about the subject. Jock Scott, Falkus and Gammon rightly state that the best spinning water occurs as the flood peak passes and the water level begins to drop and starts to lose its load of silt and sediment so that it changes from a 'semi-opaque' appearance to the colour of pale lager beer or very weak coffee – dependent upon whether the river drains an agricultural or moorland catchment. When this occurs the best conditions for flood worming have passed as the fish begin to move out from under the banks and take up station in the flatter water across the width of the river in the glides and the pool tails where they can now be covered effectively and productively with a spinner. At this stage in the recession of the flood it is likely that any fresh sea trout that were encouraged to move into the river from tidal waters will be running upriver in broad daylight to be joined by many of the fish that were already holding in the river before the start of the flood.

It is at this stage of the falling flood that spinning is the method of the moment. However, that moment may endure for no more than an hour or two on many short-spate rivers where a small flood can run off remarkably quickly. On larger rivers with substantially undrained and unafforested

153

catchments, good water for heavy spinning may persist for a day or two after heavy rain, but this is exceptional on all but the largest sea trout rivers: or in lake-fed catchments.

Although we have stated that we much prefer to fish the fly as soon as the flood water has cleared and fallen to allow it to be fished effectively, it is of course possible to spin at all river levels from a bank-high flood to extreme low-water drought conditions. Since the tackle, tactics and techniques of fishing the spinner vary with the height of the river it is perhaps best to approach our subject under the two general headings of heavy spinning and light spinning.

Heavy Spinning

The days are gone when heavy tackle was required to spin on heavy water. Double-handed spinning rods are better suited to salmon fishing than to sea-trout fishing. If you wish to derive the maximum pleasure from the typically smaller but wilder sea trout, then it is necessary to fish with lighter tackle, even on heavy water. By lighter tackle we do not imply weaker tackle, merely that it should not be so heavy and insensitive that only the larger sea trout register any fight.

Most rods used today for spinning are far too short. A short rod has advantages on small overgrown streams when a long rod would be a positive liability, but in most other situations the longer the rod the better it is for controlling the playing fish, achieving casting length and accuracy, and setting the hooks. Although Gammon used two glass fibre rods of 7 feet length, one for heavy spinning with lines up to 8lb strength and one for light spinning with lines down to 4lb strength, we would opt for something a bit longer (say 9–10 feet) for heavy spinning, although the shorter length of 7 feet is perfectly suitable for light spinning. Length is just one feature when selecting a spinning rod. Equally important considerations are weight and action. Single-handed spinning can be quite tiring after a few hours and the rod and reel should always feel comfortable in the hand. Most glass and carbon spinning rods of whatever length are sufficiently light enough to be used single-handed; although a long handle that extends down the forearm and can be tucked under the arm when retrieving is a distinct advantage with the longer rods suggested for heavy spinning.

It is surprising how few anglers give any thought to 'balance' when they acquire their spinning tackle. Every fly fisherman who has read the right books considers balance from the outset when selecting a rod or a line, but very few spinners (or wormers) seem to realise that the balance between rod, line and lure is just as important in other branches of the sport. Thus we see anglers attempting to cast tiny spinners attached to 20lb strength lines with poker-like rods of 6 feet length and then wondering why they fail to achieve any distance or control over the direction of flight. Every rod, whether fly,

Conventional heavy-water spinning. The river is still a bit too high for perfect conditions and, perhaps, the worm would be more productive until the level has dropped off a foot or so. Then fish would begin to travel in earnest and spinning would become the method of the moment.

Upstream spinning can be very productive on medium to low flows for sea trout. Hywel Morgan fishes the quill minnow at the tail of a glide. The flat water at the tail of a pool or glide is probably the best place to fish anything when the fish are still travelling in daylight as the flood recedes. (Photo: M.J. Morgan.)

155

spinning or worming, has an optimum casting weight and optimum range of line strengths. Unfortunately few manufacturers describe their products in terms of test-curves, line and casting weight ratings, and actions. Again the action of a rod is just as important when spinning as when fly fishing. Rod actions have already been briefly discussed under worming. Tip action rods are fine for casting but they tend to be too 'hard' on a fish when striking and playing and a 'medium' action represents an acceptable compromise.

Although multiplying reels have many advantages and are ideal for heavy spinning with lines in excess of 9lb strength and weights from about ¼oz (6g) they cannot be used for ultra-fine spinning on low water and so we use the standard fixed-spool reel for both light and heavy spinning. (Why have two reels when one will do?) We would stress the importance of buying well when investing in a spinning reel. A good spinning reel should have the following characteristics:

1. a high gear ratio of about 5:1 (this describes the rate of line recovery for each turn of the handle);
2. a good adjustable clutch – which is readily accessible when playing a fish;
3. a skirted spool which avoids the line becoming wrapped around the spindle;
4. a good bail-arm;
5. as few 'sticking-out-bits' as possible;
6. both shallow and deep spools for fine and strong lines respectively.

Closed-faced spinning reels which have no bail-arm have many advantages for light spinning, but they do not have enough spool capacity for a sufficient length of thicker nylon when spinning heavy water.

For most purposes, the reel should be equipped with three spools each containing about 100 yards of 12lb, 9lb and 6lb nylon to cover all water conditions from high and coloured to low and clear. There are several 'types' of nylon line and it is as well to choose a brand made specifically for spinning. Colour, texture, finish, stretch and 'memory' (or rather lack of it) are important characteristics and some brands are better than others. Fluorescent nylon lines are available which have higher visibility in air than conventional lines. This is a distinct advantage at times as the spinner, just like the fly fisherman or wormer, should always 'know' precisely where the lure is in the water and how it is fishing.

One of the greatest problems in spinning experienced by our forefathers was the problem of line-twist and kinking caused by the rotation of the spinner or spoon as it moved through the water. Various solutions were devised to overcome the very real problem of line-twist. A number of patents were taken out for anti-kink vanes and it was standard practice to have lures which spun either clockwise or anti-clockwise and to change from one to the other periodically so that the opposing action of one type removed any kink caused by the other. Fortunately today modern swivels are sufficiently efficient to remove any twist as it is created. This is just as well because no manufacturers as far as we are aware seem to make a minnow with spinning vanes set in opposite directions so that the direction of spin can be changed. Any alternation in the direction of spin seems to be a matter of pure chance within the product ranges of different manufacturers.

We come now to the weird and wonderful ironmongery available to the modern spinner. It is here that we must become slightly pedantic about the term we have been using so freely throughout this chapter. 'Spinning' is a generic term which almost defies precise definition. (It is perhaps best defined as a form of angling in which a natural or artificial bait is cast and then wound back so that its appearance and behaviour suggest a swimming fish and its action is intended to induce attack by a predatory fish. Thus, spinning does not mean merely fishing with a lure that 'spins'.) We make this point only because many of the lures used in spinning do not, in fact, 'spin'. Thus there are spinners, spoons, minnows, wagglers, wobblers and plugs – to use a very simple classification.

The most popular spinning lures for sea trout on most rivers today are the Mepps and Abu spinners and the Toby-type wobblers. However, the 'Devon', 'Irish' and 'Lane' and 'Quill' minnows appear to be enjoying a deserved resurgence in popularity in some areas and an increasing number of anglers are finding that the Rapala-type plugs (both buoyant and sinking) are attractive to sea trout also. However, despite numerous new products appearing in the tackle shops each year, most sea trout anglers remain faithful to the tried-and-tested spinner and, for this reason, it is appropriate to mention a few points about its various attributes.

The lightweight spinners (up to about 4g = ⅙ ounce) are ideal for no-splash entry. The shape of the blade determines its action in the water. The oval and round blades have greater resistance to the water and rotate in a wide arc from 45° to 60° from the axis. The 'pear' and 'teardrop' shaped

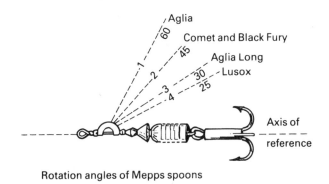

Rotation angles of Mepps spoons

Fig. 36. The shape of the blade on a spinner can affect its action. The rounder blade (e.g. Mepps Aglia) presents greater resistance to the current so that it spins well at slow speeds. The narrower oval blade (e.g. Mepps Aglia Long) offers less resistance, so making it a much better choice in fast water.

blades move closer to the axis at an arc of about 30°, with the narrow blades rotating almost parallel to the axis (see Fig. 36). The heavier the blade, the greater the inertia to be overcome and, thus, the slower and flatter the spin. Thus, for a slow rate of retrieve a light oval or round blade gives a faster spin than a heavy pear-shaped blade. One problem with spinners on heavy fast water is that they create so much drag that they rotate too fast and tend to work towards the surface. This problem may necessitate a change to a wobbler with a darting action rather than a regular spin.

There is little doubt that the Toby-type lures are excellent attractors of fish on heavy water. Unfortunately, they have a well-earned reputation as being poor hookers! This can be particularly frustrating at times when fish after fish 'hit' the lure with either no contact or the briefest of contact being made. Under these circumstances which may result from the fish misjudging the totally unpredictable random dartings and undulations of the lure, it some-times pays either to scale down by two sizes or to recover line more slowly so that the action is less pronounced in either case. Alternatively, since the fish are obviously responsive, it may pay to change to a spoon, spinner or min-now which moves in a somewhat more 'predictable' direction. Some anglers attempt to remedy the problem of the low hit/hook ratio of the Toby either by removing the tail treble and attaching it to the split ring at the head or by attaching a second treble at the head. We do not know from personal experi-ence which works best or if either works at all, as we rarely fish the Toby. There is, in our view, very little to beat the Mepps, although occasionally the minnow may be its equal or better.

Some anglers prefer to add weight to the line to achieve depth and casting distance while others prefer to achieve the same results by using a heavier lure (Fig. 37). The heavier lure without the addition of separate leads has advantages in casting in that it is far less likely to become snagged on the line, but it may not fish as effectively as a lure with the additional weight added some distance up the line (Fig. 39). This additional weight keeps the lure fishing deeper for longer and also parallel with the river bed. Unless fishing on dead low or flat clear water, when disturbance is to be avoided at all costs, or when it is not necessary to achieve any appreciable depth, we suggest that any extra weight should be added separately rather than use a heavily weighted lure.

The typical spinning rig for both heavy and light spinning consists of a swivel attached to the main line with the lure then attached to the swivel at the other end by a short nylon link of about 15–18 inches. Any additional weight is attached at or above the swivel. Many anglers spin with pierced-bullet leads threaded onto the line above the swivel. We much prefer to use the spiral or 'Hillman' leads or, for light spinning, the fold-over leads, as these can be removed or changed quickly without breaking and re-tying knots as is necessary with leads threaded onto the mainline. The three leads referred to above tend to resist line-twist and therefore act as anti-kink devices. The ability to change leads quickly when fishing a section of river

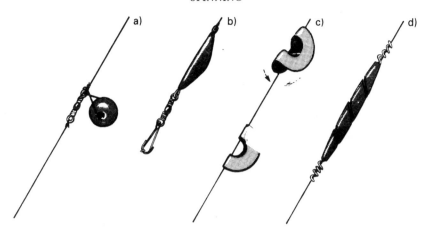

Fig. 37. The four main types of lead weight used in spinning: a) **Hillman** anti-kink lead, where the wire loop, usually threaded through the top eye of a swivel, fits into the holes in a pierced bullet so that the weight of the lead can be changed quickly without undoing knots, b) the **Wye** lead where the spinner can be attached directly to the swivel or – more usually – the lead is reversed and the swivel link on the lead is attached to a swivel on the main line, with the lure attached to the eye of the lead by a suitable (18 inch) leader of slightly weaker monofilament (This lead is widely popular on snag-free waters where frequent changes of lead weight are not necessary.), c) the **fold-over** lead, which allows a very quick change and has good anti-kink properties (one of our favourite leads, but is often not stocked by tackle shops), d) the **Jardine** or **Spiral** lead, which allows a quick change but has a bad reputation for 'flicking-off'. This can be overcome by bending the lead into a gentle curve which 'tightens' the grip of the line and improves the anti-kink properties of the weight.

where the sea trout may be lying in water varying in depth from anything in excess of 8 feet to less than 1 foot is a distinct advantage. Whereas the spinning lure itself may be changed repeatedly during the course of a day according to whim, very few anglers give any thought to increasing or decreasing the depth at which the lure is fished by changing the amount of lead. The depth at which a lure is fished can of course be controlled by the rate of line retrieve: a slow retrieve allows the lure to fish deeper than a fast retrieve. However, there are times when a lure must be fished *both* fast and deep and this can be only achieved by adding extra weight.

Spinning on heavy water which still contains some colour is relatively unsophisticated and success depends very much on being in the right place at the right time. That in turn means 'reading-the-river' and anticipating the likely movements and disposition of the fish relative to the height of the water. Perhaps the best place to start spinning on high coloured water is in the tail of a pool; preferably a pool with a long tail so that the angler can select a section where the current is not too fast for effective spinning. Sea trout seek out a favourable current where they can hold station without too much effort and, as the river level drops and the current changes the fish move station. Sea trout, and salmon, will run upstream during daylight if the river is in flood and the falling flood appears to be especially conducive to

159

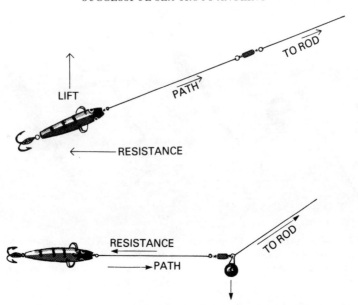

Fig. 38. The effect of the retrieve on the direction of movement of the weighted and unweighted lure.

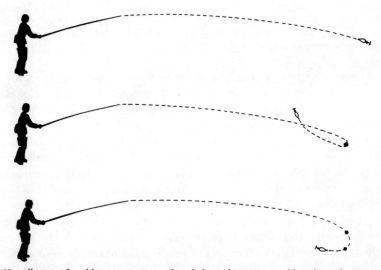

Fig. 39. All sorts of problems can arise with unbalanced spinning tackle. The rod action must balance the line strength, and this in turn must balnce with the weight of the terminal tackle. Casting distance largely depends on the weight of the terminal tackle. In light spinning no added weight may be required on the line to achieve the required distance (top). Where weight is added to produce a longer cast or to sink the lure to the required depth it should not be heavier than the lure itself as this will often result in the spinner wrapping back and snagging the casting line so that it fishes upside down (centre). Instead of using one weight that is heavier than the lure, two or three lighter weights should be used which are spread up the leader so that they do not unbalance the cast (bottom).

such movement. It is towards the tail of the pools that the sea trout tend to pause as they run upstream on high water.

Heavy spinning on coloured water tends to be fairly static – at first. Having selected a suitable location towards the tail of the pool the cast is made repeatedly across the stream in a fan-like pattern (also termed 'fishing-round-the-clock') covering as wide an arc of water as possible in an upstream and downstream direction (Fig. 40). Apart from varying the depth and speed of the lure, and changing the pattern of the lure, there is little that the angler can do to improve success until the water begins to drop off. When this occurs the angler should move progressively nearer to the tail of the pool so that any fish entering the pool from below can be covered the instant that they move into the tail. The most certain takes seem to come from these 'strangers' and the sooner they are presented with the lure the better.

As the river level continues to fall the speed of the current slackens so that it soon becomes practicable to fish the pool necks and the glides in addition to the pool tails. This now becomes spinning at its best. The river still contains some colour, the fish are still running – indeed they can be seen head-and-tailing as they move into and out of the pools and through the glides – and it is only in the fastest runs that any form of fishing is still impossible. At this stage it is wise to consider scaling down from the heavier

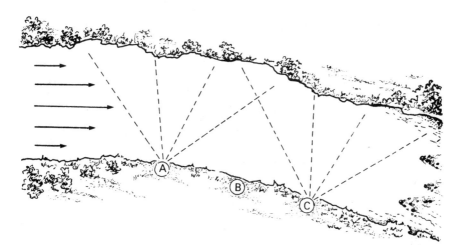

Fig. 40. Spinning on very heavy water at the peak of the flood is largely a matter of perseverance and good luck as few fish will be travelling on very dirty water that is flowing fast. Under such circumstances the best policy if you must fish a spinner (the worm would probably be more productive) is to select a pool with a long tail section, choose a position where the current is not too fast and 'fan-cast' in an arc repeatedly over the same section of water. At high flows the angler fishes from position **A**. As the river level drops the best fishing position moves to **B** and, as the level drops still further, to **C**. Position **C** is usually the best position to intercept travelling fish, usually the more certain 'takers'. As soon as you see fish showing on the receding flood move to the tail of a pool or glide and start spinning in earnest.

lures used on the higher more coloured water of a while previous and, as the colour disappears, to change to a finer (6–7lb) line.

At this juncture we would stress the difference between sea trout spinning and salmon spinning. Gammon, who fished the Tywi, a river known to us both, stated 'it is impossible to fish too fast for sea trout'. We would not disagree. Salmon spinning can be a tedious, mechanical process. The lure is cast across and slightly downstream and then allowed to swing round in a wide arc by the current to the near bank with little positive action by the angler, other than to rewind prior to re-casting. The golden rule in salmon spinning is to keep the lure working as close to the bottom as possible, with the casting lead tapping the gravel in front of the lure. While spinning for sea

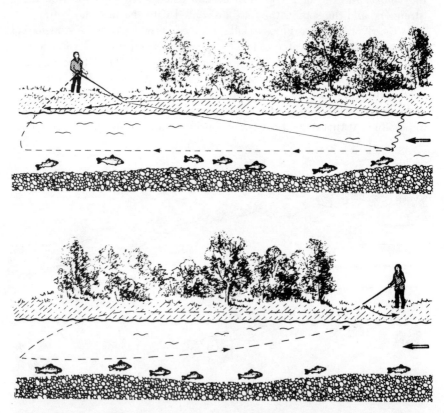

Fig. 41. Upstream and downstream spinning. When the current is not too fast and the depth is sufficient, sea trout will often lie very close to the bank where they are best covered by casting upstream (top) instead of downstream (bottom). With the more conventional downstream cast the lure tends to work upwards during the recovery so that it fishes above the fish. The upstream cast allows more control over the speed and depth of the lure during the recovery. It can be fished very close to the bottom (and the fish) over a longer distance. It is by far the more skilful method of spinning. The lure must be recovered at a speed that is faster than the current otherwise it will not fish properly and will snag the bottom; hence our preference for spinning reels with a very fast (5:1) rate of line retrieve.

trout in the early season and in very heavy water is akin to salmon spinning, it is otherwise very different at most times. The lure is fished both upstream and downstream and worked at different speeds and at different depths through every bit of fishable water. The clearer and lower the water, the faster and higher the retrieve.

There is a natural tendency among anglers to fish from the shallow bank towards the deeper water under the far bank, but it is possible to fish very effectively into deep water under a near bank by casting directly upstream virtually parallel to the bank and recovering line rapidly so that the lure fishes back at a faster rate than the current (Fig. 42). The upstream cast is often the most productive cast in sea-trout spinning. Gammon suggests that this is because 'a small fleeing fish will always head downstream and such a flight arouses the natural predatory instinct of the sea trout'. Whatever the reason, we can vouch for the effectiveness of the rapidly-fished downstream lure for sea trout. Although much sea trout spinning is practised in the downstream-and-across style, we find that we tend to fish upstream-and-down more often than down-and-across. This, to some extent, explains why we recommend a reel with a fast rate of line recovery. The upstream cast into deep holding water under the near bank is perhaps more effective than the downstream cast from the same bank or the cast from the far bank for the simple reason that it fishes over the fish longer and at greater depth than a cast from other directions (Fig. 41).

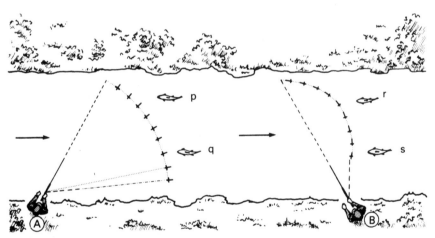

Fig. 42. Conventional salmon spinning is based on the cast being made downstream-and-across with the lure being swung across the stream by the force of the current before rewinding line to recast. The angler at A is fishing conventionally and the lure is presented obliquely to a fish at p and end-on to a fish at q. This is not the best way to spin for sea trout. Fast spinning is often more productive, and rewinding during the downstream swing of the lure presents a different profile. The angler at B starts to rewind as soon as the lure has sunk to the required depth (hence the upstream cast). The lure fishes down onto a fish at r and is presented laterally to a fish at s. It pays to vary the speed, depth, angle and direction of presentation of the lure when spinning for sea trout whenever possible.

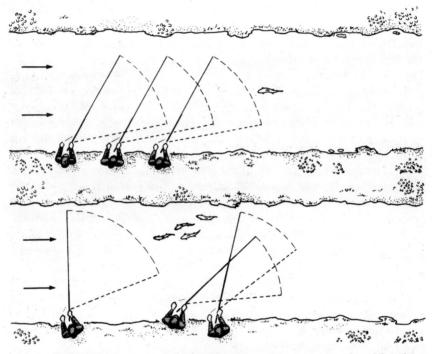

Fig. 43. When spinning on high to medium flows (when the exact position of any fish within a section of water may not be known) it is important to search the water methodically, covering every inch, if fish are not to be missed. The angler who adopts a standard 'searching' pattern of casting (top) as he moves along the bank is much more likely to encounter fish than the angler (bottom) who casts irregularly in any random direction.

Far too much spinning is done on a random chuck-and-chance-it basis. Spinning, like other forms of fishing, should be approached in a thinking way. Fish can lie almost anywhere on high to medium flows, so a methodical approach to casting which searches the water efficiently should be adopted. Do not make random casts up, across or down the river at whim as large sections of productive water may be missed. Attempt to cover the water in a systematic fashion with a regular pattern of casts (Fig. 43). A good approach to fishing a glide or a long pool tail would be to cast down-and-across at more or less the same angle, and to move down a yard or so between each cast to the end of the section; then to fish it back up again using an upstream-and-across pattern of casts. In this way the lure will cover every bit of available water twice but be presented to the fish at two different depths, speeds and directions.

In our experience the successful sea trout spinner has to be more versatile than the salmon spinner. Sea trout are far less ponderous and more reactive in their behaviour. The sea trout spinner does not merely search the water by casting like a machine but gives particular attention to varying the speed, depth and direction of the cast so that the water is searched both vertically and horizontally. There are times when the deep-fished lure works best and other times when the sea trout seem to prefer a lure which fishes high and fast. Remember that the speed at which the lure fishes depends on the speed of the current, the direction of the cast and the rate of retrieve. The depth at which it fishes depends also on these factors plus the weight of the lure itself.

Light Spinning

Light spinning on low clear water is a much neglected topic in the literature. Dawson, who was liberal minded enough to recommend spinning at night for sea trout, makes only passing reference to it. Gammon deals only with spinning on high to medium flows in any detail and Falkus deals with the entire subject of all spinning with relative brevity. It is really only Jock Scott and Holiday who embrace this branch of the sport with any enthusiasm and in any detail. Light spinning is a highly skilled method of fishing for sea trout. Let nobody persuade you otherwise until you have tried it for yourself as it is doubtful if they have ever done so!

Under conditions of low clear water the sea trout will be occupying their normal lies within the security of the pools and in the deep glides where they will seek to make the most of any cover provided by overhanging bushes and trees. Under such conditions, they are most easily alarmed and they must be approached with the utmost stealth and care if they are to be fished for successfully. Remember that the position of the sun can affect the 'impact' that the lure presents to the fish (Fig. 44). This may influence the direction and timing for fishing a particular section of water.

Light spinning tackle is now required. The rod can usefully be changed for something shorter and lighter with a more positive tip action for casting a light lure accurately over a good distance. The line has been changed to 4–5lb strength (never less) and the lure itself is smaller and much lighter.

Light spinning on low water has many similarities with daylight fly fishing under the same conditions in terms of approach but the light spinner has several practical advantages over his fly fishing counterpart on low water. First, he can cast much further and, provided that the lure is presented delicately and precisely, he can approach the fish from a greater distance so that he is much less likely to disturb the fish. Second, he can fish his lure much deeper than the fly fisherman. Third, he can fish the lure faster. Fourth, the finer spinning line will cause less disturbance on the surface after casting and as it is being retrieved that he is less dependent upon a breeze to ripple the surface and so obscure his activities. Fifth, the spinner requires much less space for casting and so can fish difficult, overgrown sections of water denied to the fly angler.

The direction of the cast can be either upstream or downstream. The downstream cast can be productive on larger rivers – especially if fished from

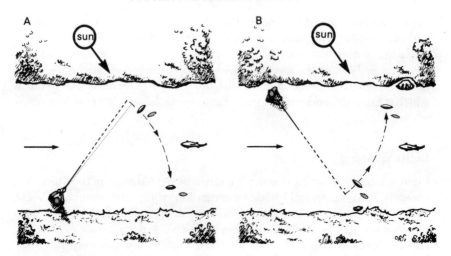

Fig. 44. The position of the sun may be very important at times when spinning on clear water. In A the angler is fishing opposite (into) the sun and casting towards the left bank to cover a fish lying midstream. The lure is illuminated from behind (and is seen in silhouette) as it moves towards the fish. Only when it passes away from the fish will it appear illuminated. Note that in A the shadow of the lure is ahead of its passage. In B the angler has crossed to the other bank and is fishing away from the sun and is casting towards the right bank. The lure is now illuminated as it approaches the fish and seen in silhouette as it moves away. The shadow of the lure is behind its passage as it approaches the fish. (The position of the angler/lure relative to the sun can be important also when fishing the fly. The thick fly line can cast a heavy shadow as it swings across the stream.)

shallow water into deeper water – but there is little doubt that the upstream cast is generally more productive on smaller rivers. The upstream cast results in the angler approaching the fish from behind so that he is less likely to disturb the fish. It also results in the lure fishing over the fish for longer at a more controllable depth and speed than the downstream cast.

The skill in light spinning is in knowing where fish lie and in the stealth of the physical approach. It is also in the accuracy of the cast. Whereas spinning on heavy water required little casting skill other than in the ability to achieve reasonable distance, low water spinning often requires pin-point accuracy in terms of direction and distance. There is little doubt that few British anglers are adept spin-casters. We doubt if more than a handful could place a lure within the same 12-inch circle with two, let alone three, consecutive casts at 25 yards – other than by pure chance. (Well – could you?) Yet this is precisely what the light spinner must often do if the fish are to be covered efficiently and effectively. There is definitely no chuck-and-chance in low water spinning.

The adept light spinner will have mastered the different casting techniques. The most commonly used and accurate cast is the 'overhead' (snap) cast where the angler 'sights' down the rod as if aiming a gun to achieve accuracy and controls distance by the power of the forward cast and 'feathering' the line as it runs off the spool with the index finger of the rod hand (or with the spare hand) to control any over-casting. However, he will also be well practised in the 'soft-cast' (for presenting a soft bait such as minnow) with a slow power build up, and the 'backhand', 'sidearm', 'pendulum' and 'bow' casts for placing a lure between and beneath overhanging bushes or for fishing in overgrown streams where there is no space to swing the rod in the normal casting arc.

The advantage of the upstream cast is, as already noted, that the lure can be fished over the fish at a more precisely determined depth for longer than with the usual downstream-and-across cast. Its principal disadvantage is that the line and swivel cover the fish before the lure, and this may cause some disturbance. The direct upstream cast can be employed successfully where fish lie in shallow water at the tail of a sweeping pool which allows the angler to fish upstream from the gravel or the bank without 'walking among the fish'. In most situations, however, the cast will be made up-and-across as in upstream fly fishing. In long pool tails and in glides it may be expedient to adopt the 'leap-frog' technique of fishing the water in sections to avoid 'pushing' fish progressively upstream so that they disturb the remainder of the shoal before they are reached by the angler (see Fig. 45). The upstream cast into any deep water lying under the near bank should never be over-looked when spinning for sea trout – especially under low water conditions as it is very likely that any fish will be tucked in close to the shelter of the bank.

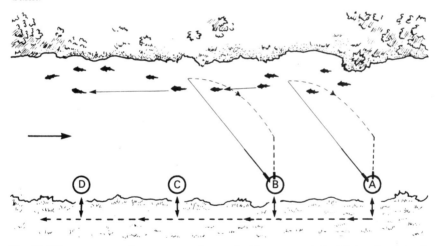

Fig. 45. When spinning on low water it is often preferable to approach the fish from behind and spin upstream-and-back. Great care must be taken to avoid disturbing the fish. Those that are disturbed and which drop downstream into water previously fished cause no problem, but any fish which are pushed upstream may disturb those fish which have yet to be covered. Instead of working steadily upstream from A to D, it is often better to 'leapfrog' up a section of water, fishing at A then B then C then D in the above example so that the angler moves ahead of any likely disturbance. (This also applies when fishing the upstream wet-fly or dry-fly in shallow pool tails and glides.)

The Quill Minnow has recently regained popularity for spinning on medium to low flows. The modern, weighted, plastic variety (left) has certain advantages as it fishes deeper without added weight and is easier to obtain than the lighter 'traditional' quill (right). Both can have one or two flying trebles to increase their (theoretical) hooking potential. (Photo: M.J. Morgan.)

The smaller sizes of spinner (0, 1 and 2) are suitable for low-water work, but many anglers prefer to use the minnow. The Quill Minnow was once very popular for sea trout but virtually disappeared from the tackle shops for over a decade. It has now reappeared in various forms made out of plastic rather than natural quill and is, in our view, an improvement on the original. The traditional Quill Minnow was armed with a tail treble and two flying trebles (nine hooks in all). Removal of one of the flying trebles *seems* to improve the spin of the lure, especially on the smaller sizes, without detriment to its hooking ability.

In recent years we have both developed an affection for the Irish or Lane minnow. We have never liked the metal Devon Minnow, and while modern Devons come in a vast array of weights, shapes and sizes (in wood and plastic also), there is something about the stream-lined shape and action of the traditional Irish minnow that makes it particularly successful (for us) under low to medium water conditions. The downstream retrieve requires a lure that works well with low water resistance. Therefore, if the spinner is to be used it is worth remembering that the broader blade spins better than the oval blade when worked downstream at a relatively slower speed ahead of the current. We rarely use plugs (other than for pike fishing) and find the Toby-type wobbling lures unsuitable for downstream spinning in low water.

Every spinner will develop a particular preference for some colour or combination of colours, stripes or spots for his choice of spinning lures. These now come in an infinite variety of colours, multi-colours and reflective surfaces. The only really noticeable gap in the range appears to be common-or-garden brass. Generally speaking we find the duller and drabber colours and hues more suitable for clear water spinning; with black and gold, green and gold and brown figuring predominantly among our minnows.

The natural minnow was very popular with sea-trout spinners during the 1930s and 1940s. Many authorities preferred it to the artificial minnow, believing that its softer body resulted in a more positive take. Be that as it may, the natural minnow is little used today, although we know of two or three local exponents of the ancient art who still swear by it and go to great lengths to lay in a supply of freshly salted minnows each year. It is still possible to buy minnow mounts which incorporate a spinning vane and the associated treble hooks. These come in a range of sizes (either leaded or weightless) but it is equally productive to forgo the spinning vane and set the trebles to produce a curve in the body of the mounted minnow so that it wobbles (rather like a Toby) rather than spins. (The wobbled sprat is a particularly effective method of fishing a dead-bait for pike).

Light spinning on low water may be prohibited on many fisheries. Always check the local rules and regulations first. Where it is permitted, take advantage of the fact to enrich your experience and improve your repertoire of methods. By and large it pays to cover as much water as possible – a few casts here, a few casts there, move on. The most likely chance of success is when fresh fish are present, so do not neglect any pools in the vicinity of the tideway if they are available to you.

We discuss playing and landing sea trout in detail elsewhere (pages 181–245). It is necessary here that we mention striking a sea trout on the spinner. The spinner should, if fishing properly, be in direct contact with the lure at all times. This is more likely to be so when sea-trout spinning than when salmon spinning, as the sea-trout spinner will, more often than not, be working the lure by re-winding whereas the salmon spinner relies more on

Light spinning on small streams requires stealth, accurate casting and an understanding of where fish are to be found in low water conditions. (Photo: G.S. Harris.)

the current to swing the bait in an arc across the stream. Thus, the sea-trout spinner will be more likely to 'feel' the take of a sea trout *sooner* than the salmon spinner. This will be perceived as a sharp pull or as a quick pluck – depending on the size of the fish and/or the speed of its movement to the lure. Rarely do sea trout take, like salmon, with a long, solid, draw. Do not overreact. The lighter lines (4–8lb) used for most sea-trout spinning require no more than a smart raising of the rod in a steady backward sweep in order to set the hooks. Over-striking, too hard and too fast, is the bane of sea-trout spinning. Most fish move to the spinner so quickly that they hook themselves. Better a missed take than an instant break! In either event the result is the same. But the latter is more costly.

The highly pleasurable act of playing a sea trout is very different on a centre-pin fly reel (or a multiplier) when compared with a fixed-spool spinning reel. Every spinner, as a matter of crucial importance, should ensure that the clutch of the fixed-spool reel is carefully set *before fishing commences* so that line is given against the clutch at a pressure which does not cause the line to break on striking or playing a fish but which allows the strike, which is made against the clutch, to set the hooks firmly without giving line too freely. How many spinners forget this basic ritual only to lose their first fish of the day (perhaps the only fish of the day) either because the line breaks against a solid clutch or because the clutch gave line too readily and nullified the strike? We have done it ourselves, more than once.

A common mistake is to wind in against the clutch of a fixed-spool reel. DO NOT DO IT! Line is recovered by the process of 'pumping'. Lift the rod towards the vertical against the pull of the fish, then drop it smoothly to the horizontal and recover slack line. Repeat the process as necessary. Rewinding line against the clutch produces twist and causes the line to bed down into the underlying coils on the reel. Both of these create all sorts of problems with subsequent casting and can weaken a fine line.

8 · THE FLY BY DAY

There is a myth, which is still surprisingly popular, that sea trout cannot be caught in daylight. This is patent nonsense. What is true, though, is that sea trout are more difficult to catch in daylight when the river is flowing low and clear; and that the lower and clearer the river level the harder they are to catch!

Night fishing is a relatively recent branch of the sport. Maxwell, Mottram and Bridgett (our earliest authors) did all, or virtually all, of their sea trout fishing in daylight. It was not until the writings of Dawson and Bluett in the 1940s that night fishing became firmly established in the repertoire of standard techniques of sea-trout angling, and it is significant that both authors fished West Country rivers.

This geographical point is quite important. In most areas of the British Isles the main runs of sea trout occur in June and July, when the nights are at their shortest. The further north the shorter the night. In the very north of Scotland there may be very little darkness in high summer unless the sky is well clouded. If it has been clear and bright, the night may be little more than an extended twilight when dusk and dawn seem to merge. However, further south into Wales and the West Country the nights are both longer and darker. Even so it is not unusual for darkness to last for but two or three hours in late June and early July. We have both fished in the northern extremities of Scotland in mid-summer and recall times when it was possible to read the print of a newspaper at midnight when we would have been confidently fishing in comfortable darkness some 400 miles further to the south.

The crux of the matter is that the adult sea trout when in fresh water is the most sensitive, easily alarmed and panic-prone of all British game fish. This basic truth can be seen at a fish farm where the different species of salmonids are reared. Whereas the rainbow trout will move towards anyone approaching their rearing tank as if expecting to be fed, salmon and brown trout tend to stay put or move towards the rear of the tank. Sea-trout fry and parr, however, go wild and swim about frantically as if looking for somewhere to hide. This behaviour highlights the problem of daylight fishing and explains why almost every author has emphasised the need for stealth, caution and guile when approaching the river in daylight and the critical importance of doing nothing by way of clumsy movement and indelicate presentation of the lure

171

to frighten the fish.

Bridgett more or less says it all: 'One fact that the angler must firmly impress on his mind is that the sea trout is a shy timid fish, very easily alarmed, and after a short stay in fresh water its innate shyness becomes more and more developed until a capture is very difficult to make'. . . 'Not only is the sea trout extremely shy, but it takes up a position in the river which enables it to take very good care of itself, e.g. in the clear glassy glides at the tails of pools and along shallow edges almost devoid of current, in places. . .where it can lie in comfort, and which at the same time are within easy reach of deep water to which it can retire when alarmed'. . . 'The angler must take every precaution that his presence remains unknown, and he cannot over-estimate the powers possessed by sea trout to detect danger. Consequently, he should beware of walking on a high bank, or standing on exposed rocks, and he should always be quick to take advantage of any cover at hand, such as a background of trees or bushes.' 'He must keep out of sight of the fish by making use of his surroundings and by throwing a fairly long line. . .'

Bridgett adds that he has often made the statement that the sea trout is nocturnal in its feeding habits but now wonders if it is justified. It may be that it merely takes better under cover of darkness when its suspicions are less easily aroused. Therein lies the truth!

The approach to daylight fly fishing depends very much on the prevailing conditions of river level and water colour. These two factors are absolutely critical as they influence both the distribution of sea trout within the river and their response to the fly. Consequently, they determine how, where and when the fly is best fished.

Daylight fishing for sea trout can be practised with either the wet fly or the dry fly. But whereas dry fly fishing normally requires low river flows and clear water conditions to be effective, wet fly fishing can be practised over a far greater range of river flows. Therefore, our treatment of wet fly fishing is best divided into two sections covering high water conditions when the river is above normal summer levels and low water conditions when it is below normal summer levels.

The Wet Fly

High Water Fishing

The period immediately after a summer flood represents, for us, the most exhilarating and potentially most rewarding opportunity of taking sea trout on the fly. In some respects it is even more pleasurable than night fishing which, while frequently far more productive in terms of fish on the bank, lacks the visual appeal of daylight fishing.

The flood peak has passed, the river level is receding, the colour is rapidly fading as the river drops its load of silt, the sea trout are still widely distributed in the pools, glides and runs and, if the water level is high enough, they may still be running up river. In fact, provided the water is not too fast or too deep, almost every bit of fishable water may contain fish and be worth fishing.

There are big floods and little floods, clean floods and dirty floods, occasional floods and frequent floods. The most favourable conditions for daylight wet-fly fishing may prevail for but a few hours or they may persist for a day or two (or three) depending upon the nature of the river system, the height of the flood and the preceding weather conditions. No matter how long these conditions last, lucky is the angler who, by default or design, is on the river bank when the daylight wet fly becomes 'the method of the moment'.

'Perfect' conditions for daylight fishing with the wet fly on most rivers known to us would be following the first flood towards the end of July or in early August after a period of low water lasting (say) two weeks. In this preceding period the peak runs of sea trout have been steadily accumulating in the estuary and lower reaches of the river. The flood provides the 'trigger' which causes these fresh fish to pour up river in abundance and so provide possibly the most spectacular sport available to any fly fisherman.

By contrast, the worst conditions for sea-trout fishing in daylight are when the river experiences a prolonged drought lasting throughout the entire season, when even the sea trout find it physically impossible to penetrate the river for any distance above the tide, or when flood follows flood every few days throughout the season, so that the fish can run straight through the river, from estuary to tributary, with hardly a pause in the main fishing sections.

In our opinion, many anglers persist with heavy-water spinning (Chapter 7) for far too long as the water level begins to drop and clear after a flood. Time and time again we have seen the heavy-water fly angler walk into the river along a bank populated by spinners and wormers all fishing away without success and immediately take fish after fish. Why this should be we can but speculate. Perhaps the spinner has become too visible or is fishing too fast or too deep. It may be that sea trout are now occupying different positions in the river that can be covered more effectively and efficiently with the fly. Whatever the reason, it is evident that the fly can be fished suc-cessfully far sooner after a flood than most anglers seem to appreciate. Gray expresses a similar view, stating that provided the fly can be seen in coloured water at a depth of about 3 inches then it can be fished with every chance of success.

Most sea-trout rivers are relatively small. Long double-handed rods of 12 feet or more are rarely necessary: except perhaps on very heavy water or on some of the larger rivers such as the Tywi or Spey where a longer rod may prove advantageous in certain situations. We much prefer to fish with a single-handed rod of 10–11 feet in length whenever possible, and rarely find it necessary to resort to our double-handed salmon rods for sea trout.

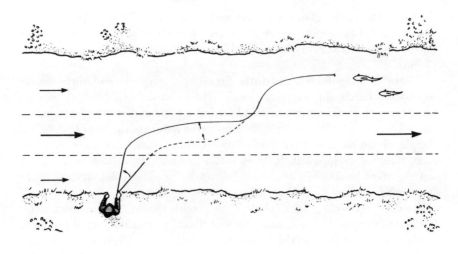

Figs. 46 & 47. Mending the line so that the fly fishes downstream without 'drag' caused by the current is an important feature of fishing the surface/subsurface fly on a floating line in daylight. Fig. 47 is an overstylised portrayal of the 'mend', which entails throwing the downstream 'bow' in the line caused by the current back upstream so that the fly fishes without drag. This is done by a carefully-timed rotation of the rod-tip from the shoulder. In practice one or more mends would have been made before the bow developed to the extent shown. Fig. 46 shows a more typical situation. Mending cannot be done after the line has sunk beneath the surface. However, when fishing the sunk line, a mend to adjust for the anticipated effects of the current may be thrown as the fly is cast (if you are very skilled) or immediately after delivery (if you are less skilled).

174

In order to achieve greater distance and, more importantly, to get the fly down to the right depth quickly when fishing very heavy water (when the river will be flowing faster and, depending on the nature of the banks, may be wider) we occasionally resort to a heavy, fast-sinking, line (a forward taper AFTM 9); but for lower water conditions a lighter (AFTM 7) line is to be preferred. The AFTM 7 is, it seems, the 'standard line' for sea-trout angling. It has many advantages in that it combines the ability to achieve adequate casting distances while being capable of handling the large lures often used for sea-trout fishing at night without loss of delicacy in presenting the smallest flies. Many anglers prefer to use a floating line as this can be picked up off the surface more readily when casting and can be 'mended' (see Figs 46 and 47) when necessary. Floating lines do, however have certain dis-advantages in that they cast a larger shadow, create surface disturbance, and may not allow the fly to sink to the required depth in a strong current. Thus, much of our fishing on high water is done with a slow to medium sinker or with a neutral density or sink-tip line *depending on* the depth of water being fished, the strength of the current, whether the surface is flat or broken, and the presence or absence of a bright sun. The floating line does, however, have its uses under certain conditions and is, of course, essential when fishing the dry fly.

In heavy water which may still contain some colour, and when it is likely that larger and heavier lures will be fished, a strong leader of 8–10lb strength is advisable. There is every chance under these conditions of connecting with a salmon or a very large sea trout, and since the thickness of the leader is not quite so critical at this stage of the receding flood, we would normally err on the side of safety.

Many authors stress that the sea trout is far more 'gut-shy' than the salmon and our own experience reinforces this view. We, like others, would stress the general principle of using the finest leader sensible for the prevailing conditions. Notwithstanding the fact that the 'strength' of the leader should be balanced with the size of fly used to achieve optimum casting distance and best presentation, we submit that it is not sensible to fish so fine that the leader is likely to break on the 'typical' sea trout which might reasonably be expected in the water being fished. Thus we would rarely go below 6lb strength on good water or below 4lb strength on low water unless we could expect to encounter only small fish of less than 2lb.

Once the colour of the flood disappears from the water, particular attention should be paid to the problem of 'flash' caused by the reflection of sunlight from the rod, line and leader. This becomes increasingly important as the river shrinks in size, and the angler must be increasingly aware of the need for greater stealth, camouflage and delicacy in presenting the fly to the fish. It is as important to avoid 'flash', particularly 'leader flash', when fishing clear, flat, water as it is to avoid a badly presented cast which splashes onto the water surface. For this reason we are careful to use nylon with a dull or matt finish and, generally, select a dark (black, green or brown) line in preference

175

to a pale (white, straw or peach) line. Nylon which is specially treated to absorb water and, thus, to sink has many advantages when fishing the wet fly on clear, flat water.

The length of leader depends on a number of factors. For most situations a length of about 9 feet is adequate for above-average water levels, but for low, clear, flows a longer leader of 12 feet (or more) may be necessary.

One, two or three flies can be used, but for heavy water two flies is sufficient. In a fast current it may be an advantage to have some weight in the fly to obtain depth. This can be achieved by using a large hook, a double hook, some lead in the dressing of the lure, or by using a Waddington shank. We do not like tube-flies for fast water as their bulk presents resistance to the current so that they tend to fish too near the surface. The Waddington shank has many advantages over the tube fly (see page 326) and is excellent on heavy water.

In high water still containing some colour we have found a good combination to be a single size 6 *Haslam* fished on a dropper with a *Tywi Peacock and Red* on a 1½-inch Waddington shank. Generally speaking, silver-bodied flies often prove very effective immediately after a flood and we have developed a liking for lures with 'Flashabou' or 'Lure Flash' incorporated into the dressing when fishing heavy water. Also effective after a flood where the current is not too fast are the *Marchog* lures. These have great hooking and holding characteristics and the Red, Blue and Yellow variants have all proved their worth under near flood conditions.

As the river level drops off, the wet-fly angler reverts from near-spinning to finer tackle and smaller flies. Perhaps the best fishing occurs in the range of flows between heavy to medium water. Under these conditions the pools, glides and runs will all hold fish and be worth fishing during the day and virtually and fly, or combination of flies, is likely to prove effective. Within this range of flows when the sea trout are still very receptive to the fly, many anglers will fish with a team of two or three flies but in smaller sizes (8–10). The slightly 'out-point' long shank treble is an excellent hooker and the *Twist Series* of double hackled flies was designed for daylight fishing under high to normal flows: the red, yellow, black and blue variants provide a basic range for use as point flies (sizes 8–12) with the Red twist being an excellent fly for the autumn. However, personal choice apart, any one of the modern or traditional sea-trout patterns, on a single, double or treble hook, may be used with equal effect. We discuss the choice of flies in some detail in Chapter 16 and it is sufficient here to deal with no more than some broad generalisations.

Several maxims have been devised which relate to the choice of fly and the method in which it is fished during daylight. 'A bright fly on a bright day and a dark fly on a dull day' is but one. We doubt if it makes much difference when the fish are fresh, and it has always seemed slightly illogical in terms of visibility to use a dull fly on a dull day. Surely a bright fly would be more obvious? Possibly the fly can be too visible to the fish at times. Another popular maxim is 'Bright flies for fresh fish, dull flies for stale fish'. Apart from asking somewhat flippantly. 'Who wants to catch stale fish anyway?', we neither agree nor disagree. We have caught fresh fish on dull flies and stale fish on bright flies. A black fly is always a good fly for sea trout by day and night irrespective of whether or not the fish are stale or fresh. The basis for this statement appears to be that fresh fish are more likely to respond to a silver, bright fly which is reminiscent of their food in the sea (e.g. herring fry), while staler fish become attuned to the duller, more camouflaged food found in, or on, freshwater. Are the animals on which the sea trout feed in the sea any duller or brighter than those which it takes in freshwater (herring fry apart)? Irrespective of the answer, what is the rule for a stale fish on a bright day?

Our views on flies are, in common with several authors, that style and size are more important than pattern. What is important also is *how* the fly is fished. In most circumstances this may be the single most important factor.

Prior to the development of the technique of greased line fishing for salmon by A. H. Wood of Cairnton and Glassel on the Aberdeenshire Dee in

Daylight fly fishing on heavy water. Many anglers would still be spinning or worming when the river is high and still slightly coloured as the flood recedes. This angler chose to fish the fly – wisely so, as seen by the bend in the rod. Fly fishing can be productive on heavy water, so do not wait for too long before commencing. (Wading can be dangerous in any river, especially on coloured water when you cannot see your feet. Take care at all times even when you know the section well.) (Photo: M.J. Morgan.)

the 1920s, the sunk line was essentially the standard method of fishing the wet fly. Certainly Bridgett fished with a sinking line, so too did Bluett, Cass and Stirling. Crossley, that arch-disciple of Wood, was among the first to advocate the floating (= greased) line for sea trout and the floating line grew in popularity during the 1940s and 1950s. Horsley was one of several authors of the period who advocated the floating line. Holiday, another floating line devotee from West Wales writing in 1960, makes the rather surprising statement that 'almost all fly fishing for sea trout is now done with the greased or floating line'. This was *not* so in Wales for the period covered by Holiday. Much sunkline fishing was still done and we note that Jock Scott, although he personally fished the floating line, stated that it was a 'non-standard' method. Currie, writing more recently about Scottish sea-trout angling, used both a floater and sinker and we suggest this is now perhaps the normal approach: a floater when appropriate, a sinker when necessary. Much depends on the water conditions and, of course, the disposition and reaction of the fish.

Another subject for debate is the depth and speed at which the fly or flies should be fished. Again, different authorities have different views and we suspect that all are 'right', depending on the nature of the river, the water conditions, the depth at which the fish are lying, their relative 'freshness' (and 101 other considerations). Holiday states, with that certain dogma, which we have come to respect (even if we usually disagree), that: 1) when warm and fine – fish shallow; 2) when cool and unsettled (some sunshine) – fish mid-water; 3) when cold and sunless – fish deep. If we combine this admonition with the general rules of 'bright day bright fly...' and 'stale fish dull fly...', we thus have 12 possible options! We make no comment other than to say that provided our fly is under (rather than in or on) the surface when fishing heavy to medium water we are happy. On lower flows the depth at which the fly is fished depends very much on the depth of the water and speed of current. With a slow sinking line in a medium current it is unlikely that a depth of much more than 12 inches will be attained before the cast is fished out. In a slow current (which may imply low water requiring a greater need for finesse) it is likely that a floating or slow sinking line will be used and, thus, that the fly will be close to the surface.

When fishing the conventional wet fly, the cast is made either across the current or across-and-down. The direction of the cast is important in that it controls the speed at which the fly moves relative to the current as it fishes down and then across the stream. It also influences the depth at which the fly is fished and the profile that the fly presents to the fish as they face upstream.

Crossley, Horsley and Holiday were all avowed greased-line anglers who fished on the basis that the fly should move downstream at the same speed as the current (or as Kingsmill Moore aptly states 'as if the fly is not attached to the line'). But in our experience sea trout (unlike salmon) generally respond better to a fly that moves fairly fast. The speed at which the fly moves de-

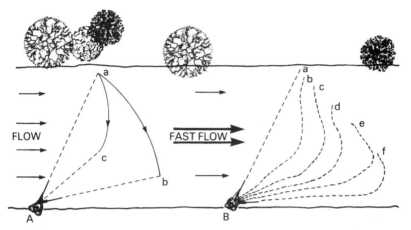

Fig. 48. The effect of the current on the speed and profile of the fly as it swings back across the stream is often of crucial importance in both day and night fishing. At position **A** the angler is casting across a current of uniform speed and the fly will swing round through the arc *a–b* at a contant rate. Recovering line will cause the fly to move through the arc *a–c* at a faster speed. At position **B**, which is a more typical situation, the angler is casting across a current which flows faster down the centre of the stream. The fly will now move through a characteristic S-shaped curve *a–f* and moreover its speed will increase progressively as it swings round from *a–e* before slowing down as it moves out of the main current at *f*. This problem (and it is a very real one) can be minimised by casting a longer line at a larger angle downstream or by throwing a 'mend' of line upstream (*see* Fig. 47).

pends on the speed of the current. A fly fished in a fast current will swing round faster than a fly fished in a slow current. This is to state the obvious. What is often less obvious, or, rather, what is often less understood, is that a fly which is cast at a smaller angle to the direction of the current will fish round slower (and tend to 'hang' longer over the fish) than one that is cast more directly across the stream.

In fast water it may be necessary to slow down the speed at which the fly moves, but in most situations it may prove more effective to increase the rate of movement of the fly rather than rely on the current and/or direction of the cast to work the fly at its most effective speed.

The rate of movement of the fly relative to the current can be reduced in several ways:

1. Casting the fly with an upstream 'mend'.
2. Throwing a 'mend' immediately the fly alights on the water surface.
3. Repeatedly 'mending line' as the fly fishes down (only possible with a floating line).
4. By moving downstream a pace or two (or three) with each cast before the fly begins to swing across the current.
5. By casting a long line at a 'smaller' angle to the current.
6. Working out additional line after casting by 'wiggling the rod' (a technique suggested by Holiday).

Increasing the speed of movement of the fly may be achieved by:

1. Throwing a downstream 'mend' on casting.
2. Employing the technique known to salmon anglers of 'backing-up'.
3. Recovering line as the fly fishes down and across.

By far the best way of increasing the speed of the fly is by recovering line – either by coiling or by the figure-of-eight retrieve. Not only does this allow the speed of the fly to be controlled more precisely but it also has the incidental but very important, advantage of maintaining the closest possible contact with the flies because any curve or bow in the line caused by the current is minimised. Close contact with the flies is important because it allows the take of a sea trout to be perceived (felt) sooner so that the strike can be made quicker than when the fly is fished on a slack line. We are firmly of the view that, as a general rule, sea trout should be struck immediately when river fishing. Not surprisingly, since they fished the greased-line method where the delayed strike is virtually a 'Commandment', Crossley, Horsley and Holiday disagree with this view. However, we take comfort in the fact that Bridgett (who has become our guide – if not our guru on the daylight wet-fly – and who did not fish the floating line) states quite un-equivocally that 'it is impossible to be too quick in responding to the take of a sea trout'. We fully agree and note that several other eminent authorities (who obviously play truant from the greased-line school) share our view : notably Kingsmill Moore.

The profile presented by the fly as it fishes down the current is thought to be important by several authors, all greased-liners. Horsely and Holiday felt that the line should be allowed to swing round with a belly in it so that the fly was presented 'broadside-on' to the fish. However, Crossley – the arch-proponent of greased-line fishing stated the exact opposite and stressed that the fly should fish round parallel to the current (i.e. tail-on). We think that the profile presented by the fish is important but that too much can be made of this point. Our belief that the fly should be worked as it swings round in fact implies an 'oblique' presentation; but this is a direct result of recovering line rather than from any deliberate attempt to present the fly with any particular profile.

Before moving on to discuss playing and landing fish, we would make a comment about overcasting. Why is it that many anglers are convinced that every fish always lies under the opposite bank? This may well be so under low water flows when the angler has contrived to approach the fish from the most distant point in order to avoid scaring them, but is frequently not so on medium to high river levels when the fish are often lying in the quieter water nearer to the sides or, if the current is not too fast, are distributed across the width of the river.

Time and time again we have seen anglers fishing perfect fly water on a river whose width has been increased by the high flows trying desperately to reach as far as possible towards the far bank. In order to attain their objective they felt obliged to cast directly across the current with the result that their flies fished round too fast and too high in the water. In most situations the proper approach was to fish a long line at a wide angle downstream so that the flies fished at the right depth and speed over the fish lying nearer to the angler. This would have meant that part of the width of the river on the far side was not covered by the cast, but it is surely far better to fish *half* of the river well than *all* of the river badly.

The take of a sea trout on the wet-fly is usually felt as a quick pluck or a short but firm pull. Rarely do sea trout take with a long steady draw like salmon, although some larger fish may take in a similar fashion.

Holiday stated that sea trout came across to the fly, rather than moving forward to intercept it, and believed that the fish should be given time to return to its lie before striking. He deliberately kept his rod tip held high ('at an angle of not less than 30° to the water') to provide slack line for the delayed strike advocated by all greased-liners. A fast-moving fly and a quick strike are, in our view, the best general policy for sea trout in daylight. Sea trout are indeed curious but they are also perceptive, capricious and shy and we think it a mistake to give them too much opportunity to study the fly. Thus our philosophy in presenting the fly is based on 'What was that?' as opposed to 'Look at this!'

The reference above to salmon brings us to an important point. The angler must decide from the outset whether sea trout or salmon are the quarry. The angler who tries to fish for both at the same time will not do well with either. There would seem to be four main reasons for this fact: 1) sea trout occupy different clear-water lies to salmon; 2) sea trout prefer smaller flies; 3) sea trout prefer a fast-moving fly; and 4) sea trout should be struck quickly.

Bridgett and others make this point quite firmly and it is widely noted that the angler who fishes for sea trout may catch salmon whereas the salmon angler is lucky to catch sea trout on clear water.

Playing a sea trout on heavy water – particularly a fresh-run fish of about 4lb weight or larger – requires nerves of steel and a major degree of good fortune. It is frequently possible to play a salmon more or less under the rod tip and, if necessary, to lead it to an area of quiet water where it can be played in safety. More often than not a sea trout will run wildly about the river in a wholly unpredictable fashion. If its first frantic rush takes it into the full force of a heavy current so that it gets downstream of the angler the ensuing scrap will not be easily won. Whenever possible contrive to keep below your fish.

Sea trout should be netted or beached. They should never be gaffed. Gaffing damages the fish. It may, arguably, be necessary for large salmon in some situations, but it is rarely, if ever, justified with sea trout. Neither should a tailer be used for landing sea trout. Apart from the fact that the thicker wrist of a sea trout results in the tailer applying a less than certain hold, sea trout come in smaller sizes than salmon and the tailer is of little use with fish under 4lb weight.

Whenever possible we prefer to beach our fish as an alternative to netting. While we invariably take a net to the river, just in case, there are many pools with nice gravel banks where the net becomes a superfluous encumbrance. However, there are times when a net is essential, such as in heavy water, when the banks are steep or when the wading angler does not wish to move onto the shore to land a fish.

There is a natural tendency, especially at night, to attempt to net a fish too soon! Don't! More decent sea trout are probably lost by premature attempts at netting, the fish going berserk at the sight of the net and making a frantic run when the line is at its shortest and when the angler is least able to respond...ping! Wait until the fish turns onto its side and allows itself to be swung round towards the bank. Move downstream of the fish and gently swing the fish into the net. Do not attempt to swing the net under the fish. The fish should move, the net should be static. If you are fishing with more than one fly, be careful not to get the spare flies tangled in the net before the fish is safely enmeshed. This is another cause of lost fish and another good reason for beaching fish whenever possible.

Beaching sea trout is relatively straightforward provided the bank slopes gradually into the river. Again, wait until the fish is properly played out and has turned onto its side. Then, from a position downstream of the fish, swing it round steadily until its head rests on the gravel. You now have two options – either to complete the full beaching operation or to tail the fish by hand. If the tension is held on the line the fish will start 'kicking' when it feels the gravel under its flank, but since its head is pointing up the bank its kicking will tend to move it progressively onto dry land. Alternatively, since fish cannot swim backwards, the tension on the line can be released. This results in the fish lying still (for a few seconds at least). Walk quickly to the fish, grasp it round the tail and, with a smooth movement, swing it smartly out of the water and walk up the bank away from the water. Sea trout can be tailed quite safely provided they are grasped with the thumb and index finger facing the tail (i.e. as if holding a beer glass). They can also be tailed with the hand in the prone position, with the thumb and index finger furthest from the tail, but the thicker wrist of the sea trout results in a weaker grip so that heavy fish tend to slip through the grasp.

Do not attempt to remove the hook from the fish until it has been dispatched by two or three sharp taps on the 'neck' with a suitable blunt object. Attempting to unhook a living fish is the quickest way to hooking yourself – especially when using treble hooks.

Before restarting to fish make a rigid discipline of checking the points of hooks, the alignment of the fly, the hang of any droppers, and the condition of the leader. Remove any wind knots. This takes only a few seconds and is worth the effort.

Tactics are very important in fishing the fly by day. In very heavy water when the current is flowing fast, it is perhaps best policy to fish the flatter water at the pool tails. The current is usually slower here than elsewhere and the pool tails rapidly become less fishable as the water level drops while the glides and runs remain fishable for longer. If sea trout are still running the pool tail is a good place to intercept fish, since they often pause for a while at the tail as they enter a pool. As the river level drops further, the pool tails may still be productive but the glides may provide better sport. Other than when fish are travelling, we usually leave the runs alone until the rest of the river becomes difficult to fish. We find that sea trout do not prefer fast broken water but, instead, seek quieter water whenever possible. The runs may well contain some sea trout during the day but the bulk of the fish are usually elsewhere. The attraction of runs on *low* water is that the broken surface provides cover for the approaching angler and, as a result, any sea trout lying therein may be more catchable.

It is often sensible to try and cover as much water as possible, especially in a wet summer when river levels have been consistently above normal and the sea trout are thinly spread out over the length of the river. Do not waste too much time casting a fly repeatedly over the same place. Try to work down a section of water by moving two or three paces between casts and be prepared to move from pool to pool, glide to glide and run to run as appropriate depending on the length of river available. The angler who roams widely when the sea trout are thin on the ground or, if plentiful, are otherwise unresponsive is usually more successful than the angler who stays put. It is better to go and find a taking fish rather than to wait for one to find you!

Low Water Fishing

The foregoing section dealt with wet-fly fishing in daylight under the most favourable conditions of high to normal river levels. We must now consider the worst conditions likely to be encountered as the river continues to fall below its normal summer level and a drought ensues. These are conditions of adversity. The pools have shrunk in size and depth and the runs have increased in length. The sky is invariably clear and bright, the sun is hot and the river seemingly lifeless. The sea trout long since stopped running up river in daylight and have become concentrated in their low-water lies.

Under such conditions the wet-fly angler faces the most difficult and testing fishing possible. But how sweet the success of rising to the challenge and taking a sea trout under 'impossible' conditions. In our view these are often the most memorable fish of the season.

The river must be approached with care and the sea trout fished with stealth and delicacy at all times on low water. Unless there is some form of breeze to ripple the water surface, fishing over the pool tails is virtually impracticable as the visible presence of the angler and the disturbance caused when casting invariably results in any fish lying in approachable positions bolting for cover into deep water or under the bank. In the absence of a breeze the best that can be hoped for is to fish down the broken water in the runs with a

On very low flows the daylight angler has very few opportunities for fly fishing. One option is to fish the fast water running into the neck of the pools and glides. The general rule is to fish fine-and-far-off and to fish small-and-fast with the wet fly. This is the run into the Fir Tree on the Dyfi on drought flows in the autumn of 1986. (Photo: G.S. Harris.)

team of two or three small flies (size 10–14) on a fine (4lb strength) leader and a floating, intermediate, or sink tip line. It may also be possible to make a few casts at the heads of the pools where the fast current may provide some limited cover. Otherwise, conventional wet-fly fishing employing the down-and-across cast is a waste of time except perhaps for an hour or so at dusk or dawn when the twilight may afford sufficient cover to allow the glides to be fished with some chance of a fish or two.

A breeze makes the world of difference on low water, especially if it blows

Midsummer idyll on the Teifi. The river is at normal level and the angler is fishing a team of three small wet-flies over a narrow gut of water under the far bank. The current is sufficient to swing the flies round as the section is fished quietly down into the pool to the left of the shot. (Photo: M.J. Morgan.)

upstream. It ripples the surface of the pools and the glides and provides some cover for the angler who can now at least approach the river with some chance of success. When an upstream breeze occurs, the wet-fly may be fished either downstream in the conventional way or it may be fished upstream. The upstream wet-fly is tantamount to dry-fly fishing except that a team of two or three flies is used. These are fished in or just beneath the surface using a floating line which is recovered either at the same speed or slightly faster than the current as they drift downstream. In practice, it is rarely possible or sensible to fish directly upstream-and-back. To do so would put the angler in a position where he was walking up river among the fish and casting a line over their backs: both of which would cause any fish in the vicinity to shoot upstream, disturbing the remainder of the shoal, and so ruin any prospect of success. Consequently, it is more likely that a cast made upstream-and – across would be employed so that the line was less likely to travel over the fish.

Having had two of the worst drought years on record in Wales in the last decades (1976 and 1984) we have had some experience of applying ingenuity to overcoming the problems of fishing dead-low water by day, as did many others. We can vouch that, provided there is a breeze to ripple the surface, the upstream wet-fly *can* produce results. Surprisingly, we have found that it was the fish lying not in the shallows at the tail of the pool, but those in deeper water (often the larger fish) that responded best to a team of small flies worked back slightly faster than the current. Interestingly, the sea trout usually allowed the fly to pass overhead before moving up from the bottom

185

and taking it from *behind*. Rarely did they move *forward* to take the fly in front of their lie. Most rises were deliberate and positive, the fish swinging up and round to break the surface with a characteristic 'swirl' as it returned to its lie. All that was required was to tighten as the line stopped or began to move away.

Several authors have discussed the question of drag when fishing the wet fly. Bridgett noted that sea trout did not like a wet fly to be fished too near the surface (he advocated pushing the rod tip below the water to prevent this happening as the fly swung round!). However, he suggested that sea trout sometimes responded better to a dry fly that dragged a little (as did Mottram). Holiday was another who abhorred any drag on the wet fly, yet Mclaren advocated working the flies loch-style with a bob-fly deliberately drawn across the surface to create a disturbance.

The wake fly technique – popularised in the 1930s and 1940s by Bluett and Dawson and rediscovered more recently by Falkus – is now a standard method of fishing for sea trout at night on rivers (Chapter 9) and by day on lakes (Chapter 13). Why it should be avoided by day on rivers escapes us. Provided the surface is not flat calm and the fly (and only the fly) breaks the surface to create drag, we have found that it may at times induce a take when all else fails. (See also page 195.)

Conventional wet-fly fishing in the downstream-and-across style can of course be practised where the water surface is broken or rippled by a breeze. The angler will be upstream of the fish and, therefore, potentially more visible than the angler fishing up and across from behind the fish. The rule for downstream fishing on clear and bright conditions should be, therefore, 'fine-and-far-off'. The advantage of the downstream style is that there is less risk of scaring fish by covering them with the line since the fly and leader *should* cover the fish before the line, a 12–15 foot leader being appropriate on dead low water under certain conditions.

It also allows the larger sea trout that usually lie at the front of the shoal to be picked off first and, on the assumption that any hooked fish will tend to run upstream away from the rest of the shoal so that they can be played without disturbing their companions, enables the shoal to be covered repeatedly without undue disturbance. (That is the theory! The practice is often very different with the fish running downstream to scatter the rest of the shoal and ruin any chance of taking another fish.) The practical disadvantage of the downstream approach is, apart from the angler being more visible to the fish, that the river bed often becomes covered in silt and algae after a period of sustained drought so that any angler attempting to work the river *above* the fish may send a cloud of filth down river onto those that are shortly to be the subject of later attention.

The approach to upstream fishing with the wet-fly can take various forms depending upon the topography of the section of water being fished. Fish lying in the tail of a pool can be approached from directly below with the angler standing in the run and casting in a fan-pattern into the pool tail;

Daylight wet-fly fishing. A team of three small flies is fished down-and-across the current and worked back quickly before stepping down a couple of paces and recasting. On low water such as this a good breeze is essential to ripple the surface and conceal the angler. The conditions here are perfect for the dry-fly! (Photo: M.J. Morgan.)

187

normally, however, the angler will work carefully up the section from below casting across-and-up. This allows the fish to be approached from behind, *but* any overcasting which results in the line crossing the fish *must* be avoided if the fish are not to be scared.

When fishing upstream over sea trout in a long glide in low, clear water, it is sometimes sensible to adopt a leap-frog approach by fishing the section in a series of blocks as opposed to working steadily up river. This tactic overcomes the problem of the angler's presence 'pushing' the fish progressively upstream to disturb the remainder of the shoal. The problem may still occur, but its effect is localised within each block as the angler then moves ahead of any disturbed fish to cover the next block of fish (see Fig. 45).

Another technique of taking sea trout under very low water conditions is by 'hanging' a fly or team of flies in the current. In certain situations it is sometimes possible to work a fly down a run and then into the quieter water at the neck of a pool by standing well upstream and merely holding the fly 'on the hang' in the current. By working the rod across the body from one side to the other it is possible to work the fly across the stream. By stepping downstream a yard or so and repeating the process every so often it is possible to work the fly over the fish very effectively without risk of disturbance, provided a long line is used.

There is a popular myth that sea trout cannot be caught in daylight on rivers. Utter nonsense! This is one of four fish averaging 2½lb taken on low water in an hour one bright August afternoon on a size 12 Silver Stoat's Tail. All were caught under 'impossible conditions' by hanging a fly in the faster water at the neck of the pool. Each fish took in a deepish gully on the right of the angler (who has sensibly led his fish well downstream) under the white stick on the far bank. (The pool is the famous 'Fridd' on the lower Dyfi—alas now a shadow of its former self as a result of gravel movement occasioned by land drainage and forestry which have changed the pattern of flood flows.) (Photo: G.S. Harris.)

It is boring work but produces results under adverse conditions and may produce a surprise salmon or two. Much depends on the nature of the run into the neck of the pool. In some situations the topography of the river is such that the technique cannot be employed. In other situations, using a very long line of 20–25 yards, the fly can be fished down virtually the entire length of a short pool provided the current is adequate.

The line can be a floater, intermediate or sinker depending on the speed of the current and, since the water surface will be broken by the current to some extent, the leader may be somewhat stronger than might otherwise be used by water conditions. The fly should be small and, since the fish will be taking on the hang, treble hooks are a distinct advantage (although we have successfully used singles and doubles also). [The *Silver Stoat's Tail* (size 12 treble outpoint) produced four fish of 3–5lb on the hang for one of us in bright sun one July afternoon during the 1976 drought.] During the 1984 drought the same technique on a different river produced three fish of 2½–7lbs at teatime in bright sun during mid-August on a size 14 *Moonbeam*.

Hanging is boring. It is not a technique to employ all day but is just one of a range of techniques within the angler's repertoire to be used when special conditions prevail.

Another technique for providing sport under adverse conditions is to strip a fairly large lure very fast over the heads of the sea trout lying in the deep water of the pools and glides. This technique of inducing sea trout to move to the surface fly from deep water has the particular appeal that the fish is often seen as it sweeps up from deep water and moves to intercept the fly. It works best when there is some breeze to ripple the surface and is most effective when fresh fish are present. The lure – a small streamer fly or a 2 inch *Marchog* with a small flying treble – is cast over the deeper water of the pool or glide and then stripped back by recovering line so that it moves just beneath the surface. The 'strip' must be very fast, so fast that the figure-of-eight retrieve is too slow and coiling or dropping the line is necessary. The direction of the cast relative to the current is not important and it often pays to cover the water by fan-casting.

The sea trout, attracted by the overhead disturbance, swing up from the depths of the pool on an interception course to meet the fly. They can often be seen quite clearly and the secret of success is to keep the fly moving whenever a fish follows, preferably speeding up its movement. Whatever you do, *do not* slow down the retrieve when a fish starts to follow the lure. Occasionally a fish will take with a great surging rush, often creating a boil on the surface. On seeing, or feeling, the take, tighten! Do not strike as such; but do not delay in tightening the line either. Usually the fish will have moved to the fast-moving fly at such speed that it has probably hooked itself anyway and, since a tight leader of 4lb strength line would have been used, probably on a floating or an intermediate line, any over-reaction in striking may lead to being broken.

Sea trout will move to a fly worked fast across the surface on drought conditions in a lake from depths of up to 10 feet or more during daylight. They will also do the same in a river at night. There is no reason why they should not do so in a river during daylight *provided* they are not disturbed, deterred or distracted in any way.

Those anglers fortunate enough to fish waters which include a section where the river rises and falls with each tide are to be envied in drought conditions: especially if the tidal section is more than just one or two pools. The Dyfi is a classic example of river where the tidal section extends for 3 or 4 miles before the estuary proper is reached, and within which are several excellent pools and runs at low-tide. Sea trout are not dependent on a flood to initiate a run into the river. A flood helps, but in its absence a large proportion of sea trout will push on through the estuary with each tide and remain in the lower reaches when the tide recedes. 'Fishing the tide' can be productive even on the lowest of river flows.

There is a view that sea trout respond to the tidal-cycle even when well upstream. Having spent some time in the sea, it is not improbable that they have an in-built time-clock closely linked to the rise and fall of the tide. Many anglers believe that sea trout in the lower reaches of rivers (i.e. the fresher fish) come on to the take for a while either side of the top-of-the-tide. The hour before the tide and the hour after the tide are widely held to be good taking times.

Fishing the tide relies on three key factors: 1) using the ebb to provide the otherwise absent conditions of depth and current necessary to conceal the angler and work the flies effectively; 2) the presence of fresh fish which moved in with *that* tide or other recent tides; and 3) the greater susceptibility of fresh fish to the fly.

The technique is rather one of logistics than style. The tackle is similar to that used for other forms of low-water wet-fly fishing: a light rod, floating or intermediate line, a glint-free leader of about 4lb strength and a team of two or three (we prefer three) flies of whatever pattern but in small sizes (normally 12, occasionally 10 or 14, and singles, doubles or trebles according to preference). Casting is normally downstream-and-across, and the critical factor is co-ordinating the precise time when a particular pool, run or glide is fished relative to the ebb of the tide and, thus, in the logistics of moving downstream from section to section as the tide recedes. It is possible to fish down behind the tide too soon or too late. Only experience will tell you if you have judged your movements correctly.

Fishing the tide may result in no more than an hour or two of good fishing; much depends on the height of a particular tide and the length of the tidal section. However, during the peak of the normal run, it would not be unusual (say) to move 40 fish, prick 10, play five and to land, if you are lucky perhaps one or two! It may not be productive fishing, but it is certainly exciting and very challenging.

Finally, a few words about whitling. There is nothing more likely to test the skill and patience of the angler than the speed with which a fresh-run whitling can move to the wet fly. This can be so fast that it give new meaning to the word 'quicksilver'. It is not unusual to fish over a shoal of fresh-run whitling and move, literally, 30 or 40 fish in as many minutes, but to connect with only one or two.

Almost every cast produces a rise but, no matter how fast the strike, frustration mounts as fish after fish is missed. This is sea-trout fishing at its most challenging as there seems to be no standard solution to the problem. Changing to a dry fly sometimes works; so too does fishing a darker or brighter fly, or fishing the flies as fast as possible. Changing the angle of the cast sometimes increases the proportion of takes that are struck successfully, either by fishing upstream, downstream or across or, if possible, fishing from the opposite bank.

All we can recommend is that the angler tries every trick in the book until some permutation of style, pattern, size and speed of movement produces a satisfactory increase in success. But bear in mind that what proved successful yesterday may not work today. There is no fish more capricious than sea trout and small whitling are no exception even if, as many authors believe, they are more likely to take food in freshwater than their larger brethren (see Chapter 1).

Whitling seem to prefer the shallower water at the tail of pools, but they will often lie in the runs if the current is not too fast. It is probable that a large proportion of the whitling that enter the tideway and the lower reaches of the river are not destined to spawn that year. These are fish which were actively feeding in the sea close to the river mouth and which were drawn prematurely into the river, perhaps by high tides or the last flood and which in the absence of any urge to spawn may return to the sea within a few days or weeks. Their sojourn in fresh water is, therefore, more a result of accident than design, and many may continue actively 'feeding' in the normal sense of the word.

The best sport with whitling is when large shoals lie the runs and open water at the tails of the pools where, even on very low flow conditions, there is usually sufficient current to swing the flies down and then across the stream. Casting down and across is easier than casting up and across as the line does not need to be recovered quite so fast in order to work the flies at the right speed. Nevertheless in some situations the upstream cast can be equally effective and it may be essential if there is a fresh upstream breeze.

When an upstream breeze does occur do not neglect the dry fly. A low river, a bright sky and an upstream breeze, when combined with the presence of large shoals of fresh whitling, provide idyllic conditions under which to practise.

The Dry Fly

Brennand states: 'If you can devise a method or find a place where sea trout do genuinely take a floating fly then you have discovered what is probably the most delightful form of fishing'. Both Chrystal and Falkus admit to being singularly unsuccessful with the dry fly such that they dropped it as a method from their repertoires, and Brennard even admits to a notable lack of success with the dry fly.

Jock Scott never fished the dry fly for sea trout (if we read him correctly) and Bridgett, Bluett, Cass, Kingsmill Moore and Holiday all refer to the dry fly in some detail but with only mild to moderate enthusiasm. Thus it is only Mottram and Dawson who extol the relative merits of the dry fly. This they fished successfully by day and by night. It is interesting to note that Mottram occasionally fished *two* dry flies on the same leader.

Whether or not you choose to fish the dry fly depends very much on your personal preferences, the type of river being fished and the weather and water conditions encountered. Some rivers are more suitable for the dry fly by virtue of their flow regimes and topography. Rivers where dead flat, slow-moving pools represent the greater proportion of holding water under low-flow conditions do not, in our view, provide good dry fly fishing. The dry fly appears to do quite well on some rivers in Scotland and the south-west of England, where it has a small number of devotees, but it is by no means a popular or widely practised technique.

A floating line is, of course, essential for dry-fly fishing. Although some anglers prefer a somewhat stiffer action in the rod when fishing the dry fly, the same rod used for normal wet-fly fishing will normally suffice for most purposes. Long-distance casting may, at times, be necessary, but precision in presenting the fly is not required since the fly will seldom be presented to a rising (and feeding) fish. The dry-fly angler will be fishing-the-stream trying to induce a rise; so pinpoint accuracy is not essential. What is essential, bearing in mind the conditions under which the angler has resorted to the dry fly, is stealth, concealment and the utmost delicacy in setting the line on the water.

In the absence of a breeze to ripple the surface of the water, dry-fly fishing will generally be restricted to the runs between the pools and the faster water entering the heads of the pools where the broken water provides some concealment for the angler. In our experience the runs are not usually the most popular lies for the sea trout but any sea trout residing in these locations may be more catchable because of the cover provided by the faster-flowing current. A good breeze which ripples the surface of the pools and glides, wherein most sea trout prefer to lie, is a distinct advantage when fishing the dry fly as it opens up more water and, thence, greater opportunities.

Classic style dry-fly fishing in the mode of the English chalk streams (once the HQ of angling purism) requires the fly to be cast more or less directly upstream to the rising brown trout. This approach is often not practicable for sea trout because, unlike the single 'territorial' brown trout, sea trout are usually aggregated together in loose shoals and do not become so 'preoccupied' with feeding. Thus, any angler who attempts to wade directly upstream when sea-trout fishing will be walking among the fish, so destroying any

The dry-fly on low water on the Afon Teifi. Two in the bag and patiently awaiting some breeze to ripple the surface of the gin-clear water. Stealth and concealment are of paramount importance under such testing conditions. (Photo: M.J. Morgan.)

prospect of success. Thus the direction of the cast will usually be up-and-across or down-and-across or sometimes across.

When fishing the broken water of the fast-flowing runs the direction of the cast is usually down-and-across or across. In fast water it may be necessary to 'mend' the line upstream once or twice as the fly fishes down to prevent too much belly forming in the line which causes the fly to swing across the current causing drag which drowns and waterlogs the fly causing it to fish wet rather than dry. The rod should be swung round to follow the down-stream passage of the fly, and as the fly starts to swing across the current it should be cast to a new position slightly downstream of the last, the angler moving a pace or two downstream so that the casting distance remains more or less constant.

When fishing long runs and glides with a moderate current where the fly drifts downstream at a manageable speed it is often possible to fish the water from the bottom to the top by casting up-and-across. This approach has the advantage that it allows the same section of water to be fishing *up* with the dry fly and then *down* with the wet fly. When fishing both dry and wet fly

193

over the same section of river it is good practice to fish the upstream dry fly before the downstream wet fly as the latter causes more disturbance.

The physical approach to fishing pool tails and glides with the dry fly depends very much on the local topography of the river and the presence and direction of any wind. Breeze is helpful as it ripples the surface and makes the angler less visible to the fish; but it is virtually impossible to fish the dry fly into a wind. Thus, in the absence of a wind the flat water of pool tails and glides is best fished from downstream casting up-and-across and recovering line as the fly drifts down. In this way the angler is less visible to the upstream-facing fish. The fish may, of course, be approached by working downstream but a far longer cast is necessary if the fish are not to be scared by the approaching angler and long-distance casting imposes certain penalties in terms of miscasting and, thus, disturbance. Never try to cast more than your natural, comfortable, distance, when fishing flat-calm water.

The downstream-and-across approach to fishing pools and glides is much facilitated by a downstream breeze, *but* a downstream breeze is often not a good breeze. Most sea-trout rivers flow to the south or west and a downstream breeze must come from the north or east, and such winds are often not propitious winds for river sea trout. Far better an upstream wind from the south or the west and such winds favour an upstream approach.

One question which looms large in the literature on dry-fly fishing is whether or not 'drag' is to be avoided. It is anathema to brown-trout anglers, but it is interesting to note how opinion differs among sea-trout anglers and

Stealth, concealment, a delicate presentation, and (above all) perseverance, are the four main attributes of the low-water, dry-fly angler. Fine-and-far-off at the tail of Lynn Morgan ('Dirty Ditch', not a literal translation) on the lower Afon Dyfi. Paul Burgess attempts (unsuccessfully) one of a 'mass of fish' to rise to the (subsurface) wet-fly (see p. 195). (Photo: G.S. Harris.)

A 4lb sea trout taken in bright sun on low flows by the first author some 15 minutes after taking the preceding photograph. (Photo: G.S. Harris.)

how dry-fly fishing may grade into wet-fly fishing. Mottram, who must be regarded as the arch-proponent of the dry fly for sea trout, first suggested that drag caused by the fly swinging across the current could sometimes stimulate a rise when the conventional approach failed. McLaren advocates working a team of flies so that the bob-fly is dragged at a right-angle across the surface in the same manner so successful for brown and sea trout on stillwater (*see* Part III).

To encourage or avoid drag? The surface and subsurface fly are both very effective at times when fishing lakes by day and rivers at night. Why should sea trout in rivers respond any differently in daylight provided that they have not been scared? Our combined experience on many different waters is that the worked fly, either dry or wet, is more effective by day and night than one that drifts passively with the current. Thus we believe that drag is frequently a good thing and only to be avoided in so far as it creates problems in causing the fly to become waterlogged. In this respect our views are perhaps more flexible than those of our predecessors because modern floatants are so very much superior than those of yore.

We have so far avoided any mention of dry-fly patterns for sea trout. The reason is that there are none that are peculiar to sea trout! Most authors used smallish brown-trout flies. Mottram suggested sized 14–17 unless the fish were taking well, in which event a larger fly up to size 8 may be tried. He named two patterns for daylight fishing – the *Black Variant* and the *Red Gnat*. Cass relied on the *Rusty Brown* and *March Brown*, while Bridgett ex-

195

pressed faith in the *Red Quill* and *Black Spider*. Dawson also expresses faith in the *Red Quill* and recommends too the *Coch-y-bondu* with a silver body, *Wickham* 'or anything else the individual angler may fancy'. Well, six times out of ten we fancy the dry *Moonbeam* and, for the remaining four times the *Dunnock*. Both are excellent flies by day and night when fished either wet or dry: on rivers or lakes. For daylight fishing with the dry fly we usually use sizes 10–16 depending on water and weather conditions. Both patterns contain a hint of yellow fluorescence: which improves our confidence (and may even improve their appeal to the sea trout).

We have previously stressed the paramount importance of delicacy and finesse when fishing the wet-fly under low water conditions. This applies equally, if not more so, when fishing the dry fly. This accepted, it follows that great care must be exercised when casting so as to create the minimum disturbance of the water surface. Accuracy is not important but the ability to judge distance so that the line is not cast over the fish is a skill to be acquired. The leader, which should be as long as the angler can handle comfortably under the prevailing conditions, should be at least 9 feet long. Often a leader of 12 to 15 feet is required under conditions of bright sun and little or no breeze. The leader should be the finest 'flash-free' nylon possible. For most purposes we would fish with a leader of 4lb strength nylon and only go as fine as 2½lb strength under the most testing conditions or when fishing for whitling.

The rise of a sea trout to the dry fly is fairly characteristic. Some fish appear to move forward to intercept the fly as it drifts downstream but the general form is that most fish do not turn to the fly until it has passed overhead. The strike should be delayed *momentarily* to allow the fish to turn down and away from the angler. By this we mean that when a rising fish breaks the surface as it moves to the dry fly, the angler should anticipate the movement of the fish and delay the strike accordingly. Not all fish rise in the same way, and not all anglers react at the same speed. Some takes are quite leisurely, others are like greased-lightning. The term *delay* tends to over-emphasize the length of time implied before striking the rise. By delay we are really referring to a momentary hesitation of maybe a second, or even a fraction of a second, dependent upon the speed at which the fish moved to the fly. In the faster water of the runs the take is often very quick indeed and an instantaneous strike is usually the best policy.

The strike should not be too violent as this may result in the fine leader being broken. A quick tightening of the line against the weight of the fish is usually sufficient to set the hook.

Since dry-fly fishing will usually be practised under low flow conditions when the sky is usually bright and clear, the good tactician will choose carefully where and when to fish in relation to the sun's position and the presence or absence of any cloud cover and also the speed and direction of any breeze.

Mottram sometimes fished two dry flies on the same cast. One or two anglers on the Teifi fish a dry fly and wet fly on the same cast. The dry fly is fished on the point (as is normal) and a small wet fly is fished on a dropper. The basic rationale is that it gives the angler the double advantage of fishing the wet and dry fly simultaneously. Fish may be attracted to either; and if they miss the one they may take the other. (See also Dapping – Chapter 14.)

The dry fly has long been a standard technique for salmon fishing in North America. Elsewhere it is the exception rather than the norm. It would be a pleasure to see it become established as a standard method for sea trout. We doubt that this will ever be so, but the dry fly will always have a few devotees to keep the method alive, and, perhaps, pioneer some advances.

9 · NIGHT FISHING: ANTICIPATION

We come now to what is for us the most exciting and generally the most productive form of sea-trout angling – fishing the fly during the hours of darkness.

By far the greatest proportion of sea trout taken by anglers on Welsh and English rivers are caught at night. On some fisheries where bait fishing and spinning are either prohibited or carefully controlled, the proportion of sea trout taken on the fly during darkness may be as high as 75 per cent (or more) of the total catch. Furthermore, the average weight of sea trout caught at night is frequently larger than for daylight fishing and, in our experience, night fishing consistently produces more specimen fish than daylight fishing. Although we fish the fly, spinner and bait during daylight in accordance with river conditions (and the local fishery regulations) it is a fact that all our double-figure sea trout have been taken on the night fly.

It is interesting to note that night fishing is generally more popular with authors from South of the Border. It is really only Currie among that impressive band of Scottish writers who discusses night fishing with any great enthusiasm and in any useful detail. At this point we should explain that when we refer to night fishing we are speaking of fishing through into the true night and not just limiting our artivities to the hour or so after dusk nor during a northern summer night when as Maxwell describes '. . . twilight, long lingering, almost joins hands with dawn'.

Night fishing is something that you either like or dislike. Some people have a well-developed fear of the dark and never, no matter how much they try, feel comfortable alone on the river bank miles from anywhere (and possibly anyone). Falkus analyses the fear of darkness experienced by many erstwhile night fishermen: 'Things do go bump in the night! There are squeaks and grunts and screeches and gurgles and rustles and plops. Stones rattle, shingle slides, bushes move and swish, eyes gleam, ripples spread across the water from unseen swimmers; a fox screams from the fellside; a deer barks; owls hoot from the shadowy woods. The creatures of the night are stirring: badger, otter, hedgehog, stoat, weasel, rat, feral mink, nightjar; all of them at some time or another will share the waterside with us. But to the novice who comes unprepared into this elemental and seemingly hostile jungle of the dark, these animals are strangers, the sound they make he does not understand – and what man does not understand he fears.' Those who cannot come to terms with the noises of the dark will never experience the true delights of night fishing.

There are still many misconceptions about night fishing. It has been described variously as 'like fishing with a bloody bucket over your head'; 'blundering about the river bank in the dark'; 'more a business of catching fish than pleasant sport'; 'a chuck-and-chance it business'; 'the opportunity of the novice and incompetent'. All this is nonsense, and misinformed nonsense at that!

There are indeed problems and pitfalls in night fishing; and it would be wrong to understate them. However, night fishing is not 'easy' 'unsporting' or a business of 'chuck-and-chance'. The only practical advantages enjoyed by the night fisherman are that the 'cover-of-darkness' enables the angler to approach within reasonable casting distance of the fish without scaring them and that, under normal conditions, the fish are more active during darkness. Everything else depends just as much on stealth, persistence and skill as when daylight fishing. Night fishing is certainly not for the novice, the incompetent nor the bungler. Anyone who bungles about the riverbank in darkness will: a) become very unpopular with other anglers; b) not catch fish; and c) more than likely break a leg or a rod.

Both Holiday and Falkus stress the importance of the correct mental approach to successful night fishing. Night fishing is just as much a matter of careful planning and preparation as it is of knowing the water being fished, understanding how the fish behave at night, and mastering the various methods and techniques of presenting the fly under a range of different river and weather conditions.

Holiday points out, rightly, that 'the angler will have to learn how to cast all over again'. The *visual* clues available to the daylight angler relating to the accuracy, distance and finesse of casting are not available to the night fisherman, who must, instead, learn to cast with a sense of rhythm coupled with instinct and intuition. Holiday notes that while the daylight angler may not *consciously* study the action of the line when casting, subconscious or 'fringe-of-field' vision is used to regulate and adjust the lift-off, back-cast, and forward delivery and then to modify the angle, distance, and presentation of the line. All this is denied to the night fisherman who must operate with a heightened sense of touch modified at times by the sense of hearing. The 'swish' of the line as it travels through the air is often an important clue when casting at night.

It is surprising how much it is possible to see at night ever when it is pitch-black. On all but the blackest nights it is usually possible to see your way dimly along the bank and to pick out landmarks which enable you to locate your position on the river. On clear nights with some moonlight it is often possible to see the line as it makes contact with the water surface and, also, to see the 'boil' of a taking fish as it moves to the surface or subsurface fly. On certain nights with clear sky and a full moon it is even possible to make up a new leader and retie a fly without the use of a torch. Night vision can be quickly destroyed by artificial light and it takes time to recover. A cardinal rule when night fishing is to keep the use of your torch to the absolute minimum. Use it only if you have to replace a leader or fly: or when you pack-up. *Never* shine it on the water when getting into position or playing or landing a fish, and *never* shine it directly into your eyes or anyone else's. It is good practice to have two torches. One should be fairly powerful and used for walking back along the bank after packing up, and the other should give only sufficient light to allow you to change a fly or undo a tangle while actually fishing.

There are several torches manufactured especially for night fishermen. Many have angled heads in flexible fibre-optic lenses that project out of a breast pocket or clip onto a belt or jacket lapel. These make lovely gifts from knowing relatives, but the best torch for night fishing is one that can be hung from a piece of old fly line around the neck and which is small enough to be held in the teeth when required for use.

A final point about vision at night is that things always seems a lot nearer than they really are. There is a natural tendency to cast short at night for fear of getting caught up on the far bank. While overcasting can be costly in terms of lost tackle, fishing time and patience, undercasting can be costly also in terms of fruitless effort spent fishing the unproductive water that is usually closest to the angler. It the fish lie under the far bank at night then you must cast to the far bank. You may lose some tackle until you become familiar with the section of water but you will ultimately catch more fish than by playing safe and casting short.

Almost every book on sea-trout fishing makes some statement about the best weather conditions for night fishing. But the most important thing about sea-trout fishing is *first* that there should be fish present in the water to be fished, and *second* that the river level should be suitable for night fishing. It matters not that weather and water are perfect if the fish are absent. It matters not that the fish are present and the weather perfect if the river is too high, or too low. Of course there are weather conditions that are more propitious than others for sea-trout fishing, but nights when everything is perfect are few and far between, and the successful sea-trout angler is the one who can catch fish when conditions are far from perfect.

We have caught fish at night in high clear water and in drought, in thunder and lightning, in a howling gale and with winds blowing from all points of the compass. We have caught sea trout under a brilliant full moon and in stygian darkness, in autumn frost and in swirling mists. Provided that you are prepared to persevere and, more important still, to adopt the method most appropriate to overcome the effects of adverse weather conditions then you will frequently achieve at least some measure of success.

It is interesting to note how different authors disagree on what constitutes the ideal conditions for night fishing. Whereas Dawson liked a moon 'the brighter the better', Gammon preferred the night to be as dark as possible, while Bluett stated 'I do not like a very black night'. To some extent the preference for a dark night or a bright night depends upon the style of fishing to be employed. The deep sunk lure seems to be more effective on a really dark night and Falkus states that the surface or wake lure fishes best under similar conditions (although we do not fully agree). However, sea trout appear to respond better to the dry-fly and to the conventional wet-fly if there is some light – perhaps because they can see it better – and these methods are certainly easier to employ effectively when it is possible to 'see' something of what you are doing.

We neither like nor dislike a bright night (we just change our tactics and our targets). However, in broad terms, our preference is for a warm night when any moon is decently veiled by high cloud. All authors agree that a mist that comes off the land, as opposed to one that comes off the water, is inimical to success. Some say that it is fatal, but that is going too far. It is not fatal – we have taken some fairly respectable bags of fish in a swirling, thick, white mist on a large, *deeply sunk*, lure fished very slowly. We would, however, agree that fishing the *surface or subsurface fly* in a persistent mist is usually fruitless because the fish seem to 'go down' as soon as the air temperature drops and the first curling fingers of mist creep along the river to slowly envelop the pool.

The mention of temperature brings us to another planning point. A summer night on a river (or lake) will rarely be as warm as you think, especially if there is a clear sky. A clear night sky usually means a rapid drop in temperature, and this can be quite marked if it has been ideal weather for the beach during the day. Although it may be possible on some nights to fish past midnight in shirt sleeves, such occasions are the exception rather than the rule. Being wet is one thing, being cold is another. The most miserable experience is being both wet and cold. Always remember to take a waterproof and a warm sweater with you when you set out at night. And wear a hat, even if you do not normally wear one by day.

It is surprisingly easy when going fishing to forget some particular item of equipment. We carefully go through a mental check-list when loading our vehicles before setting out from home to go to the river, when leaving our vehicles to go down to the water, and when packing-up to go home. This is done by a conscious ritual of starting at our feet (socks and waders), working up our bodies (sweater, waistcoat, waterproof, towelling scarf and finishing at our head (hat). We then work along our arms from rod(s) to reel(s) to leader nylon to, ultimately, fly boxes (= various). A net is included with body wear. One of the best inventions for the modern angler is the modern fishing waistcoat (ours have 20 plus separate pockets!). We then go through the compartments of both our waistcoats and our fishing bags. Organisation requires that there should be a place for everything and that everything has a place. Thus, the torch is in the top left-hand waistcoat pocket – along with the carborundum stone for honing hooks and the hot-melt wader repair kit. Spare batteries for the torch are kept in the left-hand (outer) pocket of the fishing bag; along with the butane gas lighter for the latter (matches might get soggy). Licences and permits are kept in the right upper (internal) pocket of the waistcoat, whereas leader sinkants, fly floatants, midge repellents (and other things) are in the right-hand (outer) pocket of the bag. Provided that we have not omitted anything at the start of the season and provided we remember to replace whatever we consume during the course of the season, then we should never be without anything important once we reach our chosen venue for the night. We will return to organisation and planning once we have arrived at our chosen venue later, but now to basics.

Before discussing *how* to fish at night we must first consider *where* to fish at night for the simple reason that *where* you fish largely conditions *how* you fish.

'Time spent on reconnaissance is seldom wasted'. It is always a good policy to carry out a fairly detailed daylight reconnaissance over a section of the available water to note which pools and glides contain fish and where the fish are lying within each possible venue. Reconnaissance is sensible because a pool which contained fish one night may be almost fishless the next night if the run has travelled upstream and a pool which was almost devoid of fish one day may contain fish in quantity the next morning if the run of the intervening night has, for some reason, elected to take up residence.

Runs of fish into, and up, the river are not uniform throughout the season and their rate of upstream movement may vary within and between seasons depending on a number of factors, of which the river level is probably the most relevant. Every river will have certain pools which have become established as good 'holding pools' and which will contain large quantities of fish throughout much of the season in most years. There are other pools also which can be termed 'resting pools'. These do not usually hold fish for any great length of time, perhaps because they are too shallow or lack adequate bankside cover or because the current is too fast, but they may at certain times during the season contain large shoals of fish which, if the river level drops quickly, may become 'stranded' there until the river rises. However, in normal circumstances 'resting pools' do not 'hold' fish and the fish that reside there temporarily will soon move on to their intended destination.

On the larger sea-trout rivers, such as the Spey, Tywi and Teifi, there are some magnificent pools and glides often stretching several hundred yards from head to tail. Some can be fished productively throughout much of their entire length, but in any given section of water some locations will be far more productive than others and unless these locations are known much time can be wasted fishing unproductive water. The key to successful night fishing is knowing where sea trout are most likely to be caught at a given level of river and then fishing these areas carefully and correctly (see p. 226).

Virtually all night fishing is focused on the pools and, to a lesser extent, the glides, because these are the places where sea trout choose to lie on the normal to low water conditions most conducive for night fishing. The ability to 'read' a pool or glide in terms of where and how to fish it is one of the most important skills that can be acquired by the angler. Every pool is different

A classic resting pool. Success here depends on knowing where and when to fish it in relation to the river level. The angler (top) is too far upstream and the taking-place at this height (3ft 6in) is in the 'gap' on the extreme left of the picture. In the lower picture he has moved down to the correct position and should fish down to the end of the trees. At 4 feet on the gauge the best taking-place is the open water below the trees (Chest waders required). At 2 feet on the gauge the section may hold a few fish in a deep, almost unfishable, hole under the bank on the extreme right of the lower picture. The section of water below the angler in the bottom picture is perfect for intercepting 'travellers' at night when the gauge is between 3 and 4 feet. (Photo: G.S. Harris.)

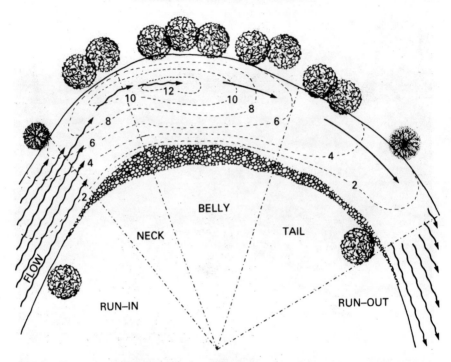

Fig. 49. The sections of a pool. The run-in and the run-out are normally too fast and/or shallow to hold fish or be fishable. The neck consists of fast, broken water where the current speed and turbulence decrease as the depth increases into the belly of the pool. The belly represents the deepest section and the current is now smoother and slower. The tail is where the depth decreases and the current increases progressively until the 'break' of the pool is reached at the run-out into the next section of river. (This description is very much a generalisation.)

within any one river and different rivers may have very different types of pools. However, in very general terms each pool can be divided into three constituent parts (Fig. 49). These are:

1. The 'neck' or 'head' which consists of a length of fast broken water flowing in from the run out of the pool above. As the neck enters the main body of the pool the depth increases and the current becomes smoother and slower.
2. The 'belly' or mid-section of the pool is where the current is at its slowest and the depth greatest.
3. The 'tail' is where the depth decreases while the current increases steadily until the pool 'breaks' into the fast broken water of the run leading to the pool downstream. The area immediately in front of the 'break' is known as the 'hang' of the pool.

Figure 49 oversimplifies the situation. Some pools may have long necks and short tails, some may have short necks and short tails, some may have short necks and long tails, others may be a series of short interlinked pools with only a defined neck to the first and a defined tail to the last.

We have mentioned that sea trout may also be caught at night in glides. A glide is, in essence, a length of smooth, unbroken water, which lacks the characteristic deep belly of a pool but which, nevertheless, is deep enough to hold fish. Some very long pool necks or pool tails may be termed loosely as 'glides'. In broad terms the ability of a glide to hold fish depends very much on the occurrence of good tree cover on one or both banks to provide security and protection for the fish in the absence of depth.

Having decided on the basis of daylight reconnaissance which pool (or pools) to fish that night, the next important matter to decide is whereabouts within the pool to concentrate your efforts. So many anglers begin their night fishing by moving sraight to the tail of the pool and then remain there until dawn breaks, even when they are not taking or even moving fish. These anglers are accepting too uncritically the view of many experts that 'the pool tail is the best place at night'.

We do *not* regard the pool tail as the best place to fish on each and every night. On some nights it may well be the best place to fish *all night*, on other nights it can be the worst place to fish, while on other nights still it may be the best place *at certain periods*. We know of several pools on the Tywi, Conway, Dyfi and Teifi where the pool tail is invariably the worst place to fish at almost all times except when fish are travelling upstream and, in a few cases, even when fish are travelling upstream. All generalisations are dangerous, but there are many pools on the Dyfi where by far the greater proportion of fish are taken at night from the neck and belly sections rather than from the tail.

There are probably several reasons why the pool tail has assumed general acclaim as being the best place to fish at night. The main reason is perhaps that this is where fish are frequently to be seen lying by day in the flat shallow waters and so it is not surprising that the angler would wish to concentrate on such places at night. Another reason may be historically linked to the fact that until the mid 1960s it was impossible to obtain fast sinking lines that enabled the angler to get a fly down quickly to fish lying in the deeper water of the belly of the pool or in the fast water at the neck. At best the fly lines of yesteryear sank relatively slowly by modern standards and could only cover effectively the shallower water located at the tail. Thus, fishing over deep water was not normally productive unless the fish were inclined to rise up from the depths to intercept a fly fished near to the surface, as sometimes occurs. A third reason may have been that the accelerating current at the pool tail enabled the fly to be swung round more effectively than in the slower deeper water of the belly and this fact suited the style of greased-line fishing which was widely popular on many rivers in the 1940s and 1950s. Whatever the reason, the belief that the pool tail is the 'best place' to fish at night is still widespread. It may or may not be so depending upon the river level, the darkness of the night, the nature of the pool and the disposition and abundance of the fish. To this we would also add two other very important factors; first the behaviour of the fish within the pool at night, and second the method of fishing the fly.

It is wrong to assume that each fish within a pool (or glide) behaves in the same way at night. In order to explain our approach to night fishing it is important that we discuss this crucial point in some detail before considering tackle, tactics and techniques.

Each fish within a shoal is an individual with its own personality and proclivities. It is just as likely to behave differently from the other members of its shoal as it is likely to behave in a similar manner. We would also add that *each shoal* of fish may be different, and react and behave differently, to another shoal within the same pool at any particular time but that, while each fish is indeed an individual, the fish within the same shoal are more likely to behave in a similar manner than the fish within a different shoal.

Here we must digress slightly to expand on the last point. There is some evidence from smolt tagging studies that the shoal should be regarded as a fairly cohesive unit. It is possible that many of the smolts within a shoal remain together while in the sea and migrate back to the river at the same time: eventually returning to their natal spawning area. Thus, the members of a particular shoal have certain common features in terms of their origin, composition, past history and ultimate destination and it is to be anticipated that they each will be subjected to a similar urge (or drive) to reach their original spawning areas and, as a consequence, may be expected to respond in a like manner to conditions within the river. A different shoal will consist of fish of a different origin, composition, past history, and ultimate destination (unless from the same tributary) and may well respond differently to the same conditions. For example, a shoal of fresh fish destined to spawn high up in the head waters of a river may feel the urge to migrate upstream more rapidly (and do so at lower river levels) than another shoal of fresh fish in the same pool at the same time originating from a tributary lower down the catchment. A third shoal of fresh fish originating from a tributary with a confluence immediately above the same pool may remain there for several months regardless of intervening spates and only enter the tributary when the increase in hormone levels that precedes spawning encourages the fish to migrate upstream.

Many good sea-trout rivers have stocks which consist of a large proportion of previous spawners. It is not known whether the kelts from a tributary reform into shoals after spawning. It would seem to be unlikely that they do so and, therefore, that each fish behaves very much independently of others on returning to the river. That shoals consisting of previous spawners do occur is a fact established from scale reading studies. The early runs of large sea trout into the Dyfi in May and June are composed almost entirely of previous spawners but it may be that these shoals are no more than amorphous aggregations of individual fish which form by chance within the estuary and which break up rapidly after entering the river.

Our approach to night fishing is to make the general assumption that any pool on the river may contain up to four different groups of sea trout, each of which behaves differently at night and which should be fished for in a different way. This basic philosophy is perhaps best illustrated by reference to one pool that we both know well on one of the best sea-trout rivers in Europe (Fig. 50). The pool in question is located about 3 miles above the tidal limit. It is one of the best holding pools on the river and usually well stocked with fish from late May until the close of the season in October. It is fairly typical in that it is on a large sweeping bend in the river and has a well-defined neck, a large belly with a deep pot of some 15 feet in depth and a very long tail which gets progressively shallower as it breaks into the run leading to the lower pool. It is heavily wooded on the 'far' (= outside bank), and has a shoulder of gravel on the inside of the bend. The only atypical feature is the large spawning stream entering the upstream run just before it becomes the neck of the pool. (See Fig. 50.)

The time is early in July. It is the third day after a small summer spate. The river is about 6 inches above normal summer level and fish are still travelling upstream under the cover of darkness. In this respect we are discussing almost 'perfect' water conditions for night fishing and the pool should, in fact, contain the full complement of four different groups of fish. These groups can be termed:

1. travellers;
2. resters;
3. stayers;
4. stoppers.

Travellers

These are sea trout which move into the pool during darkness. They may originate from the pool immediately below or from other pools some distance downstream. Some may move into, through, and out of the pool almost immediately; others may rest awhile before moving on. The distance moved during one night by a traveller may depend on several factors, notably the freshness or staleness of the fish, the nearness or remoteness of its intended spawning area, its 'internal motivation' (or hormonal drive), the 'appeal' of the pool in terms of its ability to hold fish and, above all, the river level. Some fish may be in no great hurry to travel upstream under favourable conditions, others may be very keen to do so and 'travel' at a lower river level.

It is likely that most travellers bide a while on entering a pool after moving up through the fast water of the run. It is often suggested that they do so at the limit of the pool tail on the 'hang' where the pool gives way to the broken water of the run. The route through the pool to the neck is likely to be in or alongside the main flow of the current, and it may be that some travellers

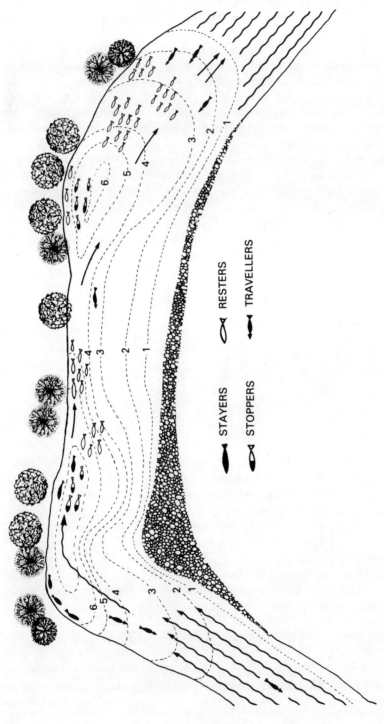

208

reconnoitre the pool, making several circuits, before deciding whether to settle in or travel onwards.

Resters

These are fish which have moved into the pool and stopped travelling either because they did not wish to progress further or because dawn intervened to arrest their migration until the next night; or because the river had dropped to a level that precluded further movement (i.e. would-be travellers have become stranded). This group of sea trout can often be seen lying at the very end of the pool-tail early in the morning. As the day progresses they may move further up into the security of the deeper water towards the belly or across to the cover provided by a high or wooded bank. The shoal is frequently graded with the larger fish to the front and the smaller fish to the rear. More than one shoal may be present and, if space allows, the shoals appear to keep apart rather than intermingle. If the fish are fresh from the sea they are usually quite active, turning on their sides intermittently in a characteristic 'flashing' roll, and leaping from the water. If they are forced to lie in insecure positions, either because the more favoured lies are occupied by other fish or because the pool lacks suitable characteristics, they are usually very unsettled and easily scared.

Stoppers

These are fish which remain in the pool until stimulated to travel by a subsequent spate. Fish may become stoppers because the river level has dropped to a point that is no longer conducive to upstream movement or because the urge to migrate further is weak and/or the pool has a strong 'holding' appeal in affording safe and secure lies. Some stoppers may ignore the opportunity to migrate provided by subsequent floods and remain in the pool for several weeks, but many stoppers may be traveller – rester fish that have become temporarily stranded by a falling river level.

Stoppers tend not to lie in the shallower water occupied by resters. Generally they choose to lie in the deep water near the belly of the pool where they are safer and, therefore, more comfortable. They have time to seek out the best lies, and can be expected to do so. The 'best lie' for a resident or semi-resident fish is *not* in the exposed shallow water at the pool tail where the fish must expend energy holding station in the fast current.

Fig. 50. Our basic philosophy in night fishing is based on the premise that: a) there may be up to four different 'types' of fish in a pool; b) each type occupies a different position based on its length of residency; c) different techniques are required for different types; and d) catchability declines with length of residency.

Stayers

These are sea trout that reside within the pool until the spawning urge compels them to run upstream. Although stoppers and stayers both tend to occupy the best lies in the slower deeper water, stoppers are fish that will remain regardless of water conditions because they have attained close proximity to their intended spawning stream or area such that any further upstream migration would be unnecessary. They are invariably the most problematic group of fish for the angler as they often take up almost unfishable lies in the depths of the pool seeking out any cover afforded by rocks and stream bed contours (such as ledges). These are the fish that can be seen week after week with their heads stuck 'ostrich-like' into the cover provided by tree roots and their tails sticking out from the bank. Such fish are easily snared and are much sought after by poachers. Stayers are oblivious to subsequent spates. They may move out from their chosen lies during a flood because the current is too fast or turbulent to make those lies habitable and so take up a different position within the pool (when they may be taken by a spinner or, more usually, a worm) but they soon move back to their original (or better) lies within the pool as the flood recedes.

Of these four groups, travellers are the most transitory, since their occurrence depends on river levels. As the flood recedes and the river drops towards normal summer level, fewer fish are inclined to travel and those that do so may not move very far, maybe no further that the next pool upstream, and the period of movement may be restricted to no more than a brief burst of activity at dusk and at dawn. Eventually, as the river drops towards drought levels, all upstream movement at night ceases and the pool contains only stayers, stoppers and resters and, as time progresses without any increase in river level, the resters become stoppers by default, taking up deeper water lies and becoming dour and unresponsive to the fly.

Whether or not a pool contains all four groups of fish depends very much on the time of year, the frequency of earlier spates, the river level at the time of fishing and the characteristics of the pool. 1985 was a very wet summer on Welsh rivers and sea trout anglers had a lean time because fish were able to travel upriver almost every night of the season. Thus for much of the season the pools on the lower sections of rivers contained only stoppers (which were virtually unfishable for at the above average river levels because of the speed of the current in the neck and belly of the pools) and travellers (which were few and far between because most runs passed through within days of entering from the sea leaving nothing to follow on ensuing nights until the next run.

At the start of a season the first fish to reach a pool will be travellers, these may take up residence as resters or as stoppers or stayers but it takes time for them to build up to worthwhile numbers of fishable fish. As we have indicated, the ideal for night fishing is when the pool contains a good head of fish in the four groups but most night fishing on low water will encounter only stoppers and stayers.

Glides do not contain good holding water and fish best when they have a good head of resters and when fish are travelling. One of the crucial skills of night fishing is to recognise the presence and abundance of these different groups of fish within the chosen pool or glide, and to select from the repertoire of possible techniques the 'right method' for the group of fish which become the main focus of attention during the night, *and then* to refocus attention and change method to fish for a different group of fish if and when things go quiet during the night. Flexibility in approach is very important when night fishing.

How does all this affect our choice of the best places to fish at night? The tail may be the best place to intercept fish *when they are travelling.* So too may be the head of the pool since almost everything that comes in must, eventually, go out, and fish probably tend to pause at both locations. The tail is a good place to start fishing at night if it *contains resters*. It is a waste of time fishing the tail if the pool *does not* contain resters or travellers. This is often the case during prolonged low water when the best place to fish is the belly. Even when the pool contains resters, the belly can also be the best place to fish, provided it is fished properly. It is certainly the place in which to catch the larger fish on low water.

Although Jeffrey Bluett was responsible for popularising night fishing and making it respectable during the 1940s it was Hugh Falkus who brought it up to date in the 1960s. He provided a basic repertoire of night-fishing techniques and presented a general system for applying them under standard conditions. The 'comprehensive' (or 'Neo-Falkus') approach to night fishing employs four general methods of fishing the fly or fly-lure:

1. the surface fly/lure;
2. the dry fly;
3. the subsurface fly/lure;
4. the sunk fly/lure.

There are several variations of technique within each method and we will deal with these as appropriate. (For convenience we will use the term 'fly' to embrace the many different confections of fur, feather and tinsel used when night fishing irrespective of whether or not they are, conventionally, flies or lures. There *is* a distinction; but we are not sure at what point in its construction a 'fly' becomes a 'lure'.)

The Surface Fly

It has long been known that a wet-fly worked through the surface wave on a lake (Chapter 13) or that a dry fly allowed to 'drag' in the current on the surface of a river (Chapter 8) can be very effective at times for sea trout in daylight. It was only logical for someone to try the same thing at night and find that it was equally, if not more, productive than by day. Thus the technique of fishing a fly so that it dragged across the surface leaving a V-shaped 'wake' was developed sometime during the 1930s or 1940s and, then, variously refined in later years.

The early forms of wake fly were little more than a piece of wood mounted with a treble hook which was, sometimes, garlanded with a few feathers or tufts of hair. The standard technique was to cast the fly across the current and hold it in check so that it swung round to the near bank against the resistance of the current (more or less as when spinning for salmon). In the absence of sufficient current to cause the fly to drag the surface properly so that it left a clear wake, movement was imparted by working the fly back by stripping line with a series of short, sharp pulls.

Broadly speaking, the wake fly was kept as a last resort when more conventional methods failed to produce results. Some anglers, however, used it faily regularly and it was recommended by Falkus and others for use on a pitch-dark night or where the pool was well shaded from the light of the night sky by bankside trees. It was held by some to be particularly efficacious on a damp, muggy night, when rain was imminent.

While semi-traditional wake flies, such as described by Falkus, are readily obtainable today (most large mail order companies can supply 'Falkus Wake-lures'), these have now been superseded by modern buoyant lures which are easier to cast and more aesthetically pleasing to the purist since they less resemble the floating 'plugs' used in fishing for pike with spinning tackle. The technique of fishing the surface fly has developed considerably since it was 'rediscovered' by Falkus. Lures dressed with bucktail and semi-buoyant deer hair (i.e. the *Muddler Minnow*) or fashioned from 'plastazote' are now widely used instead of lumps of wood or cork.

Not only has the fly itself evolved, but the technique of fishing it has been subject to considerable variation. Almost any unweighted fly will drag through the surface and create an attractive wake *if it is fished fast enough*. The fast-stripped fly can be a particularly effective method on low water conditions in the belly of the pool and along the length of the tail and, in many respects, the slower the current the better. Working the fly over slow moving water using the strip-and-coil or, where *very* fast recovery is to be employed, the strip-and-drop technique extends the possible use of the wake fly to sections of river where the current is too slow for traditional wake-style fishing.

Sea trout move to the wake fly in a variety of ways: from a violent, rod-wrenching snatch to an ever-so-gentle take which is detected as no more than a 'touch' on the line. Much depends on the mood of the fish and the speed of travel of the lure. Clearly a fish which takes hold of a fly being stripped *very* fast will be 'felt' as a very firm take; especially if it has had to move at speed to intercept it in the first place. It is also our experience that the wake fly produces more positive takes when fished over deeper water;

but this may be because it is usually fished at a faster speed to compensate for the slower current over the deeper parts of the pool and that the deeper dwelling fish have to move some distance to intercept it.

There is one pool that we fish occasionally which is one of the best holding pools on that river. On low water it is almost 20 feet deep in the belly and rarely contains less than 1,000 sea trout (many of 'specimen' status). Its configuration is such that it is virtually devoid of any current for most of its length and experience has shown that the subsurface fly and deep sunk lure are not effective methods. Here, we have found that the most sure method of taking fish lying in the depths is to cast a very long line (20 yards plus) straight across towards the far bank and, almost before the line touches the water, strip-back as fast as it is physically possible to do so, to create as much disturbance on the flat-calm surface, with a large, heavily dressed tube-fly of about 2 inches (usually with a similar tube-fly mounted as a dropper!). This technique seems, eventually, to 'aggravate' the sea trout lying on the bottom; which then swirl up from the depths to take the lure at great speed and, in so doing, to produce some of the most savage, heart-stopping, takes that we have ever experienced. This is one situation where a strong leader (12lb strength) is almost mandatory as the fish run very large on this river.

Great care should be taken when fishing the wake fly. Those made of wood or cork are far heavier than conventional flies while the lighter buoyant materials are more resistant to air when being cast. An 'open' cast is import-ant and false casting should be avoided or kept to an absolute minimum. While we do not recommend the practice of laying the line on the water surface, instead of false-casting, as a means of increasing the length of the cast, we recognise that this is the safest way of working out extra line, espe-cially in a wind.

The tackle used when fishing the wake technique depends mainly on the size and type of fly, the darkness of the night and the smoothness of the water surface. On a bright night and flat surface we would use a size 8–10 *Muddler* on a 9 feet length leader of 6–8lb strength, and an intermediate line. If the surface was rippled and the current reasonable, a floating line could be used. On a very dark night we might choose a leader of up to 10lb strength with either a 1½ tube-fly on the point and a size 6 *Muddler* on a dropper irrespective of whether the surface was broken by wind or flat-calm. Contrary to normal advice, we have found that the fast-stripped surface fly can work very well on a bright night, particularly over deep water.

Although we keep a couple of the 'traditional' wooden-bodied wake flies in our fly box (just in case), we have not used them for some years as we find that the well-dressed muddler (fished fast or slow) or the fast-stripped tube-fly is easier to cast, just as effective, and, aesthetically, more like fly-fishing!

Dry-Fly Fishing

We have discussed dry-fly fishing in daylight (Chapter 8) and noted that it is very much a minority branch of the sport with, as yet, relatively few devotees. It is, by its very nature, a technique best suited for low water and when fish lie in shallow water at the tail of pools or in flat glides. Unless a breeze is present to ripple the surface with a modest wave, fish lying in such exposed positions in daylight are very easily scared by the first miscalculated cast or incautious movement by the angler. Thus daylight dry-fly fishing is, perforce, largely practised in the runs or at the neck of the pool where the angler is better concealed by the broken water. But such places are not, as we have noted, the most favoured lies of sea trout. Consequently, good days with the dry fly are infrequent and, so, few anglers bother to become adepts.

Much can be done under the cover of darkness, provided the angler avoids clumsy movements, splashy casting and unnecessary wading. Certainly fish lying in large shoals at the tail of open pools can be approached with the wet-fly at night and we find it rather surprising that more anglers have not turned their hand to the dry fly under the cloak of darkness. Experience has shown that fish lying at the very tail of the pool can be covered by casting up-and-across or down-and-across without being panicked into scattering about the pool and that the physical problems of the approach and the presentation of the fly are really no more than when fishing the dry-fly by day or the wet-fly at night. The only problem is one of a much reduced ability to *see* fish move to the fly and, thus, to time the strike correctly. However, there are some nights when a full moon and a clear sky make fishing the dry-fly a practical proposition and, if the river is low enough and slow enough, the dry-fly can often prove to be a better option than more conventional methods.

We have found that the best conditions for fishing the dry-fly are a very low river (so that the current is not too fast), a wide pool tail that can be approached on the gravel margins *from both above and below,* and a shoal of fairly active (preferably fresh) fish swirling and showing in the shallow water. These conditions, combined with a good moon and the shorter nights of June and early July can provide productive and definitely challenging sport when other methods fail.

A floating line is essential and a fine leader of up to 12 feet in length of 4lb strength nylon treated to sink to within about 3 inches of the fly is recommended. The fly itself should be as visible as possible, and for this reason we suggest that a good standard pattern is a size 8 or size 10 sedge-type dry fly (such as a *Dunnock* or a well-hackled bi-visible variant of the *Loch Ordie* dapping fly tied with a white hackle at the front or rear). The fly should be well treated with a good floatant in advance of fishing.

The mode of fishing is fairly straightforward and whether or not you fish upstream-and-across or downstream-and-across depends very much on the topography of the pool and the position of the moon. Try if you can to fish with the moon anywhere but directly behind you. The skill in fishing the dry

214

fly is in anticipating where, within a yard or so, the fish might be lying at any moment.

It is occasionally possible to see your fly as it drifts downstream when the night is very bright and you are fishing at the best angle to the moon, *but* on most occasions it is unlikely that you will be able to do much more than judge the approximate whereabouts of the fly. Thus, you will be reacting to either the sound of a rise, the signs of a swirl, or the feel of a take; rather than to the actual *sight* of a fish breaking the surface and taking your fly as when daylight fishing.

Success in fishing the dry fly at night depends, therefore, on 'knowing' where your fly is and where the fish are so that if a rise is 'seen' or 'heard' in close proximity to the estimated position of your fly you can react appropriately. The 'appropriate' reaction in terms of the strike varies, depending on: a) whether you have seen the fly being taken (in which event pause a fraction to allow the fish to turn down with the fly), usually manifested as a 'pull' on the rod or a 'veeing' of the line as it straightens out (in which event strike immediately); or b) whether you have seen or heard a fish 'boil', 'plop' or 'splash' where you 'think' your fly should be (in which event strike quickly – you may have got it wrong but only the strike will tell).

Conventional dry-fly fishing stipulates that the fly must drift downstream with the current and that any form of drag must be avoided. That is sound advice when fishing to steadily rising brown trout with a fly carefully chosen to imitate the particular insect on which the trout are feeding. All the precepts of dry-fly fishing '*à la* English chalk stream' break down when fishing for the non-feeding or randomly-feeding sea trout as the principal purpose is to induce or stimulate a 'rise'. Many authors have noted that the dry fly dragged across the surface sometimes promotes a rise, and it often pays to 'twitch' the fly by a sharp tug on the line as it fishes downstream. The 'twitch' can be particularly effective at night, much more so than in daylight, and this is where dry-fly fishing shades into wake-fly fishing. The only difference is the refinement of the tackle, the direction of the cast (if up-and-across), and the fact that the dry fly is usually employed on bright nights while the classic wake fly is used on dark nights. By such innovations are new methods born!

The Subsurface Fly

Modern subsurface fly fishing is essentially traditional wet-fly fishing with certain variations made possible by advances in tackle technology. While the method is as old as the hills, the approach and application has changed a great deal in the context of sea-trout fishing.

Fishing the subsurface fly implies presenting a fly (or lure) at a depth of up to 12 inches or so below the water surface. This method is widely employed throughout the British Isles and remains the most popular method of night fishing. It is without doubt the most enjoyable method of taking sea trout. However, the subsurface fly should not be used to the exclusion of other methods if it does not produce results. There are nights when other methods are more effective.

The subsurface fly is primarily fished over shallow water in runs, glides and below the belly of the pool. Until the advent of modern fast-sinking lines in the 1960s that could 'get down' quickly to fish lying in deep water, most sea trout fishing was undertaken with a fly that fished near to the surface. Some of the old 'ungreased' lines sank better than others, but none could compare with the sinking rates achieved today with the range of high-density lines currently available. This possibly explains the enormous popularity of the pool tail as being 'the best place to fish at night' in a historical sense, because it was only in such shallow water that the fly could be presented at the correct depth and speed.

Larger flies are usually used at night than during the day with sizes 6–8 being widely favoured. However, it is not unusual for very large flies of sizes 2–4 and long lures of up to 3 or 4 inches (or more!) to be used in subsurface fishing, even on very low water, and for very small flies (sizes 10–14) to be used also. We use both very large and very small flies at night depending upon various considerations. We should record that we have experienced many nights in the company of other anglers when fish were being caught by *both* very large and very small flies and, also, when *only* very large or very small flies produced results. We have also had the frequent experience of fishing without success using a very large fly when a change to a very small fly brought immediate results, and vice versa. There is a general rule in fly fishing that requires a change to smaller flies when the fish are not responsive. Sometimes when fishing for sea trout it is more effective to change to something larger.

Most subsurface fly fishing is done with a floating line. We have discussed fly lines in Chapter 4, and so we need only to mention that we favour the new neutral density lines which sink just below the surface for virtually all of our subsurface fishing (by day and night) because these do not leave the disturbing 'wake' of a floating line when fished on a calm surface.

The question of whether or not to fish a dropper at night has loomed large in the literature, with widely divergent views being expressed. A dropper can be a curse or a boon depending on your casting ability and the prevailing river conditions. Unless you are a reasonably proficient caster who feels comfortable with a dropper (or droppers) at night it is probably best to fish with just the one point fly until bad casting habits have been overcome and enough experience has been gained to enable you to cope with a difficult wind. Tangles are bad enough by day but they are even worse at night.

A popular view, as expressed by some authors, is that the dropper is more trouble than it is worth because the benefits of a second fly are outweighed by the loss of fishing time spent in attempting to unravel a 'mess-of-flies' by torchlight or, otherwise, in changing the leader. (The latter course of action is usually the best policy.) Other authors, though, recommend the use of a second fly on a dropper.

The advantages of a dropper have been variously stated as being: a) a second fly 'doubles' the chances of catching fish; b) it allows the angler to fish at two different levels in the water (Bridgett); c) the fish can be provided with a choice of two contrasting sizes, styles or patterns (Dawson suggests 'one dark fly with one light'); d) it helps to sink the leader quickly and enables the point fly to fish deeper. Only McClaren recommended using a *second* dropper (i.e. fishing with a team of three flies). However, it should be remembered that he fished in the north-west of Scotland where the shorter nights are generally bright, and that his style of fishing was to fish the river like a lake by working the bob-fly across the surface of the water (see page 77).

We sometimes use droppers and sometimes we don't. We have no hard-and-fast rules when it comes to fishing the subsurface fly at night. Our preferred choice of style for a particular night is determined by the height of the river, the speed of the current, the weather conditions, the presence or absence of a moon, the abundance and freshness of the fish, the topography of the water selected, and our intuition and mood. There are nights, usually during a period of successful fishing, when the urge to experiment overcomes the urge to catch fish. By contrast there are times, usually during periods of consistent failure, when the urge to catch fish actually dictates that we experiment!

The technique of fishing the subsurface fly is basically straightforward. Apart from the odd occasion where fan-casting from a fixed position may be appropriate, the standard cast is made directly across the river or down-and-across and the fly is worked back by recovering line with a figure-of-eight retrieve or by stripping-and-coiling. This is the normal method but there is, as might be expected, much variation in the speed at which the fly is worked, and, indeed whether it is worked at all.

Advocates of the greased-line style of fishing for sea trout, such as Horsley and Holiday, used a floating line which, after being cast across or slightly down-and-across, was allowed to swing round with the current without any additional movement being imparted to the fly by recovering line. This is fine in certain situations, but it is impossible to fish the fly effectively in this manner in slow-moving water and we would assiduously avoid any form of mending the line to regulate the speed of movement of the fly (see page 175) because of the disturbance created on the surface. (Mending line properly requires careful timing and, while it is not impossible at night, it is not made any easier by the absence of enough light to see what you are doing.)

It is our experience that sea trout respond best to a fly that is worked against the current. We also believe that working the fly so that there is as little slack in the line as possible results in more sea trout being hooked than would otherwise be so. The speed at which a fly should be worked depends upon so many factors that it almost defies description. Basically, however, there are two principal determinands: firstly, the speed of the current, and secondly the mood of the fish. There is no 'ideal' speed at which the fly should move relative to the current. Where the current is itself quite fast we tend to recover line at a slower speed than where the current is slow. As a general rule we find that as the current decreases the speed of movement imparted to the fly should be increased so that, in virtually still water, the fly is worked very fast indeed.

The mood of the fish can also be important in determining the speed at which the fly should be worked. On some nights the capricious sea trout will take almost anything regardless of how fast or how slow it is fished. On other nights they will move only to a fast fly or only to a slow fly. Therefore, our practice is to vary the rate at which we work our flies as we fish down a section of water until we can determine what appears to be the 'best' speed for the particular conditions prevailing that particular night. If the fish seem to go off the 'take' after a while, we then start to experiment again – or change method!

Most anglers have a standard leader that they use at the commencement of any session. Under ideal conditions our standard leader would be a 9 feet length of 8lb strength nylon with two flies, such as a *Dark Squirrel* (size 6 single) on the point and a *Dai Ben* or a *Harry Tom* (size 8 single) on a dropper. If the river was above normal level or the night darker we would use the same leader but change the flies for the same pattern two sizes larger (i.e. size 4 point and size 6 dropper). If the river was low and the night bright we would, again, stay with the same patterns but go two sizes smaller (i.e. size 8 point and size 10 dropper) and we would change the leader for a 12 feet length of 6lb strength nylon.

That would be our choice *at the start of the night.* How we would finish up would depend very much on the mood of the fish. We do not believe in slavish persistence with the same flies (or method). We frequently change patterns and sizes if the sea trout are unresponsive and it is not unusual for us to change several times during the course of a night, trying in turn a selection of flies between sizes 2–10 (or even 14 if the river is low and the night is bright), a range of tubes and Waddingtons up to 1½ inches in length, and various streamers up to 3 inches long.

Unless the current is very slow, when we tend to cast directly across or even up and across, our usual cast is down-and-across at an angle of about 30°. We then allow a few seconds (no more) for the leader to sink and for the current to begin to swing the line back across the stream before commencing to work the flies back by recovering line. We have developed some rules-of-thumb over the years that we generally apply to our choice of fly pattern, fly size and, especially, to the speed at which we work our flies. We would stress that these are only a rough guide and that it sometimes pays to adopt the complete opposite:

1. the darker the night the darker the fly;
2. the darker the night the larger the fly;

218

3. the larger the fly the faster the retrieve;
4. the lower the river the smaller the fly;
5. the brighter the night the finer the leader.

Another technique of fishing the subsurface fly at night is to fish a team of three flies on a short line and to work the fly on the topmost dropper so that it drags or cuts the surface causing a disturbance which, like the surface fly, can prove very attractive to sea trout.

The method entails a steady, rhythmic approach to casting and, in order to keep the bob-fly cutting the surface, a short line is employed. The cast is made across or down and across (depending on the speed of the current) and the team worked across the stream with the rod-tip held high to keep the bob-fly fishing properly.

This is a delightful way of fishing at night and one that we find appeals to us more and more each season. It can be useful in certain situations where long casting is not possible because the river is either too small or the bank overgrown or very high. The method works well in long glides and at narrow pool tails; provided the current is not so fast that the flies swing round too quickly. It is, by definition, a hybrid between traditional subsurface fishing and surface or wake-fly fishing, and seems at times to give the angler the best of both worlds.

The main disadvantage of fishing the bob-fly on rivers is that the shorter casting distance means that the angler is much closer to the fish than would be normal with subsurface fishing so that there is a greater risk of disturbing the fish. This risk can be reduced by using a longer rod so that the bob-fly is fished further away from the angler (McClaren recommended a rod of 12 feet length as the ideal). The method is best employed on a bright night so that the swirl of a taking fish can be seen and the working of the bob-fly more readily controlled by visual clues, but we have used it with good result on a pitch dark night when everything was done by intuition and feel. The one advantage of darkness is that it allows the angler to get nearer to the fish.

We tend to go 'traditional' in our choice of flies when fishing this method. Thus, our typical team of three flies would consist of something like the following: point = *Bloody Butcher* or *Peter Ross*; middle-dropper = *Silver Invicta* or *Pheasant and Yellow*; top dropper = *Black Palmer* or *Brown Sedge* (both well-hackled). All flies are size 10 singles. Recently we have fished with a *Black Muddler* or *White Muddler* in the bob position with excellent results. Most fish that move to the bob-fly do so quite positively. Overstriking is to be avoided. The long curve of line from the rod tip provides scope for the fish to turn down with the fly and the general rule is to wait until you feel the fish before striking. Fish which miss the bob-fly may take either of the two subsurface flies or, if not pricked, may come again to the bob-fly.

The Sunk-Fly

The term 'sunk-fly' can mean all things to all anglers. To us it means getting a fly or lure down as deeply as possible as quickly as possible so that it is presented eyeball-to-eyeball with any sea trout lying on the bottom. The perfectly presented sunk-fly is one that fishes for as long as possible no more than about 12 inches above the river bed. This requires very careful reading of the pool or glide in relation to depth and current speed *and then* the correct choice of the appropriate type of sinking line.

For most purposes we use a line that sinks at a medium rate, but in faster-flowing or very deep water an ultra-fast or high-speed sinking line may be required, while a slow sinker or sink-tip line may be preferable when fishing over shallow water with a slow current. All our sinking lines are forward tapers as we believe that they sink with a straighter profile than double tapers. And, by allowing more direct contact to be maintained with the fly, provide a greater proportion of hooked fish.

Sunk-line fishing may lack the aesthetic pleasures and much of the excitement of fishing the subsurface fly, but there are nights when it may be far more productive and there is no doubt whatsoever in our minds that it consistently produces the larger fish.

It is now fairly common practice to fish the subsurface fly during the 'first-half' of the night and to change to the sunk-fly during the 'second-half' if the subsurface fly is not successful. However, there are nights when the sunk lure may be more productive during the 'first-half' and, indeed, when it is the best method throughout the night from dusk to dawn. There are also nights when both methods can be equally productive on the same section of water.

Whether you choose to fish the sunk lure before or after the subsurface lure is a matter of choice. As a general rule it is perhaps best left until proper darkness if only because fishing the subsurface fly is more enjoyable immediately after dark when there is still some light in the night sky and when there are likely to be fish lying in the tail of the pool. However, if the only fish in the pool are to be found in deep water then fishing the subsurface fly at the pool tail will usually be a waste of time (unless travelling fish are likely to be encountered), and in such circumstances we would commence our fishing with the sunk line in the belly of the pool.

Apart from when fishing in glides, where the speed of the current and depth of water can be fairly uniform over a long stretch of water, there are few pools where the same sinking line fishes effectively (i.e. close to the bottom) in all sections. Usually the current speed, water depth and bottom profile of the pool are such that a fast-sinker fishes best at the neck, a medium-sinker at the belly, and a slow-sinker at the tail. For most purposes we use a medium-sinker as our standard line, it provides optimum flexibility in fishing the greatest range of depths and current speeds without having to change lines (always a chore when night fishing unless you have set up two rods.) By varying the amount of time allowed for the line to sink before recovering line and by speeding up or slowing down the rate employed to recover line it is possible to control the depth at which the fly is fished to a significant extent; and this can be further extended by changing the angle and distance of the cast and by wading to different depths.

As a general rule the deep-sunk fly should be larger and fished much slower than the subsurface fly. This is where flies give way to lures. Although we still fish conventional flies (singles or doubles) of sizes 4–6 at certain times, much of our sunk-line fishing is now with large Waddington shanks, tube-flies or Marchog lures. Tube-flies seem to have held their popularity in Wales more than elsewhere and there are few occasions when we do not use one at sometime during the night. We have two favourite patterns – the *Dyfi Phantom* on a bright night and an *All-black* for a dark night. Usually, however, we use the Waddington shank as we think that this has many practical advantages over the bulkier tube-fly (page 326). Our two favourite patterns of shank-fly are the *Moonbeam* and *Tywi Peacock and Red*; but we have several other patterns in reserve and often alternate the above with a *Badger and Orange* or a *Red Streak*.

Our standard leader for sunk-line fishing is a 9 feet length of 10lb strength nylon. Large lures require stronger leaders and we do not believe in fishing too fine when large fish are likely to be encountered.

In heavy water (when night fishing was only just possible) we would fish a 2½ inch shank. In normal water a 1½ inch shank and in low water a ¾ inch shank would be used at the start of fishing but we would experiment with larger or smaller sizes as necessary if the fish were unresponsive. If the sea trout were moving to the lure but 'taking short' we would change to a *Marchog* lure with a long flying treble. We strongly advocate the use of treble hooks when fishing the deep-sunk lure hence our preference for lures rather than flies for this style of fishing.

Broadly speaking, most fish taken on the sunk-lure tend to hook them-selves, and there is more chance of this happening with the needle-sharp outpoint trebles used on our lures. The typical take on the deep-sunk lure is a good solid pull. Striking as such is not necessary; all that is required is to tighten on the fish and pull back. Some takes can be amazingly gentle in that there is no discernible pull on the line. All that happens is that everything 'stops', – i.e. you find that the line can no longer be worked back and the rod tip starts to curve down to the surface as you attempt to recover line. It is as if you have caught up on the bottom or in weed (you may well have done so!) but it is always surprising how often the snag begins to pull back as you raise the rod tip. This form of take is quite common when fishing the lure very slowly on very dark nights.

Fishing the deep-sunk lure requires method and discipline when casting. It is important to let the fly work round and to recover enough line before attempting to recast. One of the worse faults in fishing the sunk line is to try to lift off for the backcast before the line has been brought to the surface. To do so results in a badly mistimed backcast (which is both dangerous and messy) and it is the easiest way to overstrain and break a rod.

Although on some nights sea trout will respond amazingly well to a lure stripped across the surface some 5, 10 or 20 feet above their heads (page 213), fishing the sunk line is the only way to fish the deepest water at the belly pool with regular success. However, the presence of a back-eddy between the angler and the main flow of the current can cause problems and effectively render some of the most productive water unfishable. It may be possible to wade out and cast over the eddy, but the back-current often scours out a deep pot which makes wading impossible. Hence, we now introduce you to the technique of 'pot-fishing' which has been developed to a fine art by certain anglers on some of the 'gravel' rivers in mid-Wales. We can attest its efficacy at times of low water when fish are lying deep in the belly of the pool. It has certainly saved us from many a blank night when more conventional methods and techniques have failed.

Pot-fishing cannot be practised in every pool as it depends on being able to wade out into the neck of the pool so that a long line can be cast downstream and fished back in the slower current at the edge of the main stream. This is often made possible in gravel rivers by the spur of shingle (often termed a 'whaleback') that protrudes out into the belly of the pool from the neck (Fig. 51).

Extreme caution must be exercised when wading in the fast broken water entering the neck of the pool and this technique should be reserved for low-water conditions for two reasons: firstly, it is dangerous, if not impossible, to wade the neck other than in low water; secondly, the current will be too fast to fish the lure properly when the river is flowing at a higher level.

The angler wades out as far as possible on to the gravel spur, (taking great care not to step off the edge!) and settles into position. A long line is cast as far downstream-and-across as possible and allowed to swing round to a position almost directly below the angler. If the main stream current is reasonably strong, a few extra yards of line can be worked out from the reel to achieve greater distance and, ultimately, depth. A medium or fast-sinking forward-taper line will be used (depending on the depth of the pot) and this is allowed to sink for as long as possible as the line moves out of the main current, The general idea is to work the fly back as near to the bottom as possible through the slacker water. Some experimentation is usually necessary to determine how long to delay the retrieve so that the fly sinks to the correct depth. In deep pots this may be 10, 20 or 30 seconds and the fastest sinking line possible is obviously to be preferred to reduce delay and increase the actual number of casts that can be fished out over a period of time. As a general rule the lure should be worked back *very* slowly by gently drawing and coiling line; but fish will sometimes take the lure when it is fishing high in the water and when it is being recovered at a slow to medium speed. It is not unusual for fish to take as the lure swings across the main current, such takes usually being so savage that striking is unnecessary. They sometimes take 'on the drop' as the lure starts to sink. Again, such takes are usually

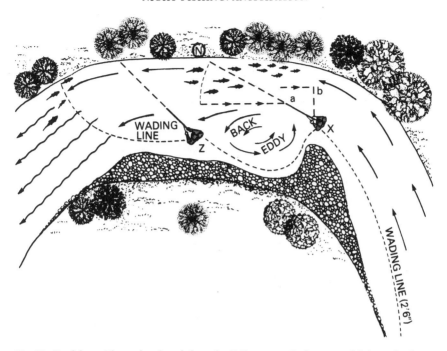

Fig. 51. Pot fishing. The wading line defines the 2′6″ contour. On low water fish lie in the deep pot on the far side of the back-eddy, which makes a conventional cast across or down-and-across impracticable as the line is carried upstream. The angler at Z cannot fish up-and-across to cover the fish as the fast current sweeps the fly back before it can sink anywhere near to the fish. If he casts downstream he is covering fishless water on low flows. The only way to fish this pot effectively is from X by casting a very long line downstream to the 'gap' on the far bank at N and then let it sink to the bottom before retrieving *very slowly* along the line of the slower flow between the main current and the back-eddy. The pot is some 12 feet deep and is best fished at normal flows with an ultra-fast sinker and at low flows with a medium sinker. By holding the rod out at position b it is possible to work the fly back into the main current, but this tends to cause it to work up to the surface. Chest-waders can be worn on low flows to move further out into the stream, but the current is too fast for deep wading on normal flows. (Position Z is an excellent place to be when sea trout are travelling as they tend to rest awhile at the tail of the pool before moving on.)

quite sharp but, since the lure is not yet being worked, they are invariably missed. This style of fishing is also characterised by very gentle takes.

When recovering the line, keep the rod tip well down to maintain direct contact with the lure. Since the lure is often directly downstream the rod should not be pointed at the lure but, instead, held down across the body over the current so that there is an angle between the line and the rod tip. This keeps the lure working in towards the main current, maintains it at depth for as long as possible, and provides a better spring for striking or as security against a 'smash-take'.

Although the lure is fishing mostly on the 'hang', we have not experienced

223

any great problem in connecting with fish. (Many authors maintain that it is difficult to connect on striking when fish take a lure that is directly below the angler.) This may be because the fish move across to the fly or because we are almost certain to be using a large Waddington shank, a tube or a Marchog, all of which are mounted with our favoured outpoint treble hooks.

Pot fishing can be dull, repetitive work and unless you are interested only in 'specimen' fish it is perhaps best left as a last resort in order to save 'blanking-out'. If practised long enough it usually produces a fish, eventually. A regular change of lure (every 20 or so casts from the fixed position) is a sound policy (page 328).

Playing a fish from the waist-deep water on the tip of a gravel spur can present problems if the fish is large, lively, or heads off downstream. Some fish are well behaved and may be played-out and netted in the quieter water of the back eddy well away from their companions. But others are less co-operative and it is often necessary to back out of the water so that they can be played from the bank. *Whatever you do make sure that you back out the way that you went in.* Do not attempt to reach the bank by the shortest distance. You will get very wet if you try to do so as the back-eddy can be very deep!

Having discussed the various methods and styles of fishing the fly at night, we must now consider some general tactics. As we have shown, there is a basic repertoire of four different methods (wake-fly, dry-fly, subsurface fly and sunk fly) from which to select in accordance with the prevailing conditions of water, weather, and fish. Remember, however, that your *preferred* style of fishing may not always be the best method for a particular location or combination of conditions.

We have stressed the importance of daylight reconnaissance to determine the location of the fish and, hence, which pools or glides to fish at night. However, there is much more to reconnaissance than just seeking out the fish. The next few paragraphs are written mainly for the novice or visiting angler, but some points are relevant to those who regularly fish the same water for sea trout at night.

Among the many considerations affecting the night fisherman is where to park the car and the best route down to the river bank. Very often cars must be left in narrow country roads where parking can cause difficulties. Always park safely and do not leave valuables on display in an unattended vehicle. The actual route to the fishery is also an important consideration. The shortest route may be to scramble down a steep bank, or negotiate a wood, bog, or ditch on your way to the water. However, this will be done in daylight and it may not be quite so easy coming back in pitch darkness laden, if you are lucky, with 20lb or 30lb, weight of fish. Note the crossing points (gates or stiles) through hedges and wire fences and the exact position of bridges over drainage ditches. Note also the routes to them. Fishing rights have been lost to clubs because thoughtless anglers crossed through fields of unharvested crops. Go round hay meadows and corn fields until they have been cut. This all sounds very much like common sense but it is very easy to lose your bearings at night and to become disorientated, especially in a heavy mist. [We have several times encountered visiting anglers stumbling about the countryside in the dead of night a mile or so from where they should have been frantically looking for their cars. And in one instance doing so on the wrong side of the river!]

Having reconnoitred the way to (and from) the river bank, the next thing to consider is the fishability of the water. Some pools may hold a lot of fish but may be physically difficult to fly-fish because of high banks and bankside trees and shrubs. The easiest pools to fish at night are those with gravel shoulders on the inside of bends, but it only requires the odd tree, gorse bush, or stand of bracken strategically located behind the angler to make fishing the most likely lies so difficult that it may be better to go elsewhere.

Wading should always be approached with caution, particularly at night and especially on rocky rivers, and should be avoided if at all possible as it will clearly create some disturbance. But many pools must be waded if they are to be fished properly. Therefore, try to work out *beforehand* where to enter and leave the water and the route through the pool. Look also for the tell-tale mark of clean gravel which shows where the previous occupants have waded and, especially, *where they have not waded*. Another factor to consider is where to play and land your fish and whether or not you will require a net. We much prefer to beach our fish whenever we can (page 182) but this is not everywhere possible, and it is advisable to take a net to the river irrespective of apparent need. You may change venue because your chosen pool proves unproductive, or your 'fish of a lifetime' may run down to the pool below (or above) where it cannot be beached.

If you are fishing a section of river where you have access to both banks you may need to cross to the other side to fish another pool or to fish the same pool in a different section. Check carefully where to cross and, very important, where to cross back. In some situations the flow of the current and topography of the stream bed may be such that you can cross in one place *but cannot wade back* at the same place. Most anglers get wet or stranded for this reason, rather than any other. Be warned!

All the above advice relates to selecting a particular section of water for night fishing. But before actually deciding whether to opt for section A or B or C of the water, there are several other important considerations to take into account quite apart from the presence of fish and the fishability of the venue. These are the presence of a moon, a wind, the afterglow of the setting sun and the light from cars and buildings. All these factors can affect where and when you fish a stretch of water.

We have shown a fairly typical section of water on a river in mid-Wales known to us both (Fig. 52). The approach to fishing this series of pools and glides is explained in the caption but a few words by way of amplification are appropriate here.

A clear sky with a full moon shining down onto the water behind the angler is the enemy of good night fishing. It forces the angler to employ

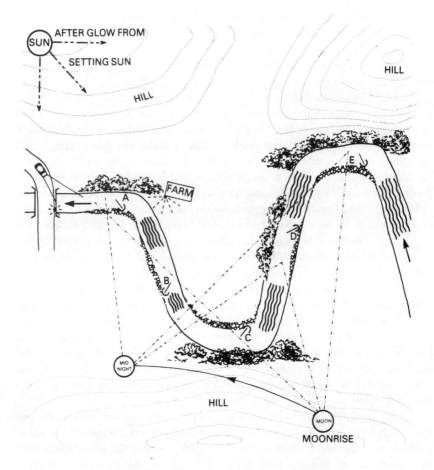

Fig. 52. Night fishing tactics. The setting sun, the moon, the amount of cloud cover, the wind strength and direction, the river level and the disposition of the fish are all important in deciding where and when to fish at night.

Section A is a long flat glide that normally holds a lot of fish. It is protected from the afterglow but receives the full light of any moon all night. On a dark night the moon is no problem but the angler fishing down has to contend with the bridge lights and the swing of car headlights as they turn onto the bridge. It can be fished upstream on low flows but the lights in the farmyard shine into the eyes until around midnight. It is not seriously affected by the wind.

Section B is a lovely pool but it is badly affected by both the afterglow, the moon and any downstream wind. The lights from the farm are also a problem. It is really only fishable on a dark night after midnight.

Section C is a much-loved pool. The main part is rarely affected by the moon but any afterglow delays fishing by up to an hour in July. A downstream wind helps and an upstream breeze is not too difficult unless 'very brisk'.

Section D is a nice glide that fishes well (for travellers) on higher flows. It is protected from the afterglow and any upstream wind but may be affected by the moon as it rises. Later in the night it is sheltered by the trees. A downstream wind helps.

Section E is a fantastic pool/glide fishable at most flows. It is sheltered from the afterglow but badly affected by the moon. An upstream wind causes problems.

more stealth and finesse in approaching the fish than would otherwise be necessary. We would much prefer no moon at all or for the moon to be partly obscured by high cloud. Remember that: a) the moon waxes and wanes with a regular periodicity so that you can expect a full moon every 28 days and that 14 days later there will be a new moon; b) the moon rises in the east; c) that it moves across the heavens during the course of the night; and d) the trajectory of the moon varies with the season. Thus, when planning a fishing trip check the lunar (and tide) tables; by altering your plans by no more than two weeks you fish with a new moon and so lessen the impact of a clear sky. The fact that the moon moves from east to west during the night may mean that a pool that was affected after dusk may become fishable later on during the night as the moon moves behind a stand of trees, or conversely, that a pool where the moon was obscured by the hill or by trees early in the night becomes illuminated later on.

The sun sets in the west, but in a clear sky the afterglow of the setting sun once it has dropped below the horizon may delay nightfall by a significant length of time. Careful choice of venue can allow you to start fishing half an hour or so earlier, while other less river-wise anglers are still sitting on the bank waiting for darkness.

A breeze can be very welcome on a clear bright night as it ripples the surface and obscures the presence of the angler; especially a warm breeze from the south or west. A wind, however, is a very different matter, particularly one that blows upstream and makes casting difficult and, if fishing a large lure, positively dangerous. Given the choice between fishing in either full moonlight or a strong wind we would always choose the moon. There are a number of pools and glides on several Welsh rivers where the fishing has been 'ruined' by artificial lighting associated with bridges, new highway improvements, hotels and various private dwellings. A light from the uncurtained windows of a bungalow on the hillside, even if it is almost one mile distant, can be very disconcerting if it is shining *directly* into your eyes as you fish down a pool. Neon street lights are worse still and the periodic flash of car lights as they sweep across the river are something that we avoid like the plague. Fortunately most decent people go to bed before midnight (at least in rural Wales they do) and the frequency of car traffic on country roads dwindles after closing-time at the local hostelries so that some sections of river become fishable during the 'second-half'. Unfortunately street lights stay on until after dawn and this particular limiting factor is one that can only be endured or avoided.

We never like arriving at the pool chosen for the night in darkness, irrespective of how carefully it may have been reconnoitred during the day. Unless we are *very* familiar with the water to be fished, we arrange to arrive at the river an hour or so before dusk while there is still enough daylight to tackle up and to study the water carefully in more precise detail.

When fishing new water or water that we have not fished for some time we usually try a few careful 'test-casts' at each of the main positions likely to be fished that night in order to determine the effect of the current on the speed and depth at which the fly swings round. This also helps us to confirm wading distances, water depths, casting lengths and casting angles relative to the current at each particular point. Where necessary we mark the position on the bank where we should enter and leave the water with a suitable stick or a small pile of stones. We try also to memorise the number of paces out to the 'correct' wading position, along with the number of pulls of line from the reel to achieve the optimal casting distance at each point, and we also take note of any reference points that will be discernible at night on the far bank that help to indicate casting angles or hazards, such as over-hanging branches.

These test-casts are performed with the utmost stealth and caution in order not to disturb the water unduly. However, experience has established that they are a risk well worth taking as it is often surprising, especially on gravel rivers, how a pool can change subtly but significantly after a flood, and, furthermore, how much difference an inch more, or less, of flow can make to the speed of the current, and, hence, the speed and depth of movement of the fly from one night to the next. Although the night fisherman may be practising his art in total darkness without any clear visual clues as to how his line and lure are behaving, he should endeavour *at all times* to 'imagine' exactly where his lure is and how deep and how fast it is fishing. Just as the daylight angler uses visual clues to focus his concentration on the passage of his fly through the water, so too must the night angler employ a heightened sense of judgement, reinforced largely by touch, to provide a 'feel' for what his fly is doing. This is critically important. A major part of the skill in night fishing is 'knowing' how the fly is fishing, and in this respect it is arguably more skilful than when fly fishing in daylight!

A sound piece of advice when rain is about or imminent is to place a marker at the edge of the stream before starting to fish and then, at intervals during the night, to check whether or not the river is rising. It is surprising, even on small catchments, how local the rainfall can be and, bearing in mind that small catchments are usually more subject to sudden, violent spates, there is always the risk of being stranded on the wrong side of the river by a rapid rise in water level. If you have the misfortune to be night fishing when the river starts to rise - *pack up*! Night fishing on a rising river which is starting to show colour is hopeless. You are best advised to go to bed and look for an early start the next day.

Having reconnoitred the pool (or glide) carefully and done the required number of test-casts to get the 'feel' of the water, the night angler should retire to the bank and get properly organised for the main event to come. 'Getting organised' means just that. Night fishing is difficult enough without loading yourself down with fly boxes, spare spools, bags, nets and all the etceteras that you may have carried to the river bank 'just in case'. One obvious priority is to tie up a few spare casts ready for a quick change in the event that what you start off with gets caught up on the opposite bank! It is all too easy to misjudge distance at night and much time can be wasted in tying up a new cast by torchlight. Much fishing time can be wasted also in retreating periodically from the water and trudging back to the fishing bag to change a fly that has lost its point on the stones or, as a result of faulty or misjudged back-casting, has been lost altogether or which no longer inspires confidence and is to be replaced with something 'better'. We always carry a small selection of replacement leaders and alternative flies so that a quick change can be made *in situ*, without leaving the water.

Another aspect of getting ready is to store any food within your fishing bag, safe from the depredation of bankside rodents and the attentions of slugs. The bag should be located alongside some very obvious bankside landmark as it is very easy to become disorientated at night and waste time flashing a torch about looking for a bag which is some 20 yards elsewhere next to *another* alder tree or alongside *another* patch of heather.

Unless we intend to be highly mobile at night and fish several pools and glides (a sensible strategy when the sea trout are scarce and widely distributed), we would normally tackle-up two rods – one for subsurface fishing and one for sunk-fly fishing. In our view the ideal rod for night fishing on the medium to large rivers that we mostly fish is a single-handed carbon rod of 10–11 feet length. The rod for subsurface or surface work should have a softer action, while that for sunk-line work should be stiffer and more powerful for lifting off a partially submerged line when recasting and, generally, for coping with larger fish. (All our rods are fitted with 4-inch detachable extension handles. Welsh sea trout run big and the extension handle makes playing a large or lively fish so much easier. It also keeps the reel clear of sand and gravel when the rod is placed upright against the bank.)

The advantage of having two rods set up ready for different methods of fishing is not so much that it saves time later on when you wish to change but that it makes it more likely that you will in fact bother to change. Of course you will not wish to change from a floater to a sinker (or vice versa) if whatever you are using is producing results. However, it is when whatever you are using *is not* producing results after a reasonable period of perseverance that you should change. But changing a reel, threading a new line and tying on a new leader and flies takes time and is a fiddle in the dark. If a second rod is tackled up ready-and-waiting then change is easy and you are more likely to try a different approach. We use our second rod *repeatedly* on most nights. It is surprising how often a few casts with a sinker in the pot or a quick flick across the tail with a subsurface or surface fly produces more than just the odd fish and the facility to change and then change back from one method or another with regular frequency during the night may, at times, be exactly what is required to produce a respectable bag of fish.

Fishing literature is variously interspersed with advice on when to start fishing. Gammon states that it is best to wait until the fish have begun their evening movement and suggests waiting quietly on the bank until at least three fish have jumped. Others state that you should wait until the bats appear and Falkus believes that there is no greater mistake than 'to steal a march', as no disturbance of any kind will be tolerated until the shadows have lengthened sufficiently. Jock Scott counsels in a similar vein, while Mottram states, perhaps more helpfully, that the night angler should 'wait until it is too dark to read the time on your watch'. All this is sound advice, as sea trout are readily scared. It is all too easy to let enthusiasm override common sense and to start fishing too soon. But it is just as much a mistake to wait too long as it is to start too soon. There are nights when the best fishing is to be had at dusk *before* actual nightfall and the angler who waits for maximum darkness before putting a fly on the water may miss 30 minutes or more of superlative fishing, especially if fish are travelling as they often do at twilight. In any event it is difficult on some Association waters to find a pool or glide that has not been disturbed recently by another angler. The precise time when you should start night fishing at your preferred location is a matter of judgement based on experience.

On a bright night with a full moon and a clear sky the 'correct' time may be an hour or so after the 'correct' time the *next* night when there is heavy cloud obscuring the moon. (See also page 225.) However, our general advice is to suggest that you hold back until the shadows of the night make it impossible to see the junction of the far bank with the water surface so that the casting distance is solely a matter of judgement.

Waiting for twilight to give way to darkness before entering the chosen pool or glide does not necessarily mean that you cannot fish elsewhere. Provided you have access to a reasonable section of water, and provided also that the other pools or glides within the available section are not occupied by anglers who, like you, are waiting for darkness, it is often possible to pick up a fish or two as dusk falls by fishing the faster, broken water entering the head of the pools or by carefully fishing the shaded water of the glides with either the dry fly or the wet fly. This helps to get the angler 'tuned up' for the night; and there is nothing more likely to boost confidence (and confidence breeds success) than to start fishing in earnest with a fish (or two) already in the bag. It serves to take the 'urgency' out of the proceedings so that the angler adopts the more leisurely approach that is more conducive to successful night fishing and which, regardless, makes night fishing that much more enjoyable.

We have stated that the actual tactics, techniques and approach to night fishing at the selected venue will depend upon various considerations, of which the topography of the pool, the river level and current speed, the presence or absence of the moon or of wind, and the disposition of the fish are among the most important. Bearing in mind the four basic methods of fishing and the four different types of fish that may be present in the selected water (if you are lucky) it is then necessary to adopt some systematic and planned approach in order to achieve the best result.

You can of course occupy one part of the pool all night and fish away from dusk until dawn with one preferred method without movement or change, but this becomes exceedingly boring even at the best of times. In our experience it is usually more productive, and it is certainly much more enjoyable, to fish each section of the pool methodically during the course of the night and, in so doing, to fish whichever method or style is most appropriate for the conditions prevailing at each section.

This emphasis on adopting a varied approach was, perhaps more than anything else, the most important message imparted by Hugh Falkus. We would not disagree with his division of the night into four 'time blocks' and his general approach of fishing each 'block' at the *appropriate* section within the pool with the *correct* method in relation to the expected 'typical' behaviour of the fish under *'standard'* conditions. Thus, Falkus divided the night into four parts:

1. first-half: from dusk until about midnight;
2. half-time: from midnight until roughly 1 am;
3. second-half: from about 1 am until just before dawn;
4. extra-time: a variable (but short) period around dawn.

In addition to these four main periods we would add two others which, while not related to night fishing in the true sense of the word, can form an important part of the total experience. Thus, continuing the sporting idiom of Falkus, we include:

5. *warm-up*: the period before dusk when, having arrived early, you are disposed to experiment with some particular method at an appropriate nearby location;

Night fishing – the warm-up. It is a mistake to start fishing the main section of water chosen for the night too soon. The hour or so before darkness can be productive, however, with small flies fished in the broken water of the run entering the neck of the pool. Twilight on the Cottage Pool in the middle reaches of the Dyfi. (Photo: Emyr Lewis.)

6. *kick-off*: a short period of failing light equivalent to dusk. This is of variable length depending upon weather, season and geographical location.

We would stress that Falkus was careful to point out that his *generalisations* about the periods of the night *were just that*: and 'intended only as an indication of what might be expected' – not, we stress, what *could* be expected, but what *might* be expected.

As he points out, the first-half may not occur at all on some nights, or it may last for just a short while, while at other times it may occur all through the night '. . .and an exceptional bag is taken; but such nights are rare'.

Thus, while we agree wholeheartedly with the structured approach to night fishing as developed by Falkus, we must again emphasise the need to be flexible in its application. *It is for guidance only.* The worst possible trap that the aspiring night fisherman can fall into is, in our view, to adopt a stereotyped and ritual approach to the sport. Conditions can vary from night to night in so many ways and there is little that is 'standard' or 'typical' about sea trout or sea trout angling.

The modern approach to night fishing is based on using the subsurface fly at the shallower water of the pool tail during the first-half until the fish 'go down' and then moving up to the deeper water in the belly region and fishing a sunk-fly during the 'second-half'. The general rule is to fish the subsurface fly high-and-fast and to fish the sunk-lure slow-and-deep. Half-time is a period for reflection, relaxation and re-orientation. Wake (or surface-fly fishing) usually forms an ancillary to sunk-lure fishing during the darker second-half, but it may be used at any time during the night if there is not too much light. (Falkus does not recommend as such the inclusion of dry-fly fishing and classic-style wet-fly fishing in his basic repertoire – *we do*.)

This, then, is the modern (or Neo-Falkus) approach to night fishing. However, there are nights when it all breaks down. If the night is cold the sunk-fly may be the best choice from start to finish. Some of the best nights we have had in recent years have been back to front, with the sunk lure taking the fish first and the subsurface fly being effective only after mid-night. Such is the essence of sea trout fishing!

10 · NIGHT FISHING: REALISATION

Our general approach to night fishing can best be illustrated by considering how we would fish a 'typical pool'. The pool we have chosen (Fig. 53) is one that is well known to us both. It is *not* our favourite pool by any means (it is too far from the tideway and fresh-run fish) but it is one that has all the main attributes without any peculiar features that complicate the narrative. This pool fishes best at night when the river level is about 2 ft 9 in on the nearby gauging post. Drought levels would be approached at about 1 ft 6 in on this gauge. We will start our sequence at the tail-end of a small summer spate with the river clearing and falling rapidly. Thus:

1st Night (Gauge Level = 4 ft). Fish are still travelling in daylight but the

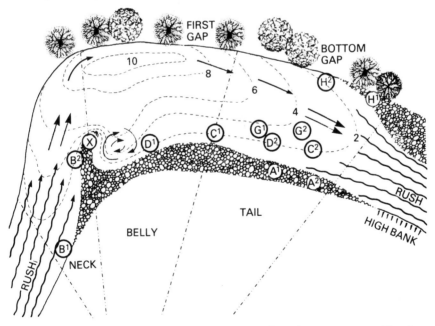

Fig. 53. Night fishing tactics based on the example of a single pool at various stages of flow from heavy fly water to drought levels. (See pp. 233–8 – remember that there is a difference of 2½ feet in the water levels and that the current speed and depth characteristics of the pool will change as a consequence.)

prospects for night fishing are hopeless as the current is far too fast in all sections.

2nd Night (Gauge Level = 3½ ft). River still too high for good night fishing. The current is still too fast and turbulent in the neck and belly for any form of fly fishing and the tail is unsuited for conventional subsurface fishing as the current speed is both too fast for fish to rest there and to fish the fly properly. Fish will still be travelling at night and there is a good chance of picking up a fish from dusk by using a large lure on a medium sinking line and repeatedly casting across the tip of the tail from position A1–A2. We would fish this either in relation with similar tactics at the tail of another nearby pool or by fishing '10 minutes on' and '10 minutes off' for an hour or two (but no more if we met with no success). The bulk of any travelling fish should normally appear during the first period of darkness. Casting would be down-and-across with a fairly long line at a big angle to reduce drag and to hang the fly across the tail for as long as possible. The current would be plenty fast enough to swing the fly round and line would be recovered with a slow 'figure-of-eight' retrieve sufficient only to keep in direct contact with the lure. Under such conditions we would expect to catch the odd fish and, if we were lucky with a good run of fish travelling, more than just a few.

Night 3 (Gauge Level = 3 ft). Almost perfect river conditions. Fish still travelling at night, but there are now fewer of them and the main movement is shortly after dusk. The pool tail is now fishable, as is the belly. The neck is still rather too fast – but is worth a few casts. However, the pot is not yet fishable. We would anticipate a productive night; perhaps not the best of nights but our hopes would be high.

We would probably warm up with the wet-fly in the long glide above our pool and then kick off at dusk with a team of two or three (size 8) flies on our intermediate line from B1 to B2 at the neck. Casting would be down-and-across; and the flies allowed to swing over to the 'hang' position without being worked. There is every probability of taking sea trout that are getting ready to travel upstream (and the possibility of a salmon) and so we would almost certainly fish the neck section down again a second or third time. (This pool is affected by the afterglow of sunset and unless the sky was well clouded there would be no urgency to move to the tail.)

As dusk gives way to darkness we would move to the tail where fish should now be showing (they should also be showing in the belly and neck), but unless it was cold or there was more activity in the belly we would choose to fish the tail section first from C1 to C2 with the subsurface fly. Thus we would change the flies on the 9 feet length leader of 8lb strength nylon used to fish the neck for a size 6 point fly and a size 8 dropper and carefully fish down to C2 casting across or down-and-across (varying the speed and depth at which the fly is worked) and taking a pace or two between each group of, initially, experimental casts. The final few casts would be fished out in

Night fishing – the 'second-half': the deep sunk lure fished slowly in the 'pot' or in the belly of the pool invariably produces the larger sea trout, in this case a beautiful 12lb fish taken by the second author from the Dyfi. (Photo: G.S. Harris.)

anticipation of contacting a 'traveller' that had paused to rest after entering the pool at dusk.

Very careful note would be taken of exactly *where* any fish were moved and *what* length of line, angle of cast and speed of recovery was being used at the time. On some nights sea trout can be very specific in their reaction to a fly fished in a certain way. The normal taking place when the gauge level is between 2½ and 3 feet is 'opposite the bottom gap' (under the bushes on the far bank). This zone would be fished *very* methodically.

The section C1–C2 would be fished a second and third time, perhaps changing the flies for something different in terms of pattern and size (going either bigger or smaller) if there was no response to each pass down the section. Each pass would take *about* twenty minutes, and so after an hour of unproductive fishing it would be timely to move to the belly.

For our sunk-line fishing at this river level we would select a medium sinking line and a 9 feet length leader of 10lb strength nylon with, initially, a 2-inch Waddington shank on the point and a size 4 (single) fly on the dropper. The belly section would be fished from D1 to D2 by casting down-and-across and allowing the line to sink before recovering line with a slow *but steady* strip-and-coil movement. The taking area is, basically, down to the first gap, and by the time we have reached D2 the cast is made directly across and the recovery has become faster. Fishing down below D2 is not possible with a medium sinker because the fly begins to snag the bottom. We would normally fish D1–D2 at least twice, and probably a third time, changing fly pattern and/or size each time if we were not moving fish.

If our third pass failed to produce fish then we would take 'time out' and retire to the bank for a review of options. The pot is unfishable as yet and the neck is still too fast to fish properly for a traveller. In any event, if there were travelling fish about we should have made contact with them earlier at the tail of the pool. The river is too high for the dry fly and the tail rather too fast for the bob-fly/wet-fly technique. What are we to do for the best? Everything is near perfect; but for some reason the fish are not responsive.

This is when many anglers decide to go home. They have fished the pool more or less from top to bottom and exhausted their limited repertoire of subsurface/wet-fly and sunk-fly techniques. However, there is still every chance of a fish (it is probably about 1 a.m. by now), and so we decide to fish on.

Our first preferred option would be to fish C1–C2 again with the subsurface fly, in the hope that a travelling fish may have moved into the tail sometime during the last hour. If that did not work and fish were not showing or moving to the fly we would change our subsurface leader for one of the same length and strength but with either a large Muddler (size 6) or a lightweight tube-fly (1½ inches) and fish the *belly and tail* quickly from D1 to C2 (casting directly across and stripping line back very quickly so that a wake was created). The fast stripped 'wake' fly has saved many a blank night and can be just as effective on a bright night as on a dark night. If *that* did not produce results we would then fish the belly again with a sunk fly: and then, as dawn approached, we would quickly fish the neck and the tail with small (size 8–10) wet flies.

Night 4 (Gauge Level = 2½ ft). Although very few travelling fish are to be expected at this river level (which seems to be the 'holding' level for this pool), prospects are still very good as the tail should still contain resters, the flow at the neck is perfect and the pot is now fishable. Warm-up would consist of fishing the upper two-thirds of the glide above with the dry fly working upstream and then as dusk approached fishing it down from neck to tail with a team of small wet-flies (size 10–12). (This glide is heavily wooded on the far bank and so sheltered from the setting sun and its afterglow.) At dusk, as before, we would kick off with a team of two or three small wet-flies (size 8–10) on a 6lb strength standard leader and fish the neck very carefully down from B1 to B2, and then, because the current is slower, to X. The level is now perfect for fishing this neck and we would probably fish it again before moving directly to the tail and fishing the same team of flies from C1 to C2. Resting fish now tend to be lying in deeper water but we would anticipate catching whitling and the odd traveller in the lower tail section. We would work the flies very fast and be heartened by the presence of any breeze. Although there is every chance of picking up fish on the subsurface fly (the taking area has now moved upstream to the vicinity of the 'first gap' by the way) we would have to choose between starting off with the sunk-fly or with the subsurface fly. If fish were more active in the belly or not showing in the tail, or if the night was cold, we would start with the sunk-fly in the belly. However, the tail should still be productive to the subsurface fly, but we would now consider using a finer leader and small flies (size 6–8). We would fish down from just above C1–C2 two, or maybe three, times before moving up to the belly and fishing the sunk-fly. Again, we would use a finer leader (8lb strength) and, initially, smaller flies. If the sunk-fly brought no response after fishing D1–D2 at least twice, our next option would be to fish the pot very carefully with a range of Waddingtons, Tubes and Marchog lures for 30 minutes or so, as it usually fishes well at this river level. If success still eluded us we would now call 'time out' and reconsider our options. There is still a chance of a fish as the river is still in good order after the recent flood, even though the resters have now moved into the deeper water in the upper tail and only the odd traveller is moving into and out of the pool.

We could fish the big lure that we had been using in the pot through the belly section – it is some 40 minutes since it was last fished. We could fish the fast-stripped wake fly from D1 to C2 if the night was dark enough, *and*, if fish had been moving at the tail, we could wade out *very carefully* to position G1–G2 and fish the bob-fly/wet-fly technique. If fish had been moving at the tail *and* the night was bright with a gentle breeze, we could cross to position H1–H2 and fish the dry-fly up under the bushes and up-and-across the tail. Or we could continue to fish the belly and tail in rotation by conventional means with the occasional quick fish at the pot and neck to break the monotony. We could, of course, go home.

If conditions were right and we were not absolutely desperate for fish, we would be tempted to try the dry fly at position H1–H2. It is possible to wade this section, provided it is done quietly, and so fish quite a large area of water on the far side of the main stream that is rarely, if ever, fished at all.

Under normal circumstances with the river at this level the conventional subsurface fly at the tail and the sunk-fly in the belly should produce results to the perseverant angler. Those less inclined to experiment could fish both sections on and off until dawn with every chance of eventual success.

Night 10 (Gauge Level = 1½ ft). We are now approaching drought levels. No travellers have moved in (or out) for some nights. Most of the resters have now accepted that they are destined to remain behind in this pool until river levels increase again and so have moved up to join the stoppers and stayers in the deeper water of the belly or have taken up whatever secure lies that they could find elsewhere towards the cover of the far bank. Prospects for night fishing are not good. But, recognising that *you* are on holiday and may have no option, our approach would be to fish a team of small flies (size 10–12) on a fine leader (6lb strength) down the neck at dusk. Then, as darkness falls, we would move straight to the belly and fish a slow sink line down from D1 to C2 with a 6lb leader and a small ¾-inch Waddington, and then, after two or three passes, change from a slow to medium sinker with an 8lb strength leader and a 1½ tandem lure or small Marchog and fish from D1 to around C1. (The change of lines and distance fished along the bank is necessitated by the fact that the river level is now much lower and the current very much slower so that our standard medium sinker now touches bottom much sooner than before.) After two or three passes down the section with each line (changing pattern at each pass) we would then move to the pot and fish our medium-sink line with our usual range of Waddingtons, Tubes and Marchogs.

If we had to stay until dawn, our tactics for the night would be to fish round from neck, to belly to pot, with the occasional quick fish down the pool tail with our small wet-flies used to fish the neck.

One option that we would seriously consider during each of the many 'time out' periods called during the night is the fast-stripped surface lure. This would be fished from D1 to C1 and from position X at the pot. However, we would need the inducement of the odd fish 'sloshing' on the surface, preferably in about the same position, to tempt us to mount up a leader with a Muddler or a Dyfi Phantom Tube and try to induce a rise to the surface-fly.

In normal circumstances the first few fishable nights after a summer flood should produce good catches with the subsurface fly and sunk-fly in this particular pool and the angler would rarely need to leapfrog about the pool trying every method in the book. In this respect, however, the above scenarios have been exaggerated somewhat to emphasise our most important point. BE FLEXIBLE IN YOUR APPROACH IF YOU WISH TO ACHIEVE CONSISTENT SUCCESS. Do not commit yourself to fishing *just* the sunk-lure or *just* the subsurface fly. We have little respect for the angler who says with great pride 'I only fish a floating line' or 'I *never* fish a lure'. We all develop a preference for a certain style of fishing, and there is much to be said for so doing, but it is as well to develop some degree of proficiency in other methods if you wish to catch sea trout consistently under adverse conditions. Remember that it is these adverse conditions that usually represent the *normal* situation in sea trout angling.

We have mentioned previously that much time can be wasted fishing unproductive water and we have alluded also to the fact that some sections of water have very specific places where, given the presence of fish and the

238

right water level, the probability of taking fish is much higher than elsewhere within that section of water. We would add that some of these localised taking places may fish well over a wide range of river levels (and, therefore, of water depths and current speeds) but that others may fish well only at a narrow range of river levels. Much of the success in night fishing resides in knowing where the best taking places are within any pool or glide at different river levels; and then how best to fish them. There is much local mystique attached to these taking places, and we should stress that if they are not fished properly they will not produce fish and, thus, they will not, by definition, be taking places – *for your style of fishing*.

In order to illustrate the fundamental point about fishing taking places properly we will refer to one particular section of water near the tail of a small pool that we both fish regularly (Fig. 54). There are in fact two very distinct taking places on this section of water, but both require a different style of fishing. One (in local parlance) is 'opposite the last gap' and is only worth fishing when 'the rock is submerged' (which means when the river level is above 3 feet). This is a well known and popular section of water on normal summer flows. It is best fished with a subsurface fly cast straight across and worked fairly fast from A1 to A2. The taking area is anywhere along this length as the fly swings round into and out of the main stream.

The other taking place is productive only on low water when the river level is below 1½ feet on the gauge ('when the rock is stranded'). As the river falls to drought levels, any fish in this section move progressively up into the deep water of the small 'pot' below the spur of bank. They are fairly visible to the angler in this position and many are tempted to try a few quick casts from B1 to B2 in the hope that the fish may respond. They never do because the fly is wrongly presented. It sweeps round too high and too fast. The correct way to fish this lie is in chest-waders using a fast-sink line and a largish fly.

This is one situation where exact length of line, angle of cast, and speed and depth at which the fly fishes are each of critical importance. There is no room for manoeuvre other than perhaps a pace or two down from position C, as the actual taking place is no larger than about the size of a bath towel. This is where knowing your water really counts on a pitch dark night. Thus, position C is *exactly* opposite the tall sycamore tree and is eight paces out from the water's edge. On reaching position C turn 45° downstream and cast a long line directly short of the 'last bush before the first gap'. Allow 6–8 seconds for the line to sink and swing round with the current and then start to retrieve line slowly and steadily in short coils (about 2 feet of line). If a fish is going to take it will do so between the third to sixth coil. If nothing happens after coil six, recover line and recast as your lure has now swung past the taking place.

Fishing this lie with anything other than a fast-sinking line fails to produce consistent results as the lure does not fish round at the correct depth. Too much deviation in the length of line or the angle of the cast and the lure does

A

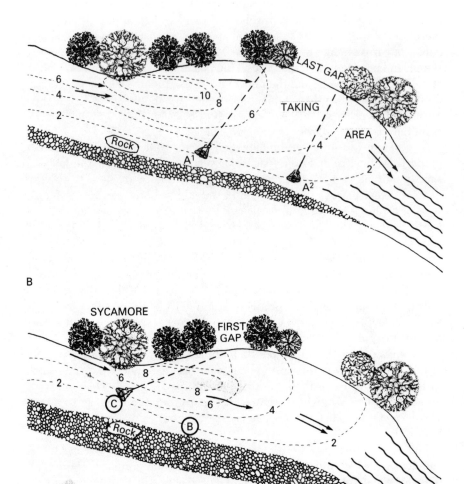

B

Fig. 54. Taking places are sections of water where fish are most likely to be taken if they are fished for properly. The top diagram shows a typical 'taking place' with the river level at 3–4 feet on a pool known to us both. It is fished from A^1 to A^2 with a subsurface fly fished across the current and recovered fairly fast as it swings round. The taking zone covers a large area 'below the last gap'. The lower diagram shows the same pool at low flows. Now the taking place has moved well upstream to the tail of the deep pot. This can only be fished 'properly' from position C by wearing chest-waders and fishing a medium to fast sink line with a long cast towards 'the first gap'. Most anglers try to cover the fish from position B but the current, even on low flows, is too fast for the fly to sink to the correct depth and swing round at the correct speed.

240

not fish at the correct speed. Recover line too fast and the fish will rarely respond. Everything has to be just *spot-on*. Knowledge of this particular taking place *and how to fish it* has saved many a blank night for those few anglers privileged to know its secret.

Night fishing can become very lonely. That apart, there is practical merit in fishing with a companion, and we often choose to do so whenever we can – preferably, but not essentially, one that we know reasonably well. One of the pleasant aspects about fishing Association waters is that it is possible to become acquainted with like-minded anglers from all walks of life, from all parts of the country, and from overseas. We much enjoy these bankside acquaintanceships and have spent many memorable nights in the company of visiting anglers whom we shall probably never encounter again. We frequently fish together at night and our usual plan is to divide the water into sections and fish turn-and-turn-about. Thus, if we are fishing a pool, one of us starts at the tail with a subsurface fly while the other starts in the belly or the pot with a sunk-fly. This is good policy because sometimes the one or the other method is the most efficacious depending upon the particular night. Then, once we have ascertained which method seems to be the most productive for that period of time, the other angler adopts the same approach and we both fish down the same section of water using the appropriate method.

Fishing with another angler down the same section of water requires a certain discipline and protocol if companionship is not to be abused by selfish behaviour. Fishing turn-and-turn-about usually entails moving a pace or two between each cast so that the section of water is covered progressively from top to bottom. On reaching the bottom of the section the angler then starts again at the top. In this way it is possible for two anglers to fish the same water simultaneously; one starting a few yards above the other and both moving downstream at about the same rate so that neither is disadvantaged. (This protocol is necessary on heavily-fished Association waters and, provided discipline is maintained, it is surprising how many anglers can be accommodated on a small section of water without too much difficulty.)

Many authors admit to being perplexed about what to do when the sea trout are 'not on'. Indeed it can be very frustrating to fish a section of water that is well stocked with sea trout for several hours without moving a fish or, as often happens, to be enjoying good sport when, just as if someone has thrown a switch, the fish suddenly go off the take. Gray (who was never one to mess about) tended to pack up and try again another day if the fish did not respond to his flies after about 15 minutes or so. Interestingly, Dawson and Bluett, who both fished the same river at about the same period during the 1930s and 1940s, give contradictory advice on what to do when the sea trout are not taking. Bluett (quite correctly) disagreed with Dawson's assertion that 'if sea trout are taking in one place they are taking in all' and suggests that when they are *not* taking in one place the correct action was to move elsewhere (and perhaps return later) or to fish finer or to fish differently, rather than go home to bed as Dawson and Gray counselled. This is sound advice with which we agree wholeheartedly, but rather than go elsewhere we would first change method. We have noted above that sea trout often 'go down' after the initial burst of activity that usually constitutes the 'first-half' of an all-night session. The important point to note is that they have gone down, not that they have gone off the take. They can still be taken provided that they are fished for properly (with a sunk-lure in deeper water). Another point to bear in mind when fishing the tail of the pool is that one of the reasons why fish may stop taking is, quite simply, because they are no longer there – the tail-dwelling resters may move up into the belly and neck of the pool as the night progresses looking for safer and more secure lies or, if the river level is such, travelling upstream into the next pool.

We discuss the over-complicated subject of when and how to strike sea trout in our treatment of daylight fishing and lake fishing and we also refer to the matter in the context of night fishing in the preceding paragraphs. Consequently, all that we need to do here is to mention some of the more salient points.

No angler can reasonably expect to hook 100 per cent of all the sea trout that move to the fly. We reckon that if we can maintain an average for the season of hooking about one in four, or one in five, of the sea trout that move to our flies at night then we are doing quite well. An average means that sometimes we may do better and sometimes we may do worse. Much of the character of sea trout fishing is about extremes. At one extreme there are nights when you may move, hook and land (say) six fish. At the other extreme you may move (say) 20 or 30 (or more) fish and never hook one.

It is our experience that the problem of 'short-rising' fish which move to the fly without being hooked is most likely to occur: a) when fresh-run fish are present that have just moved in from the sea; and b) when fishing the surface or subsurface fly. It *seems* to be far less of a problem when fishing the deep-sunk lure, but this may be for the simple reason that any sea trout that merely 'touch' the lure are less likely to be felt when the line is deeply sunk. It may, for all we know, occur quite often.

Our general approach in dealing with sea trout that 'take short' is to consider two possible causes: first that the fly or lure may be fishing either too fast or too slow; and, second, that it may be too visible to the fish. Our first approach to dealing with the problem would be to alter the rate at which the fly is fished by recovering line at a faster or slower speed. If that did not work we would try to hang the fly over the fish for longer by either wading deeper or casting a longer line at a greater angle downstream so that it fishes round over a smaller arc of water; or doing both. Another method of fishing the fly more slowly which is sometimes possible when fishing from the bank is to cast across the stream, and walk several paces down the bank as the fly fishes round. Remember that the speed of the current and the rate at which line is recovered will affect the depth at which the fly is fished and that the angle of the cast will alter the profile that the fly presents to the fish.

We find that the problem of short-rising fish and missed takes can usually be overcome by speeding up the movement of the fly on low water and, conversely, slowing it down when the river is flowing high and fast. Many other options have been suggested, such as scaling down to smaller flies, using flies dressed on long shank hooks, small doubles or using lures incorporating flying trebles. You may, if you wish, even go so far as adding maggots to your fly (page 247), but in most situations the first approach should be to change the speed at which the fly is fishing. This may not cure the problem altogether, but it can usually be relied on to minimise it appreciably.

Most readers should by now have got the message that, in our view, the best approach with sea trout is to strike on the 'feel' of a fish. Our maxim on striking is basically 'if you see it, time it', but 'if you feel it, hit it'. Since night fishing is, to state the obvious, undertaken in the dark you will inevitably 'feel' rather than 'see' the take. To say very much more on the subject would be to repeat ourselves unnecessarily. We would, however, stress again that the actual strike is never a 'back-arching arm-wrenching rod-bending surface-ripping hook-straightening leader-snapping' arc of the rod through 180°! It is no more than a firm but positive 'pull' into the fish done with a quick movement from the elbow.

The strike to the surface or subsurface lure is somewhat more positive than when fishing the deep-sunk lure. In the former instance it is perhaps more necessary for *you* to hook the fish. In the latter instance, by the time that the 'take' has been transmitted and discerned (= felt), the fish has more than likely hooked itself (Fig. 55). A strike to the take on a deeply sunk lure should be no more than a smooth, firm, 'pull' into the fish. 'He pulls you: you pull him.' Anything more than this is likely to result in a broken rod! The strain on the rod presented by the resistance of the water when attempting to lift several yards of deep-sunk line 'upwards' towards the surface when striking is quite considerable.

Playing a fish in the dark is no different to playing a fish by day, except for the important distinction that you cannot actually see what is going on! The tussle with a fresh-run, fighting-fit, sea trout of a respectable size in complete darkness is one of the most exhilarating experiences we know.

Playing a fish in the deeper water at the head of the pool is often less critical than in the shallow water at the pool tail as it is less likely to disturb other fish. In the latter situation it is always good practice to try to manoeuvre the fish so that it is played in the deeper water upstream of the tail and well away from its companions. This is often easier said than done as sea trout are much less well behaved and predictable than salmon.

Most sea trout will be hooked downstream of the angler. There is a natural tendency for most fish to head for the refuge of deeper water (albeit not always immediately) and this fortuitous behavioural propensity should not be discouraged when fishing the pool tail. After the hook has been set, any fish which strives to move upstream should be encouraged to do so. When fishing a pool tail the best position for an angler to be is below the fish. Sea trout, like salmon, tend to move in a direction opposite to the pull of the

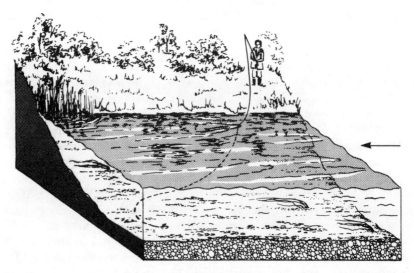

Fig. 55. A certain amount of 'slack' is inevitable when fishing the sunk lure, even if line is being retrieved as the lure fishes down-and-across. Firstly there is the arc from the rod tip to the water surface, secondly there is the downstream curve of line caused by the current, and thirdly there is the curve in the line beneath the surface of the water. The amount of slack can be minimised by keeping the rod tip pointing at the water and at the fly as it travels downstream; and by using a forward taper line where long-casting is practised. Deep wading, where safe and desirable, can reduce the effect of the current in relation to the downstream curve in the line.

line; with the result that a fish played from upriver will tend to run downstream whereas a fish played from below will tend to run upstream. It is always safer to play a fish from below and in deep water. The remarkable display of aerial aerobatics that sometimes characterises the fight between angler and fish is thrilling. But it is definitely something to be discouraged. We find that fish played in deeper water tend to jump less frequently than those played in shallow water. This is perhaps because those played in shallow water cannot go down and must, therefore, look for freedom in the air.

The initial rush of decent-sized sea trout at night can be a climactic experience. But don't panic! Whatever the fish does, you should do no more than strive to maintain positive contact until both you and the fish settle down. Keeping in contact means no more than maintaining a 'positive' curve in the rod tip. It does *not* mean bending the rod double in an effort to get the fish onto the bank in the shortest possible time. This is a common tendency at night when it is not at first certain whether *you* are playing the fish or the *fish* is playing you.

After the first rush of a hooked fish has been dissipated you can start to assume control of subsequent events. One of the first objectives should be to play the fish from the reel by winding back the loose line that is probably either trailing on the bank or, if you were wading, drifting downstream with the current. In the latter situation the safest way to dispose of this loose line is to back out of the water quietly and steadily (if possible) feeding the loose line out through the rod rings as you do so. If this cannot be done then you must attempt to reel in the slack while maintaining contact with the fish. This is achieved by trapping the line beneath the index finger and rewinding up the slack as and when you can. The pressure on the trapped line can be adjusted to let the fish take more line if it wishes to do so and any reduction in tension on the rod-tip tells you when to start recovering more line. (This is when an automatic reel is a blessing: but see page 86).

There is one aspect of playing a sea trout by night or day that deserves special mention. This is how to deal with a 'head-shaker'. Falkus describes such fish as being lightly hooked and characterised by coming straight to the surface and splashing about on their sides. He says that when this occurs 'the fisherman's heart sinks'. We agree! We have seen this behaviour with salmon and large sea trout in daylight under perfect conditions for observation. The fish stands still in the water (not necessarily on the surface) and literally shakes its head repeatedly from left to right in what seems to be deliberate and methodical response as if to rid itself of some minor irritation.

Falkus suggests that, since the fish and the fisherman are soon to part company, the best advice is to get the fish ashore as quickly as possible. Many head-shakers are indeed lost, but when we have been lucky enough to land them we have usually found that the hook-hold is tenuous and situated at the tip of the jaw rather than back towards the scissors. This behaviour seems to be encountered most frequently when a fish takes a fly which is more or less directly below the angler and fishing on the hang. It is fairly common when pot-fishing. (See page 222.)

Falkus suggests several tactics for dealing with fish that exhibit this behaviour:

1. apply maximum pressure in an attempt to get the fish ashore as quickly as possible;
2. move to one side or the other of the fish, preferably downstream, in an attempt to improve the hook-hold by pulling from a different angle;
3. drop the rod point, pushing it below the surface if necessary, in order to stop the fish flapping about on the surface;
4. strip off extra line and give the fish plenty of slack so that it goes down;
5. play the fish very gently.

We find that the best general approach is to give line quickly, either by walking down towards the fish or, if that is not possible, by releasing 2 or 3 yards of loose line. It sometimes works – but not always. We find that we now lose far fewer fish since we have used sharp-outpoint treble hooks on our Marchogs, Waddington Shanks and tube-flies.

Even the most proficient night fisherman can make bad casting mistakes at night and it is a sensible practice to check the leader and flies carefully every so often to ensure that everything is in order. Wind knots seem to appear as if by magic at times and it is always surprising how easily the points on hooks can be blunted and turned even when you would swear on oath that you had not touched either the bottom or the bank behind you.

The sound of a fly that has hitched back on the leader so that it is fishing back to front can often be detected when casting because, as Holiday says 'it whistles like an express train'. What does not make a noise, however, is a fly that is no longer there! One of the most disconcerting things that can occur (and one of the most unnecessary also) is to come out of the water after fishing the whole length of a long glide without a touch for an hour or so and then run your hand down the leader to secure the fly only to find – no fly! The question is when did you lose it? In the last few minutes? Or the first? We always check our leader and flies at regular intervals during the night, especially when fishing into a wind. It is a minor fiddle at the time but well worth the effort in terms of peace of mind and fish on the bank.

We must here mention the use of maggots in conjunction with the fly for night fishing. This is a standard method on some English and Welsh rivers where it has limited if not widespread acclaim and has been referred to by Falkus as yet another technique for dealing with short-rising fish. We have both used it on occasions and include it here more for completeness rather than from conviction. Many of the waters that we fish prohibit the use of maggots in sea trout fishing by local regulation, and while maggots can be purchased locally in a few localities where the demand from coarse anglers is sufficient to justify them being stocked by local tackle dealers, they are virtually impossible to obtain in most rural areas.

We could of course breed our own, but this is quite frankly more trouble than it is really worth. Maggots pupate quickly in hot weather and there are so few occasions when we might be tempted to give them a try that the effort in laying down a constant supply of maggots could not be justified.

However, this is remarkably easy to do if you want to. All you need is a deep biscuit tin, a piece of chicken and some bran. Leave the container in the open for a fly to 'blow' (lay eggs on) the meat and then cover the contents with the lid, which should be perforated, and leave in the shade for 5–10 days. Remove the maggots while they are tender and greyish and showing the dark feeding mark through the skin. The ideal hook maggot should be long and active with the feeding mark obvious. Store your maggots in a cool place and dispose of them quickly when they turn into casters (pupate).

We have not been able to trace when the maggot was first used in concert with the fly at night. Cass, writing in the mid-1940s, appears to make the first reference to maggots in the context of sea trout, but this was in relation to normal bait fishing. Although the fly-cum-maggot was used during the 1950s on several rivers in the English Lake District and in parts of North Wales, the first detailed description of the technique appeared in 1960 when Holiday gives two paragraphs to the subject. Falkus describes the fly-maggot technique in some further detail and gives the dressing for a special fly (appropriately named the 'Maggot-Fly') designed to be fished with the real larvae attached. He notes that under certain conditions sea trout manage to tweak the maggot without taking the fly, and suggests that when this occurs (usually when rain is imminent) the problem can be reduced by attaching the maggots to a small (size 14 or 16) flying treble attached to a lightly dressed fly tied on a single hook (size 8).

This fly, which he named his *Secret Weapon* was devised to deal with the problem of short-rising fish. When used in association with the maggot there are two options. The larvae can be impaled either on the treble point or on the front (main) hook. The latter option is used when fish are coming short, as any fish that tries to tweak the maggot must (in theory at least) ingest the wee treble first.

An earlier design which employed the same concept was the BRA Night Fly Series. This series of flies was designed by W.H. Lawrie (a well-known author and angler) for use with the 'beef maggot'. This was basically a standard dressing (*Woodcock and Yellow*; *Grouse and Claret*) tied on a longshank double-hook but with a small single hook projecting from the underside near to the head of the fly. The maggots were impaled on the anterior single hook when the sea trout were being tiresome and nipping the maggots on the tail hook.

There is a right and a wrong way to hook a maggot. The correct way is through the blunt (head) end with the point protruding from the side (i.e. in at the head and out at the side; *not* the other way round). The hook points should be needle-sharp and made from fine wire with a small barb so as to avoid bursting the maggot (Fig. 56).

Casting should be without effort and any false-casting is to be avoided if fly and maggot are to continue their associations. The fly-maggot combination is not really cast at all. It is somehow 'lobbed' rather than cast.

Proponents of the fly-maggot technique, and there are several, claim that the smell or texture or luminescence of the attached maggot enhances the appeal of the fly to the fish. Each is plausible. Falkus discounts the theory that it is the maggot (and only the maggot) of the maggot/fly combination that attracts fish; stating that he has often caught fish on the fly/maggot combination when the separately fished fly or maggot has been declined. We have too little familiarity with the technique to debate the matter further. We would, however, mention in passing that Gray (who disapproved of all forms of bait fishing for salmon and sea trout) referred, briefly, to the practice of some 'local' anglers who fished the *worm* at night on the point of a leader mounted with two flies on droppers. Gray also mentions the fly/ maggot but did not think it would be efficacious on *his* water.

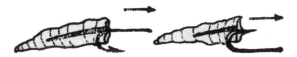

Fig. 56. There is a right way of hooking a maggot. This is with the barb emerging from the side (left). If the hook is inserted into the side (right) the maggot may squirm up and mask the point.

If often amazes us that so many anglers seem to let caution go to the wind as night falls. By day they are as careful as possible in avoiding any action likely to disturb the panic-prone sea trout. They fish fine-and-far-off, they avoid wading if at all possible and proceed heron-like, they use every bit of available cover to hide their approach and present their lines with the utmost delicacy. But at night they stumble up and down the bank, splash in and out of the river, swish their lines on and off the water when re-casting, use double-strength leaders and, generally, behave as if the cover of darkness excuses every kind of bad habit. *It does not!*

We see no reason why the sea trout should be any less readily scared at night than by day. Darkness merely allows the angler to approach within a reasonable casting distance of the fish and the physical approach to night fishing should still be subject to the same degree of discipline and stealth as daylight fishing. Falkus counsels that if you must wade then wade deep. This is good advice. It is impossible to wade quietly in ankle-deep water without splashing – so don't! If you cannot wade at least to knee depth, then try not to wade at all.

Casting at night should be a comfortable, rhythmic process employing the minimum of physical effort. Every angler has a natural length of line that can be cast without undue effort. Discover what yours is and practise to improve it if you need extra distance, but whatever you do never indulge in repeated false-casting at night in order to increase the length of line being fished. It inevitably leads to all sorts of problems, and can be positively dangerous when fishing a large lure or bulky wake fly, especially in the wind.

We find that our standard cast when night fishing is 12–15 yards. The ideal cast is one that entails no more than a smooth lift-off, a standard back-cast and then a direct forward delivery. It is necessary to extend any line that has been recovered in working the fly or bringing a sinking line to the surface prior to recasting in order to maintain distance. The greater ease with which this loose line can be 'shot' on the delivery with a forward taper line is one of the main reasons why we favour such lines for night fishing.

Although false-casting should be avoided as a general rule, there are times when it is necessary to false-cast in order to work out a longer line. Some anglers (doubless fearing the problems of false-casting a long line at night) attempt to minimise the risks by laying the line onto the surface of the water between each movement rather than keeping it working through the air. While this is the safest way of handling large lures and does help to expedite the process of working out the line, it is a very bad habit to lay the line on the surface of the water that is actually being fished, especially at the tail of the pool or in the flat, shallow water of a glide. If the line has to be laid onto the surface then do it over the unproductive water near to the bank from which fishing is taking place. Having worked out the required length of line, the final presentation is made by switching the direction of the forward cast back across the river (Fig. 57). This technique is often quite useful in situations where obstacles behind the angler make the conventional back-cast

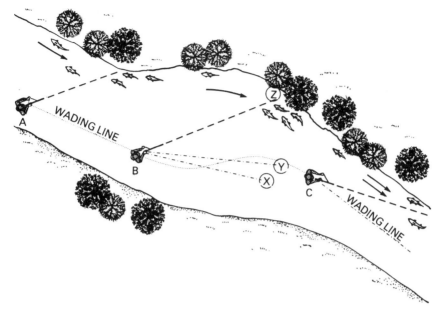

Fig. 57. It is normally a bad habit to lay the line on the surface of the water as an alternative to false casting when trying to lengthen the distance of the cast as this may disturb fish. However, it may be necessary or sensible under certain circumstances. The angler at A can fish normally with a fairly short cast and has no problems in back-casting. The angler at B has problems as a very long cast is required and the trees behind make back-casting impossible. He fishes this position by casting to X, recasting a longer line to Y, and then switching direction to present the fly to Z. The angler at C also requires to cast a long line to fish lying in a narrow gully. Here back-casting is possible, but the safest option if fishing a large sunk lure or wake lure, especially if there is a wind, would be to work out line by casting onto the surface inside the wading strip so as not to disturb fish.

problematic and the alternatives of a roll-cast or steeple-cast are not appropriate because of the extra distance required.

Finally, a word of caution. Look after the fish that you catch at night and do not leave them scattered about the bank to be picked up later. You may not be able to locate precisely where you put them that easily. And when you do they may have done a vanishing trick! We know of more than a few anglers who can recount experiences of disappearing fish that were casually left on the bank in their enthusiasm to continue fishing. Hedgehogs, pigs, otters, mink, foxes, itinerant sheepdogs, and members of the human species have variously been accused of participating in a free meal at the expense of a disgruntled angler. Unless we can slip the fish into a pocket or retain it temporarily in our landing net while we fish out a section, we now take it back to our bag and wrap it securely in a proper receptacle (page 355). We say 'securely' because there is nothing more likely to ruin a night's fishing than to return to your bag at dawn and find that your entire catch of fish has been partly eaten by rats! [We speak from experience – and lessons learned.]

11 · FISHING IN TIDAL WATERS

When viewed overall, it is apparent that only a small proportion of the total rod catch of sea trout in the British Isles is taken in estuarial or coastal waters. This is particularly so in England and Wales, where few anglers fish purposefully for sea trout in the sea: this is also a fair generalisation in respect to Scotland and Ireland, but is not applicable to Orkney or Shetland where, for reasons discussed below, fishing in tidal waters is standard practice and yields the bulk of the regional catch.

We should mention that the title of this chapter was carefully chosen to cover sea trout fishing in *both* the sea and in estuaries. We must stress from the outset, however, that fishing in the full salt water of the sea requires a somewhat different approach to fishing for sea trout in the changing salinity of estuaries. And, after much thought, we have finally included the chapter within our section on 'River Angling'. This is partly a matter of editorial

Fishing in estuaries is a somewhat different branch of tidal water angling. A small streamer lure fished very fast through the surface wave on the ebbing tide produced this sea trout during a period of severe drought when the river itself had become unproductive. (Photo: G.S. Harris.)

convenience, for although the sea can be regarded as one enormous 'lake' it is necessary to note that the effect of the tide causes water levels to change regularly and the currents caused by the ebb and flow of the tide create parallels with river fishing. While estuary fishing is, in major part, in many estuaries an extension of river fishing, saltwater fishing is really a distinct branch of the sport in its own right.

The single most important piece of ancillary equipment when fishing tidal waters is a good tide-table! Try if you can to find one that gives the time and height of both the *low* tides and the *high* tides for each day and which has been produced specially for your chosen district. Do not forget to make the necessary correction for British Summer Time if the 'lost hour' between mid-March and mid-October has not been incorporated into the tidal times; and do not forget either to make the essential plus-or-minus correction for the time of the tide at your chosen location. The time (and height) of the tide is not the same at all points around the coast. Even within a small geographical area of (say) Cardigan Bay in West Wales there is 90 minutes' difference in the time of high and low tide between Fishguard and Portmadoc – and 90 minutes can be crucial if you are to be in the *right* place at the *right* time when fishing in tidal waters.

The first thing necessary to understand relates to the phases of the moon as it is the gravitational pull of the moon and the sun that causes the tide to rise and fall in the first place. Almost everyone learns that the moon increases (waxes) and decreases (wanes) in size every 28 days, so that there are 13 new moons and 13 full moons in each calendar year of 12 months. Within each 28-day (lunar) month the moon waxes in size from newness to fullness for 14 days and then wanes back to the next new moon for a further 14 days. As the moon increases in size its gravitational pull increases and the tides become progressively larger – and vice versa at it wanes. The highest tidal range occurs on the full moon and the new moon. The lowest tidal range occurs on the first and last quarters of the moon. This is an important point for estuary fishing as it means that the tide will penetrate further upriver on a full or new moon so that, depending on the profile of the estuary (Fig. 58), long sections of fishing may or may not be affected by the tide on certain days within the lunar month. It also means that, since the higher the tide the longer it takes to run-in (flow) and run-off (ebb), the time available for fishing the lower sections of long estuaries may be very limited either side of the new or full moon. Indeed some pools within the estuary may only be fishable at low water on one or two days a month and some pools in the upper estuary may only be affected by the tide on one or two days each month. However, much depends on the configuration of the estuary. There are many rivers in Scotland, Ireland and 'the Islands' that fall straight into the sea and do not have estuaries in the normal sense of the word. At best they have no more than one or two sea pools (e.g. the Ogwen in North Wales; the Erriff in Co. Galway) where the transition from fresh to salt water is almost immediate. Elsewhere, such as the Dyfi, Conwy, Teifi, Mawddach (Wales), the zone of

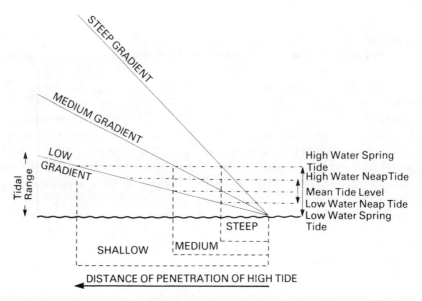

Fig. 58. The gradient or profile of the estuary determines how far the tidal rise and fall affects water levels (and salinity) within the river channel. Any given tide will move much further into a river with a shallow gradient than into one that falls steeply into the sea. The key to successful estuary fishing is understanding the effects of the tide. At certain times during the tidal cycle some sections of water may be unfishable or not worth fishing at all.

tidal rise and fall may cover several miles of 'river' channel.

Since the lunar cycle of 13 months must be accommodated within the calendar cycle of 12 months (of between 28–31 days), it should be fairly obvious that 13 into 12 'won't go' and that, consequently, the time of each tidal cycle will be phased so that it is a little later each day. Exactly how much later depends on many factors, including strength and direction of the prevailing wind and the rate of discharge of river flows, but the main point to note is that: (*a*) there are typically two full tides each day, and (*b*) each tide is roughly 25 minutes later than the preceeding tide. This is an important point in terms of logistics of when, where and how to fish since it means that the tide will be 50 minutes later each day and the time of high or low water on one day will be *roughly* 6 hours late on the same day one week later. *But*, since the tide may be higher or lower 7 days later (depending on where you are in the cycle) the effective 'best-time' for fishing at a certain point with a certain method may be longer or shorter than the week before. It may not even occur at all depending on the profile, configuration and composition of the estuary.

The tidal range is greatest at the spring and autumnal equinoxes, though 'spring tides' are not restricted to the spring. There are two *spring* tides and two *neap* tides each lunar month. The terms spring and neap refer, respectively, to the greatest and smaller range of tidal rise and fall within each monthly cycle. Thus, there are 26 spring and 26 neap tides each year!

At this juncture, we should, perhaps, pause briefly to consider also the various types of coastline and estuary to be encountered in the British Isles. It is relatively easy to categorise coastlines and beaches, as these fall into three main types – rock, pebble and sand. Beaches – where they exist – may be steep or flat and, generally speaking, sandy beaches occur only where the shoreline is fairly flat. Rocky coast – such as found in the west of Scotland, the Islands, and Ireland – may be studded with inlets where sand or fine gravel predominates. Estuaries are far more complicated. There are short estuaries and long estuaries – where the rise and fall of the tide can be measured in either yards or miles. Irrespective of length, there are rocky estuaries, sandy estuaries, muddy estuaries and estuaries where there is a variable mixture of rock, sand, gravel and mud. All may be favoured by sea trout and the only 'safe' generalisation is that sea trout do not linger long in muddy estuaries.

Some rivers, usually flowing steeply into the sea in mountainous locations, may have no estuary to speak of. The estuary, where it exists, may consist of no more than one or two sea pools. However, in some regions this 'sea pool' may consist of a large tidal lake of several hundred acres such as Lough Furnace on the Burrishoole (Co. Mayo) or it may consist of a long, narrow *voe* or *stome* (such as Killary Bay on the Erriff, Co. Galway) where depending on the height of the tidal cycle, salt water may give way to fresh water over a considerable length of channel at low tide.

Finally, before moving on to the basics of fishing for sea trout in tidal waters, we would draw attention to the fact that apart from the type of estuary, another important consideration in fishing tidal waters is how sea trout behave on migrating to sea as smolts or as kelts. We have discussed elsewhere (Chapter 1) the information derived from tagging studies relating to the marine migrations of sea trout. In some areas, notably Wales and the north-east coast of England, sea trout appear to move well out to sea and feed a long way from the coast. In other regions, such as parts of the west coast of Scotland and Ireland and in the Hebrides, Shetland and Orkney, they appear to feed in the estuaries and close to the shore for much of the year. In the former instance coastal fishing is not productive and the sea trout are only available for capture when they approach the coast and penetrate the estuary in order to run upriver to spawn. In some areas, where the runs of migrants begin in the spring, estuary fishing can be productive for much of the season, but in those areas where the runs of spawning fish are late, the season may be restricted to just a few weeks in the autumn.

There is some evidence that the sea trout from several rivers may, at times, congregate in certain estuaries if food is plentiful. One such estuary is claimed to be the famous Ythan (Aberdeenshire). The Teign (South Devon) may be another.

In general terms fish which move well out to sea usually return at a larger size than those that choose to feed in estuaries or along the coast. However, while they may be larger they are much harder to catch; the spawning urge usually inhibits feeding. Certainly it is a rare occurrence to find food in the stomachs of sea trout taken by commercial fishermen in the estuaries of most English and Welsh rivers. This is not the case where the in-shore feeding habit is established and fish of this type attack a lure or bait voraciously. The main problem here is to locate their precise feeding areas along the vast length of coastline that surrounds the British Isles.

And now to the basics.

Saltwater Fishing

Successful saltwater fishing for sea trout depends in the first instance on locating those parts of the coastline where fish feed close to the shore. Such knowledge is often hard-won unless you are able to tap whatever local knowledge exists. In Orkney sea trout appear to feed around much of the coastline from about August until April. It appears that the smolts and kelts move seaward during the late spring and return to the shoreline to feed in late summer. August and September are often the best months as the fish are in the peak of condition. Many of the fish taken in the spring are mending kelts but, because their sojourn in fresh water for spawning was brief because of the lateness of the runs and the shortness of the rivers, it is often impossible to distinguish them from a 'fresh' fish.

Although sea trout *can* be caught from large sandy and shingle beaches, most saltwater fishing is associated with hard rocky or stony shorelines usually studded with small sandy bays and inlets into which the feeding fish forage on the flood tide. By and large the more productive sections of coastline are near to the freshwater inputs of rivers and streams. Why this should be so is difficult to explain other than such inputs may serve as homing points for fish waiting to run upstream. But this does not explain why fish that have no intention of beginning their spawning migration should choose to linger close to fresh water. Perhaps they don't – and such places are more popular with anglers than with sea trout!

The simple reason for the successful rock or stony shores is seaweed! Seaweed does not grow on the unstable substrate provided by shingle, sand or mud because it cannot gain a permanent foothold. Rocky shores composed of large stones provide a good 'holdfast' for innumerable species of seaweed (greens, reds and browns) and it is the larger brown seaweeds (*Phaeophyceae*) that provide the greatest attraction for sea trout. They offer protection, cover and security for the feeding fish.

The problem caused by seaweed for the angler is that it often creates an impenetrable environment that causes much grief in terms of lost tackle – and fish. The problems of dislodging a chalk stream brown trout that (having taken your duly preferred dry-fly) immediately takes refuge in a vast clump of *Ranunculus* palls to insignificance compared with coaxing-out a fighting-fit saltwater sea trout that has gone to ground in a clump of *Fucus* (bladder-wrack). It often seems easier to uproot a willow tree than remove a hook that has snagged in a single strand of kelp!

Falkus refers to the practical benefits of removing seaweed from a chosen fishing venue during low water. This is a daunting task and not something to be contemplated lightly unless you are, as he was, a local resident who fishes a section of coast very regularly. Seaweed soon regenerates and any cleared zone does not remain fishable for very long!

Seaweed presents its densest jungle, and the greatest problems, at low water. As the depth of water increases progressively with the rising tide, the problem reduces – but it still remains a problem in most locations even at the 'top' of the highest tide. The problem of seaweed can often be minimised by fishing as close to the surface as is possible and practical under prevailing conditions. In most situations, conventional bait-fishing on the bottom is (*a*) singularly unproductive as the bait has little movement unless 'worked' and (*b*) impossible in any event.

One technique worthy of trial was developed in Orkney where it yields many fish. This is the 'cocktail' of earthworm and mackerel strip fished on a floating fly line. The standard technique is to use a double taper line with a short (6 feet length) leader of 10lb monofilament to which is attached a round bend (size 4) single hook. A largish lobworm is carefully threaded onto the hook and eased up over the hook eye. The cocktail is provided by a 2–3 inch strip of skin from the silver belly of a mackerel which is mounted on the exposed hook. Under normal circumstances a fairly long cast is required for saltwater fishing (irrespective of whether fishing the bait, spinner or fly): hence the use of the double-taper line, because it is necessary to employ the laconic roll-cast in order to avoid shaking off the relatively soft earthworm (see page 100). The second author has used this technique in Orkney (without success) – but has fished with local experts and can attest to its efficacy. Since then, he has experimented with the technique in other locations and suggests that, by using a 3-hook Stewart-mount, the amazing tough strip of mackerel skin can be mounted so securely that it it possible to dispense with the roll-cast, the double-taper line, *and the superfluous earthworm* and fish with no more than the mackerel strip and a conventional shooting-head (floating) line. The effort required to achieve the same (or greater) distance is less and, while the force may be greater, the holding power of the 3-hook mount and the loss of the basis of the cocktail does not seem to impose any penalties in terms of success. Tradition apart, why be complicated when you can simplify matters to the same effect?

While not dismissing the efficacy of spinning as a means of taking sea trout in salt water, our preference is for fly fishing wherever there is a reasonable chance of taking fish by such means. Again, we would endeavour to fish the fly/lure in, on or just below the surface of the wave to minimise the problem of seaweed and would choose a floating, neutral density, or slow sinking line; and, because greater distance casting is usually necessary than on river or lake, we would opt for a shooting head rather than a conventional forward taper or double taper line. Long casting with a large streamer lure is often necessary and this is much simpler with a shooting head. Our normal choice would be an AFTM 9 or 10 floater or neutral density line with 100–150 yards of 25lb nylon shooting line specially developed for the purpose – and preferably 'memory-free'. We do not normally recommend shooting heads for conventional sea trout angling. But there is nothing conventional about saltwater fishing in this respect, and we would even go as far as to recommend the use of a line-tray strapped around the waist in which to store the shooting line during the retrieve so that it does not get tangled in seaweed – or assorted flotsam and jetsam – between casts.

Our favoured lures for saltwater fly fishing are long streamers. Most are about 1½–3 inches long and nearly all have bright silver bodies of mylar tubing. We use tubes, tandems or Waddingtons and find the lightweight Marchog streamer with its flying-treble particularly efficacious: we recommend the Marchog Glas (Blue Knight) and the Marchog Goch (Red Knight) – and anything that looks like a sand-eel (such the Marchog Melyn (Yellow Knight).

In addition to the shooting head, one other concession we make in our tackle for saltwater fishing is to use a much stronger leader than when fishing in river or lake. This is usually shorter also. For most situations we would use about 6 feet of 10lb nylon: When sea trout are 'shy' and are seen to be following the lure without taking, or when the sea is flat calm we scale down to 9 feet of 6lb line *but* add about 6 inches of 'shock gum' between leader and flyline. The take of a sea trout when it is actively feeding in salt water is often a savage, high-speed slash quite unlike anything experienced by most fresh water anglers. A strong leader able to absorb the shock of a smash-take is a sensible precaution.

Sea trout respond best to a fly or lure worked fast against the current when fishing the wet fly in daylight. This is equally applicable when fishing the fly/lure in salt water. A fast retrieve helps to keep the fly fishing high in the water, as far above the seaweed as possible. The fast retrieve, coupled with the invariably savage take of the fish, makes any advice on how to strike saltwater sea trout irrelevant. Either they hook themselves or they don't! It all happens so quickly that any positive response by the angler is either too late or superfluous. If they hook themselves, then all you have to do is hang-on for as long as possible. Accommodate, as best you can, the first mad dash for freedom and, as rapidly as possible, attempt to assume control over ensuing developments. Some fish will attempt to run for the nearest bed of weed, others head out to sea at a rate of knots. In the former situation you may have real problems: in the latter you are lucky. Provided you have enough backing on your line, let the fish go. It is much safer to play your catch at a distance in deeper water than under the tip where weed is likely to be most dense.

For spinning in salt water we use the same tackle as for river fishing and usually employ lines of 8–10lb. Generally speaking, as with fly fishing, a fast retrieve is more attractive to sea trout and this, combined with the use of a buoyant lure, helps to keep the bait nearer to the surface and away from the weed.

The choice of lure is a matter of preference. We frequently opt for 'something silver' and can recommend the Mepp and the Rapala-type of plug. While silver is indeed a good colour in salt water, do not neglect to include something drab in your tackle-box, as the sea trout will at times favour a blue, brown or green minnow.

Spinning has an advantage over fly fishing in that it is possible to cast further and to cover a greater expanse of water more quickly and efficiently. If intending to spend more than just an hour in pursuing saltwater sea trout then we usually tackle up both our spinning and our fly rods. Experience has shown that spinning can be very effective in finding sea trout in salt water. However, having located taking fish and with a one in the bag we are usually tempted to give the fly a go.

The best time for taking saltwater sea trout is generally acknowledged to be when the tide turns and starts to flow. Good fishing can sometimes be had

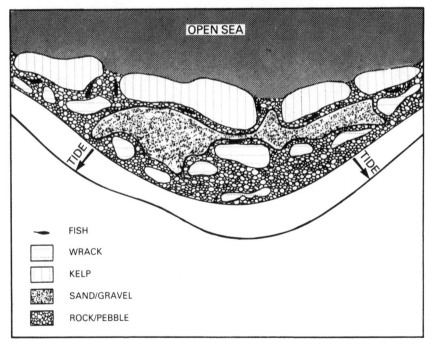

Fig. 59. At low tide sea trout lie close to the cover and protection afforded by the jungle of kelp and bladderwrack. The larger the fish the denser the cover sought. In rough conditions they may move out to feed in the open areas of water between the weedbeds. As the tide flows up the beach the sea trout forsake their low water lies and move into more exposed (and fishable) positions to feed on any items of food displaced by the waves or moving in with the tide.

on low water, but the flowing tide usually provides the more productive fishing. When the turn of the tide coincides with dusk then you can expect some superlative fishing!

As the tide starts to rise, sea trout move out of their low-water positions in and around weedbeds and move up the beach, foraging on whatever food is displaced by the action of the waves and tidal currents, and also pursuing the various food species that do likewise. Not only do the fish move *up* and *down* the shore, they also move *along* it – and penetrate the various coves and inlets. The saltwater angler requires good eyesight and a well developed sense of intuition. Sea trout which were marked down and fished for at low water rarely move in a straight line directly up and down the shore as the tide rises and falls. While the water level rises vertically and appears to move in a straight line, the tidal current may hit the shore at an angle as the tide flows: and it moves back in the opposite direction as the tide ebbs. The sea trout will follow the tide – and so must the angler.

The feeding behaviour of the sea trout in its natural environment is often capricious and challenging. Because a trout is actively feeding does not mean it throws caution to the wind or that its natural instincts for self-preservation

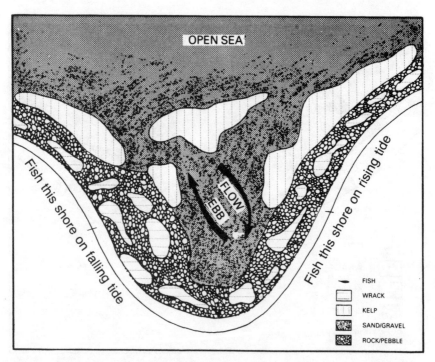

Fig. 60. While the tide appears to rise and fall vertically up the shore, it is important to remember that the tidal current will usually ebb and flow *at an angle* to the shoreline. Fish move into and out of bays and inlets with the direction of the current. In this situation the shore to the right of the inlet will usually be the most productive as the tide flows while the opposite shore is the best place to fish as the tide recedes.

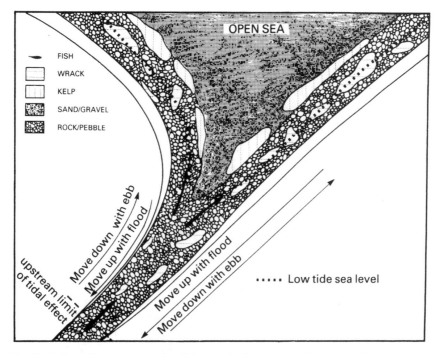

Fig. 61. At low tide sea trout may lie off the mouth of an estuary and move in and out with each tide. Since weed growth becomes less dense in estuaries because of the inhibiting effect of fresh water on growth, the fishing becomes much simpler. In this situation, the best general policy is to follow the tide upstream on the flood and then to follow it back out to sea on the ebb. Of those fish that move into the estuary with the tide, some may continue to run upstream into the river proper, some may remain behind in the estuary (provided there is suitable depth and cover) and others may move back out to sea again.

and survival are ignored. The fish still seeks cover and sanctuary from its many marine predators; and this may be why sea trout are associated with rocky shores and seaweed rather than sandy beaches where seaweed is lacking.

While sea-trout fishing from sandy beaches is not normally productive, sea trout appear to have taken the place of the majestic (and grossly over-exploited) bass in the surf beaches of Donegal: where some of the best marks are Ballyness Bay, Tra-na-Rossan Bay and the narrows at the mouth of Mulroy Bay.

Estuary Fishing

While our saltwater fishing has been focused mainly on rocky shores and coastlines, our estuary fishing has been concentrated, almost exclusively, in long 'sandy' estuaries – the longer the better. There are several rivers in Wales with long, wide estuaries of this type, where the tidal rise and fall affects several miles of channel: the Conwy, Mawddach, Dyfi, Teifi and Tywi being classic examples. Sadly, sea trout in Wales do not dwell in such estuaries to feed to anything like the same extent as in similar estuaries in parts of Scotland and Ireland: and so estuary fishing is only a practical proposition when the adult fish are running into fresh water in order (ultimately) to spawn. Fortunately this is from April to the end of the season in mid-October in the larger Welsh rivers.

Sandy estuaries come in many shapes and sizes. Most that we fish have well defined low water channels that are relatively stable from one season to the next in terms of the location, size and depth of the pools and runs. (It is our view that sea trout try to avoid resting in sections of river and estuary where the channel is unstable.)

We rejoice in fishing sandy estuaries. Estuaries have a particular fascination which is hard to explain. Our two main requirements (in addition to the presence of fish) are that the estuary should contain at least one or two (preferably more) well developed resting or holding pools in which fish can settle as the tide drops back: and that it should be as remote as possible from any popular bathing beach. 'People-pressure' is a serious problem in many English and Welsh estuaries during the peak months of the holiday season!

Our broad approach to estuary fishing is to fish the receding tide as we would a declining spate when river fishing. The only real difference is that, while a spate may take several days to run-off in the river, the twice-daily tide runs-off in a matter of hours so that the time when a particular technique of fishing is 'the method of the moment' may be telescoped into a matter of minutes rather than into hours.

Whenever we can, we arrive on the estuary at the top of the tide – or just as it starts to turn and flow back to sea. We rarely bother to fish a tidal pool for more than a few minutes after the arrival of the flooding tide unless, depending on the height of the tide and our location within the estuary, the rise in level is small and the tide runs in and out very quickly. It is difficult to fish a fly, spinner or bait properly when the current is flowing upstream at a fast rate. It may be possible to fish a worm in certain locations, provided a heavy weight is used, but we find that we catch very little – other than eels or flounders – in the rising tide. The period *just before* and *just after* the tide reaches a pool can, however, be very productive. It is as if the fish sense the imminent arrival of the tide and become so excited at the prospect that they become more active – and so are more receptive to a well-fished bait or lure.

As with spate fishing, worming, spinning and fly fishing all become – in turn – the best method as the river level drops off from peak flow to normal flow: the receding tide also favours a particular method depending on the water level and speed of the current. As the tide starts to ebb, it runs off quickly and then slows down as low-water level is reached. At low water the only current is occasioned by the natural river flow of fresh water. The first stage of the ebb usually favours spinning as the fish may be well distributed over the length and breadth of the channel and may still be moving in from the sea. In sandy estuaries the water can be coloured with suspended solids during large tides and, as noted above, spinning allows a lot of water to be covered effectively and efficiently – in both the vertical and surface planes. At a certain point during the ebb, usually just before the characteristics of the low water channel begin to emerge, conditions often favour the fly. The fish are now more concentrated and begin to move towards their low water lies. Much, if not all, of the colour disappears and there is usually enough current and depth to make fishing a fly worthwhile in the glides, runs and pool tails. Then, as the tide has more or less run off completely, the low water worm comes into its own – provided that there is current enough to work it round so that it can be presented properly to sea trout now settled in their low water lies.

Successful fishing in estuaries depends on learning *how* fish behave and *where* they lie in relation to the ebb and flow of the tide: and also on understanding the effects of the tidal cycle in relation to a particular estuary. One strategy is to leap-frog *upstream* ahead of the incoming tide and to fish a worm in each successive pool for a few minutes or so until it starts to be affected by the rise in water level. Another strategy is 'to fish the tide out', moving downstream from section to section and fishing the spinner or the fly for a while in each section as appropriate, moving seaward to the next section when the current, depth and disposition of the fish no longer favours the chosen method. More suitable on small estuaries where the ability to roam is restricted, is to fish one pool using several different techniques according to the water level and state of the tide. This can prove productive in large tidal pools when the sea trout are present in quantity. However, when fish are scarce early and late in the season the best policy is usually to cover as much of the estuary as possible.

Much of our estuary fishing employs the tackle and lures that we use in river fishing. Estuary sea trout that are newly from the sea can take a bait, fly or lure with extreme savagery. Since they are also usually in the peak of condition we err on the side of caution and fish a slightly stronger line or leader than we would under similar water and weather conditions when river or lake fishing.

Estuaries, by their very nature, are open and exposed to the wind, so it pays to take more warm clothing than you think you will need, especially during the early and later part of the season. A good stiff upstream breeze can often occur on low water when conditions for the dry fly may be perfect for an hour or so.

Estuaries can provide good night fishing if they have sufficient holding water at low tide and if the time of the tide is such that the final stages of the ebb and low water occur at or after dusk. A rising tide shortly after dusk is to be avoided unless you wish to waste time sitting on the bank – cursing your failure to consult or comprehend the tide table!

Estuary fishing on low tides can be very good also when there is a spate in the river and the estuary is wide enough to dissipate the full force of the current. Spates usually mean coloured water, so the emphasis is either on bait fishing or spinning; but heavy fly fishing can also be productive if colour is not too strong.

We discuss the law relating to fishing in tidal waters elsewhere (Chapter 2). A few other words of caution are appropriate here. It is all too easy to get cut off by the tide, so make sure that you have an alternative route of escape if you are fishing in small bays and inlets around a rocky coastline. Your life – or the lives of those in the emergency services who are called out to rescue you – may depend on it. Many of the larger estuaries are surrounded by marshland or rough grazing land interlaced with complicated networks of deep drainage ditches. The rising tide may sweep back several miles into these ditches necessitating either a long detour or a very long wait for the ebb tide. In some estuaries there may be the risk of 'quicksand' or of becoming surrounded by the tide when fishing from reefs or islands of sand or gravel.

In concluding this chapter we should, perhaps, refer to the food of sea trout in tidal waters, as this is relevant to the lure or bait chosen by the angler when fishing in both fresh water and salt water.

It is now accepted that the sea trout, like the salmon, does not feed actively when in fresh water and this has led to the hypothesis that the most effective fly, lure or bait when fishing in lake or river is one that evokes the memory of its diet within the sea. Since it is widely believed that sea trout feed on sand eels, sprats, young herring and other fish species, the use of silver-bodied fish-like lures is advocated by many authors as being the best choice – at least as far as fresh-run fish are concerned.

Relatively few studies on the marine feeding of sea trout have been undertaken, and while these have established that they do feed on fish, they have also established that they will devour many other organisms also. One recent study examined the diet of some 1,200 sea trout from sea lochs in the west of Scotland. The most frequently occurring items of food were crustacea (present in 43% of stomachs), followed by insects (31.1%), fish (30.6%), annelids (5.1%) and the occasional mollusc. While fish made up the greatest part of the diet in terms of weight of food ingested (69%), compared with crustacea (17.5%), insects (8.9%) and annelids (4.4%), the actual numbers of individual fish eaten were almost negligible when compared with the number of much smaller crustacea and other species contained in the diet.

The point to bear in mind is that the sea trout is an opportunistic feeder likely to eat whatever is most readily available. It certainly does not feed exclusively on fish, and is just as likely to take a drab, non-silver lure that bears no resemblance to a fish as it is a carefully contrived imitation of a sand-eel. Nevertheless, silver is without doubt an effective colour for sea trout, irrespective of any evocative connections; but do not let its widespread popularity prevent you from trying something different.

PART III
Stillwater Angling

12 · INTRODUCTION

Angling for sea trout in stillwater is regarded as a somewhat abstruse branch of the sport by many English and Welsh anglers, for the simple reason that there are very few lakes containing sea trout within these regions. Only four lakes in Wales contain sea trout. There are more, but not many more, in England and these are confined to the Lake District. Fortunately there are many areas in Scotland and Ireland where sea trout have ready access to stillwaters and where as a consequence these fisheries are very popular. Indeed in some parts of the country stillwater fishing is the norm and produces many more sea trout than taken from the rivers in the area.

For clarity and consistency we propose to use the term 'lake' for any standing body of freshwater. Thus, we include here the loughs of Ireland, the lochs and lochans of Scotland, the Llynnoedd (= plural of Llyn) of Wales and the lakes of England.

Lake fishing for sea trout has several forms of which the wet-fly and dapping are by far the most common. Nevertheless lake sea trout can be caught by any legitimate means and there are a number of other techniques which, while not widely practised, are worthy of mention. It is convenient therefore to divide our treatment of the subject into three chapters covering:

1. Wet-fly (Chapter 13);
2. Dapping (Chapter 14);
3. Other methods (Chapter 15).

The classic sea-trout lake is one situated a short distance from the sea with little more than a short connecting length of river. Lakes of this type are likely to contain fresh-run fish right from the start of the season, and it is these fish which usually provide the cream of the fishing. A number of Irish and Scottish rivers have lakes within their catchments, but some are too far upstream to provide the best fishing while others which in theory are ideally located within a short distance from the sea do not, for some peculiar reason, afford good sea trout fishing. Examples of the former are Lochs Tay and Earn; while the Grimersta system on the Hebridean Isle of Lewis and Loch Shin are examples of the latter.

The bulk of the lake fishing for sea trout is geographically skewed to the western Highlands and Islands of Scotland and to the west and north-west of Ireland, where as a result of fortuitous geological phenomena the terrain is such that many good lakes occur within the river systems.

Perhaps the best known sea-trout lake of all is Loch Maree in Wester Ross. This is an enormous lake by any standards (12,000 acres), and is deservedly famous for both the large size and number of fly-caught sea trout taken each year. Some excellent bags of sea trout have been taken from Maree. In 1948 two anglers caught 17 fish with an average weight of 5lb in one session and sea trout of up to 20lb weight have been taken here on the fly. Other well-known Scottish venues are Loch Lomond, one of the most southerly Scottish sea trout lakes, Lochs Hope, Shiel, Eilt, Stack and Assynt – to name but a few. These are large waters.

There are in addition many smaller lakes where excellent sea-trout fishing occurs. Indeed, in the Hebrides lake fishing on countless lochs is standard practice, largely because the rivers are mostly too short and too small to provide worthwhile sport other than when in flood.

The West of Ireland is endowed also with a wealth of good sea trout lakes. The many loughs of Connemara and Mayo are perhaps among the best known Irish sea trout lakes. Furnace, Feagh, Beltra, Doo, Tawnyard are just a few of the many available to the angler. The counties of Donegal, Kerry and Sligo have their share also, and Lough Currane is widely recognised as one of the better Irish sea trout fisheries.

Most sea trout lakes are situated amongst some of the finest and rugged scenery in the British Isles, and since lakes are not affected appreciably by fluctuations in water level, angling can continue productively long after the river has shrunk to a trickle and the frustrated river anglers have been obliged to hang up their rods until the next rain. Moreover, the lake offers its best fishing during the daytime when the river sea trout are usually far less responsive to the fly. Why sea trout should take a fly more readily on a lake in daylight in contrast to their behaviour in a river is a curious phenomenon. It is, however, a simple fact that they do.

The best months for sea-trout fishing in lakes are generally the same as on most rivers; provided that they are not too far from the sea. July and August are often the most dependable months, with September being good in some seasons. June can also be a good month on some lakes and the larger waters may have a small stock of fish in May or even in April.

Generally speaking, there is much less *available* lake fishing than river fishing. Although the lakes may have many miles of perimeter bank, they are better fished from a boat, and it is the limited availability of the boats that tends to regulate access to the water. Good lake fishing for sea trout is deservedly popular. Many of the better fisheries tend to be booked several seasons ahead during the peak months, and it is always a good practice to check in advance that the fishing and boats are available for the period required.

The ideal weather conditions for boat fishing are a steady wind which creates a good surface wave of about 6–9 inches in height and which blows down a long shore. The presence of a breeze and a wave on the lake surface are important for three main reasons. First, the breeze allows the boat to be drifted downwind to cover the water. Second, it aids casting and the action of the flies as they are fished. Third, it provides cover to make the boat and the angler(s) less visible and less likely to disturb the fish. It also seems to make the fish more responsive – but this may be a circular argument.

Temperature seems not to be that important, but light and cloud cover are. The best sky has a good high cloud with an occasional glimpse of the sun. A low cloud or a mist are not propitious: neither is a grey light. The worst wind is one that comes and goes, changes direction every so often and creates 'blackwater' as it gusts down *onto* the surface. Rain is not a problem unless you are dapping – when it soaks the line and is disastrous. A wind with some south or west in it is widely regarded as a 'kind' wind, and is generally preferred on most lakes. However, some lakes, either from geographical location or perversity, may actually fish better with a wind from the north or east! Lack of cloud cover is not a serious problem provided there is a good wave on the surface of the lake.

There is nothing quite so daunting as arriving on the banks of a new lake for the first time and being faced with a vast expanse of water. Where are the fish to be found? If you are wise you will hire a professional boatman who can take you directly to the most productive areas. Boatmen leave the angler free to concentrate on the fishing, they do all the hardwork of controlling the drift of the boat, and their judgement and experience can make all the difference to the success of the day and your comfort and safety while on the water. In the absence of a boatman or local advice gleaned from the nearby

A good boatman who 'knows the water' is a wise investment at the best of times. Becalmed on Lough Furnace (Burrishoole Fishery, Co. Mayo) and Tommy contemplates where to go and what to do next! (Photo: G.S. Harris.)

267

hostelries you must work things out for yourself!

A few words here about safety and personal comfort while boat fishing.

Safety is a matter of anticipation, preparation and common sense. Anticipate the worst, prepare for the worst and don't be stupid. Water is dangerous, boats are inherently unsafe and the weather is always unpredictable. Both of us admit to having experienced genuine fear for our lives when caught out by the weather in little boats on big lakes.

Never fish alone. Make sure that someone knows where you are going and when to expect you back. Wear a life-jacket or buoyancy aid even if you can swim. Avoid standing up in a boat while fishing, and if you do stand or move about the boat do so with extreme caution. Never wear studded footwear.

Check that the boat has a suitable bailer and that the rowlocks are safe and secured to the boat (carry a spare pair if you can).

Most boats on large lakes will be fitted with an outboard. Make sure that it is securely fixed to the transom and that you have enough fuel for the day plus about 25 per cent more than you think you will need. Carry a tool kit containing a spare plug, plug spanner, a screwdriver and some pliers, along with a spare prop spring and shear-pins. A spare pull-cord may be required unless the engine is of modern design.

Try to check the local weather forecast before setting out. *If in doubt don't go out!* If you do get caught out in a heavy wave and strong wind try to keep the bows into the wave. Never, turn the boat across a heavy wave. Try to keep to the sheltered shore even if it means a long detour to your landing point. If you have any doubt about making it back to the landing point then do not try! It is better to walk than drown, so head for the *safest* landing point no matter how distant it is from where you wish to be.

If you do capsize, avoid the temptation to swim for the nearest shore. It is probably far better to stay with the boat while it is still floating as it will eventually drift ashore somewhere.

Beware of submerged rocks when moving under power and when drifting. Some fisheries provide very detailed maps of the water. Check to see if one is available. Finally, as a general principle on a new water of any appreciable size, hire a local boatman if you can.

Comfort when boat fishing is often neglected. It may be a lovely warm day when you set out but the weather can be very changeable and you will be very exposed to the sun, wind and rain while out on the water. A warm jumper is advisable even on a warm day. Knee boots (unstudded) are useful if you want to go ashore and to keep your feet dry in the boat (which invariably has some water sloshing about in the bottom). A good waterproof hat and jacket (preferably with a hood, because you fish with your back to the rain) are essential. So too are waterproof over-trousers to keep the legs and backside dry.

Fishing should be carried out while sitting down. Very few boats have adequate or comfortable seats so something soft to sit on is a must if you wish to delay the inevitable 'numb-bum' syndrome familar to all boat fishermen for as long as possible. A buoyancy cushion is a sensible choice.

Sea-trout fishing in a lake is not, as it might seem at first, a technique of mere chuck-and-chance. The same understanding of the habits and be- haviour of the fish combined with experience and the ability to 'read' the water are as much required on lakes as on rivers – perhaps more so! The river angler often has the distinct advantage that it is frequently possible to observe the shoals of fish lying in the shallower confines of a pool or glide and can mark down their general position in the sure knowledge that they are unlikely to move much during the course of the day. The lake angler does not have that advantage. The lake itself *is* the pool. One enormous pool! It may have a surface area of several thousand acres and may be more than 100 feet deep in places. So where are the fish?

Fortunately, sea trout (and salmon also) do not distribute themselves at random throughout the entire lake. Sea trout, whether in a lake or a river, are subject to the same instincts of self-preservation and the same need to avoid wasting energy by unnecessary swimming. Although fresh-run fish may spend some time 'exploring' the lake, they eventually select a particular holding area where they may remain for some considerable time until they decide to move off in search of their natal spawning streams.

Although sea trout can occasionally be caught over very deep water, such fish are likely to be 'explorers' only temporarily available at that location and encountered by pure good luck. It is widely accepted that sea trout (and salmon) tend to seek out and take up semi-permanent residence in the relatively shallow parts of the lake. Some anglers suggest that sea trout congregate in water of up to 10 feet in depth, others suggest that water up to 20 feet deep can be equally productive. Consequently, sea trout are most likely to be found lying along the shoreline, around islands and close to rock outcrops rising up from the bottom, in shallow bays and inlets and, parti- cularly, close to the mouths of any spawning streams entering the lake. Within these areas they appear to favour a rocky bottom over a sandy or silty bottom and, generally, to avoid mud. They will lie close to any underwater cover afforded by rocks, reed beds and submerged weeds (see Fig. 62). Sea trout will often lie in remarkably shallow water, so it pays to fish right up to the shoreline. A good test to check for 'correct' depth is when a fully extended oar held vertically downwards just touches the bottom. When this occurs the depth is just about right.

Clues to the depth of water in a lake can be provided by the contours of the surrounding land (Fig. 63). A high, steeply-sloping bank indicates deep water inshore: the steeper and higher the bank the deeper the water. A flat low bank suggests shallow water for some considerable distance into the lake. Reeds cannot survive in deep water and weed beds rarely occur in water more than 20 feet deep. Shallow, and often very productive, water usually occurs where streams enter the lake, as the gravel washed down by countless floods over the centuries tends to form an elevated delta extending some distance into the lake.

269

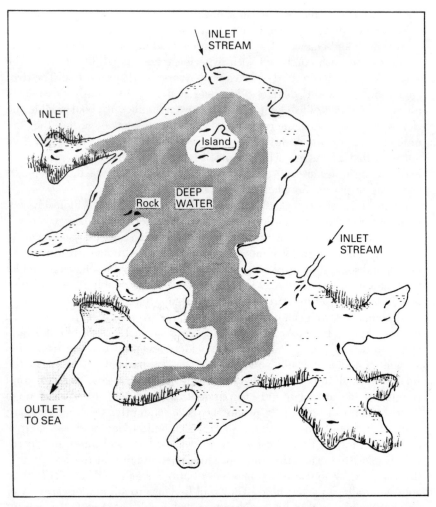

Fig. 62. A (not so) hypothetical sea trout lake. The shaded area indicates water with a depth of more than 20 feet. Fish lie in the shallower water near to the shoreline, off promontories, in bays and inlets, around islands and close to tributary streams. We would expect fish to be disposed as shown any time after June in most lakes near to the sea.

Fig. 63 (Opposite). Reading a lake. The first time out on a large and new lake can be a daunting experience. Where are the fish? The most productive areas for sea trout and salmon are the shallower waters of less than 20 feet in depth (at the most). The contours of the land surrounding the lake can provide useful clues as to the depth of the water. So, too, can the presence of emergent reeds and submerged weeds. Learning how to *read* any body of water irrespective of whether it is a river, lake, estuary or the sea is a prerequisite of the complete angler.

270

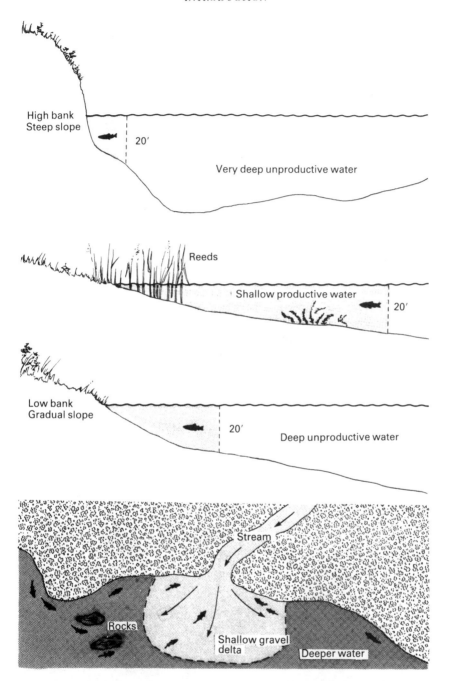

High bank
Steep slope

20′

Very deep unproductive water

Reeds

Shallow productive water

20′

Low bank
Gradual slope

20′

Deep unproductive water

Stream

Rocks

Shallow gravel
delta

Deeper water

13 · THE WET FLY

Wet-fly fishing from the bank is discussed in Chapter 15, and we are concerned here with only wet-fly fishing from a boat. This is by far the most efficient and effective way to fish any but the very smallest 'ponds', since it gives free access to every section of productive and fishable water no matter how obtuse the wind and how distant the holding water from the shoreline.

A necessary prerequisite to successful boat fishing is a decent wind to drift the boat across the surface of the lake and to create a wave which hides the boat and its occupants from the fish. As the wind drops and the wave becomes smaller, stealth and caution in handling the boat and presenting the fly to the fish become increasingly important. In the absence of wind and wave the angler has to resort to a different approach and style of fishing, but given the presence of a decent ripple there are two basic styles of fishing the wet-fly that will be employed generally: the surface/subsurface fly and the sunk fly.

The surface/subsurface fly is by and large the most popular method of wet-fly fishing and on many waters represents the 'classic' or 'traditional' style of

fishing well known to brown-trout anglers. However, the sunk-fly has its adherents and it may be the standard method on a few waters. It is often employed under certain 'adverse' conditions and is often used later in the season when the sea trout have become stale and are less responsive to the surface/subsurface fly. It also comes into its own when the wind fails or when the fish are unresponsive to the classic style for some unexplainable reason. Both styles may be equally effective at times when fished side-by-side under the same conditions by two anglers sharing the same boat. In our view, classic-style fishing has more appeal and interest than the sunk fly in that many of the rises are seen rather than felt, and given the correct weather and water conditions this would be our favoured choice of method.

Traditional style wet-fly fishing entails working a team of two or three (sometimes even four) flies just beneath, in and on the surface. The topmost fly on the leader is termed the 'bob' and particular attention is given to promoting the action of this particular fly through the surface of the water in an attractive 'bobbing' or 'dibbling' fashion by gradually raising the rod up towards the vertical position as the flies are drawn in towards the boat (Fig. 64). This style of fishing goes way back in time. The bob-fly may represent the original form of the 'wake-fly' employed in river fishing for sea trout (page 211). It is generally stated that a long rod allows the bob-fly to be worked at a greater distance from the boat and, hence, to be fishing effectively for a longer period of time following each cast (Fig. 65). This is a matter of fact and longer rods have certain other advantages in playing and fishing out the cast. However some anglers who fish in the International Trout Fly Fishing championships believe that long rods also have penalties in striking because of the bow of line which curves down from the rod-tip and militates against an instantaneous strike (Fig. 66). Thus, it may be that we should consider a trade-off between the advantages of a long rod in raising fish and a short rod in hooking fish, and opt for something of an intermediate 'compromise' length.

This style of fishing covers a range of options with the members of the team of flies fishing variously under, in and on the surface. The bob-fly is frequently the most productive member of the team, and its action in and on the surface provides the added pleasure that most rises to this fly are visible. Some anglers focus their efforts and attention solely on the working of the bob-fly and dispense with the middle fly of the conventional team-of-three and regard the tail (= point) fly as little more than an anchor to provide for better control over the movement of the bob-fly (see also page 300).

The bob-fly itself is a characteristically bushy concoction designed to create a disturbance on the surface. It is replaced by something more streamlined when fishing the sunk fly, as this method entails casting a longer line and fishing the flies at a greater depth beneath the surface. Consequently a bob-fly cannot be worked effectively and is superfluous as such. Some anglers fish just one or two flies when 'going-down' to the fish on a sunk line. The longer line usually employed in this method has two advantages: it

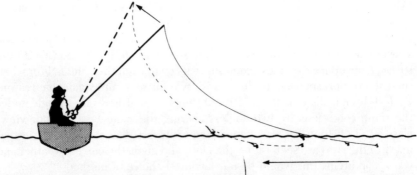

Fig. 64. Most lake fishing is practised from a drifting boat with a team of three wet-flies fished in or just under the surface. In this style of fishing the topmost fly (nearest the rod) is the bob-fly. It is often the most effective hooker and attractor in the team and is worked back across the surface to create a disturbance by raising the rod steadily to the upright (vertical) position as the cast is fished out.

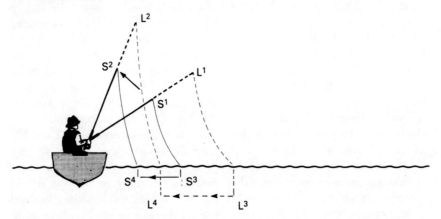

Fig. 65. Long rod or short rod? A long rod has several advantages for working the bob-fly. The cast L^1–L^3 is worked back to L^4 as the rod is raised to L^2. The distance L^3–L^4 obtained with a long rod is greater than the distance S^3–S^4 obtained with a shorter rod. Thus the bob-fly fishes more efficiently.

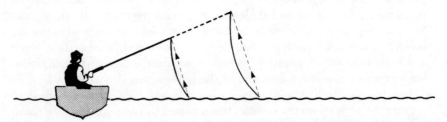

Fig. 66. Long rod or short rod? The bow of line that forms between the rod tip and the water surface is less pronounced with a short rod and so allows more immediate contact with the fish on striking. But a quick strike is often to be avoided when fishing the bob-fly or the dap and a greater bow of line obtained with a longer rod may be an advantage in letting the fish turn with the fly before it feels any resistance.

274

Doolough on the famous Delphi Fishery in Co. Mayo. A nice sea trout comes to the net. (Photo: John Wilshaw.)

allows more water to be covered with each cast and, by regulating the rate of retrieve of the line in working the flies back towards the boat, allows the flies to fish at various depths. To some extent, the style of wet-fly fishing influ-ences certain features of the tackle. We have just mentioned the merits and demerits of long and short rods in covering the water and striking fish. The long rod has distinct advantages when playing a fish especially when it heads for a weed bed or attempts to take refuge under the boat. A long rod also avoids that worrying feature of the knot which joins the line to the leader 'see-sawing' in and out of the top rings of the rod when playing a fish close to the boat or when it is being netted.

At the bottom end of the scale a normal trout rod of 9 feet in length can be used for both styles of wet-fly fishing. At the other end of the scale some anglers prefer long rods of 12–14 feet for traditional-style fishing with the bob-fly. A rod of about 10–11 feet approaches the ideal for both styles of fishing. Since it is also our preferred length for river fishing, it allows the same rod to be used on both still and running waters – an obvious advantage.

The reel used for lake fishing should be loaded with plenty of backing line. Sea trout often tend to run for deep water in lakes and since they cannot be pursued until the boat has been brought under control they must be given their head during their initial break for freedom. It is sensible to allow for this eventuality and provide the latitude and reassurance of 100–150 yards of backing.

The ability to recover line very rapidly when a fish turns and heads towards the boat is also an advantage provided by a reel with a geared (multiplying) re-wind. Although the line can be stripped rapidly in to the bottom of the boat, this is a bad habit and one likely to cause grief sooner or later. Try to play the fish from the reel at all times and not from the tangle of line in the bottom of the boat where it can get trodden on and damaged and where it inevitably gets caught up at a critical time when you desperately require to give line to a running fish.

Casting takes place downwind of the boat and is usually over a shorter distance than when river fishing. Heavy lines for achieving distance and for 'punching' a fly into the wind are unnecessary. We much prefer forward-taper to double-taper lines for river fishing (page 92) and find these perfectly suitable for lake fishing, although we tend to use lighter lines (AFTM 6–7) when fishing. The roll-cast (page 100) is quite useful at times and it allows a reasonable length of line to be cast with the minimum of effort.

For traditional-style fishing a floating, neutral density or slow-sink line is recommended. Much bob-fly fishing is done with floating lines but we find the new generation of almost neutral buoyancy lines equally suitable and they have the distinct advantage that, unlike the floater, they can be fished in the most delicate ripple or dead flat water without creating a disturbing wake on the water surface.

It is stating the obvious to say that sunk-line fishing requires a sinking line. However, the flies do not need to be fished too deeply – perhaps no more than 12 inches below the surface – so a sink-tip or slow-to-medium sinking line can generally be used.

The choice of line depends very much on the prevailing wind and wave conditions – as too does the style of fishing employed. A stronger wind means a faster rate of drift by the boat so that the flies have less opportunity to sink to the required depth before they have to be recast. For sunk-line fishing under these conditions a faster sinking line would have obvious advantages. Conversely, a light breeze means a slow drift and a slower sinking line would be used to achieve the same depth of fly.

Most lake fishing is practised with a leader of 'standard' length (about 9 feet). A longer leader of 12 feet (or more) may be required under conditions of bright sun and minimum ripple. A leader of less than 9 feet in length is not recommended. We have discussed droppers and dropper knots previously (Chapter 5). We prefer our droppers to stand out from the main line as opposed to hanging down almost parallel to the leader. We also prefer the top dropper to be slightly longer than normal when fishing the bob-fly. Dropper spacings are usually set at about 3 feet and 4 feet from the tail fly on a three-fly leader. Some anglers prefer slightly different spacings but as a general rule the top dropper should not be closer than about 5 feet to the fly-line. Use tapered leaders if you wish; they give a better presentation, but this is not quite so crucial when fishing a shortish cast in a decent ripple.

The problem of line and leader 'flash' is even more critical on lakes than on

In some parts of Scotland and Ireland the majority of sea trout are caught in stillwaters, usually on the wet-fly. A sequence from the Burrishoole. *Top*: Playing a fish is often a matter of 'hanging-on' and following with the boat after the first frantic run by a decent fish. But do not let the fish play you; keep a good bend in the rod and try to make the fish move against the pull of the line. *Centre*: The fish is brought round to the windward side of the boat just before netting so that the boat does not drift over the fish. The boatman ('PJ') does the rest. A generous net has many advantages when boat fishing. *Bottom*: A nice fish, just over 4lb, at the end of a very difficult day when everything (wind, rain, light) was 'wrong'. (Photo: Tom Quinn.)

rivers as there is absolutely no shelter or shade in an open boat out in the middle of a lake. Thus we prefer darker lines (brown, black or green) to pale lines (white, peach or straw) when boat fishing and earnestly stress again the importance of a dull or matt, 'flash-free' finish to the nylon used in the manufacture of the leader.

For perfect to near-perfect conditions of wind and wave the strength of the leader nylon should be about 6lb. In conditions of bright sun and gentle ripple a finer nylon of about 4lb strength may be appropriate, while in a really good wave under dull conditions a stronger nylon of 8lb or more may be appropriate – especially if large sea trout or salmon are likely to be encountered. *Never fish too fine*. Sea trout are undoubtedly 'gut-shy', but the use of ultra-fine leaders of less than 3lb strength is, in our view, rarely justified and generally irresponsible. Better a lost take than a leader break!

And now let us move on to the choice of fly. Almost every lake angler will have a particular preference for certain patterns of sea-trout fly based on experience, local tradition or prejudice. Among the traditional brown trout patterns, the *Black Pennell, Zulu, Grouse and Claret, Butcher, Teal and Red Teal and Green, Peter Ross, Mallard and Yellow, Grouse and Green,* and *Dunkeld* are more often than not included in the recommended top ten Scottish sea trout flies. For Irish waters we see a few changes, with the *Blue Zulu, Kingsmill, Green Peter, Connemara Black* and the *Fiery Brown* making an appearance.

As noted above, the bob-fly has its own very characteristic dressing. It is usually a bushy affair with a heavy hackle tied Palmer-style down the body. The middle dropper and tail flies are usually more streamlined in appearance and less heavily dressed: although they are still fairly bulky when compared with the popular vogue in river sea-trout flies.

For sunk-line fishing a less bushy fly is popular. Some anglers use double or treble hooks to provide extra weight to sink the fly to the required depth quickly; and to provide greater hookability. Several traditional patterns of salmon fly have proved effective for sunk-line fishing – such as the *Silver Doctor, Black Doctor, Thunder and Lightning* (Irish dressing), *Hairy Mary* and *Haslam*.

Many new patterns have achieved popularity in recent years and several traditional patterns of both brown trout and salmon flies have been adopted and adapted for sea trout in lakes. The *Daddy-Long-Legs, Rob Roy, Kate McLaren* and *Loch Ordie* (sedge style) are all good bob-flies. The *Bibio* fishes well on first and second dropper while the *Dark* and *Red Mackerels* are both good point and second dropper flies. So too are the *Moonbeam, Dunnock* and *Orange and Black Twists*.

The general range of sizes recommended for lake sea trout is 8–12 for 'standard' conditions. Sizes up to 6 may be used on a very big wave, while sizes down to 14 may be appropriate on a very light ripple. On the largest waters, such as Maree and Lomond, bigger flies of sizes 6–8 are often used (perhaps because larger waters get a better wave) but on smaller waters size

10 seem to be the favoured size for normal conditions.

It is somewhat curious that in lake fishing smaller flies are frequently used for salmon than for sea trout. This may be because sea trout tend to lie in somewhat deeper water than salmon and a larger fly is necessary to 'bring them up' from a greater depth.

Before leaving the topic of fly patterns, we wish to mention the *Red Stuart*. This consists of a silver body with a tail, wing and hackle of red Ibis. Hamish Stuart, the founder of modern sea-trout fishing, used this pattern with great success in South Uist at the turn of the century and it would be fitting to his memory to see it in general use today.

The incorporation of fluorescent and luminescent materials into fly dressings has once again become popular following a brief vogue in the 1950s. Some anglers swear by it, others believe it does not make any difference to the efficacy of a fly. The conditions of light often experienced when lake fishing are sometimes such that a small amount of fluorescence incorporated into the dressing of a bob-fly, dry fly or dap-fly may enhance its appeal in drawing fish to the surface and, equally relevant, in making the rise more positive. Visibility and attraction are important in lake fishing and we always carry a few patterns which incorporate a hint of fluorescence in their dressings – in the tag, body or hackle. The *Bibio* with fluorescent orange seal's fur in the mid-body section and the *Rob Roy* with an interwound fluorescent red hackle are both good flies in our experience.

We attach considerable importance to working the fly while it is being fished to impart both movement and direction. This applies to both classic-style and sunk-line fishing. The technique of imparting movement and direction to the fly depends very much on the style and length of line being fished.

Many anglers cast a short line when fishing a bob-fly and merely raise the rod from the horizontal to vertical positions to provide movement – hence the benefit of a long rod. The direction of the movement of the fly can be altered effectively by swinging the rod in an elevated arc across the body, either to the left or the right, as the rod is raised up to the vertical (Fig. 67). A short line can be effective under certain conditions and it is always surprising how close to the boat some fish will take a fly if not scared (literally under the oars). However, it is often necessary to cast a longish line – especially when fishing the sunk-fly – and then work the flies by recovering line with a figure-of-eight retrieve or by stripping-back. Some anglers favour a fast recovery; others prefer a slow recovery. Some favour a steady retrieve while others work the fly back in a jerky (sink-and-draw) fashion by stripping line with a series of short, sharp pulls. The method adopted is a matter of choice and it often pays to experiment on the day if fish are unresponsive or otherwise tentative in their approach to the fly.

We use the terms 'fast' and 'slow' for the recovery of the line in a comparative sense in relation to the speed of the drift. It is not unusual for the boat to drift at a rate where it overtakes a fly worked slowly. In such circum-

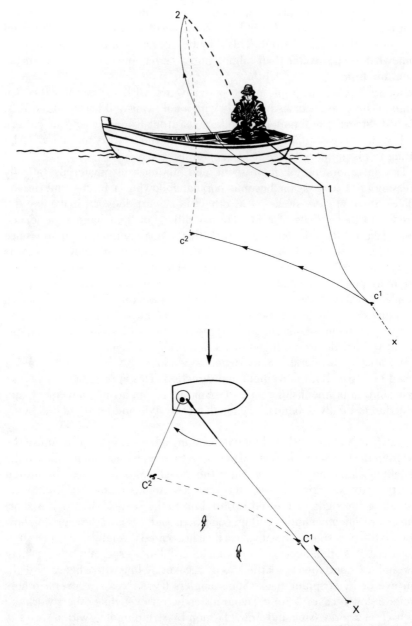

Fig. 67. When fishing the wet-fly from a boat it often pays to present the flies laterally across the line of the drift rather than working the cast straight back (see also Figure 68). In the above the cast is made to position x and, depending on the length of line cast, the flies are worked back to position C^1 at which point the bob-fly begins to drag the surface. The rod is raised steadily to the vertical from position 1 to position 2 and simultaneously swung from left to right (or vice versa) across the body (top). The flies then move from C^1 to C^2 and are presented to the fish with a different profile.

280

stances a fast recovery may only impart a slow movement to the fly. It is often necessary to recover line very fast in a good stiff breeze in order to work the fly effectively. It is difficult to recover line quickly with the figure-of-eight retrieve and, therefore, stripping-back is required.

The direction of the cast is also important. The most unproductive cast is one directly downwind with the flies worked back in a straight line. It is assumed that fish generally face into the wind and this assumption is quite plausible for a fish near the surface where the flow of the wave may be equivalent to the direction of a current in a river. *If* fish lie facing into the wind then a straight-out-and-back cast will be moving the fly directly away from the fish with an end-on profile. A cast made at an angle to the line of drift presents the fly with a lateral side-on profile and is invariably more productive. Working the flies so that they tend to move obliquely across the line of drift may also maximise the benefits of any effect of the sun (as discussed under spinning – page 166) since it may allow the fly to be presented in both illuminated and silhouette profiles (see Fig. 68) either of which may be effective depending on the mood of the fish.

As a general rule try to avoid fishing with the sun directly behind the boat when it will be 'dazzling' any fish facing directly upwind. Any good boatman will carefully plan the sequence of drifts over the course of the day to make

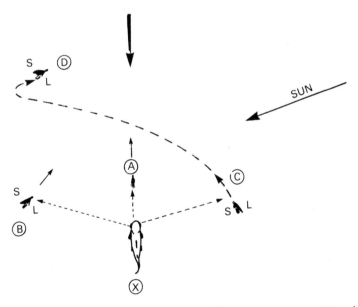

Fig. 68. Varying the profile that the fly presents to the fish can improve success. Here the boat is drifting directly down onto a fish at X with the sun shining from the right. A fly cast to A will appear end-on and in semi-silhouette to the fish. At B it will appear illuminated and at C it will be seen in silhouette. If the fly cast to C is worked back across the line of the drift from A to D it may suddenly appear illuminated just before it is recast. Fish often move to the fly just before the lift-off. Is this why?

the best use of any sunlight. A badly-lit drift in the morning will become fishable later in the day as the sun moves across the sky.

For most purposes the conventional overhead cast can be used and it is a distinct advantage to be able to cast over the left *and* right shoulders when fishing two anglers in a boat. Each angler then casts over the outside shoulder in order to minimise the risks of catching the other's line on the backcast. When two anglers are both fishing the same style and retrieving at the same speed it is possible to synchronise actions so that only one rod is casting at the same time. But this happens so rarely that to suggest it as standard practice would be a counsel of idealism (see Fig. 69).

False casting is a bad habit when boat fishing – particularly on a sunny day and with a minimal ripple – as it increases the risks of line-flash and any avoidable movement in the boat is best avoided. The roll-cast has several advantages when fishing with a companion. Not only does it require a mini-mum of physical effort, since the rod is approaching the correct position any-way as the cast is fished out when working the bob-fly, but it also avoids the problem of catching up on your partner's line during the back-cast since any rearward movement of the line is largely avoided. It is best achieved off the outside shoulder. Always check whether your partner is left-handed or right-handed. If both of you are opposite handed you have the first basis of a lasting relationship as you can each fish with your rod-arm on the outside of the boat. It is very trying for any angler to fish off the 'wrong' shoulder for any period of time. If your partner fishes with the same hand as yourself try to ensure that you change around every so often so that each in turn fishes off the favoured shoulder.

The way the boat is handled during *and after* a drift is of the utmost importance in fishing the water efficiently and effectively. An uncontrolled boat will drift at the mercy of the wind, which rarely blows steadily in the required direction of drift and at the right speed to allow all the potential holding water to be covered properly.

The value of a good boatman becomes very apparent in a contrary wind which takes the boat out into the middle of the lake and away from the productive margins if left to drift naturally. It is very difficult to fish effec-tively without someone in permanent attendance on the oars to hold back the boat when necessary and make regular minor adjustments to the line of drift. Two anglers fishing together without a boatman can be a recipe for a short friendship as both will wait – and wait – for the other to attend to the drift. It is good policy when two anglers are fishing a difficult wind for each to take a turn on the oars while the other fishes for a pre-arranged period of (say) 30 minutes. With only one angler fishing and someone on the oars at all times the ideal situation prevails.

Fishing without a second angler in the boat has several benefits. First, it allows the boat to be fished with its bow into the wind, which reduces its resistance and results in a slower natural drift. In a strong wind the rate of drift is readily controlled by gentle rowing against the drift so that it drops downwind at a controlled rate. Second, it provides the single angler with a far greater arc of fishable water (roughly double in fact when compared with a sideways drift fished by two anglers) and so increases the probability of success. Third, it rides the wave better and is less uncomfortable in a choppy wave or swell. Fourth, it overcomes any back-casting problems and competition for a fish which has shown in front of the boat (see Fig. 70). However, it is very likely that two anglers will be fishing together in order to share the costs of boat-time (and boatman). In this case the 'Northampton drift' may be better than the side drift in a strong wind.

In a contrary wind a good boatman can correct the line of the drift with a series of controlled tacks achieved by rowing across the line of movement. In this way the boat can be kept over the productive water close to the shore and shallow bays can be covered thoroughly by a series of lateral, crosswind, drifts as opposed to the alternative of drifting down and then motoring (or rowing) out to repeat the process and in so doing disturbing much fishable water.

Outboard motors are a great advantage on a large lake but they should be

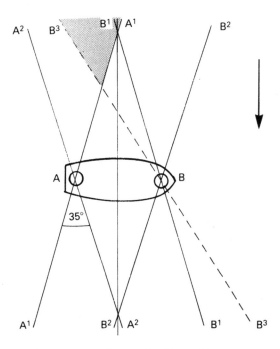

Fig. 69. Two men in a boat can cause all sorts of problems if their casting is undisciplined and they try to poach each other's water. Anglers at A and B are fishing a conventional drift with the boat side on to the wind. The effective arcs of trouble-free casting are A¹–A² and B¹–B². The arc of the backcast covers A¹–A² and B¹–B². If angler B casts to a rise at B³ his backcast will interfere with A over the zone B³–A¹. A policy of alternate casting overcomes the problem of tangled back-casts but it requires understanding and discipline. A fish at B³ could be covered with a roll-cast without affecting A.

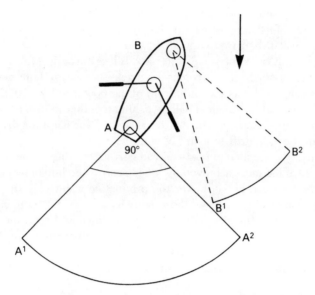

Fig. 70. With only one angler fishing from the boat at A a much wider arc of water can be fished and the boatman can better control the rate and direction of the drift. The boat can be let downwind on the oars at a controlled rate and it may be manoeuvred across the wind also. A second angler fishing at B would be at a distinct disadvantage here. If he casts too square his line will be blown downwind as his effective arc of water is B^1–B^2 and he will be fishing water that has been largely covered already by A. His presence will also much reduce the water available to A because of interference with the backcast.

used sparingly. A chosen drift should be approached over the deeper, un-productive parts of the lake – even if this necessitates a detour to avoid going through water likely to be fished by yourself or another boat later in the day. Cut the engine off well before the start of a drift and move into position on the oars. Whenever possible row out of shallow water on the oars after com-pleting a drift or, otherwise, cruise out slowly with the engine at low power. The thoughtless and unnecessary use of the engine may well reduce the catch of your boat and will certainly make you very unpopular with other boats on the same water.

It is the height of bad manners to cross in front of any boat while it is fishing. (A good standard for general adoption is the 100-yard rule used in the International Trout Championships. Even if local rules stipulate a lesser distance always err on the side of courtesy.)

Always remember that sea trout are easily scared and that sound travels a long way through water. Try to avoid clattering and bumping about in the boat. Don't tap or shuffle your feet and do not wear studded boots. Squeaking and creaking rowlocks should be silenced immediately.

The traditional way of controlling the speed of the drift when brown-trout fishing is to use a sheet anchor or drogue. English reservoir anglers have devised a number of devices for controlling the direction and rate of movement of the boat which, while very effective, are not available on the boats available for hire on any Scottish or Irish sea-trout lakes. These devices are relatively bulky to transport about the British Isles but the drogue can be folded up and stored for transit with no difficulty. Although we fully recognise the practical benefits of a drogue in controlling the rate of drift (most competition trout anglers will have two or three in different sizes), we have mixed feelings about their introduction to sea-trout lakes. While they may be used without too much disturbance to the fish on very large lakes we feel that their use on smaller or heavily-fished waters should not be encouraged. Sea trout are easily scared and lie in shallow water, preferably rocky water. In such situations a drogue is likely to be a positive liability and encumbrance. Far better to employ a boatman to do the same job just as effectively. He can also row the boat!

We have suggested above that casting across rather than down the line of the drift is often very effective. This lateral presentation of the flies, along with their speed of movement, can be further enhanced by the technique well known to reservoir anglers of fishing 'round-the-corner'. This technique was first advocated by R.C. Bridgett who wrote several books on brown trout fishing in addition to his seminal work on river sea trout. Fishing round-the-corner entails casting as directly across the wind as possible and then letting the flies swing back in an arc behind the boat as it drifts forward so that the line swings round and the speed of the flies accelerates as they move through the water in response to increasing drag (this is precisely what river greased-liners seek to avoid). Round-the-corner fishing can be particularly fruitful on certain days and is much facilitated by the technique of rowing the boat across the wind and casting the flies at an angle downwind. As the boat proceeds the cast swings round in a curve to a position parallel to and behind the boat. They can be retrieved either during the swing or after they have fished round. The forward movement of the boat combined with line retrieval imparts a faster rate of movement to the flies than would be achieved with a downwind drift (Fig. 71).

Possibly more has been said and written about the subject of how to strike sea trout when lake fishing than any other single aspect, but even today, some 75 years after the first pronouncements by Hamish Stuart, opinion still differs on whether or not to strike. We both came from river fishing backgrounds where missed takes are a frequent occurrence. We find the perennial debate on the correct way of coping with short-rising lake sea trout (a term often erroneously applied to any fish which has moved to the fly but not been hooked) somewhat amusing and rather unproductive. *Very* lucky or *very* skilled (probably the former) is the angler who achieves 100 per cent success in connecting with every fish that moves to a fly on any particular outing. When river fishing there are days (and nights) when we would be very happy to connect with one in twenty of the sea trout that move to our fly. We would be happier still to achieve the one in ten contact rate which, as judged from

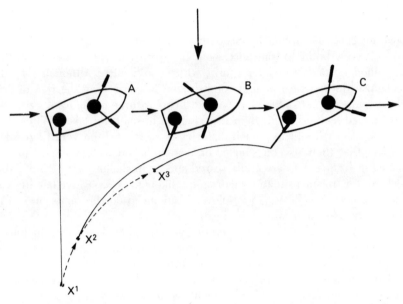

Fig. 71. 'Round-the-corner' or 'crosswind' fishing can be very productive at times. The boat is rowed slowly across the line of the drift from A to B to C. A longish cast is made downwind at A to X^1 and swings round in an arc through X^2 to X^3 as the boat moves to C when the line is recovered and recast downwind of C. Line may be recovered during the swing to speed up the rate of movement of the fly. A long cast is necessary and the oars should create the minimum of disturbance.

the literature, seems to cause so much despair among lake fishermen.

The literature itself is not much help in resolving the longstanding conflict. Indeed some of the advice given by the experts is so contradictory that it is not in the least bit surprising that less practised sea-trout anglers become confused. Hamish Stuart stated '. . . it is equally certain that more trout are missed by too quick striking than by late striking, or by not striking at all'. He added 'The morality of the strike is thus summed up in the categorical imperative 'Thou shalt not strike'. Chrystal largely agreed with the views expressed by Stuart and Jock Scott, who like Chrystal tended to fish the sunk line rather than work the bob-fly 'traditional-style', and suggested that the strike should *not* be instantaneous. On the other hand, however, Bridgett, who strongly advocated keeping in close contact with the flies at all times by recovering line and raising the rod, seems to suggest a quick strike. Currie states 'Sea trout, in complete contrast to salmon, need to be hooked by the angler' and also states quite clearly that the strike should be 'fast and positive' with a 'sincere pull'. Kingsmill Moore puts it even more explicitly: 'With white trout the strike must be quick, controlled, delicate *and must be varied according to the way in which the fish takes*. . .' The emphasis on this last point is ours because we think that it highlights the crucial point. Currie, whose views on striking seem to correspond with our own more limited

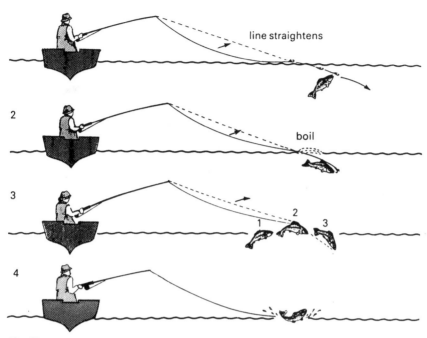

Fig. 72.

1. The *stop*. Principal form of take to the sunk fly. Line straightens, 'stops', and the fish may be felt drawing line as it turns away or down.

2. The *swirl*. A common form of rise to the surface/subsurface fly. The fish creates a disturbance ('boil' or 'swirl') in the surface as it moves to the fly.

3. The *show*. Occurs with the surface/subsurface fly. The body of the fish breaks the surface to a lesser or greater extent appearing as: 1) a head; 2) head-and-shoulders; or 3) head-and-tail rise forms.

4. The *splash*. Occurs mostly to the surface dap or bob-fly. Body of fish clears the surface of the water and drops back with a 'splash'. (An exaggerated form of 3.)

5. The *smash*. Occurs with the surface/subsurface and sunk fly. Fish takes fly at high speed. Striking is not possible as the fish hooks itself or is missed. A break ('smash') may occur on light tackle (very common with rainbow trout).

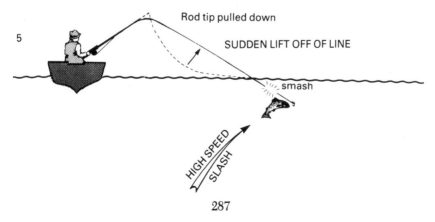

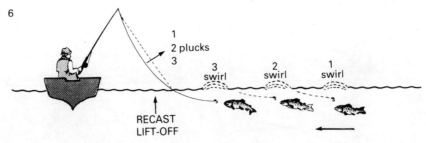

6. The *swat*. Fish follows the fly making a series of light plucks and/or swirls on the surface as the line is worked back. Angler eventually 'runs out of water' and must recast. Common rise to the bob-fly in calmer conditions.

Plugs Finnish 'Rapala' diving plugs – increasingly popular for trolling and low water spinning in rivers.

1. 'Original' floating – Rainbow Trout (3½ inch).
2. 'Countdown' sinking – Gold (2¾ inch)

Minnows These come in all shapes and forms and are enjoying a resurgence in popularity on several rivers.

3. Plastic 'Quill' minnow with single treble (2½ inch)
4. Plastic 'Quill' minnow with one flying treble (2¼ inch)
5. Natural 'Quill' minnow with two flying trebles (2¼ inch)
6. Weighted Irish 'Lane' minnow (2½ inch)
7. Weighted Irish 'Lane' minnow (1¼ inch)

8. Weighted metal one-piece 'Devon' minnow (2 inch)
9. Moulded (high density) plastic 'Devon' minnow (2¾ inch).

Spoons

10. Abu 'Salar' – Zebra (15g: 2 inch)
11. Abu 'Koster' Silver (18g: 2¼ inch)
12. Abu 'Toby' – Copper (10g: 2¼ inch)
13. Abu 'Toby' – Silver (4g: 1¾ inch)

Spinners

14. Mepps 'Aglia' – Copper (9g: size 4)
15. Abu 'Droppen' – Gold (8g: size 4)
16. Mepps 'Aglia Long' – Silver (7g: size 2)
17. Italian long-bladed 'Ilba' – Copper (size 2)
18. Italian long-bladed 'Ilba' – Gold (size 1)
19. Abu 'Droppen' – Zebra (2g: size 0)

The Ironmongery of Spinning.

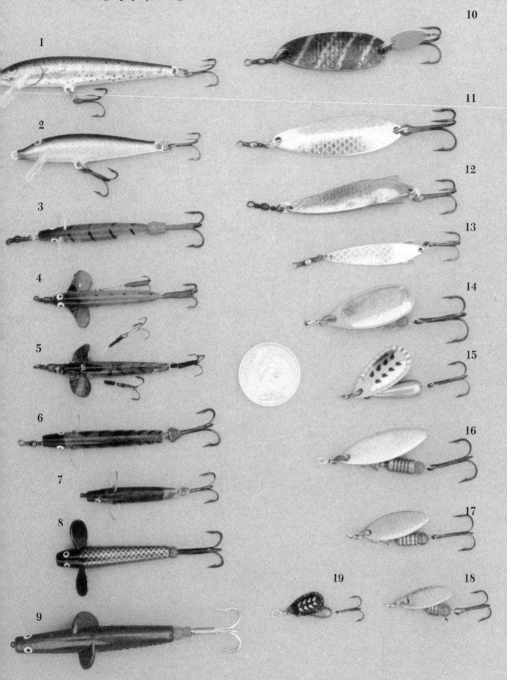

A selection of popular plugs, minnows, spoons and spinners for sea trout.

Although we have used all these – and many more in the past, we now find that virtually all of our spinning is done with spinners or with 'quill' and Irish minnows.

Manufacturers please note! It would be helpful if you could give the weight of your products rather than stamp them with some arbitary scale. The weight of the lure can be crucial to successful spinning.

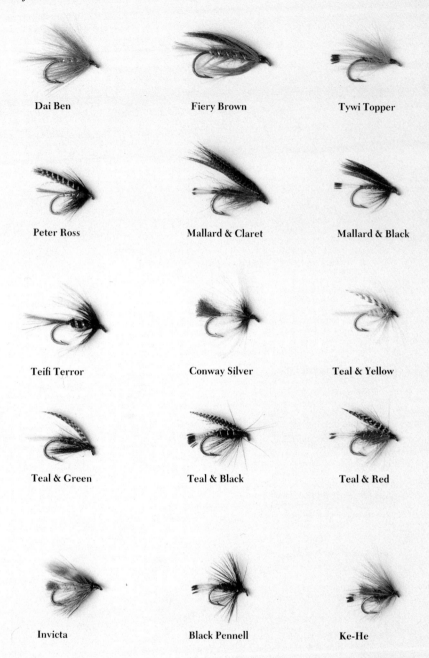

Dai Ben

Fiery Brown

Tywi Topper

Peter Ross

Mallard & Claret

Mallard & Black

Teifi Terror

Conway Silver

Teal & Yellow

Teal & Green

Teal & Black

Teal & Red

Invicta

Black Pennell

Ke-He

A selection of traditional wet-flies used mainly for subsurface fishing in lakes and rivers (mainly Scottish in origin)

Included here are some of the more popular in the Mallard and Teal series of traditional brown trout flies popular with early authors for sea trout in slightly larger hook sizes.

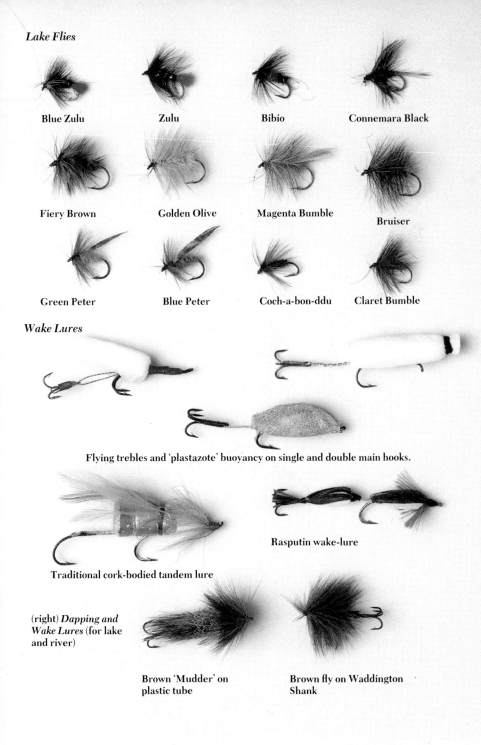

Lake Flies

Blue Zulu	Zulu	Bibio	Connemara Black

Fiery Brown	Golden Olive	Magenta Bumble	Bruiser

Green Peter	Blue Peter	Coch-a-bon-ddu	Claret Bumble

Wake Lures

Flying trebles and 'plastazote' buoyancy on single and double main hooks.

Rasputin wake-lure

Traditional cork-bodied tandem lure

(right) *Dapping and Wake Lures* (for lake and river)

Brown 'Mudder' on plastic tube

Brown fly on Waddington Shank

A selection of surface flies – ancient and modern – for lake and river fishing.
(The Bibio, Connemara Black and the Blue and Green Peters can also be fished as subsurface flies at the second dropper or point position of a 'traditional' 3-fly leader with equal success.)
  Wake Lures – used on the surface at night when fishing rivers (and, increasingly, on lakes at night!). With single or double main hooks and traditional cork or modern synthetics incorporated to provide buoyancy.

Wet-flies

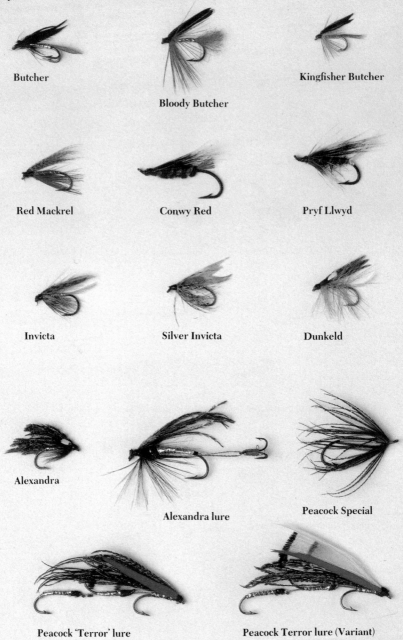

Butcher

Bloody Butcher

Kingfisher Butcher

Red Mackrel

Conwy Red

Pryf Llwyd

Invicta

Silver Invicta

Dunkeld

Alexandra

Alexandra lure

Peacock Special

Peacock 'Terror' lure

Peacock Terror lure (Variant)

Modern streamer lures are not new! The two Peacock 'Terror' lures shown here were copied from the catalogues of Messrs. Hardy Bros (Alnwick) Ltd for the 1930s!

(below left) Black & Grey Squirrel

Black, Blue &
Black Squirrel

(above right) Blue, Black & Grey Squirrel

All-Black Squirrel

(above left) Silver, Blue & Brown Squirrel
(above right) Silver, Blue & Black Squirrel

(above left) Silver, Blue & Brown Squirrel
(above right) Silver, Black & Brown Squirrel

Blue, Black,
Silver & Peacock Squirrel

Blue, Black & Silver Squirrel
(Longshark treble)

Blue, Black & Silver Squirrel
(Waddington)

Moc's Cert (Single)

Moc's Cert (Tube)

Moc's Cert (Waddington)

(above) Haslam

(left) Dyfi Black & Orange

(above) All rounder

Teal & Black (Palmered)

Peter Ross

Teal, Silver & Blue (Palmered)

Dwrgi

Tanycoed

A mostly modern and predominantly Welsh selection incorporating the effective 'Squirrel Series' of hairwings.

Lures

Peacock & Blue sunk lure

Peacock & Blue surface lure
(with 'plastazote' buoyancy)

(right) Gold T.C.

(below) Silver T.C.

(below) Tandem Blackie

(above) Silver Muddler
(treble mount)

(left) Tandem Muddler

(below) Blue Waddington

(below) Black Waddington

(right) Black Lure (Tandem)

(left and right)
Prepared tandem mounts with buoyancy

Teifi Terror (Tandem)

Red Pearly

Red Waggler

A selection of the modern generation of lures for surface, subsurface and deep-sunk fishing.

(below) The completed Marchog mount (size 2 single main hook and size 10 treble)

(left) Blue Knight
(Marchog Glas)

(right) Red Knight
(Marchog Goch)

(left) Black Knight
(Marchog Du)

(right) Yellow Knight
(Marchog Melyn)

(above) Brown Knight
(Marchog Coch Ddu)

The 'Marchog' or 'Knight' series with remote (outpoint) flying trebles and maximum hooking
power – especially for fish that are 'coming short'.

The lures here have been tied for photographic purposes. The 'Working lure' would be
tied with the feather wing alongside, rather than over, the mount and soft, floppy, hackles
would be tied-down Matuka-style to prevent them becoming 'trapped' under the main hook.

experience of stillwater sea trout, puts it another way 'The key to the whole operation of the strike is seeing what the fish are doing.'

The way in which fish take exhibits an infinite variety of forms which, for practical purposes, we would classify here under six major headings as: 1) the *stop*; 2) the *swirl*; 3) the *show*; 4) the *splash*; 5) the *smash*; and 6) the *swat* (Fig. 72).

1) **The Stop** This is by far the easiest to deal with. It occurs when a fish takes the fly beneath the water surface. There is no visual clue in terms of surface disturbance. The first indication of a take is a straightening of the bow of line from rod-tip to water surface (often not detected) followed by resistance to the further recovery of line (a 'slow take') or an obvious pull as the fish turns away or down with the fly. This form of take will be very familiar to river anglers using a sunk line and the best policy is to strike on feeling any resistance. The *stop* is a very reassuring take and provided that close contact is maintained with the flies and the rod-tip is not held too high, it is about as certain as any take can be. It is the most frequently encountered form of rise when sunk-line fishing but occurs also when fishing traditional-style when a fish takes the deeper moving tail or middle dropper fly.

2) **The Swirl** The swirl occurs when a fish moves to a fly just beneath the surface and in so doing causes the water to 'boil'. The fish itself is not actually seen, merely the after-effects of its movement. The swirl may be fast or slow depending largely on the speed of movement of the fish to the fly. The ideal

A heart-stopping moment – and a very difficult shot! A head-and-shoulders 'show' as a sea trout breaks the surface in the immediate vicinity of the flies. Has he, hasn't he? Will he, won't he? To strike, or not to strike? In this case wait a moment until the trout turns back down. (Photo: Chris Mills.)

swirl take consists of a boil in the vicinity of the fly followed by the sight of the line beginning to straighten and then the feel of a fish (all telescoped in time to a mere moment). The best policy is, as with the *stop*, to strike firmly and quickly. The *swirl* is more common with traditional-style fishing but can also occur when sunk-line fishing if the flies are being worked close to the surface.

3) **The Show** This, like the *swirl*, is a pleasing rise-form but it does require a degree of self-control. The *show* often occurs in slow motion (or so it seems at the time) and is more common when the flies are fished in or on the surface. In its classic form it entails the head of the fish emerging from the water to be followed by the body and then the tail in a 'porpoise-like' arc; but various degrees of *show* can occur when only the nose, head, or head and shoulders appear above the surface. This form of rise requires a slow, leisurely strike with some element of delay. How much delay depends on the speed of movement of the *show*. The slower the action the longer the delay. The best policy is to avoid striking the instant the fish is seen and to delay for only as long as it takes for it to disappear beneath the surface of the wave. Then strike surely and quickly; do not wait for the line to straighten or until the fish is felt. It is widely held that the fish takes the fly on the way down rather than on the way up. If it does take on the way down then an instantaneous strike as soon as the fish is seen will result in pulling the fly out of its line of movement. If it takes on the way up it is unlikely to reject the fly until it re-submerges, and to strike a fish in mid-air would seem the best way of smashing a light leader that we can think of.

4) **The Splash** Nothing can be more exciting than the spectacle of a sea trout hurling itself from the water like a submarine-launched missile to drop back with a great splash in the general vicinity of the fly. Unfortunately the thrill of the rise is not often followed by the thrill of the fight as these rises (we avoid calling them takes) are invariably the most difficult to connect with. Jock Scott states that he can give no advice on how to deal with the '*splash* rise' as it is all over in a flash. Hooked or missed! Others counsel, as with the *show*, waiting until the fish re-enters the water and turns down with the fly. Still others believe that any strike at all is a mistake since the fish has no intention of taking the fly at all but is trying to swamp or drown it so that it can take it at a more leisurely second attempt. Consequently the fly should continue to be fished as if nothing had happened. It may be that each view is correct at times, some fish behaving one way, others behaving another way.

It is therefore advisable to have a standard policy to deal with this spectacular form of rise. The practical options are: a) to do nothing but await a second attack on the fly (which may not happen); b) to wait until the fish starts to take line and can be felt; or c) to strike as it splashes back into the lake. Our policy is to treat this rise form as an extended *show* and strike firmly and promptly as the fish re-submerges. It does not always work but is on balance fairly successful. The worst policy is to have no policy, as each strike tends to be a vacillatory, half-hearted, 'Shall I, shan't I?' affair which only succeeds, if it succeeds at all, by pure luck. The *splash* is not encountered when sunk-line fishing. It sometimes occurs to the bob-fly when fishing traditional-style, and is most frequently encountered when dapping (Chapter 14).

Perhaps 99 per cent of the rise forms encountered consist of the above four types. The two following forms are, however, worthy of mention and are well known to brown and rainbow-trout anglers.

5) **The Smash** The 'smash-take' is well known to reservoir anglers – where it is a characteristic of rainbow trout. It occurs when a fish moves to the fly at great speed, either in the horizontal or vertical plane, from a distance. (If it occurred to the surface fly with the fish surging up from the depths it would manifest itself as a *splash* rise.) When it occurs in the horizontal plane it happens so quickly that there is a sudden heavy 'bang' on the line and the fish either hooks itself or is gone in a flash – sometimes taking the fly (but not the line) with it! No advice on striking is necessary: it is over in a trice.

6) **The Swat** This is very frustrating rise, well known to reservoir anglers, consisting of a series of pecks or swirls at the fly as it is drawn towards the boat. It can happen with both sunk-line fishing (when it is felt) and when working the surface/subsurface fly (when it may be both seen and felt). The frustration lies in the fact that as the line is recovered you steadily run out of space, and are eventually forced to lift the line out of the water to re-cast *knowing* that there is a fish in the near vicinity of the line. Slowing down the retrieve does not seem to work. All you can do is to re-cast along the same line in the hope that the boat has not drifted past the fish and that it will move again to the fly which, if worked faster or moved in a different direction, may induce a positive take.

The strike itself should not be over-violent. It is no more than a quick firm pull of the line into the fish. It is not a savage snatch. Over-striking leads to breaks – the finer the leader the greater the risk. Currie puts it succinctly: make the strike 'inversely proportionate to the violence of the rise'. Sound advice!

Every angler will inevitably experience bad days when every rise is missed. The fault may be *yours* because you are over-anxious or just unable to concentrate properly. It may be a facet of the light or it may be just the mood of the fish. Sea trout can be capricious. On days like this there are three options: a) try something different – fish smaller flies faster or change to a dry fly; b) move to another part of the lake where the mood of the fish may be different; or c) go ashore for an hour or so and have a complete break in the anticipation that when you start fishing again things will have improved. They often do.

Bridgett believed that it was important to decide from the outset whether to fish for sea trout or salmon. This is a very relevant point. Lake-dwelling salmon generally prefer shallower water, prefer smaller flies fished slower and should not be struck too soon. By contrast, sea trout in lakes generally inhabit deeper water, prefer larger flies fished faster and should be struck promptly. The angler who attempts to fish for both simultaneously fishes well for neither.

Playing a sea trout in a large lake is as exciting as in a river. Once hooked, the fish may head off in a frantic rush away from the boat towards deep water. This is where the security of ample backing line is very important. Don't panic! Let the fish take line against steady pressure – which maintains a good curve in the rod – while the boatman or your companion (who in any event should wind in his line) takes to the oars and turns the boat to follow after the fish, allowing you gradually to recover line and begin to play the fish at a safe distance from the boat. Many anglers attempt to play the fish much too close to the boat – literally under the oars. This is a mistake that can cost dearly if the line is fouled by the oars or if the fish attempts to take refuge under the boat. Try to keep it outside the sweep of the oars at a distance which allows the direction of its movement to be anticipated by the oarsman so that there are no sudden panics when it heads for the far bank or decides to run towards the boat. Avoid the tendency to hold the fish too near the surface as sea trout have a proclivity to jump when so played. Treat a jumping fish the same way as in a river and neither give nor take line.

Fish hooked in shallow bays will often head for the cover of any nearby weed or reed beds. If this occurs, a mild degree of panic is permissible. Try to manoeuvre yourself into a position in the boat that allows the greatest angle of side strain to be exerted on the fish. The fish is more readily led away from the obstacle than dragged back from the rear. A good boatman will assist the manoeuvre by placing the boat to put you in the most favourable position to apply the maximum lateral strain – if he can.

Eventually, the fish tires and turns on its side. It can now be brought alongside the boat ready for netting. A good sized landing net with a long (6 feet plus) handle is essential. As a general practice try to position the fish so that it is netted behind (= upwind) of the boat. The net should be well sunk and the fish drawn over the net. Do not try to sweep the net over the fish. If you are fishing a team of flies, take special care to ensure that in drawing the fish over the net you do not snag the other hooks in the meshes before the fish is encircled. The sight of the net often elicits a sudden final lunge by the fish and many fish have been lost at this stage because the dropper or tail fly had snagged the net.

Make sure that you have equipped the boat with a suitable 'priest' or some other means of humanely killing the fish before you set out. Such materials are not readily to hand when boat fishing. Finally, remember that the wind and sun will dry out rapidly any fish left uncovered in the bottom of a boat so that it looks singularly unappealing by the end of the day. Be prepared with a suitable cloth or bass to cover the fish.

14 · DAPPING

Dapping (or blowline fishing to use the original, more descriptive, but now defunct term) is an exotic form of dry-fly fishing. It can be done from the bank but it is primarily a boat-fishing method on lakes.

Dapping entails no casting whatsoever. Instead the large dapping fly is blown downwind through the air on a special ultra-light line (= blowline) and then 'dapped' onto the surface of the water some distance from the boat by carefully controlled movements of the rod.

It is not a method widely employed, but given a well-stocked lake, a good *steady* breeze, a high wave, and the sea trout in a favourable mood (a rare combination), a day on the dap can be a memorable experience. It is a very visual form of fishing where the rise of a fish to the fly requires concentration and good eyesight. There is little that is more rewarding than to see a fish take a fly.

The art of dapping is, by origin and evolution, primarily associated with the lakes of Scotland and Ireland. These regions are well endowed with many lakes suitable for dapping, although its popularity seems to be confined to the larger waters. It is not clear where and when dapping evolved. Several authors writing in the 1920s accept it as an already established method. Henzell, writing in 1949, refers to 'this dapping business, which has come into such vogue for sea trout during recent years, has caused such argument that anyone might think it was a new theory, whereas any Irish man will tell you that it is old enough in all conscience'. According to Henzell it was developed on Lough Derg and then adapted on Loughs Mask and Corrib as a means of presenting the crane fly (*Tipula gigantea*) to the very large brown trout in those venues as 'there is no method of representing the insect's passage across the water with any sort of verisimilitude except by dapping'.

Irrespective of origin, someone, somewhere, somewhen, established that the crane fly (locally termed the 'Jenny' or 'daddy-long-legs') or the natural mayfly was effective in taking sea trout and also salmon and devised an artificial fly to overcome the practical problems of collecting enough of the natural product when it was out of season or in short supply. Dapping was eventually imported to other waters in the British Isles and in some locations – such as Loch Maree in Scotland where McLaren recalls it being established by the late 1920s – soon became a very popular method of fly fishing. The method has endured on Loch Maree and this magnificent water is often considered as being the dappers' 'Headquarters'. According to McEwan (who should know) dapping has, curiously, never caught on at Loch Lomond.

Dapping has three characteristics which, more than anything else, explain its general appeal. First, it is reputed to be more effective in bringing the larger sea trout up to the fly. Second, it is thought to be more effective in attracting fish in deep water. Third, it is possibly the most leisurely form of fly fishing. The fact that it is practised from a drifting boat combined with the lack of any physical effort in casting makes dapping a method particularly suitable for disabled or elderly anglers.

The tackle used in dapping has certain peculiar characteristics but is otherwise fairly unrefined. The most important features are the line, the rod and the fly.

Dapping line is very different from the modern plastic-coated lines used in other forms of fly fishing. Conventional dapping line, once made of silk, now consists of a polyfilament made up of very many ultra-fine strands of nylon thread which are loosely braided to form a gossamer-like 'floss'. Since the whole purpose of the line is to catch the wind, its resistance (= sail area) and lightness are important. Modern nylon flosses, which are either brown (preferred), white or light green, are far superior to the old silk lines in these respects: while also being stronger, waterproof and quicker drying when

Loch Maree in Sutherland (Northern end, near Poolewe). Probably the most famous of all British sea trout lochs and Mecca for dappers everywhere. Boat safety is of singular importance on such a large sheet of water. (Photo: Gordon Carlisle.)

wetted. This ability to shed water is crucial as a wet floss line is virtually unfishable.

Some exponents maintain that the nylon floss lines are an example of modern technology over-surpassing itself in that they are *too efficient* in terms of lightness and wind resistance to be fished in the strength of wind classically favoured for dapping. The secret of successful dapping is in controlling the billowing line so that the fly sits on–*but never in*–the water for as long as possible. The dapper must, therefore, be able to adjust his line and technique to cope with a range of wind speeds and also with that curse of dappers – a gusting, changeable wind.

Some anglers split their floss lines in half to reduce the sail area for use in a strong wind. Others achieve better line control by knotting the line (with an overhand loop) every foot or two. Others still make up a range of different lengths of floss line which can be readily interchanged: a shorter length for a strong wind and a longer length for a light breeze. Another option is to knot together 6–10 strands of 2lb strength nylon monofilament line of the required length. These home-made dapping lines work well in a good stiff breeze, they are very water-repellent, and have virtually no 'shadow' – a particular problem with the thicker floss lines.

The length of rod used for dapping is another important feature. A long rod has many practical advantages. It makes the best use of the available wind, it enables a longer line to be fished so that the fly is worked further from the boat with less chance of the fish being disturbed and, within limits, it permits the movement of the fly laterally across the line of the drift so that it fishes a greater arc of water. Some of the early dapping rods were up to 20 feet in length! Since these rods were made of bamboo or greenheart they must have weighed a tonne by the end of the day. Modern dappers have many advantages. Glass and carbon are so very much lighter and modern lines are so much better that such fearsome wands can remain in the collectors' cabinets where they belong.

The 10–11 foot fly rod generally recommended for most other forms of fly fishing might suffice in a strong wind provided that it is fitted with a long (18-inch) extension handle for double-handed use or so that the butt can be rested comfortably on the thigh when dapping single-handed. However, the length of rod generally favoured by modern exponents is between 13–17 feet. Some anglers deploy their double-handed salmon rods for dapping but these are somewhat heavy and far too powerful to get the best out of playing a small sea trout. Another option is the range of (very cheap) telescopic rods currently available for coarse fishing. These are up to 17 feet long and have very large rod rings. Their main advantage (possibly their only good point) is that they readily fit into the boat or car-boot when not in use!

Carbon is the ideal material for a long dapping rod. It is strong, sensitive and above all, supremely light. We suggest that any wormer tempted to try dapping can do no better than to dap with the 13–14 foot carbon-fibre rod recommended for low-water worming (page 145). This coarse fishing rod has

Three in a boat. But the angler in the centre is fishing the dap while his companions fish the wet-fly. He does not need to cast and so does not interfere with their casting. His dap may bring fish to the surface and establish where the sea trout are lying in a large body of water. Any fish that miss the dap may take the wet-flies. (Photo: M.J. Morgan.)

the advantage that the fittings allow the reel to be located on the long handle at any point so that the outfit can be adjusted for balance and convenience. (Its one major disadvantage is that it is intended for use with fine nylon lines and has small-diameter rod rings with the result that the dapping line and the knot to the backing do not pass through the top rings smoothly. However, the original rings can be replaced quite simply with something larger and more suitable for dapping without affecting the continued use of the rod for worming.) Apart from its length, a dapping rod has no other peculiar characteristics. Its action is irrelevant for casting because no casting is done, but it should, of course, be suitable for striking and playing a good size fish. Provided that it is light enough to handle without strain all day, virtually anything will do. It is generally stated that any old reel will do for dapping. It must, nevertheless, have sufficient spool capacity to hold about 150 yards of 20lb strength backing line. The most sensible approach is to use the same reel as when fishing the wet-fly and have a spare spool loaded for dapping. (Why carry two reels when one will do?) The only problem is if you want to put up two rods so that you can change method periodically during the day.

The length of the dapping line that is fished is a matter of choice and skill. Some anglers prefer to fish close to the boat while others choose to stream out a very long line. A short line allows a more positive strike and has the further advantage that the fly is more easily seen and controlled. A longer line (provided it can be controlled) makes better use of the wind and results in less disturbance from the boat – although this is not usually a limiting factor in the good wave generally preferred for dapping. It is quite common to see much longer dapping lines fished today than in the past.

Some early writers held that the length of floss attached to the backing should be less than the length of the rod so that the joining knot to the backing was always outside the top rod ring when playing and netting a fish. The knot did not then jam in the rings and the floss did not become abraided and weakened by see-sawing in and out of the ring. Jock Scott fished close to the boat with some 4 yards of aerialised floss, Henzell recommended 8–10 yards of floss, while McLaren, who grew up on the banks of Loch Maree, suggested that only about 14 feet was necessary. Many of today's dappers load 20 yards or more floss onto their reels so that they have immediate flexibility in fishing a shorter or longer line as appropriate to the wind and the fish.

The leader which attaches the fly (or flies) to the dapping line is much shorter than in other forms of fly fishing. Henzell suggests a leader length of 3 feet, Jock Scott suggests 26 inches as the best length, while Balfour-Kinnear recommends 30–36 inches. Thus, on the basis that an inch or two is of no great consequence we usually employ a leader of about 3 feet. A long leader is not necessary when dapping since both the line and the leader are (or should be) *above* the water and *never on it*.

Since dapping tends to attract the larger sea trout, a stronger than normal leader is a wise precaution; we usually fish at about 8lb strength under most conditions, and a thicker, stiffer, nylon allows somewhat better control of the fly. As the line billows and rolls in the wind, the risk of 'flash' from the leader is increased, and with it the risk of scaring the fish. We are, therefore, very careful to choose dull or matt finished nylon when dapping.

There are several methods of connecting the backing and leader to the floss. The simplest method, which allows a quick change when required, is the loop-knot (see Chapter 5). Alternatively, a large-size cast-connector may be used for the backing-join provided it will pass freely through the rod rings or both ends of the floss may be attached by more conventional knots (see Fig. 73).

Dapping usually takes place on a good wave and dapping flies are invariably larger than normal wet flies, with sizes down to 4 being used in a good wave. The general rule is 'the larger the water the bigger the fly'. Size 4 or even 2

overhand knot
at 24" intervals
for line control

Leader loop

8-10 lb
strength

overhand
knot

c. 36" leader
to fly

Fig. 73. The simplest means of connecting the dapping line to the leader.

would not be too big under certain conditions. We find that most of our dapping flies are size 6 or 8, with the larger flies being the most widely used.

The typical dapping fly is like nothing on earth! It is, traditionally, a large, very bushy confection designed to be as buoyant and visible as possible. It comes in all sorts of weird and wonderful shapes. The 'standard' patterns are very heavily hackled at the head or tied Palmer-style with a generous body hackle. Then there are the 'hairwings', the 'fore-and-afts' and the new generation of lightweight tube-flies. Perhaps the best known dapping fly is the *Loch Ordie*, but the *Blue Zulu*, *Black Pennell* and *Red Palmer* are, perhaps, more widely used today – along with a whole host of locally tied 'nondescripts'. Some have flying-treble attachments to improve 'hookability'; Some are tied on lightweight Waddington shanks with treble hooks.

The availability of new materials for the modern fly-dresser has led to many innovations in style and pattern of wet and dry flies, and this has now extended to dapping where highly buoyant and virtually waterproof materials – such as cork, deer hair and 'Plastazote' – have been incorporated into the dressings of new and traditional dapping flies. We like our dapping flies for the 'non-feeding' sea trout to contain a touch of fluorescent material in the dressing to improve their visibility and, hopefully, appeal to the fish. (If fluorescence is going to work, it works in air and not under water: so its use in dapping flies seems logical.)

A range of four or five patterns tied on light hooks for a light breeze and

Playing a sea trout taken on the dap in Doolough on the Delphi Fishery in Co. Mayo. (Note the excellent pin-hole rowlocks – much safer than the standard U-shaped type.) (Photo: John Wilshaw.)

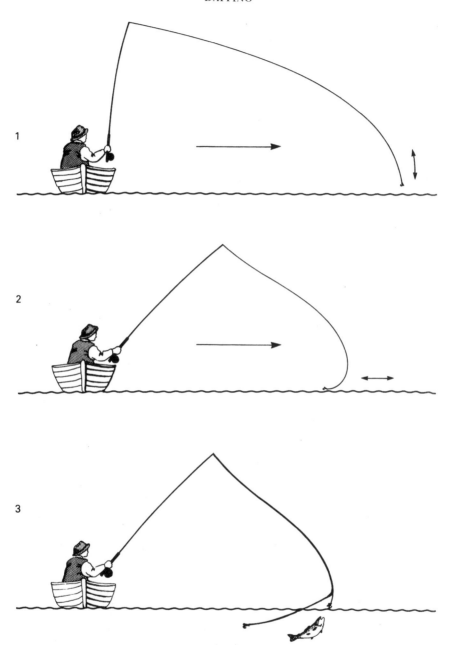

Fig. 74. Dapping has many pleasures. The fly must be kept on the surface (never in or under it) for as long as possible. By raising and lowering the rod it is possible to dap the fly on and off the surface (top and middle) and to move it from one side of the line of drift to another so as to cover as much water as possible. The addition of a point-fly (bottom) in a strong breeze helps to anchor the dap and provides more control over its movements; any fish that misses the skittering dap-fly may turn to take the subsurface point-fly.

299

heavy hooks for a heavy breeze is an advantage (say sizes 4, 6 and 8). Under some wind conditions it is difficult to control the movement of the fly onto the surface of the water, and a heavy fly helps. Another trick useful in controlling the gyrations of the dap fly is to fish it on a long dropper with a second fly on the tail of the leader (which should be about 18 inches longer). The tail fly, which is a conventional lake pattern such as a *Turkey and Gold* or a *Dark Mackerel*, is fished beneath the surface and tends to act as an *anchor* to steady the dap fly and make its movements more subdued and predictable. The problem of 'lift-and-slap' of the fly in a gusty wind can be particularly aggravating and necessitates drying out the fly so that it floats properly every few minutes, which wastes fishing time. The use of an anchor fly gives the angler the best of both worlds (at least in theory) in that it allows one fly to fish wet and one to fish dry. A fish which has risen to the dap fly and missed may turn to take the wet fly. (Fig. 74).

There are two very basic skills in dapping: control of the erratic, billowing, movements of the line so that the fly sits on or just above the water for as long as possible without wetting the line or water-logging the fly; and hooking a consistently high proportion of the fish that are raised to the fly.

It is arguable whether or not it is best to hold the dap fly on the surface for as long as possible, in the manner of conventional dry-fly fishing, or to 'bounce' it intermittently over the waves – a few seconds here, a few seconds there. To some extent this debate is academic since it is virtually impossible to hold the fly in any particular position for any extended period of time before it lifts, off of its own volition. We find that there are days when it pays to let the fly stay for as long as possible, and other days when it pays to impart extra movement to the fly – especially on a small wave when the movement of the fly seems to elicit a better response.

In addition to working the fly up and down by raising and lowering the rod tip, the fly can also be moved laterally across the line of drift by moving the rod from side to side across the body. However, since the line is controlled by the wind, the arc of water that can be fished is relatively small and determined by the length of the rod. An important point to remember when dapping is that the fly cannot be dried out by false casting as when fishing the conventional dry fly. Therefore line control is of critical importance and a good floatant is an absolute essential.

The various ways in which lake sea trout move to the wet fly have previously been categorised under six broad headings and discussed in some detail (page 289). The three most commonly encountered rise-forms when dapping are the *swirl*, the *show* and the *splash*. The *smash* and the *swat* may also occur, and we could add a seventh category – the *search*. This occurs when a fish has either risen to the dap and missed or when it was moving to the fly which, as a result of some injudicious movement of the rod tip or a perverse gust of the wind, suddenly disappeared. In either event the fish is left near to the surface still full of intent cruising around looking for the original fly that 'fell off the plate'. However, if it moves again to the fly it will usually take with a swirl or a show, so this form of behaviour is already covered. The form of take categorised as the stop may occur to the submerged anchor fly when a two-fly dap leader is fished.

The timing of the strike when dapping requires nerves of steel and an ability to control reflex muscle movements on seeing a great swirl or head and shoulders appear at the fly. It is important to remember two things in judging when to strike. First the line will be stretched out in an arc with no straight line contact between rod tip and fly, second, the fish must be given time to turn down and away with the fly so that it is not 'pulled out of its mouth'. It is also worth remembering that the dap often induces the larger fish to rise and that these larger fish are often more ponderous in their movements. Much of the problem with the high percentage of missed rises often experienced in dapping – leaving aside problems of the light and the vision of fish for a moment – results from bad timing by the dapper. The dapper expects to see the rise, and the senses may become so highly tuned that the reflexes take over and the strike is made instantly there is any movement in the vicinity of the fly *before* the fish has taken it properly. At other times when the fish are thin in the water, or present in quantity but unresponsive, it is very likely that concentration waivers and the sudden rise at the fly takes the angler by surprise with the result that the strike is too slow. Dapping requires a highly tuned eye combined with a relaxed mentality which subjugates the naturally honed reflex to a carefully calculated raising of the rod as the fish turns down. There are no hard and

Dapping on Lough Curreel in the heartland of Connemara. A good water noted for the quality of its sea trout. (Photo: Peter O'Reilly.)

fast rules on the timing of the strike, each fish is an individual and behaves as such. Many anglers have disciplined themselves to recite a favoured incantation which is phrased to provide the appropriate delayed response. For example (gleaned at random). 'Did you see that? – Strike!' 'God save the King/Queen – Strike!' 'One, two, three (four, five . . . ?) – Strike!' 'About xxxxxx time too – Strike!' This may or may not improve success.

Currie discusses the problem of missed takes and short-rising fish in some detail. He concludes that the dapper must expect to miss a high proportion of the fish which move to the fly, and suggests that the phenomenon of 'chasing' or 'following' fish which fail to take the fly or which attempt to take it but miss is common to both sunk-fly and surface fly fishing, *but* that the problem is more obvious with dapping and bob-fly fishing because fish which behave in a similar fashion to the sunk-fly *are not seen* by the angler. He states: 'It is probably just that sea trout *must show* to the dap which makes it appear that the dap moves more fish than the wet fly' (our emphasis). We derive much comfort from this very plausible explanation of the seemingly low proportion of successful takes often experienced when dapping.

McEwan refers to the problem of missed rises when dapping, and suggests that this may result from the fish losing sight of the fly 'at the last moment'. The subject of trout vision in relation to their response to the fly was discussed at length by Kingsmill-Moore. It is a highly technical subject which has recently been admirably presented in a non-technical way using underwater photography by John Goddard and Brian Clarke in their definitive work *The Trout and the Fly: A New Approach*. Although this dealt with feeding brown trout in the crystal-clear and smooth waters of the English Chalk streams, the physical principles apply everywhere. The only difference is the motivational behaviour of their feeding brown trout.

We summarise the main discoveries about fish vision in Fig. 75 *a–e*. All we can add is that, given the disturbance and distortion caused in the fishes' 'window' on the surface, combined with the erratic movements of the dap fly as it moves, or those of the bob-fly as it skitters across the surface, sometimes on the wave, sometimes through the wave, it is surprising not that so many fish miss the fly *but that any manage to take it at all!*

Dapping is a visual form of fishing requiring supreme concentration in observing the fly *at all times*. It is very demanding; especially on a dour day when the fish are unresponsive. It is fatal to let concentration lapse.

Give dapping a try when the opportunity arises and, above all, *persevere*. Do not be put off at the first attempt by failure. Nothing in angling comes easy – especially dapping. There are days when it works and days when it doesn't. On some days when two anglers fish the dap and the wet fly side-by-side in the same boat, the one or the other method may be more successful. On other days both are equally successful. Even when the dap is not producing fish, it can be useful in promoting rises which indicate where the fish are holding so that their location can be marked down and they can be covered subsequently with the wet fly.

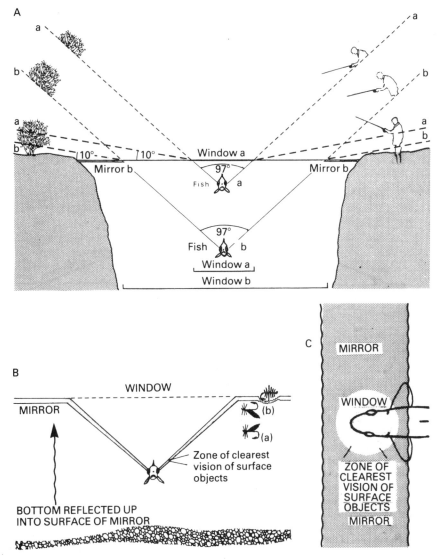

Fig. 75. Sea trout vision is a complicated subject and we do no more than attempt to cover the salient points in A–E (*see also over page*). The effects of refraction, reflection and wave action are of paramount importance. The basic principles to be understood are 1) light is bent downwards as it passes through the interface between air and water 2) those rays, striking the surface of the water at the smallest angle, are bent the most and reach the eye of a fish at an angle of 48.5° 3) any external object that lies below an angle of about 10° to the surface is virtually invisible to the fish because the image is so weak 4) the fish-eye view of the external world appears on a slope projected above its head 5) anything outside an angle of 48.5° to the eye is invisible to the fish as the undersurface of the water effectively becomes a mirror reflecting the bottom and any objects that lie between the surface and the bottom 6) within the angle of 48.5° the fish has a circular window through to the external world 7) the deeper the fish lies in the water the larger the area of the window and so the more it sees of the outside world.

303

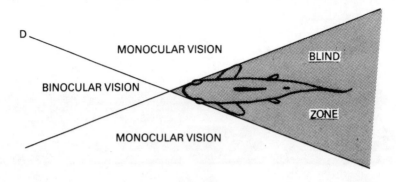

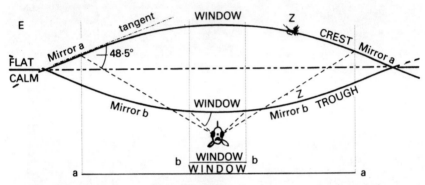

Fig. 75 (cont'd). At the periphery of the window there is a narrow band in which vision is clearest (B & C) and where the surface fly will be seen in full colour rather than in silhouette. The mirror may have a confusing effect at times. A fly/lure at position **a** in figure (B) will be seen in two different ways – either directly at its true position or mirrored on the undersurface of the water. The nearer that it is to the surface, the closer the reflected and true positions.

Fish have both monocular (unfocused or awareness) vision and binocular (focused) vision that enables distance to be judged precisely (D). Each eye can be moved independently of the other and this fact is very important in 'awareness' vision. Fish cannot see behind – hence the 'upstream' approach advocated in river fishing in clear water.

The effect of wave action (E) is to increase and decrease the area of the window (and hence what the fish sees of the surface and external world) as the crest and trough of each wave passes overhead. A fish at position X is lying at a fixed height above the bottom *but* its depth relative to the surface will vary dependent upon the height of the wave. If the fish is 18 inches below the surface on a flat calm, then a 12 inch wave will mean that it is only 6 inches below the surface on a trough but it will be 30 inches below the surface on the crest of a wave. Since depth determines the area of the window, the fishes' view of the external world will expand and contract dependent on the frequency and height of the wave and the depth of the fish. Thus any dap or bob-fly on the surface at **Z** will be lost from view as the trough develops (and the window decreases) only to reappear again as the next crest passes overhead. These transitory and intermittent glimpses of the surface fly may explain the quick upward rolling lunge of the fish that increases in occurrence as the height of the wave grows – and why so many fish miss the fly. Considering that the surface of a large wave is frequently broken up into smaller wavelets it is surprising that so many fish do, in fact, actually manage to take the fly! (The above figures are composites based on, and redrawn from, Clarke & Goddard and Kingsmill Moore).

304

15 · OTHER METHODS AND TECHNIQUES

This chapter covers methods of lake fishing which will be unusual and un-familiar to most anglers. 'Not for them', perhaps, for a variety of good reasons. However, other anglers more disposed to experiment may find them useful at times. Thus we include here: dry-fly fishing; bank fishing; night fishing; spinning; and trolling.

The Dry Fly

When the breeze fails and the wave dies to nothing, leaving the boat be-calmed on a flat mirror-like surface and highly visible to any fish within the vicinity, many anglers pack up and go home. Others put ashore and wait dis-consolately for the breeze to pick up again. Some may persevere with the wet fly on a sunk line, fishing clockwise around the boat with a very long line, an ultra-fine leader of 12–16 ft length, and small flies. The dry fly pre-sents one further option.

The approach to the dry fly varies according to whether the lake surface is flat calm, or there is sufficient breeze to create a half-decent ripple and so cause the boat to drift slowly. (The dry fly can be fished on a normal wave but there are very real difficulties in line control and keeping the fly dry.)

The best policy in a flat calm is to manoeuvre the boat into an area of the lake which, from past experience, is known to hold fish at most times and which ideally has not been fished previously that day. Under these cir-cumstances, a fly cast out on a long line and left for a long time may stimulate a rise from a resident or cruising fish. How long it is left in the original position before recasting depends on your boredom threshold. Some anglers adopt the practice of recasting every ten seconds or so; others are content to let the fly ride in the same position for as long as ten minutes. Whatever is done, it must be done with the utmost delicacy and with the absolute mini-mum of disturbance from the boat and its occupants.

Any fish which show within casting range may be covered with the fly, but it is important that this is done quickly. It may be possible to fish around the boat in a complete circle, but the water should always be searched methodically in a systematic pattern. Once the pattern has been fished out, the process can be repeated using a longer line to cover water that has not been disturbed by the first pattern. Alternatively you can move elsewhere.

If the water has some surface ripple, so much the better. The boat will be less visible and the disturbance of the line less important. Under such conditions it may help to 'twitch' the fly every few seconds by recovering line with a short, sharp, pull. This often induces a fish to move to the fly, but it is important to avoid any action which drags the fly under the surface.

As with dapping, the lightning, instantaneous strike is to be avoided at all costs. Not only will such intemperate action probably pull the fly away from the fish, but it will almost certainly also result in the fine leader used in dry-fly fishing under these conditions being broken. Strike *swirl* rises promptly, but allow the fish time to turn down with the fly if it makes any form of show at the fly. The speed of the rise when dry fly fishing is usually much slower than with other methods. Try to respond accordingly.

A floating line is, of course, essential for dry-fly work. Some anglers may prefer a shorter, stiffer, rod to that generally used for boat work, and a finer leader of about 3lb strength may be advisable in calm, bright water. It is under these conditions that any 'flash' from the rod, line or leader will be most hostile to success.

Various patterns of dry fly have been used with good effect – such as the *Olive Quill*, *Wickham*, *Greenwell* and *Black Pennell*. The last two patterns were recommended by Henzell who used them on size 10 hooks.

Larger dry flies up to size 6 can, and have, been used on a good wave as an alternative to the wet fly or dapping. The fly is cast out on a long line downwind, and line recovered at the same rate as the boat drifts towards the fly – giving the fly an occasional twitch if required. The dry fly remains more or less static in the position to which it was cast, moved only by the wind and wave, whereas the dapped fly is constantly moving across the wave at the same speed as the drift of the boat and thus covering fresh water and fish all

Three of a kind – all within a whisker of 1lb 12oz – taken in bright sun and a flat calm on the dry-fly from Lough Beltra (Co. Mayo). (Photo: G.S. Harris.)

the time. The disadvantage of dapping, however, is that it is impossible to move the dap fly any distance *across* the line of the drift against the direction of the wind to cover a fish showing to the left or the right. It is also impracticable to shorten or lengthen line quickly to cover a fish showing more than a yard or two upwind or downwind of the drift. The dry fly has the advantage over the dap that it can be recast quickly on a longer or shorter line to cover a rising fish over a far greater arc of water than is possible when dapping.

We anticipate that the innovative techniques developed on reservoir fisheries over the last 20 years or so, combined with modern, highly buoyant, fly dressing materials which have enabled a virtually unsinkable dry fly to be produced, will provide scope for much experimentation in the general field of dry-fly fishing for lake sea trout. One particular direction for experimentation is in the use of the fast-stripped buoyant wake-fly used at night on rivers. It works well with rainbow and brown trout on reservoirs in daylight and we can think of no good reason why it should not work for sea trout in lakes. Whether it is dry-fly fishing, extended bob-fly fishing, or pseudo-spinning is another matter.

Bank Fishing

The angler who fishes a lake for sea trout from the bank, either from choice or necessity, is at a distinct disadvantage compared with the boat angler. The bank angler is very much at the mercy of the direction of the wind. Unless he is able to put out a reasonable length of line into the wind, his movements will be restricted to that limited area of the lake where he can cast with the wind or at an angle across it. Any fish which lie outside casting distance cannot be covered, whereas the boat angler has access to every single inch of water. Whereas boat fishing is leisurely (unless long-distance rowing is required), bank fishing can be physically arduous. The topography of the lake may well be such that very long detours over rough or boggy ground are necessary around bays and inlets to reach fishable water: and reed beds and weed beds may even then make fishing impossible.

Nevertheless, apart from the savings on boat hire costs, there are a few advantages to bank fishing. It is safer than boat fishing (better to break a leg than drown) and the angler can fish on into darkness after the boats have finished their working day (this is usually between 9 am and 6 pm on many fisheries). Indeed, not all lakes have boats on them and bank fishing may be the only method of fishing some of the smaller and more remote lakes.

Two words of warning. Bank fishing may not be permitted on some fisheries. Where it is permissible, be sure to have a generous supply of midge-repellant. Midges and other man-eating insects do not seem to be a particular problem when boat fishing, but they can be extremely unpleasant under certain conditions when fishing from the bank.

Fortunately, salmon and sea trout tend to lie in the shallower waters within a lake and this largely means around the shoreline where they are accessible to the bank angler. Given reasonable casting ability, a respectable wind, a wave which moves along the shore, and a suitable depth of water within casting distance, the bank angler will be able to search every inch of potentially productive water far more effectively and with less disturbance than would be possible from a drifting boat. The technique of fishing the bank is akin to fishing a river with the angler moving down the bank a pace or two after each cast is fished out.

It is usually necessary to cast a much longer line from the bank, and this makes it impossible to fish the bob-fly effectively. Thus, the standard method will be the subsurface or sunk fly. Whereas it is difficult to achieve any great depth with the sunk fly when boat fishing because of the drift of the boat towards the fly, the bank angler is not so inhibited and can fish the fly as close to the bottom as desired by selecting a suitable line with the appropriate sinking rate. Much of our bank fishing has been done with a sink tip or slow sinking line, but floating or intermediate lines can be used equally well. The shooting-head has little practical use in sea-trout fishing on rivers or when boat fishing. Its use may, however, be justified when bank fishing when extra distance is required. If properly cast, using the double-haul technique and a suitably powerful rod, the shooting-head can add up to 50 per cent to the distance of a cast. This extra distance may be useful at times, especially over rather shallow water (when the head should be a floater or slow sinker).

Tackle is generally no different to that used when boat fishing: although a more powerful rod may be required for long-distance casting. One, two or three flies may be used but, as a general rule, we suggest that, unless you are a master-caster, it is best to reduce the number of flies from three to two and then from two to one as casting distance increases.

The bank angler can fish the dry fly also. He can also fish at night, when the standard technique is to fish either a surface (wake-type) lure, a 'twitched' dry fly, a team of subsurface flies, or a large sunk-fly, in the 'around-the-clock' fashion. The bank angler is far less mobile at night than during the day. The key to successful bank fishing on a lake at night is to choose the fishing station very carefully after due consideration of the likely location of the fish, the direction of the prevailing wind *and*, of considerable importance, the position and brilliance of any moon. Whenever possible, try to avoid fishing at night with the moon behind you, or directly in front of you. The best moon is no moon. The next-best moon is one shining between you and the fish (i.e. from the side).

The bank angler will be at some disadvantage when playing a fish because, unlike the boat angler, he cannot row after it. Plenty of backing line on the reel is absolutely imperative. Remember that the best method of playing a fish in this situation is not to hang on like grim death with the rod bent double, but to use the resistance of the line in the water to play the fish. Instead of raising the rod vertically, hold it down *parallel* to the bank and so keep as much line as possible in, or on, the water. The drag caused by 25 yards of thick fly line plus backing line is more likely to stop a fish than a direct pull through the rod. When a fish heads directly away from you at a rate of knots, try to turn him off course by walking along the bank in order to increase the angle of lateral pull. This often works.

Night Fishing

While the majority of river-caught sea trout are taken at night in many areas, the reverse is true on stillwaters, where the proportion of sea trout taken in darkness is insignificant. This is simply because very few anglers fish at night on lakes. To some extent this is as a result of tradition; the fishing hours on many prestigious lake fisheries are from about 9 am to 6 pm and it is, somehow, not quite done to seek leave to fish outside the 'working day'. It is, perhaps, also due in part to the fact that on more northerly waters the night is long-coming and relatively short. It is also partly because it is hardly sensible to fish through the night when excellent fishing is to be had by day and when a good night's sleep is conducive to success. We know from long experience that the biggest mistake any sea-trout angler can make is to try to fish all day and then all night. Sea trout can be caught by day and by night but everyone needs to sleep some time. The adept sea trout angler decides his options in relation to conditions. Twelve hours fishing for sea trout is enough for anyone in a 24-hour day. If you are going to fish by day forgo the night, and vice versa.

Stillwater night fishing, where allowed, can be undertaken from the bank (see above) or from a boat. Anyone contemplating boat fishing at night should be very much aware of the safety implications. It is difficult to navigate and orientate a boat at night unless there is a clear sky and a reasonable moon. Many lakes are in remote locations with few visible landmarks on the bank to fix precise position. BOAT FISHING IS DANGEROUS; ESPECIALLY AT NIGHT. It is a foolish angler who fishes at night from a boat in a strong wind!

Having said that, night fishing from a boat has its own particular appeal. The cover of darkness overcomes many of the practical disadvantages of daylight fishing in that the angler is less likely to disturb the fish and, if lake fish behave in the same way as river fish (which they seem to do) they are likely to be more responsive to the well fished fly at night).

Night fishing techniques on lakes encompass the whole gamut of techniques available by day: the sunk-fly surface/subsurface fly, dry fly or wake fly. Tackle is the same as by day; save that stronger leaders (8lb strength) and larger flies/lures are practicable.

It is in a flat calm that boat fishing at night comes into its own, since the physical presence of the boat is least likely to disturb the fish, provided due regard is given to the position of the moon and any afterglow from the setting sun. A good tactic is to take the boat quietly into a shallow bay and, if there is no breeze to influence the direction of the cast, fish 'around-the-clock' (figuratively, not literally), moving *quietly* to a new station after a circle of water has been fished-out.

Night fishing, whether on lake or river, is predominantly a tactile rather than visual activity. A taking fish is 'felt' rather than observed. For this reason we much prefer the worked fly to the static fly, and recommend the sunk-fly or surface/subsurface fly (see Chapter 9).

Playing and landing a large, fresh-run sea trout on a lake at night is something never to be forgotten!

Spinning

Conventional spinning techniques similar to those used on rivers can be productive either from a boat or from the bank, although the lure must be worked at all times as there is no current in a lake. The main advantage of spinning over fly fishing is the greater distance covered by the cast and the fact that the lure can be fished directly into the wind and fished very much deeper if so required. Depth is not always an advantage, however, as sea trout more frequently reside in shallow water in lakes.

The same tackle used for light spinning on rivers (page 165) will usually suffice on lakes, but a fine line (4lb strength) may be advisable in clear water. In a good wave large lures and stronger lines can be used, but under most circumstances a small lure is appropriate. The small 'Mepps' and 'Droppen' spinners (sizes 0, 1 or 2) and the 'Toby' or 'Lurgan' wobblers (sizes 7–12 grams) are good stillwater lures. The spinners work at a slower rate of retrieve than the wobblers and are generally to be preferred. The smaller sizes of Devon, quill and Irish minnow could be used also but we prefer the Mepps for most purposes.

The standard shape of spinner (e.g. Mepps Aglia) is better than the less resistant 'elongated oval' (e.g. Aglia Long) as it spins better at a much slower rate of retrieve since it has more resistance to the water. Since lake spinning is undertaken in clear water, the more subtle hues and colours are normally preferred, such as the zebra, gold or copper blades, but silver (so loved by river anglers) can produce results on certain days – especially when fresh-run fish are in residence.

Casting from the bank is best undertaken employing a round-the-clock search pattern as this presents the lure from a range of directions to any fish in the vicinity and makes the best use of any available light (page 166). The shallow water close to the bank should not be overlooked and should be fished first. Avoid fishing too deep in shallow water. Lures are not cheap and many lakes are very rocky! The lure fished close to the surface with a fast retrieve is often most effective, but do not be afraid to experiment with fishing depths and rates of retrieve.

When spinning from a drifting boat the cast can be made in any direction except directly behind, as the passage of the boat is likely to have 'scared' any fish as it passed overhead. Generally speaking approach this form of spinning as if fly fishing. The diagonal or lateral cast across the line of the drift allows full use of the forward movement of the boat to swing the lure 'round-the-corner' with a slow rate of retrieve. This achieves greater depth, allows more water to be covered than the straight-ahead-and-back cast, and achieves an attractive change of direction in the passage of the lure.

Trolling

Trolling entails trailing a lure (usually a spinner; but sometimes a 'fly') on a long line behind a boat which is moved under power (by rowing or on an engine) over the likely fish lies. The correct term for this form of pseudo-spinning is 'trailing', but the term 'trolling' is now widely employed. It is essentially a technique used on the larger lakes – such as Loch Lomond. It is prohibited by regulation on many waters.

The advantages of trolling are that it often produces larger fish than other methods, allows far more water to be covered, and exploits fish which may have become 'stale' and unresponsive to other methods by long residence in the lake. Its disadvantages are that it is *boring* and is essentially a technique of skilled boat handling rather than angling.

The basic skill in trolling is to fish the lure at the 'right' depth and speed over the potential holding water. The depth at which the lure fishes depends on three main factors; 1) the speed of the boat; 2) the weight of the lure (plus any lead attached to the line); and 3) the length of line extended behind the boat. A heavy lure fished at speed will fish nearer the surface than the same lure fished slowly. A shorter line results in the lure fishing close to the surface.

On some of the larger lakes it is not unusual to fish two or three rods simultaneously with the lures working at different depths (Figs 76 and 77).

Standard spinning tackle may be used for trolling with 10–12lb strength nylon line. The lure is fished for sea trout at a depth of up to 5 feet beneath the surface some 30–40 yards behind the boat. When fishing two or three rods it is wise to fish each line at a different length and at a different depth to 'search' the water more effectively. We believe in quick-change rigs, and use a 'Hillman' lead attached to swivel so that the weight can be quickly increased and decreased according to need. Almost any lure can be used when trolling, from natural sprats to plugs (such as Rapalas and Kynock Killers) to artificial minnows, Toby-type lures and standard spinners. The large 'Marchog'-type streamer flies with long flying trebles are also effective when trolling and are becoming increasingly popular also for rainbow and brown trout on reservoirs. The colour of the lure is usually irrelevant. There is, however, much sense in the general maxim that a dull lure is better when fishing slow and deep and a bright lure when fishing high and fast.

The rod is rested at an appropriate angle against the side of the boat,

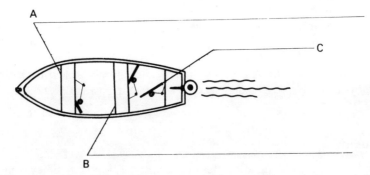

Fig. 76. Trolling a spinner (or fly) behind a moving boat is permitted on some waters and banned on many more. Up to three rods may be fished at one time with the lures carefully weighted to fish at different depths. Trolling enables a lot of water to be covered in a day and is useful in large lakes when fish are scarce in the early part of the season.

Fig. 77. The main skill in trolling is in handling the boat to fish the lure in the right place and at the right depth and speed according to the mood of the fish. Different lengths of line are fished from each rod and different amounts of weight are used to fish the lure at different depths. Each rod much be securely positioned in the boat so that it does not go overboard when you hook a fish (or the bottom).

either in a rowlock, wedged under a seat or inserted in a secure rod rest specially designed for trolling. Do make sure that the rod is secure. Line must be given freely when a fish hits the lure. This is done by lifting the bail-arm (on a fixed spool reel) and laying a stone or piece of wood across the line to prevent it running free. This weight is 'flipped off' when a fish takes. As soon as a fish is on, the boat should be brought under control and any additional lines wound in. This is often easier said than done. It always pays to have two people in the boat!

When fishing the single troll, and with someone manoeuvring the boat, the rod can be held over the stern and worked from left to right and up and down to vary the direction of movement and depth of the lure. Striking as such is rarely possible when trolling. The fish is either hooked or it isn't.

Quite apart from the skill of handling the boat, the other principal skill in trolling is knowing the water so that the lure fishes over the favoured lies for as long as possible.

Shallow weedy lakes or those with rocky bottoms are a troller's nightmare. Snagging the bottom can be very costly and trailing a lure for 30 minutes festooned with weed is not conducive to success – or good temper. It pays to check the lure periodically.

We mentioned earlier that trolling was becoming popular on trout reservoirs. It is (where allowed) – but only with the fly or streamer-type lure. Various reservoir anglers have developed the technique to a very fine art, and we anticipate that some at least will apply the technique to sea trout with interesting results in the not-too-distant future. If they are as successful with sea trout as with brown and rainbow trout we may see trolling outlawed on those waters where it is now permitted!

PART IV
Fur and Feather

16 · FLIES: GENERAL CONSIDERATIONS

We now come to the one aspect of fly fishing that usually holds the deepest fascination for most anglers – the fly itself. The first question invariably asked by another angler when you admit to catching a fish is 'What on?' – not 'Where?' or 'When?' or 'How?' but 'What on?' (meaning what pattern of fly were you using?) Yet *if* we take heed of the advice of most of the experts, and *if* we accept the established fact that sea trout do not feed in the river on returning from the sea, the actual pattern of fly used in sea trout fishing should be the least of our concerns.

The conventional view is that the size and shape of the fly and the way that it is fished are of far greater importance than its pattern. This is largely true. Nevertheless there are times when the pattern of the fly may be the key to success when others about you fail. That is not to say that the other characteristics of the fly as presented to the fish – its size, shape, profile, depth, speed of movement, direction of movement, etc – are not important, because they are. The 'right' pattern fished at the 'wrong' speed or depth or size is just as likely to be as ineffective as the 'wrong' pattern presented and fished correctly.

The sea-trout angler's choice of fly patterns depends to some extent on whether or not it is believed that adult sea trout 'feed' in fresh water. Most early authors believed that sea trout were no more than brown trout which, having spent some time feeding in the sea, continued to feed like brown trout when they returned to the river. Thus, much early sea-trout fishing was based on an approach similar to that adopted for brown trout in rivers and lakes. Since much of the early literature on sea-trout angling originated from Scotland, it is not surprising that Scottish patterns of river and lake 'trout' flies dominated the formative period of sea-trout angling.

Mottram, who was essentially a dry-fly exponent, believed that sea trout 'undoubtedly fed in freshwater before and after spawning' and (not unnaturally) adopted an 'imitative' approach in his choice of flies. This 'imitative' approach of employing patterns designed to copy the life-cycle stages of the submergent and emergent natural food of the brown trout was prevalent among devotees of the 'English school' of sea trout fishing, and was continued by Dawson (another dry fly angler) in the West Country. Dawson stated that 'sea trout, of course, feed in fresh water – when they can find anything to eat', and then makes the rather amazing and contradictory statement that 'daytime fishing for sea trout differs little, if at all, from when brown trout are the object' adding that 'a variety of patterns is unnecessary'. He recommends no more than the *Red Quill, Coch-y-Bon-ddu* with a silver body(?) 'or almost anything else that the individual angler may fancy'.

Bridgett, who, even though he wrote his seminal *Sea Trout Fishing* some 60 years ago, must still be regarded as 'authoritative' as far as river fishing in daylight is concerned, states 'there are still people who cannot allow themselves to be persuaded that salmon do not and cannot feed in fresh water. It is fortunate that I am saved the task of proving a similar peculiarity in sea trout. They will feed grossly and voraciously when opportunity offers.' However, Bridgett goes on to qualify this by noting that 'nevertheless it seems to be under no great necessity to take food, being able, and in certain streams compelled, to subsist, principally if not altogether, on the accumulated store of fat provided from the inexhaustible waters of the estuary'.

He then makes a statement which was to set the general tone of sea-trout angling for more or less the next half-century by adding that 'thus it is a creature of moods, often answering an impulse other than appetite, inquisitiveness or acquisitiveness, the same, whatever it is, that urges the salmon to its doom. Consequently, the sea trout occupies a sort of intermediate position between the salmon and the brown trout.' Thus he recommends 'an artificial trout fly fashioned in imitation of a natural fly' when the river is low, the surface calm and the light strong and 'the flies are hatching out', and, by contrast, a salmon fly when the river is running full but clear and the sea trout shows little shyness, and when 'it is...fearless...launching itself with eagerness upon a salmon fly, attracted by the glittering body of the lure or the flashing blends of silk, feather and tinsel'. On lakes, Bridgett notes a similar situation with large flies 'cast in hope of a salmon' often welcomed by sea trout in 'a brisk breeze which raises an ample ripple', whereas 'there will be no response to anything but small flies delicately presented...when only the gentlest of breezes tempers the heat of the sun'.

Bridgett was widely experienced on many different waters in Scotland and Ireland. Despite this fact – or perhaps, more exactly, *because of it* – he stated in his characteristically undogmatic way that he was 'not qualified to recommend which flies were the most serviceable for sea trout'. He, like Brennand some 25 years later, noted that different flies fished well on different waters and stated that 'style was more important than pattern'. Bridgett's view was that the bushy wings and bulky bodies widely popular with the brown trout anglers of his day were to be avoided for sea trout 'since the fly should enter the water smoothly and pass without disturbance'. In this he was the first to declare a preference for the slender-winged, sparse-bodied, lightly hackled sea trout flies of later years.

Bridgett evidently fished with a wide range of different patterns. He noted, as have many, that sea trout – especially fresh-run fish – liked flies with silver bodies but that, in his view, their fascination (to sea trout) was surpassed by a yellow body followed by a glowing claret or red.

318

'Every sea trout angler requires several different sorts of flies about his person.' 'Scruff' Oliver makes his selection for the Slebech water on the Eastern Cleddau (South-West Wales). (Photo: Martin Cavaney.)

Bluett, another widely recognised authority, stated that sea trout do not rise readily except when fresh run *or* as whitling *or* after they had time to revert to the river feeding habit. While we would agree with the first statement generally, and would not dispute strongly the second statement, we must disagree with the final statement. Bluett seems to have been the originator of the still-popular belief that dull, drab, semi-imitative brown trout flies are better for sea trout that have been in fresh water for some time. There is no evidence whatsoever that sea trout eventually 'revert' to feeding in the river after a period of re-acclimatisation. In our experience, the longer sea trout have been in the river the harder they are to catch on anything – be it bait, spinner, bright fly or dull fly – *unless* they are motivated by the complex hormonal drives that presage spawning or are reinvigorated by the effects of a flood.

Horsley was another who believed that sea trout fed like brown trout on returning from the sea. Cass, on the other hand, disagreed, saying that sea trout like salmon survived without feeding by utilising their reserves of accumulated fat. Kingsmill Moore asserted that 'the feeding of whitetrout in fresh water is spasmodic and limited'. This view was based upon an examination of the stomach contents of about 100 fish of which about 95 contained next to nothing. He makes the point, later to be taken up by Falkus, that sea trout have their 'taking times' and *if* a hatch of fly coincides with this time they will take the natural fly '*but* a rise of natural will not necessarily bring them on the take'. He adds that the taking time seems to be the result of a sudden burst of activity quite unrelated to the availability of food.

The question of taking times for the non-feeding salmon has stimulated authors for almost a century and much is still speculative even if some of the theories are very plausible. Falkus makes the very relevant point that the angler can adopt one of two assumptions when deciding what approach to adopt for sea trout:

1. that sea trout remain active feeders on returning to the river;
2. that sea trout *do not* feed actively on returning to the river.

Thus, a decision must be made on whether to approach sea-trout fishing like either brown trout or salmon fishing. Since we must now accept the evidence (Chapter 1) that sea trout, like salmon, do not feed in fresh water as adults, it follows that the angler who adopts the 'imitative' approach of the brown-trout angler in terms of choice of fly pattern and style of fishing will only catch sea trout successfully when they are rising to the natural. Since such rises are infrequent, and seem to decay with time after the fish enters fresh water, it is to be expected that the angler who adopts salmon-style tactics suitable for non-feeding fish will be more successful than the angler who adopts an approach more suited to the feeding brown trout.

Bridgett and Brennand, as mentioned above, both noted that different flies assume a local popularity on different waters. On some rivers the *Peter*

Ross is acclaimed as *the* fly for sea trout. On another river the *Teal, Silver and Blue* is accepted as *the* best fly. Even within a single river system individual anglers will develop their own personal preferences and prejudices in respect of a particular fly pattern. Thus angler A will invariably fish with (say) a *Mallard and Claret* while angler B chooses a *Black Pennell* and both appear to be equally successful.

Brennand states 'I think in sea trout fishing it is very necessary to have plenty of different sorts of flies'. He observed that sea trout sometimes show a marked preference for some particular pattern for a period and then change to some quite different pattern for another period. He also observed that one pattern may fish well during one year and another pattern fish well the next year. He suggests that the best thing to do is to use three flies of different patterns during the first few days on a water and note carefully which pattern is favoured, adding that 'the preference for one fly will usually be quite marked'. Having found the right fly, he suggests using two of the same pattern but of different sizes on the leader. This is not, we think, especially good advice for sea trout, although it may make more sense when fishing for brown trout when they are selectively feeding on a particular item of food.

Bluett also suggests having plenty of flies. He states: 'Some modern writers, and many experienced fishermen, go so far as to declare that it is quite unnecessary to use more than two or three patterns. With this I am not in agreement.' He believed that 'conditions of light, environment, height, colour, temperature, and rate of flow of water, and condition of fish vary so greatly that it must, I think, be necessary to have some half-a-dozen patterns in varying sizes to meet all eventualities'. We agree with the general opinion expressed by Bluett, but would not restrict ourselves to just half-a-dozen patterns. Bluett fished largely on just *one* section of *one* river where half-a-dozen different patterns in different sizes may have been sufficient for his needs. We are both fortunate to fish widely on several different rivers and lakes throughout the British Isles and have noted that different flies are indeed successful on different waters. The half-a-dozen that we would select for the crystal-clear gravel rivers of mid-Wales would not be the same as the half-a-dozen chosen for the peaty moorland rivers of Scotland or Ireland. Nor would the same half-a-dozen be chosen for lake fishing. Even on the same river, our original half-a-dozen for the first half of the season might be very different by the end of the season; and they would probably differ from year to year, depending on whether it was a wet or dry summer. Further more, our selection for sunk-lure fishing would not be identical with that chosen for surface/subsurface fishing, and so on.

It will have become apparent by now that we believe in having 'plenty of different sorts of fly' about our person when fishing for sea trout. This is perhaps because we are both keen fly dressers. As such we take more than just a passing interest in our flies and those used by others. Aided by the earlier 'researches' of Bluett, we have prepared a list of the various patterns of fly recommended for sea trout by various authorities (Table 16).

The list is of *either* just passing interest *or* more than passing interest, depending on your view as to whether pattern is important or not. It covers a period of some 50 years of authoritative opinion by seven very worthy experts and shows, among other things, firstly the marked preponderance of Scottish patterns, and secondly the prevalence of 'trout' as opposed to small 'salmon' patterns.

We could spend the rest of this chapter (if not this book) discussing this list and commenting on the various omissions and inclusions and orders of preference (not that these were everywhere stated). We must not do so: but some comment is relevant to what follows.

If we accept that there is not much difference between Woodcock, Grouse and Mallard as feathers for winging, and that silver (= grey) Mallard has a barred effect similar to Teal, we cannot fail to note the broad similarity in most of the above lists. They more or less all contain a claret or red fly near the top of the list, yellow and blue figure largely in most lists(the *Teal and Silver* having a blue hackle), all contain a silver-bodied fly, all contain a black or blackish fly and, if we exclude the *Alexandra*, the only notable (and surprising) omission is a green fly from all lists other than Stuart's.

The style of dressing shown in the various illustrations given by several authors is for a bulky, heavy fly – save for Bluett's selection for West Country rivers which is refreshingly different and surprisingly modern. It is here that we see the inception of the lightly winged, slender-bodied, open-hackled flies that were to become the vogue in later years. We also see in his 'frontispiece' the large 2 and 3 hook lures that were to be popularised by Falkus some 20 years later. His Alexandra lure with its silver body, blue hackles, peacock herl wings and red varnished head is, for all practical purposes, identical to the sunk-lure advocated by Hugh Falkus. In this context it is noteworthy that Bluett, writing in the 1940s, was apparently the first to recommend a very large demon-type lure for sea trout. Clapham also recommended large tandem-mounted lures as a useful addition to the fly box for sea trout; so did Holiday, and Gray. However, credit for recommending the use of the now standard two-hook lure must go to Maxwell who, at the turn of the century, declared 'there is nothing that has more attraction for sea trout than a large red palmer; if tied on two hooks, one behind the other, so much the better'.

The lists given by Bridgett and Jock Scott (Table 14) were obtained by writing to Scottish tackle dealers asking for details of their best-selling sea-trout flies. They were not in fact patterns which these two expert sea-trout anglers necessarily chose to use themselves and, as Bridgett states, it is not clear whether his listings were the preferred choice for river or lake. Jock Scott, who was in some respects rather radical in his 'salmonistic' approach to sea trout, stated that after many years' experience he preferred to use small salmon flies for his sea-trout fishing and listed as his personal choice *Hairy Mary, Thunder and Lightning, Green Highlander, Dusty Miller,*

Table 16: 'Recommended' sea trout flies by different authorities 1917 to 1969

Hamish Stuart – Lochs – [1]	Bridgett 1 – Top 10 –	Bridgett 2 – for Hebrides –	Bridgett 3 – for Connemara –	Clapham – Estuaries –
Mallard & Claret	Butcher	Teal & Silver	Blue Zulu	Black & Orange
Woodcock & Green	Peter Ross	Mallard & Claret	Blae & Black	Black & Silver
Zulu	Teal & Silver	Pheasant & Yellow	Pheasant & Yellow	Claret & Mallard
Teal & Blue	Dunkeld	Butcher	Mallard & Claret	Connemara Black
Grouse & Purple	Mallard & Claret	Silver March Brown	Mallard, Claret & Yellow	Francis Fly
Red Stuart	Silver Doctor	Mallard, Claret & Yellow	Black & Silver	Heckham Peckham
Cinnamon & Gold	Grouse & Claret	Woodcock, Teal &	Alexandra	Silver March Brown
Silver Zulu	Pheasant & Yellow	Yellow	Bloody Butcher	Ramsbottoms Favourite
Butcher	Blae & Blue	Black Zulu	Brown Turkey	White Tip & Claret
	Blae & Black	Blue Zulu	Grouse & Claret	
		Black & Silver	Connemara Black	
			Thunder & Lightning	

Bluett 1 "Standards"	Bluett 2 "West Country Choice"	Dawson[2] – Elsewhere –	Jock Scott – Top 10 –	Holiday – Rivers –
Peter Ross	Mallard & Claret	Mallard & Claret	Black Pennell	Alexandra
Butcher	General Eagle's Fairy	Teal & Silver	Claret Pennell	Black Pennell
Teal & Silver	E.R.B.	Teal & Red	Blue Zulu	Butcher
Woodcock & Red	The Martyr	Blae & Black	Invicta	Fiery Brown
Pheasant & Yellow	The Magpie	Mallard & Yellow	Teal & Silver	Grouse & Purple
Pheasant Tail	Bluett's Fancy	Butcher	Alexandra	Teal & Claret
Mallard & Claret	Jackson's Palmer	Alexandra	Grouse & Claret	Invicta
Yellow Bustard	The Butcher	Bradshaw's Yellow	Silver Butcher	Mallard & Claret
Alexandra	The Owl	Zulu	Soldier Palmer	Silver March Brown
	Fancy Pheasant Tail	Peter Ross	Red Palmer	Peter Ross
	Alexandra Lure		Fancy Palmer	Pheasant & Yellow
	Tavy Lure			Teal & Blue

[1] Stuart listed separately his river flies as Teal & Silver, Grouse & Yellow, Grouse & Purple and March Brown with a silver bodied, blue hackled fly with a greyish 'blae' wing being 'always a killing fly'. Bluett in comparing various selections failed to make this distinction (quite easily done) and thus misrepresented Stuart's selection.

[2] This list is, again, derived from Bluett who has, again slightly misrepresented the quoted author's choices. Dawson includes the first 8 patterns as general flies of wide acclaim. He does not necessarily recommend them for West Country use.

323

Silver Doctor, and *Yellow Eagle*. Crossley and Maxwell also favoured small salmon flies; but the general preference of most of our experts is overwhelmingly for trout patterns.

During the 1940s and 1950s there was a noticeable shift away from the traditional 'Scottish' patterns and style of fishing that had dominated sea-trout angling for generations. This was due largely to the strong West Country influence on the literature of the period, and particularly to Jeffrey Bluett who did so much to popularise night fishing and make it 'respectable'. Thus the use of much larger and non-standard flies became quite common 'south of the border' in the post-war period. This was especially so in Wales, where 'sewin' fishing had been hardly affected by what went on elsewhere since time immemorial. Here, many 'new' patterns, such as the *Haslam, Conwy Red, Dyfi Black and Orange, Penybont, Mallard and Silver*, had become generally popular, and many anglers were using large lures and tube-flies of anything up to 3 inches as a matter of routine.

The progressive breakdown of traditionalism in sea-trout angling continued in the early 1960s with the publication of Hugh Falkus's definitive work on sea trout. Not only did he popularise the current vogue for slender flies as recommended by Bridgett and Bluett and for large flies at night as recommended by Bluett but he also advocated the use of the large multi-hook sunk lure as previously mentioned by Clapham, Bluett, Gray and Holiday. While tipping the pendulum further towards 'big' flies, he also added weight at the other end of the scale by restoring to favour the very small Loch Leven-style 'wee doubles' so popular in the 1920s and 1930s with some authors and first mentioned as being 'desirable' by Bridgett. In addition, Falkus also revitalised the 'wake fly' technique of fishing a surface lure at night. Dawson mentions this technique in the 1930s and credits its 'invention' to F. M. Warhurst of Ulverston in the English Lake District. This buoyant surface lure must have been fairly popular at one time for it to have been marketed commercially by Messrs Hardy Bros in the 1950s but, for some reason, it fell into almost total obscurity until rediscovered by Falkus.

The final stage in the evolution of the modern sea-trout fly began in the late 1960s when, for various reasons, reservoir fishing in England and Wales took off in a big way. The techniques of fishing large man-made waters where rainbow trout form the mainstay of the fisheries developed rapidly, as too did the patterns of flies employed in reservoir fishing, and we have seen an enormous range of new patterns evolved which have eventually become adapted or adopted for sea trout. This has been a rich, colourful, and sometimes bizarre inheritance! But it has resulted in such new patterns as the *Sweeney Todd, Viva, Missionary, Dog Nobbler, Muddler Minnow* and *Undertaker* being just as likely to be used today for sea trout on river and lake as the old favourites, such as *Mallard and Claret, Black Pennell* and *Peter Ross*, by a new generation of anglers graduating from a very different school.

While much early sea-trout angling was done with the standard-sized flies more typical of brown-trout fishing, the usual advice being to fish 'two sizes bigger at night', the larger flies and lures so popular today with many night fishermen are nothing new. Although Maxwell recommended flies in the size range 8–12 and Stuart advocated size 8 'if sea trout are at all in the mood', Bridgett sometimes fished as large as size 4 at night. (Chrystal nowhere mentions hook sizes for sea trout but we can assume that he probably followed Stuart.) Bluett mostly fished size 10–12 flies but suggested that size 5 was suitable on coloured water by day and often fished down to size 4 at night when it was very dark. Although Falkus also recommended large hooks in the size range 3–5 for his Mallard, Silver and Blue, *Medicine* fly, MacLaren had previously noted that sea trout sometimes preferred a size 1 or 1/0 salmon fly at night and, even earlier still, Crossley had fished size 1 to an enormous size 5/0 fly for the large sea trout encountered in Sweden. Thus large flies are nothing new for sea trout.

Jock Scott and Currie suggested that the size 8 flies used by Stuart are still the standard for sea trout, and they are probably right. But it is interesting to note that Stuart recalled using much larger flies for sea trout in his youth (the late nineteenth century), stating '. . . you would now probably, indeed assuredly, angle in vain for sea trout in certain waters if you used the flies that your angling forefathers employed'. It seems that his assurance was wrong since things have come full circle and sea trout are again being caught on large to very large flies today. By contrast, they are also being caught on flies much smaller than the standard sizes 8–10, with singles, doubles and trebles down to size 16 increasing in popularity for daylight fishing on several waters.

By and large, the single hook is still the most popular. Although Maxwell drew attention to the use of a long shank double to overcome the problem of short-rising fish (Bluett suggested a long shank single dressed 'short'), the double hook was, surprisingly, not popular with most experts. Jock Scott alone stated a clear preference for double hooks. In recent years the long-shank treble has become popular and many patterns of wet fly and dap fly are being modified for tying on treble hooks.

The treble hook, particularly the outpoint version, is an exceptionally good 'hooker-and-holder'. We find that we lose very few fish on the treble when compared with a single hook and it is not unusual when using the smaller sizes (12–14) to have all three points firmly impaled in the tip of the jaws of a fish that has taken 'on-the-hang' so that the mouth is locked solid and the fly impossible to remove without recourse to a knife. However, apart from the fact that flies dressed on trebles somehow never look as aesthetically pleasing (to the angler), we would *suggest* (no less) that they may not be quite so effective in attracting fish. Single and double hooked flies seem to produce more offers.

We mentioned previously that the tube-fly was once very popular, almost predominant, on some Welsh rivers in the 1950s and 1960s. It still has many adherents in Wales but is rapidly being replaced by the Waddington shank which, in our view, has many advantages over the tube.

Falkus discusses the demerits of the tube-fly compared with the large single hook. He argued that the thicker body of the tube resulted in fewer offers, it was more inclined to hook back on the leader in a wind, and the treble was inclined to stick out at an angle. For these reasons he preferred a large single hook which, he claimed, held on to a sea trout better than the treble.

While the problem of the treble fishing out-of-line with the fly can be overcome by using needle-eye hooks inserted into the body of the tube, or by using a small rubber sleeve to join the tail of the tube with the shank of the treble (which is of course tied to the leader threaded through the tube!), and while the problem of hooking back may be resolved by a more open style of casting, we agree that the much more bulky tube-fly produces less offers – but not that it is any less good in its hooking power than a single. Another disadvantage with a large tube is that its resistance through the air (especially in a wind) may cause casting difficulties and lack of distance.

While there are times when sea trout seem to prefer the bulk of a tube-fly to anything else, much of our fishing is now done with Waddingtons rather than tubes. The Waddington shank comes in sizes from about ½ to 2 inches and can be a single or double strand of metal. The dressed Waddington fly is far more streamlined than the tube-fly, its lesser bulk minimises casting problems and its greater weight can be an advantage in a wind. Being slimmer (= less resistant) and heavier it also sinks quicker and deeper and fishes better in a current than a tube-fly. (It is possible to obtain weighted tubes but we dislike them intensely other than for early or late season salmon fishing.) By selecting single or double shanks it is possible to fish higher or deeper in the water for a given size of fly than would ever be possible using different weights of single hook. The treble hook is held in line either by a rubber-sleeve or by whipping a short nylon link between the shank and the mounted treble. This provides an articulated hinge. But some anglers prefer to allow the treble to swing freely from the shank on the basis that it will in any event fish 'in-line' as the fly is worked through the water.

Generally speaking then, *we* much prefer the Waddington shank to the *large* single hook lure and recognise the advantages of both over the tube-fly. Nevertheless there are times when the more buoyant and bulky tube fly is more effective than either and there are not many nights when we ignore the tube altogether. In fact, one of the most effective 'wake' lures known to us is a 1½–2 inch lightweight tube-fly (*Dyfi Phantom*) stripped *very* fast over the surface of a deep pool.

We have previously noted that all the good books say that the pattern of fly is not important, but what matters is the way that it is fished. A.H.E. Wood, the originator of the greased-line technique for salmon, fished throughout one entire season with a *Silver March Brown* to prove his belief that pattern mattered not at all – and apparently caught his usual share of fish. But we all collect flies, don't we? Most of us seem to derive great comfort from the knowledge that we have about us plenty of different patterns to cover every conceivable need – plus a few extra sorts just in case – and we all spend much time carefully pondering what particular pattern to use, and when to change it for another. Very few sea-trout anglers would fish with just one pattern *throughout the week*, let alone an entire season. We all have favourite flies. Usually they are patterns that served as well on one particular, memorable, occasion and which inspire us with that very important ingredient – CONFIDENCE.

Is it true, then, that the pattern of fly is not important? We think that it is, if not false, a dangerous over-statement. There are times when, in our view, the pattern of fly can be very important and can mean the difference between success and failure.

There is now little scientific argument that trout have excellent vision and are well able to distinguish between colours and even between shades of the same colour. They can see contrasting shades or patterns, such as stripes and spots, with exceptional clarity. The colour most visible to fish is red followed by orange, yellow, green, blue and violet. These basic facts explain certain phenomena well known to fly fishermen, and the consequential popularity of fly patterns with contrasting barred wings of mallard and teal and with red and yellow butts, tags and bodies. It also explains the appeal of silver tinsel and the use of black wings, hackles and bodies to achieve contrast. The *Peter Ross* with its teal wing, red and silver body and black hackle is, in theory, one of the most visible of all patterns.

Several authorities suggest that it is good policy to have one dark fly and one light-coloured fly on a leader and, if fishing three flies, to include a silver or flashy fly as an added attractor. This is fine and covers the main options, but leaves much to chance. A light fly becomes a dark fly when seen in silhouette and the visibility of any fly depends on the turbidity of the water, the amount of sunlight/moonlight and the spectral content of the light.

Every angler will experience days when one pattern of fly *and only one pattern of fly* raises and/or hooks fish (it is usually in your companion's fly box and *not* in yours). The angling literature is liberally littered with such anecdotes. Why should this be? Why should an 'orange' fly succeed on one day when everything else fails and on another occasion it is a 'blue' fly – or some other specific confection of fur, feather and tinsel?

The sea trout is a fish of many moods and these moods dictate its threshold of response to a fly (or spinner or bait). Each fish is an individual with its own separate threshold of response, which may or may not be the same as that of its associates in the shoal. Some fish may be 'switched-on' while others are 'switched-off'; and there may well be a range of receptivity within any group of fish. Sometimes it may be that a fly is *too visible, too obvious*. At other times it may not be obvious enough. We firmly believe that the pattern of a fly – its form, colour, shade, texture, contrast and, in a word, 'appearance' – can at times be as important as its style and the size and manner in which it is fished. Pattern dictates whether or not the fly appears as a flat, solid object which reflects or absorbs light or whether or not it appears as an ephemeral, translucent object. The secret of success is to hit on the right combination of pattern, style, size and *movement* for the conditions prevailing at the time.

Sea trout are undoubtedly shy, but they are also curious. Falkus vividly demonstrates that a worm fished persistently over a salmon may eventually stimulate a positive response provided that the lie is not disturbed. The same approach with the less ponderous and more capricious sea trout will, more often than not, result in the fish moving elsewhere – *very soon and very fast*. We have noted time after time when fishing wet fly, dry fly and worm on low clear water that sea trout seem to have a very obvious 'boredom threshold'. A lure (fly/bait) presented anew to a shoal of fish under perfect conditions for observation usually results in some interest being shown, with several fish moving towards the lure/bait as it fishes past. Repeated presentation of the *same* lure/bait results in a clearly visible decay in group interest. If (say) six fish turned and moved with the fly the first time it fished over the shoal, only two or three would do so the second time the same fly was presented, and then for a shorter distance. The third presentation of the same lure would promote only marginal interest by one or two fish, and by the time it was on its fourth presentation the fish would show no interest whatsoever. As this stage, we have noted that a change of fly, say from a *Mallard and Claret* to a *Silver Stoat's Tail*, has a marked effect on reawakening interest by members of the shoal – but whether they were the same fish that responded before or different members of the same shoal we cannot say.

We are, as we have stated, both keen fly dressers and we have, naturally, taken an interest in 'who' was catching what with what: especially under adverse conditions. We have been pleasantly surprised to find that those anglers who seem to catch fish when others fail are often those who 'tried something different' – usually visitors who knew no better and tried the 'wrong' fly. This is a significant observation on the increasingly heavily fished waters of today, especially club waters. Sea trout that have become sick to death of, and wholly accustomed to, seeing *Teal, Silver and Blues* or *Green Peters, Mallard and Clarets* (or any one of the popular and 'recommended' flies on that particular water) may develop an unhealthy interest in, and so fall foul of, a *Missionary*, or an *Ace-of-Spades* or some other outlandish pattern that probably had never before set hackle in *that* particular water.

As a matter of policy we frequently change fly when our favoured pattern fails to produce the required reponse after a decent period of fishing. More often than not, a change produces a fish. Whether or not persistence with the favoured fly would have eventually produced the same result is open to conjecture. We think not.

So on the matter of patterns, we would say: '*enjoy your flies*'. They are works of art lovingly created by someone for a particular purpose. Each pattern, every variant, was born in hope, baptised in faith and christened in reward. Do not be afraid to have plenty of flies about you and do not be ashamed to change pattern when you feel the need. *The pattern may at times be important.* If it is not then a change can do no harm and the confidence so generated may, in itself, provide the key to success.

17 · FLIES: PATTERNS AND DRESSINGS

No selection of sea trout flies could ever be comprehensive. Every year new patterns or variants of old patterns are created which should be included in any list as being 'useful for sea trout'. The following patterns have been selected to illustrate the range of flies which may be used for taking sea trout. Many of the patterns are included in the accompanying colour plates (1–6). We have deliberately avoided classifying them into river or lake flies for good reason. While some patterns achieved their original fame as either a river fly (*Teifi Terror*) or as a lake fly (*Kingsmill*), the sea trout themselves make no such distinction. The *Peter Ross* is just as likely to catch sea trout in either environment and this applies to virtually every other pattern given the correct circumstances and a half-competent angler at the other end of the rod.

This chapter is divided into three sections, covering:

1. surface flies and lures;
2. subsurface flies and lures;
3. sunk flies and lures.

We recognise again that this classification is somewhat arbitrary. The *Muddler Minnow* was originally designed as a sunk lure and fished in a way to emulate the dipping and darting movements of a small fish. It can be, and is, fished successfully for sea trout as a deep sunk and mid-water lure in rivers, but it is perhaps best known as a surface and sub-surface lure for sea trout in both lakes and rivers.

We have carefully avoided listing our own recommended selection for rivers or lakes. The reasons for this are, quite simply, that the two lists would be completely different for rivers – although they may overlap for lakes – and because our recommended 'top ten' or 'top twenty' would probably be very different to that which we would propose this time next year or would have proposed a year ago. *Of course* we have particular favourites: but that does not mean that we always use them. We would both never be without a *Red Palmer* or *Silver Invicta* in our fly boxes, but it must be several seasons since we last used either. Thus, our preferences and prejudices are our own. We leave you to develop yours and merely give you a selection of patterns on which to start!

Surface Flies and Lures

It has long been recognised that a fly skittered or dragged across the surface so that it creates a disturbance can be attractive to sea trout, brown trout and salmon alike. This knowledge has led to the development of several methods of fishing a fly or team of flies, each of which has its own characteristic range of patterns. Thus we have dapping with its characteristically large, bushy and buoyant flies fished 'dry' on and off the surface of a lake. There is the technique (used principally on stillwaters) of working the topmost fly (the bob-fly) in a team of two, three or even four flies across the surface so that it drags and creates a small wake. There is the technique (used principally on rivers at night) of fishing a large floating lure downstream and swinging it round against the flow of the current to create a wake, or of fishing a buoyant or semi-buoyant fly or lure very fast by stripping it back across the surface or just under it so that it creates a disturbance. Finally there is the technique of fishing the dry (floating) fly in the classic style on rivers and, not so classically, on lakes.

Drag Lures

Recent developments in reservoir trout-fishing techniques, combined with a more innovative approach to fly dressing facilitated by the availability of new waterproof and highly buoyant materials, have brought about several advances in the pattern and style of the modern surface fly/lure. We anticipate many new developments in this area over the next few years.

The Wake Lure

This lure (it can hardly be called a fly) was rediscovered by Hugh Falkus and enjoyed a new popularity in the 1960s. It may have originated in the English Lake District in the 1920s or 1930s (page 324).

Silk:	black.
Hook:	4–8 single: usually with flying treble (size 10–14).
Body:	Ethafoam strips – shaped like a minnow.
Back and tail:	dark pheasant tail fibres.
Hackle:	short ginger cock.

This is a distinct improvement on the original. It is far easier to cast than the original lump of wood, cork or porcupine quill, although a smooth 'open' action is still required with little or no false-casting. After a while the lure tends to settle in the water. This is no disadvantage as it still creates a good wake and, for some reason, the takes seem to become more certain.

A slight modification in style entails the eye of the hook emerging from under the middle of the body. This results in the front section of the lure fishing above the water surface to create a better wake.

Muddler Minnow

    Silk: black.
    Hook: 6–10 (usually long shank single or double).
    Rib: oval silver tinsel.
    Body: flat silver tinsel.
    Wing: natural deer hair and grey squirrel.
    Head: deer hair tied tightly and clipped to style.

The use of deer hair in fly dressing is now widespread for reservoir patterns, but sea-trout anglers (both river and lake) have been slow to appreciate the opportunities provided by this hollow, buoyant and versatile material.

The original American version has undergone many changes. The above pattern is, arguably, the best variant, but many anglers prefer the original gold body for a moonlit night, and the black and the white variants are also popular. It is usually fished quickly through the surface to create a wake but may be used (in smaller sizes) as a useful dropper fly in conventional wet-fly fishing. In its smallest sizes it makes an excellent bob-fly for stillwater sea trout.

Muddler Head

Almost any conventional fly can be adapted to fish in or just under the surface by the addition of an attached Muddler head. The head is dressed and formed on a short length (about ½ inch) of light plastic tubing. This is then mounted on the leader (like a tube-fly) and slipped down to fit over the eye of the fly. (A muddler head can be useful when using a fast sinking line to keep the fly/lure fishing clear of the bottom.)

Floating Snail

    Silk: black.
    Hook: 10–14 wide gape.
    Body: pear-shaped cork covered with peacock herl.
    Hackle: one turn of black cock.

This lure is simply made. The shaped piece of cork is carefully slit along its middle and glued onto the hook shank. The body is then coated lightly with glue and the peacock herl (stripped on one side) is wound closely around the cork. The herled body may then be soaked in thin varnish *before* tying in the hackle.

The snail is an effective mini-version of the surface wake lure. It creates a small wake and is useful for fishing runs and glides on small rivers. It is good for small fish in the 1lb weight class. The use of plastazote for the body gives a more stylish lure.

331

Jumbo Palmers

Very large and very bushy flies are traditional for dapping. Some early patterns were so heavily hackled that they looked like feather dusters. Some had a very dense front hackle only, but most had a hackle wound round the length of the body also in the classic 'Palmer' style. The best known fly of this genre is probably the *Loch Ordie*. [We recently dissected one that was nearly 50 years old and which had no less than six hackles wound round a size 4 hook.]

More recently the large palmered flies used as dapping flies and as bob-flies on the larger lakes have been improved by the incorporation of deer hair, bucktail and squirrel hair into the dressing to improve their buoyancy. The use of two contrasting colours in the hackle to create a 'bi-visible' effect (e.g. blue and black: black and white) is now fairly standard.

Loch Ordie

> **Silk:** brown.
> **Hooks:** 4–6 (single or in tandem – with or without a size 12–14 flying treble).
> **Hackles:** large ginger cock tied palmer-style with a dense white cock head hackle.

The flying treble is intended to improve the hooking potential of the fly. A single 1-inch Waddington shank or a light 1-inch plastic tube with a size 8 treble may be used instead of the large single hooks. Other good dapping patterns are the *Black Pennel, Blue Zulu, Lock Maree*. The Loch Ordie in a half-and-half dressing on a size 8–12 single hook is a good bob-fly on some lakes.

Palmers

The smaller-sized palmer hackled flies are designed to fish on, in, and just under the surface so that they create a light wake. They are excellent bob-flies and are usually fished on the top or middle droppers of a three-fly team. Most of our dry flies for river and lake fishing are in this category.

Zulu

> **Silk:** black.
> **Hook:** 8–10.
> **Tag:** red wool or floss.
> **Body:** black seal's fur, floss or silk.
> **Rib:** fine silver wire.
> **Hackle:** Palmered black cock.

The *Black Zulu* is a very old favourite on many lakes. It is an excellent bob-fly, but often fishes well on a middle dropper. The *Blue Zulu* is equally favoured. This has a royal blue hackle. It is held to be a better fly early in the season than later on.

Bibio

> **Silk:** black.
> **Hook:** 8–12.
> **Body:** black seal's fur with a thin centre band of orange (traditional) or red seal's fur.
> **Rib:** fine silver wire.
> **Hackle:** Palmered black cock.

This near relative of the Zulu is a good bob-fly and also fishes well on a second dropper. Most of our patterns are modified to include a small tag of red fluorescent floss (Zulu) or orange or red fluorescent seal's fur in the central section (Bibio). It is to be noted that if fluorescence is to have any appeal it must be fished in air or *just* beneath the surface in daylight.

Rob Roy

> **Silk:** black.
> **Hook:** 8–10.
> **Tail:** red cock fibres.
> **Body:** alternate bands of red and black cock hackle – wound very closely.

We have used a modification of this good bob-fly with notable success. We use a fluorescent red cock hackle for the tail and body and dress the fly (like a Bibio) with a mid-section of red hackle sandwiched between a front and rear black hackle and bound in with fine silver tinsel. (The variant is more 'open' in the palmering than the original.) We have another variant – which we have named *MacGregor* – where the red is replaced by fluorescent phosphor green hackle.

Bumbles

We now come to the bumble series of 'translucent' lake flies created (once more) by Kingsmill Moore for use as surface (bob-flies) or subsurface flies. They are characterised generally by the careful blending of the colours of the double body hackles (wound together) in order to obtain the best effect from the available daylight. The shoulder hackle is of softer hen hackle and should be slightly longer than the stiffer cock feathers used for the body hackles. We give five of the seven original dressings.

Claret Bumble

Silk:	claret.
Hook:	size 10–12.
Tail:	four strands golden pheasant tippet.
Rib:	fine gold oval.
Body:	medium claret seal's fur.
Body hackles:	natural black cock and dyed medium claret cock.
Shoulder hackles:	blue jay.

The *Magenta Bumble* is equally popular and differs from the above only in the use of magenta seal with a silver rib.

Grey Ghost Bumble

Silk:	black.
Hook:	8–12.
Tail:	golden pheasant topping.
Tag:	black ostrich herl.
Rib:	fine oval silver tinsel.
Body:	light grey seal's fur or silver monkey.
Body hackle:	dyed Irish grey cock and natural black cock (Palmered).
Shoulder hackle:	teal or grey partridge.

This is another of Kingsmill Moore's 'gifts'. In recent years there has been a tendency to reduce sea-trout flies to the minimum of dressing. This fly is re-freshingly complicated to dress. Its originator states that it is a good lake fly when the water has a milky or grey tinge and when a hazy or bright sun affects underwater visibility. Under such conditions he would fish it on a dropper with a small black fly on the point.

Bruiser Bumble

Silk:	blue.
Hook:	8–12.
Tail:	flax blue wool.
Body:	rich gentian blue wool.
Rib:	fine silver wire.
Body hackle:	natural black cock and dyed gentian blue (Palmered).

Described by its creator as 'good on a dark day with low clouds and showers'.

334

Fiery Brown Bumble

Silk:	brown.
Hook:	8–12.
Tail:	Indian crow.
Tag:	golden brown floss.
Rib:	oval gold tinsel.
Body hackle:	fiery brown and blood red cock.
Shoulder hackle:	dark grouse.

Originally designed for coloured water, it failed to please its creator. We like it!

Silver Blue Bumble

Silk:	black.
Hook:	size 8–12.
Tail:	golden pheasant topping.
Body:	fine oval silver tinsel wound closely.
Body hackle:	bright medium blue dyed cock and natural badger cock hackle (Palmered).
Shoulder hackle:	teal.

This is almost an Irish version of the Teal, Silver and Blue adapted for surface work.

Hackled Surface Flies

Many flies used as bob-flies and for subsurface fishing lack the palmered body hackle.

Coch-a-bon-ddu

Silk:	black.
Hook:	8–12.
Rib:	fine gold wire.
Body:	peacock herl.
Hackle:	Furnace or Coch-a-bon-ddu.

An old fly. This is one of the few Welsh patterns to achieve international fame on river and lake as both a wet fly and a dry fly. It may be tied with a palmered body hackle.

Green Peter

> **Silk:**   green.
> **Hook:** 8–12.
> **Rib:**   fine gold wire.
> **Body:** green seal's fur.
> **Wing:** hen pheasant.
> **Hackle:** ginger cock – tied full in front of wing.

This is one of the better-known Irish lake flies and a particular favourite of ours. It fishes well on the bob and middle dropper. There is a variant with a blue seal's body called (not surprisingly) *Blue Peter*.

Dovey Bumble

> **Silk:**   black.
> **Hook:** 6–12 (also 10–12 doubles).
> **Tag:**   golden pheasant crest.
> **Rib:**   fine silver tinsel.
> **Body:** green peacock herl tied full.
> **Hackle:** Barred Plymouth Rock.

This is a classic bumble in the original English style. It lacks the double body hackle. It originated in the Dyfi valley where, in the smaller sizes, it is an excellent fly for whitling on a bright day when fished fast. In the larger sizes it fishes well at dusk or on a bright night.

Subsurface Flies and Lures

We now come to the vast range of general-purpose patterns used by day and by night, in sizes small and large, and fished largely – but not exclusively – as subsurface flies in rivers and lakes. This may be further categorised into 'Flashers', 'Standards' and 'Traditionals'; but this is an arbitrary classification, and they are best treated as one amorphous group consisting of patterns both ancient and modern from all parts of the British Isles and, increasingly, from abroad. Thus:–

Random Choice

Alexandra

> **Silk:** black.
> **Hook:** 4–10 single (also in tandem and as a tube).
> **Tail:**   red ibis (substitute).

Rib: silver wire.
Body: flat silver tinsel.
Wing: green herl from peacock sword with a thin strip of red swan along each side.
Cheeks: jungle cock eye feather.
Head: black (or red) varnish.

This pattern was once thought to be 'so deadly' that it was banned on many lakes. This Royal fly, apparently named in honour of Princess Alexandra, is some 120 years old. It is often used as an 'attractor' in point position on a two- or three-fly leader. It is good in heavy water (rivers) and in squally conditions (lakes). We have a particular variant of this traditional fly, the *Tywi Peacock and Red*, tied on a tube or, preferably, a Waddington shank (½–2 inches in length) which has a blood red throat hackle and a wing of silver 'Lureflash' mixed with peacock sword tail, which has proved *very* effective for large sea trout in medium to heavy water at night.

Butcher (Bloody and Kingfisher variants also)

Silk: black.
Hook: 8–10 (single or double).
Tail: Red ibis or wool.
Rib: silver wire.
Body: flat silver.
Hackle: black hen (Butcher).
Wing: blue mallard.

The standard *Butcher* dressing is given above. The *Bloody Butcher* has a dyed red throat hackle. The *Kingfisher Butcher* has a tail of blue fibres, a body of gold tinsel ribbed with gold wire, and a hackle of hot orange. It is a remarkably popular fly for lake and river work and usually fished on the point of a leader. The *Bloody Butcher* is popular with some anglers and the *Kingfisher Butcher* has a local reputation as a good fly for a moonlit night on some rivers in South Caernarfonshire.

Red Mackerel

Silk: red.
Hook: 4–10.
Tail: bronze mallard.
Body: red lurex tinsel.
Hackle: blood-red cock (Palmered).
Wing: bronze mallard.

Originally a fly for heavy water after a flood, this very obvious fly is widely popular for both river and lake fishing (as it is a close relative to the *Dark Mackerel* which has a darker furnace hackle).

Conway Red

Silk: red.
Hook: 6–8.
Rib: flat red tinsel.
Body: black floss silk.
Wing: hair from the back of a badger.

This North Wales fly has a very characteristic hair-wing in the original dressing. The badger hair is tied in to protrude over the eye and then doubled back before forming the head. It creates a bulky wing which is thought to cause more underwater disturbance and so enhance its attracting power.

Badger and Red (Pryf Llwyd a coch)

Silk: black.
Hook: 6–8.
Tail: golden pheasant topping.
Rib: red tinsel (flat).
Body: black seal's fur.
Hackle: badger cock.
Wing: badger hair.

This is also a good salmon fly! The body is usually tied rather full and loose, and the tinsel pulled tight to cut into the fur. A good fly for fresh fish in the lower and tidal sections. Red is a good colour for sea trout by day and night, on high and low water and in rivers and lakes. Many of the earliest flies were predominantly red. Hamish Stuart based his *Red Stuart* on silver and red and the *Red Palmer* is perhaps one of the most loved of all surface flies.

Moc's Cert

Silk: black.
Hook: 4–10 (also tube and Waddington).
Body: rear half – flat silver tinsel; front half – black seal's fur ribbed with flat silver tinsel.
Hackle: black cock.
Wing: black squirrel hair with overlay of green peacock sword feathers.
Cheeks: jungle cock eye-feather (optional).

This is an 'experimental' fly devised by...guess who?!...after discussion with several sewin experts about the 'ideal' fly for sea trout. It was used extensively since 1985 by day and night and proved its worth. The fairly bulky seal's fur body is intended to 'open out' the wing to provide life and movement to the fly. It is 'designed' to create 'underwater disturbance' – hence the stiff cock hackle tied round the body instead of the normal soft hen hackle tied 'false'. We have already developed a marked preference for the Waddington version – in fact we like anything on a Waddington!

Blackie

Silk:	black.
Hook:	6–8 single or in tandem.
Rib:	silver tinsel.
Body:	black seal's fur.
Hackle:	black cock.
Wing:	black squirrel.
Cheeks:	jungle cock eye-feather (optional).

Black flies have always been popular and 'highly recommended' by the experts. Given a choice of just *one* fly for sea trout (on river or lake) we would choose something black.

This pattern is a good work-horse at night, fished either as a subsurface fly or as a sunk lure. The tandem Blackie (size 4 hooks and up to 4 inches long) is a *very* good sunk lure at night. It is a good subsurface and daylight fly when tied on size 12 doubles, and a dry fly version is also efficacious.

Haslam

Silk:	white.
Hook:	4–10 single or (larger sizes) double.
Tag:	flat silver tinsel.
Butt:	white wool or floss.
Tail:	small golden pheasant crest.
Body:	flat silver tinsel.
Rib:	oval silver wire.
Throat:	blue jay.
Wing:	hen pheasant tail.
Horns:	blue/yellow macaw curving along wings and crossing over behind tail.
Head:	black varnish.

As good Welshmen (by birth or adoption) we love this fly. Next to the Coch-a-bon-ddu (*sic*), it is the second Welsh fly to achieve more than a local reputation. McEwan, that great Loch Lomond angler, used it from time to time as a lake fly for salmon and sea trout. This is interesting as it was originally tied as a salmon fly for coloured water but achieved far greater fame as a sea-trout fly on the Dyfi under medium to low water. The original pattern has been subjected to many modifications. The 'traditional' dressing had a white butt but the most popular mini-variant has an orange butt and a Palmered badger hackle. We give here the 'original' pattern.

The Dyfi is one of the 'best' sea trout rivers in the world! It is not unnatural that it should have been the inspiration for a number of dressings. We have mentioned the Dovey Bumble already, but another local pattern of perhaps greater renown is the DBO.

Dovey Black and Orange (DBO)

Silk: black.
Hook: 4–8 (usually doubles).
Tail: red swan.
Rib: silver thread.
Body: black floss silk.
Hackle: orange hen.
Wing: black squirrel.
Cheeks: jungle cock eye-feather (optional).

The DBO fishes well by day and night and is best at medium to high flows. It is also a good fly at night fished subsurface or well sunk.

All-Rounder

If you believe in persistence with a single fly then this is, perhaps, the fly to use. It combines many of the recognised attributes of the 'ideal' sea-trout fly: black, with red and with silver and with peacock, *plus* that 'absolute essential' for sea trout – jungle cock eye!

Hook: 6–8.
Tail: golden pheasant topping.
Rib: silver tinsel.
Body: black seal's fur.
Hackle: black cock.
Wing: black squirrel overlain with red squirrel.
Topping: peacock sword.
Cheeks: jungle cock eye-feather.

The All-Rounder is usually fished near to the surface or mid-water. A modern subsurface variant replaces the 'flash' of the jungle cock cheeks with the contrast of a Muddler head. This is more buoyant and, therefore, fished *in* or just *under* the surface. The basic All-Rounder also fishes well as a tube.

Traditionals

There are many flies in the traditional series. We include here those of which we have personal experience. We think that they are fairly typical of the genre.

Huw Nain

Silk:	black.
Hook:	8–10.
Tail:	golden pheasant tippet.
Rib:	silver wire.
Body:	rear half – golden olive; front half – grey seal's fur.
Hackle:	partridge back feather.
Wing:	sandy hen.

This is a fairly old fly, still popular on the Conway and other North Wales rivers. It was originally devised for fishing the fast-flowing runs in daylight, and the originator was noted for his success with large sea trout.

Dai Ben

Silk:	black.
Hook:	6–10.
Tail:	honey dun fibres.
Rib:	flat silver tinsel.
Body:	rabbit fur.
Hackle:	honey dun.

A fly from the Tywi valley. Less popular today than in the 1950s and 1960s when it was widely used by day and night and achieved some fame as a good fly to fish behind the ebbing tide in the estuary. It is usually fished in the point position. The body should be tied with plenty of the guard fibres sticking out to give the fly an animated effect when it is drawn through the water. The rabbit fur is taken from the back and the blue under-fur should be excluded as it lacks 'sparkle'.

Harry Tom

Silk:	black.
Hook:	8–12.
Rib:	gold wire.
Body:	dark hare's ear fur.
Hackle:	blue dun.
Wing:	bronze mallard.

Originally tied for use in the blue-grey slate rivers of North Wales, this fly
has travelled well to other regions and has proved equally as productive on
lake as on river. As with its stable-mate the Dai Ben, it is best fished as a
subsurface fly at dusk when its moth-like appearance produces results. It is
usually the point fly in a team.

Connemara Black

Silk:	black.
Hook:	8–12.
Tail:	golden pheasant topping.
Rib:	gold tinsel (flat).
Body:	black seal's fur.
Hackle:	black cock with blue jay in front.
Wing:	bronze mallard.

This Irish fly is popular on lakes and rivers and is good by day and on a dark
night. The black hackle is usually Palmered on larger flies.

Kingsmill

Silk:	black.
Hook:	8–10.
Tail:	golden pleasant topping.
Tag:	enamel blue floss.
Rib:	silver wire.
Body:	black ostrich herl.
Wing:	secondary feather of rook – rolled.
Cheeks:	small jungle cock eye-feather.
Topping:	golden pheasant topping to curve over top of wing and meet tail.

This pattern was slowly evolved by trial and error by Kingsmill Moore from a
blackish *Heckham Peckham* and was, in its creator's view, 'a new fly superior
to most current patterns' in almost all conditions. It is still popular as a lake
fly.

Teifi Terror

Silk:	black.
Hook:	6–10 in tandem.
Rib:	gold wire.
Tail:	furnace cock fibres (optional).
Body:	black floss.
Hackle:	furnace.

Once a traditional fly on a three-fly leader, it is now usually fished on the point as a tandem lure. In its traditional form on a size 8–10 single it is usually fished subsurface during daylight on the falling flood. This drab, traditional-style fly is also an effective sunk-lure when fished deep.

Towy Topper

Silk:	black.
Hook:	8–10.
Tail:	golden pheasant tippet.
Rib:	thin silver wire.
Body:	well marked peacock quill.
Hackle:	blue or rusty dun.

Much less popular today on the river that spawned it, this is a good daylight fly when fished on normal flows as a downstream wet fly.

The Teal Series

We dislike teal! We speak as fly tyers. Good teal feathers in large sizes are difficult to obtain and, when you have got them, they are prone to 'splitting'. Many of our teal patterns have been 'adapted' to use silver mallard, which looks similar. The barred teal feather, with its alternating bands of black and white, represents the ultimate 'contrast' (and thus 'visibility') in a *moving* fly. We start with perhaps the most 'famous' in the series.

Teal, Silver and Blue (TSB)

Silk:	black.
Hook:	4–10.
Tail:	golden pheasant tippet.
Rib:	silver wire.
Body:	flat silver.
Hackle:	blue hen.
Wing:	teal flank.

Some modern dressings use natural grey squirrel as an alternative to barred teal without apparent loss of effect. The TSB can be tied in tandem, using longer badger hair, to give a lure of some 3 inches in length.

The TSB fishes well as a subsurface and mid-water fly and, in lure form, fishes well in deep water. It has a deserved reputation as being particularly attractive to fresh-run fish and is widely used everywhere. It is perhaps the single most popular (and over used) sea trout fly of all time!

Teal and Black

    Silk: black.
    Hook: 6–14.
    Tail: golden pheasant tippets.
    Rib: silver wire.
    Body: black seal's fur.
    Hackle: black hen.
    Wing: barred teal flank feathers.

This useful member of the Teal family is more popular in the North than in Wales and Southern England. It is generally claimed to fish best on a dark night. It is a good fly for whitling in daylight when fished small (12–14).

Teal and Green

    Silk: black.
    Tail: golden pheasant tippets.
    Rib: silver wire.
    Body: green seal's fur.
    Hackle: black hen.
    Wing: barred teal flank feather.

This, like the equally effective Green Peter (page 336), has a better reputation as a lake fly. It seems to be much less popular today than it was at the turn of the century.

Peter Ross

    Silk: black.
    Hook: 6–10.
    Tail: golden pheasant tippet.
    Rib: silver wire.
    Body: rear half – flat silver tinsel; front half – red seal's fur.
    Hackle: black hen.
    Wing: barred teal flank feather.

The Peter Ross is basically a *Teal and Red* but with a half-body of silver. Many Scottish anglers much prefer this fly to the TSB and the records show that it has produced some excellent sea trout, many in double-figures. It is particularly effective in peaty waters.

Mallard Series

There is bronze mallard and there is silver (= grey) mallard. Good-quality large bronze mallard is very expensive and difficult to obtain. There are some hairwing substitutes (e.g. Parey Squirrel) but these are also not readily available at times. Silver mallard is often used as a substitute for teal (a smaller duck) on the larger flies. Both mallard and teal are difficult to tie without breaking the fibres so that the wing disintegrates. This creates a feather 'hairwing' which offends the artiste but has no discernible effect upon the appeal of the fly to the fish. While bronze mallard and grouse feathers are interchangeable on smaller flies, so that the 'Grouse series' parallels the 'Mallard series' (other than to the purist), the smaller grouse feather cannot be used to wing the larger flies.

Mallard and Claret

Silk:	black.
Hook:	8–10 (12).
Tail:	golden pheasant tippets.
Rib:	gold wire.
Body:	claret seal's fur.
Hackle:	black.
Wing:	bronze mallard.

Many trout fishermen were brought up on this ancient fly. It has long been recognised as a standard for sea trout and brown trout and is still widely used today. It is a good lake fly and low water river fly for daylight and dusk and it invariably fishes subsurface. There are several variants. Some dressers add a pinch of black seal fur just beneath the wing. Others use a Coch-a-bon-ddu hackle, or a hackle of claret or ginger. We would never be without it. Nor the next in the series.

Mallard and Silver

Silk:	black.
Hook:	4–12.
Tail:	golden pheasant tippet (topping).
Rib:	silver wire.
Body:	flat silver tinsel.
Hackle:	black hen (or cock).
Wing:	bronze mallard.
Cheek:	Jungle cock eye-feather.
Topping:	golden pheasant.

This is a great sea trout fly. The variations to the standard dressing that we include on our pattern are shown in parentheses. It is a widely-used fly in Wales for night fishing where it is fished as a point fly (size 4 double) or as a dropper (size 6) in conjunction with a large tube or Waddington. It is a popular Dyfi fly and has produced many large sea trout.

345

The Squirrel Series

Hairwing flies for sea trout and salmon have grown in popularity over the last 20–30 years. The 'fibre' wings advocated by Bridgett and Horsley to present a slender profile have become standards for much sea-trout fishing today: but fibre has given way to hair – and quite rightly so. Although a hairwing fly is not quite so aesthetically pleasing to the dresser, the sea trout do not seem to mind a bit! Many anglers believe that the diffused action of a hairwing fly in water is much more attractive to fish.

The squirrel series of flies is now a popular standard for many anglers. Squirrel tail can be dyed to all colours and the following dressing is the more popular of the stable.

Black Squirrel

Silk:	black.
Hook:	6–10 (single or double, sometimes long shank treble).
Rib:	silver wire.
Body:	flat silver tinsel.
Hackle:	black (or blue).
Wing:	black squirrel.

The Grey, Red, Orange, Yellow, Green, Blue and Purple Squirrels cover the range of the spectrum. The hackle may be black or complementary (blue hackle with a blue wing) or contrasting (orange with a black wing). The Grey (= natural) Squirrel tied on a size 6 double or a tube or a Waddington is a particular favourite of ours.

The Squirrels are essentially point flies. *The Grey Squirrel* represents an alternative to the *Silver March Brown* so loved by some sea trout anglers. When tied with a blue hackle, it is not too different to pass off as a *Silver Invicta*.

The Twist Series

The Mallard and Teal series consists of a basic dressing where one key feature, the body, varies. All of the variations relate to providing a basic range of colour effects (Teal and Green, Teal and Red, Teal and Orange, Teal and Blue etc, etc). From time to time a new series of flies emerges which is based on the philosophy of variation-on-a-theme. One such recent theme is the *Twist* series. We give the basic dressing below.

Red Twist

Silk:	black.
Hook:	8–14 long shank treble (outpoint).
Butt:	red fluorescent floss.
Body:	flat silver tinsel.

Hackle: inner – blood red cock; outer – black cock.
Head: red varnish.

This series was devised to overcome the problem of missed takes when daylight fishing on high to medium clear water. The standard characteristics of the fly (which was to be fished fast in, or just under, the surface) are the fine outpoint treble which has maximum 'all round' hooking potential, the touch of fluorescence to improve visibility to the fish, and the black *outer* head hackle (black always being a good basic colour element in a sea trout fly by day or night). The variants are all based on the *inner* hackle colour; the Blue, Yellow, Orange and Green variants have an appropriately coloured inner hackle. The head is varnished black or the same colour as the variant to provide added contrast.

The dressing could not be more simple. The inner and outer hackles can be wound separately to provide an inner and outer ring or they can be wound together to provide a mixed hue (as on the Bumble series). The overall effect is readily varied by the number of twists around the shank given to each hackle (e.g. two turns yellow, four turns black, or vice versa), and the style of the fly can be varied by tying the head so that the hackles lie back along the shank at various angles to create a narrow streamlined fly or an open bushy fly. Cock hackle was chosen in preference to hen so that the stiff hackle created more disturbance as it was worked through the water in order to draw attention to its presence. Soft hackle has little advantage in a fast-worked fly presented to non-feeding fish. Not only has the Twist series proved its worth in relation to the original design concept, but it has also produced sea trout in lakes when fished at the point of a team of flies. It has also produced fish at night when fished as a subsurface fly.

Sunk Fies and Lures

The advent of modern line technology has now enabled the angler to get a lure down to a fish lying in deep water far more readily than with the silk lines of yesteryear. The deep-sunk lure fished slowly and presented 'eyeball to eyeball' with the fish is recognised as being particularly effective in taking the larger sea trout.

Sunk lures are to be had in all sizes and colours and they invariably entail two or three single hooks tied in series or a large single or double front hook with a flying-treble. Some of the sunk lures available in the 1930s were as colourful as the built wings of salmon flies. Many were based on the *Alexandra* but liberally embellished with blue jay and golden pheasant tippets and toppings. Some that appeared in Hardy Bros' Coronation catalogue of 1937 were very similar to those popular today. In addition to the Demon and Terror lures listed in the catalogue, some patterns were dressed 'Matuka-style' (with the anterior section of the streamer feathers tied down onto the top of the hook). Experience with Matukas has shown that although the long waggling tail seems to be quite a good attractor it is subject to a lot of bottom pinching and few firm takes. (The Matuka is thought by some to be the antecedent of the modern Frog and Dog Nobblers.)

The standard sunk lure of today has an infinite variety of forms. The following pattern is highly popular. So is a black variant.

Alexandra Lure

Silk:	red.
Hook:	4–6 single tied in tandem – sometimes with the rear hook mounted 'upside-down'.
Body:	broad tinsel ribbed over with silver thread, sometimes thin silver mylar piping.
Wings:	two, four or six blue cock hackles tied in pairs along shank.
Topping:	2–6 long strands of peacock herl.
Head:	red or black varnish.

A good all-purpose lure for most conditions. Best fished deep and slow.

Dog Nobblers

Silk:	black.
Hook:	4–8.
Tail:	white marabou.
Body:	white chenille.
Rib:	silver tinsel.
Head:	peacock herl over lead (substitute) shot.
Varnish:	black.

The Dog Nobbler has gained enormous popularity among some reservoir anglers since it was introduced some three or four years ago by Trevor Housby. Latterly some more adventurous sea trout anglers have given it a trial; with outstanding success. Other good colours are orange and black marabou. The Nobbler is fished at all depths, from low and slow to middle and fast. It tends to fish in a sink-and-draw fashion when retrieved in long draws with a pause in between. Smaller versions of the Dog Nobbler are called Frog Nobblers.

Frog Nobbler

Silk:	black.
Hook:	10–12.
Tail:	black and white marabou.
Body:	gold mylar or flat tinsel *over* weighted body of fine lead foil.
Head:	black varnish.

This is a good bi-visible version. So is green. The appeal (to the fish) is the open waving action of the marabou in water. An all-black nobbler has proved *very* effective on an exceedingly wet and pitch-black night.

Dyfi Phantom

Silk:	black.
Mount:	1–1½-inch semi-transparent (slipstream type B) tube (size 8–10 outpoint treble).
Body:	no dressing whatsoever.
Wing:	squirrel or badger hair tied around tube.
Cheeks:	folded slips of bronze and grey mallard.
Crests:	a few fibres of yellow bucktail.
Head:	black or orange varnish.

Probably the simplest of all tube flies to tie. Fished at night with some moonlight slow and deep (or subsurface into neck of pool).

Moonbeam (Shank)

Silk:	black.
Mount:	1–2-inch Waddington shank (single or double depending on weight required).
Butt:	yellow floss.
Rib:	oval silver tinsel.
Body:	black floss.
Wing:	yellow bucktail tied round with black bucktail over.
Head:	black varnish.

A personal favourite, especially on a dark night when fished very deep and slow. A silver-bodied variant is also effective. The double shank fishes best in faster or deeper water.

Marchog (= Knight) Lures

The 'flying-treble' has long been used as a device to trick sea trout that develop the annoying habit of just nipping at the tail of the fly. The traditional Loch Ordie dapping fly often has a wee flying treble at the head to improve its hooking potential when fish come short. Hugh Falkus created his 'secret weapon' to deal with the problem by attaching a small (14–16 treble) on a short nylon link to a standard size 8 single hook.

It is important that the treble mount should be as invisible as possible and it should, therefore, not be dressed. The theory is that the fish goes for the tail of the body dressing on the main hook, and in so doing takes the unseen treble.

The problem of short rises and missed takes also occurs with large sunk

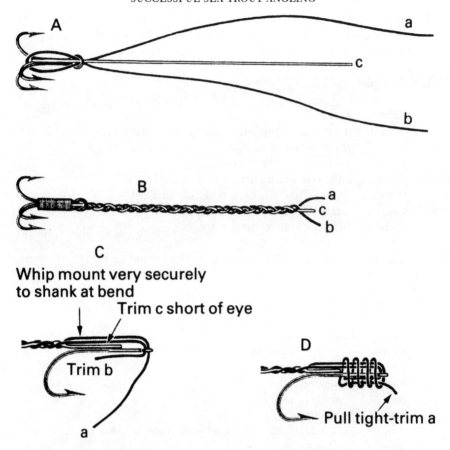

Fig. 78. Preparing the Marchog mount.

1) Mounting the treble (A). Place a size 10 or 12 outpoint treble in the vice and lightly whip to form a bed of silk. Cut a 15-inch length of 20lb nylon and pass one end through eye of treble, taking it back round the rear of the hook and back up through the eye of the treble from the opposite direction. Pull so that the ends of nylon a and b are of equal length. Pull very tight and whip down. Cut another length of nylon about 8 inches long (c) and whip one end on to top of treble. Finish off neatly. End c should be shorter than a or b for later recognition.

2) Preparing the link (B). Plait the three ends a, b, c, passing left over centre, right over centre, left over centre etc for about 1–2 inches. The tighter the plaiting, the stiffer the link. Place the three ends of nylon in hackle pliers to prevent unravelling. Remove hook from vice and varnish head of treble.

3) Mounting the link (C). Place a size 2–4 single (or double) hook in the vice and lightly whip over. Present the mount along the top of the shank of the single, remove the pliers and adjust for length and style. Whip over tightly, especially at the rear of mount. This is very important.

4) Connecting the link (D). Cut end c short of the eye and pass both ends A and B down through the eye and pull back along shank. Cut end b about half-way along shank and form a four-turn needle knot with end a. Ease the knot up to the eye, pull very tightly and trim. Whip over neatly and tie off.

This mount, if tied properly, is the strongest we know!

lures and the modern Marchog series (the name means 'Knight' in English – so called because the lure was well armoured) was devised to improve hookability – especially when fish take a fly almost directly downstream below the angler (as when pot-fishing).

There are several Knights around the table, the Marchog Glas (Blue Knight) and Marchog Goch (Red Knight) being well know locally. We give here just one dressing which has become a particular favourite since it has produced several fish in excess of 10lb weight over the last few seasons.

Marchog Coch Ddu (= Brown Knight)

Silk:	black.
Mount:	size 2–4 single with 1½-inch link to size 8–10 outpoint treble.
Butt:	orange floss silk.
Body:	flat silver tinsel with oval copper tinsel over.
Hackle:	orange cock fibres tied false.
Wing:	two pairs of matched furnace cock feathers.
Cheek:	cock pheasant back feather.
Head:	black varnish.
Tail:	black varnish.

Fished slow and deep. The hooking potential of the light treble makes this lure effective when fishing on-the-hang. The preparation of the Marchog mount – possibly the most secure and strong tandem link so far devised – is shown in Fig. 78. The link has taken salmon in excess of 20lb weight and is, therefore, probably dependable should you encounter a new British record sea trout!

PART V
Tail Pieces

18 · CARE AND COOKING

To adapt the immortal words of Mrs Beaton; 'Before you can cook it, you have got to catch it.' Before giving a few recipes for cooking (or, in one instance, of not cooking) your sea trout that we have 'tried-and-tasted' and can recommend, it is appropriate to say a few words about how to care for your fish in the interval between killing it and cooking it.

We have both caught a lot of sea trout in our time and we have seen very many more caught by others. It grieves us greatly how so many anglers treat the most sporting of fish having played it, landed it and killed it. We have seen sea trout almost folded double and stuffed into bags and pockets to emerge stiff, horseshoe shaped and covered with assorted rubbish some hours later. We have seen fish left all day in the blistering sun, to be carried off as stiff as a board, wrinkled with dessication, and very far from beautiful. We have seen the flesh of magnificent sea trout falling off their bones because they were left all day in a black plastic bag in full sunlight so that they had almost cooked.

Plastic bags have many uses but they are not suitable receptacles for fish on a warm day (or night), as they cause the fish to sweat and excude mucus. Old straw 'basses' are better. They can still be obtained if you shop around, and if kept moist they will keep the fish fresh until the end of the day with no problems. However, they tend to absorb blood and slime and can stink to high heaven after a while if they are not washed with a mild disinfectant. By far the best receptacles that we have encountered are the 'traditional' fish basses manufactured in a man-made synthetic fibre (trade name Samlin, and produced by J. Barbour & Sons Ltd in the UK) which do not absorb moisture and are loosely woven to allow the air to circulate. They also fold up much smaller than the old rush or straw basses and can be stowed neatly in a bag or a jacket pocket for ready use when required. We have used these for several seasons now and are well satisfied. A quick rinse the day after use and they are as fresh as new.

Before we go on we must go back. Having netted or beached your fish, the first priority is to kill it cleanly and quickly. We always carry a priest or 'nocwr' for this purpose, and two or three sharp taps at the back of the head are usually sufficient to dispose of the catch cleanly. The hook is then removed and the next priority is to store the fish properly in the bass. This may mean leaving the river for a minute or two to walk back to the bag and

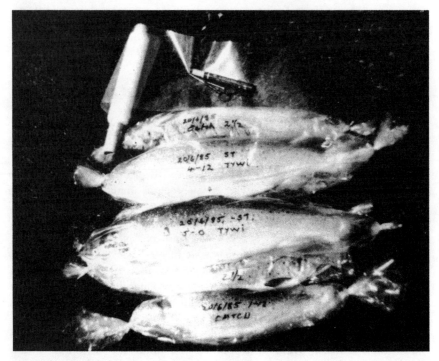

Ready for the freezer: properly labelled and packaged in polythene tubing to prolong freezer-life. (Photo: G.S. Harris.)

retrieve the bass but it is well worth the inconvenience,especially at night (see page 249). If the day is hot or the night is warm then soak the bag first before inserting the fish, and then keep it moist over the period of the fishing session. The subsequent evaporation of the water has a cooling effect and keeps the fish much fresher.

Having got your fish back home they must be stored properly for later use if you are not going to eat them the next day. This invariably means deep freezing, and there is a right way and a wrong way to prepare fish for the freezer.

Our approach to storing the catch on arriving home is to remove the fish from the bass and wipe them down with a paper towel to remove any slime, leaves, grass or grit adhering to the skin. We then place them on a white surface (a fish plate, newspaper or china sink) and cover them with a white teatowel that has been moistened with water. Then we leave them until we have had some sleep.

There are several reasons for this ritual: 1) if you have fished through the night the last thing you want to do on getting home is to fiddle about putting fish in the freezer and risk waking the other occupants of the house; 2) it does much to improve the appearance of the fish; and 3) it is biochemically wrong to freeze a fish too soon after capture. The first reason is fairly obvious. The main concern after six or seven hours' night-fishing is bed! The other two reasons merit some expansion.

The ability of a fish to adapt its colouration to its background continues for some time after death, and the appearance of a stale fish can be very much improved by leaving it on a white background. We learnt this trick many years ago from the wife of an angler acquaintance. She could make the blackest of October fish look as if it was almost fresh from the sea.

Sea trout have two very different types of muscle. The flesh of the fish is largely composed of white muscle, but under the skin on each side is a layer of dark-coloured meat with a characteristic strong and oily taste. This is the red muscle. It has a rich blood supply and contains myoglobin – a dark oxygen-binding pigment. It is this muscle that does much of the work in normal swimming behaviour. The white muscle is used for fast swimming and occupies some 90 per cent of the bulk. It is rich in glycogen – a sugar that provides an instant energy source.

The fight of a sea trout when it is being played results in the sugar being converted into lactic acid. The endurance of the white muscle is very limited and there is a rapid build-up of acid within the muscle as the energy-giving sugar is rapidly depleted, so that the fish becomes immobilised and turns onto its side in a state of 'exhaustion' (when it can be netted or beached). The normal process of reconverting the acid back to sugar takes time and continues after death. Fish that are frozen too soon after death are not at their best when thawed as the high acid levels affect the flavour and texture of the fish. We try to delay for at least 12 hours between catching and killing our fish to allow partial restoration of the acid-sugar balance.

Most books on deep freezing suggest that the freezer-life of sea trout and salmon is six months, after which the texture and taste begins to diminish. We have eaten fish which have been frozen for up to two years without noticing anything untoward, but suggest that it is best to try to consume your fish within the year. Proper packaging is important in order to prolong freezer-life and prevent those unsightly 'freezer-burns' where the flesh has dried out.

We now use 'layflat' polythene tubing for wrapping our fish ready for freezing. This comes in rolls of several widths and can be obtained from most freezer stores or by mail-order. We normally use three sizes: the 4-inch for whitling and fish up to about 1½lb; the 6-inch for fish up to about 6lb; and the 8-inch for fish up to about 12lb. (We have some 12-inch also, but it seems to last a very long time!)

A length of tubing some 6–8 inches longer than the fish is cut from the roll and the fish is inserted into the tube. This can be surprisingly difficult, and the best way is to slide your arm down through the tube, grasp the fish about the head and draw it head-first up into the tube. Before sealing off the tube at either end *as tightly as possible* with the special wire-ties obtained at your freezer store, make sure that you squeeze out as much air as possible from the tube.

357

The fish is now ready for freezing, but before doing so we record the date, place, weight and location (river and pool) relevant to its capture on the outside of the tube. This ensures that you can consume your fish sequentially within the recommended period of time and find one of the required size without undue difficulty. It also has one other advantage, at least as far as we are concerned. The fishing season is effectively limited to about five months of the year and there is nothing much to do in the remaining seven – except think about fishing. The details recorded on our frozen fish when we take them out one by one for eating over the intervening months allow us to recall the circumstances of its capture; to relive the pleasures of taking the fish of '4lb 12oz, 26/7/86, Catch Pool, Dyfi' or '2lb 4oz, 3/9/86, Lough Furnace, Burrishoole'; to remember how we caught it, who we were with at the time, the other fish that we caught that trip – and the ones that we didn't; and so much more besides.

We always try to avoid cutting our fish in any way prior to freezing. This exposes the flesh to the air and much reduces their freezer-life. Since sea trout rarely contain food in their stomachs it is not necessary to gut them first. In fact it is much easier to gut and clean them when they are partly thawed: it is certainly less messy as they do not bleed. One of the incidental advantages of sea trout is that they come 'naturally packaged' in a wide range of convenient sizes which will serve anything from one to twelve people. A 3lb fish is normally just right for four people and our preferred range is 3–5lb, especially if the fish is a fresh-run 'maiden' that has not spawned previously, as these are of the finest flavour and texture and have the best colour to the flesh.

The greatest mistake with salmon and sea trout is to cut the fish into cutlets prior to freezing. It may be sensible to cut a very large fish into useful-sized pieces (for four or six people) before freezing rather than thawing it out later to cut off the required portion, and being left with a large section of fish that you are obliged to give away or cook and freeze. *Never* refreeze anything that has been thawed: unless it has been cooked prior to refreezing. The only other option is to saw a section off the large fish while it is still frozen solid.

We will discuss later the biological importance of conserving large sea trout that have survived several spawning visits to fresh water (p. 385). The flesh of these repeat spawners usually becomes progressively coarser, paler and more insipid after each spawning. We tend to be very wary of any heavily spotted and coloured fish weighing upwards of 6lb and normally take them to be cold-smoked if we doubt the quality of the flesh. This applies also to any large fish remaining in the freezer at the start of a new season.

Anyone who has been on a fishing holiday to distant waters will be familiar with the problem of getting the catch home from one deepfreeze to another without defrosting during the course of a long journey. A sensible purchase is an insulated 'cool-bag' with the requisite number of freezer packs. Having successfully brought some fish back from the west of Ireland recently which remained solidly frozen after a 20-hour journey by car and ferry we can recommend the ASW Cool Fish bags (available in the UK from ASW Sales & Marketing). The 36-inch size will hold a 20lb fish and has sufficient capacity for as many fish as any angler could decently want to take.

We must admit that we like our sea trout to taste of fish rather than what it was cooked with or cooked in. We therefore abhor heavily condimented dishes which use the fish as a basis for added taste. Nevertheless, a good sauce can, as it should, compliment and enhance the dish and a 'rich' sauce may be necessary to make the best meal out of an old fish that has become colourless and tasteless as a result of repeated spawnings.

The following recipes are recommended. They have been chosen to cover a range of fish sizes and cooking methods and to cater for a range of tastes.

Sewin A Gig Moch – Sea Trout with Bacon
(Serves 2)

Mochin = Pig. This is a variation of a very traditional Pembrokeshire recipe.

2 sea trout about ¾lb weight
4 slices middle cut bacon with rind
    removed

For the stuffing
2oz coarse brown bread crumbs
2 chopped shallots
2oz chopped ham
2oz shelled prawns
1 tablespoon chopped parsley
1 beaten egg
White wine
Salt and pepper

Mix together in a bowl all the ingredients for the stuffing, binding with white wine if necessary. Leave to stand for 30 minutes. Clean and gut the fish and fill the body cavity with stuffing. Wrap each fish in two slices of bacon and secure with wooden cocktail sticks.

Place on a greased baking tray and cook in a preheated oven 350°F, 180°C, Gas mark 5, for 30 minutes. Finish off under the grill to crisp the bacon.

Buttered Sea Trout
(Serves 2)

2 small sea trout about ¾lb weight
Or
2 steaks (from a larger fish) about 1 inch
   thickness
5oz butter
Juice of 1 lemon
Milk
Seasoned flour
Chopped parsley

Clean and gut small sea trout. Wash and dry the fish or steaks, dip in milk and coat with flour. Melt 2oz of the butter in an ovenproof dish large enough to take the fish. With 1oz of the butter fry the fish quickly on both sides. Place in the ovenproof dish and cook in a preheated oven 350°F, 180°C, Gas mark 5, for 10 minutes. Meanwhile heat the remaining 2oz of the butter in a pan until golden brown, and blend in the lemon juice. Remove the fish from the oven and place on a heated server, pour over the sauce and garnish with chopped parsley and lemon wedges. Serve immediately.

Sea Trout with White Wine and Cream
(Serves 2)

2 small sea trout about ¾lb weight
Or
2 steaks (from a larger fish) about 1 inch
   thickness
1 glass dry white wine
1 glass water
6 shallots peeled and chopped
4oz mushrooms, sliced
1 level teaspoon mixed herbs
¼ pint cream
Lemon
Parsley
Salt and pepper

Place cleaned and gutted fish or steaks in a shallow pan. Sprinkle over the mushrooms, shallots, mixed herbs, seasoning and some grated lemon rind. Pour wine and water over and poach gently for 15 minutes. Remove the fish and keep warm on a serving dish. Strain the liquid and place the mushrooms and onions over the dish. Boil the liquid to reduce by about half. Cool slightly and add the cream, reheat carefully but do not boil. Strain and pour over the fish. Garnish with parsley sprigs and lemon wedges.

Breakfast Sewin
(Serves 2–3)

6 fillets of sea trout from 3 small fish of
    about ¾lb weight
6 rashers of smoked bacon with rind
    removed
6 shallots peeled and chopped
1oz butter
1 lemon
2 glasses dry white wine
Salt and pepper

Butter an ovenproof dish. Cut the bacon rashers into 2-inch strips. Layer the fillets and bacon in the dish, sprinkle with chopped shallots. Add a generous squeeze of lemon juice, seaon with salt and pepper and pour the wine over. Cook in a preheated oven 400°F, 200°C, Gas mark 6, for 12 minutes. Remove from oven and serve immediately.

This makes a great breakfast as it tastes as if the fish has been smoked (who needs kippers?). It may also be served as a supper dish or as a fish course.

Alfresco-style (as the sun rises after a night's fishing), the fish may be prepared on the river bank over a wood fire. All you need in your tackle bag is a frying pan, some lard and some rashers of bacon! Having made a wood fire with a good hot base, place some lard in the pan. Add the fish (previously cleaned and gutted), and cook gently on each side. About halfway through the process, add the bacon and continue until both are cooked. (The fish is ready when the flesh starts to flake off the bone when teased with a knife.) Eat from the pan with the fingers. Be careful not to burn the mouth! The organised and *confident* angler expecting to partake of his sewin breakfast on the bank will have provided for half a lemon (goes with gin-and-tonic also) and some buttered brown wholemeal rolls, as well as a flask of breakfast coffee. Then to bed (or to work!!).

Sea Trout with Almonds
(Serves 4)

1 sea trout (3lb weight)
1 tablespoon of seasoned flour
3oz butter
3oz flaked almonds
1 tablespoon fresh lemon juice
Parsley

Clean and gut the sea trout. Crimp the skin and wipe with water or lemon juice. Coat with seasoned flour. Melt 1oz of butter in a frying pan until it is

361

'smoking' and add the flaked almonds. Fry until lightly browned and then remove and keep warm. Add the remaining 2oz of butter and the oil to the pan. Fry the whole fish gently for 10–15 minutes, turning repeatedly, until nicely browned. Remove from the pan, drain on a kitchen towel, place on a warm serving dish, and sprinkle with almonds and lemon juice. Decorate with lemon wedges and parsley or with fresh dill.

Poached Sea Trout

There are several ways of poaching sea trout. This is ours. We allow (roughly) 1lb of fish per person and the size and number of cutlets depends on the size of the fish. Allow 2 × ¾-inch cutlets from a 3lb fish and 1 × 1-inch cutlet from a 5lb fish per person.

Clean the fish and prepare cutlets. Wrap each cutlet in baking foil adding a knob of butter, salt and black pepper, along with a *thin* slice of lemon before sealing each package as tightly as possible. Bring a pan of water to the boil – adding a bouquet garni if you wish. Put the foil-wrapped fish into the gently boiling water and cook for ten minutes. Then, *if eating cold*, turn the heat off and leave the fish in the cooling water for a further ten minutes. *If eating hot*, keep the water gently boiling for a further five minutes.

Remove the package and open. Peel off the skin and serve hot or cold (preferably cold).

Unless you have a fish kettle you are going to have problems poaching a large fish if you want to serve it whole. Baking or roasting is a practical alternative – depending on the size of your oven – for fish of up to 5 or 6lb weight.

Baked Sea Trout
(Serves 4–6 plus)

1 large sea trout 4–6lb weight (cleaned
   and gutted)
4oz butter
1 dessertspoonful of vinegar
½ orange
½ sliced lemon
Salt and pepper
6 Bay leaves
3 Rosemary sprigs
6 cloves

Butter the bay leaves and place with the rosemary and cloves inside the fish. Season the fish inside and out and rub the butter over the fish until very well coated. Cover with foil in an ovenproof dish and bake in a preheated oven at

350°F, 180°C, Gas mark 5, allowing 20 minutes for each pound of weight. Place the cooked fish onto a serving dish and remove the skin. Take the cooking juices and add a tablespoon of butter, the slices of orange and lemon and the vinegar. Boil quickly to reduce the volume by half. Remove the slices of orange and lemon and serve the sauce separately.

Pickled Sea Trout
(Serves 4)

This is a rather complicated dish to prepare since it takes some time, but it is well worth the effort! It is based on the Scandinavian salmon dish *gravad lax*. Once the sewin has been pickled the actual preparation time is about 30 minutes and relates to the sauce.

4 cutlets of about ½–¾ inches thick
    from a fish of about 6lb (preferably
    from the tail immediately behind
    the vent).

Pickle

1 heaped tablespoon of sea salt
1 rounded tablespoon of granulated
    sugar
1 teaspoon crushed black peppercorns
1 tablespoon brandy
1 rounded tablespoon fresh dill
    (preferably) or 1 *level* tablespoon of
    dried dill

Mix together all the pickling ingredients and spread about a third of the mixture on a flat dish. Lay two cutlets on this base and spread a third of the mixture over the top. Place the other two cutlets on top of this and cover with remaining pickle. Cover the fish with a flat board weighed down with a brick or something of similar weight. Store in a cool place or a fridge for 3–5 days and turn each cutlet daily.

On serving, remove the skin and lay cutlets onto plates.

Sauce

2 rounded tablespoons of French
    mustard paste
1 rounded tablespoon of granulated
    sugar
1 large egg yolk
6 tablespoons of olive oil
2 tablespoons of wine vinegar

1 rounded tablespoon of fresh dill (or
   level tablespoon of dried dill)
Salt and pepper

Beat the egg yolk, mustard and sugar together until smooth. Then mix in oil and vinegar gradually. Season with dill, salt and pepper. Serve with brown bread and butter and the sauce separately. Garnish with fresh dill, lemon or chopped parsley.

Fried Sea Trout with Herbs
(Serves 2)

2 sea trout of 1–1½lb (cleaned and
   gutted)
2oz of seasoned flour
4oz butter
1 level tablespoon chopped sage
1 level tablespoon freshly chopped
   parsley
1 level tablespoon freshly chopped
   thyme
Lemon wedges

Wipe the fish dry, coat with oil and dust in seasoned flour. Melt half the butter in a frying pan and then cook the fish for about 5 minutes on each side. Remove and drain fish on kitchen paper. Melt the remaining butter in a clean pan, add the chopped herbs and gently fry for about 2 minutes. Spoon the garnish over the fish and serve with lemon wedges. With crisp brown rolls – a marvellous quick meal.

Sometimes, when you have cooked more than you need to avoid having bits of fish cluttering the deepfreeze, you are at a loss to know what to do with it. Here are three suggestions for avoiding waste.

Kedgeree of Sea Trout
(Serves 4)

8oz of cooked sea trout (poached or
   baked)
6oz of rice
2 shallots or a small onion
2oz butter
2 hard-boiled eggs
Salt and black pepper, cayenne pepper

Carefully flake the fish into a bowl avoiding the addition of any bones. Prepare the rice separately with a pinch of salt, pepper and cayenne. Chop the shallots finely and fry with some of the butter until soft. Set aside. Remove the yolks from the hard-boiled eggs. Chop the egg whites coarsely and the egg yolks very finely. Drain the rice and then add the butter, fish and egg whites and mix together. Season and heat gently. Place in a dish and garnish with the egg yolks and parsley. Serve with hot brown toast. A quick and tasty dish.

Sea Trout Fishcakes
(Serves 4)

The secret of a memorable fishcake is a high proportion of fish to potato, combined with a creamy sauce to bind them together.

1½lb cooked sea trout
12oz of peeled potatoes
½ pint of milk
Bouquet garni (parsley, thyme, bay leaf)
2 shallots or small onion
2oz butter
1½oz flour
2 tablespoons cream
1 tablespoons chopped parsley
Salt and pepper
1 tablespoon lemon juice
1 beaten egg
8oz of breadcrumbs

Heat the milk with the bouquet garni and shallots. Bring almost to the boil and then remove and cover. Boil the potatoes until cooked and then mash. Now continue with the sauce. Melt the butter and stir in the flour. Strain the herbalised milk and mix in gradually. Bring slowly to the boil with constant stirring to make a smooth sauce. Simmer for 2–3 minutes, remove from heat and blend in the cream and chopped parsley. Now *fold* (don't beat or mix, just fold) the sauce into the mashed potatoes. Then add the flaked sea trout and lemon juice. Add salt and pepper to taste. Then, and this is important to the flavour, leave to cool overnight or refrigerate for several hours. Making up the fishcakes requires no more than some floured hands to form 8 cakes about 3–4 inches wide. Brush with beaten egg and coat with breadcrumbs. Fry in butter or hot oil until crisp and golden. Serve with chips, peas and ketchup (for the kids), or, if you want to be more sophisticated serve with a piquant sauce (sorrel or ginger cream) and an exotic vegetable – fresh asparagus or butter spinach. Left-overs can be very tasty!

Fish Pie
(Serves 4)

1½lb sea trout cutlets or tailpiece
4oz butter
1 pint milk
2oz plain flour
4oz shelled prawns
2 hard-boiled eggs – roughly chopped
1 level tablespoon capers
3 tablespoons fresh chopped parsley
1 tablespoon lemon juice
Salt and freshly milled black pepper

Topping
2lb freshly cooked potatoes
1oz butter
¼ pint soured cream

Preheat oven to Gas mark 6, 400°F, 200°C. Place the fish in a baking tin and season well. Pour over with ½ pint milk. Dot with 1oz butter and bake in oven for 15–20 minutes. Drain off and retain cooking liquid. Remove the skin and flake the fish into largish pieces, carefully removing any bones.

For the sauce: melt the remaining 3oz butter in a saucepan, stir in the flour and gradually add the retained cooking liquid – stirring well. Slowly add the remaining ½ pint of milk, and season. Mix the fish flakes into the sauce, along with the prawns, egg, capers and parsley. Taste and season as required. Stir in the lemon juice and pour contents of saucepan into a 2½-pint baking dish which has been well buttered.

For the topping: cream the cooked potatoes with the butter and soured cream and spread over the fish. Bake on a high shelf for half an hour or until heated through and browned on top.

Finally, we recommend to anyone who fishes regularly and is likely to take a number of small sea trout over the season that they invest in a do-it-yourself hot-smoker. There are several on the market at a reasonable cost and, if you follow the instructions, hot-smoking is surprisingly quick and simple. There is nothing nicer than hot-smoked whitling of up to 1lb in weight when served cold-and-skinned with a salad. It makes a great starter for a dinner party.

Bon Appetit!

19 · CONSERVATION AND THE FUTURE

There is no *scientific* evidence available at the present time to show that our *stocks* of sea trout are in decline and at risk from over-exploitation. Indeed it would *seem* that our sea-trout fisheries are reasonably healthy!

In making this rather provocative statement we would stress that we are speaking of the British Isles *as a whole*. Several fisheries appear to be going through a bad patch at present, but these problems are probably only local and so are not symptomatic of a more general and widespread malaise affecting the stocks of sea trout throughout the British Isles.

We do not know how many rivers in the British Isles contain sea trout and support sea-trout fishing – either commercial, recreational or both. There are 52 in Wales; and perhaps slightly fewer in England. If you then include Scotland, Ireland and the Hebrides, Shetland and Orkneys, the total increases significantly. There must be 500, and maybe many more.

Whatever the total, it is singularly depressing to have to admit that there is only one river system in the entire British Isles where we have any useful information about the true status of our sea-trout stocks over a period of years. This river system is the Burrishoole Fishery in Co. Mayo. To describe it as a river, as far as fishing is concerned, is incorrect. It is a lake fishery of the classic Irish west-coast type, consisting of two large loughs (Furnace, which is tidal, and Feeagh). Adult fish (salmon and trout) running out of Furnace into Feeagh are trapped, counted and then released. The smolts migrating seawards into Lough Furnace are also trapped and counted as they move out of Feeagh. The fishery has been the subject of much research for over 30 years by the Salmon Research Trust of Ireland. Much of our understanding about the factors affecting stock abundance, population regulation, survival rates and other fundamental topics relevant to the better management of our salmon and sea-trout fisheries has been developed on this fishery. *It is unique to the British Isles.*

'So if this river is unique and we do not know how many adult fish are present in any other river system at any time, then how on earth do we manage fisheries and regulate fishing to prevent over-fishing?' The answer is that, in the absence of information on the numbers of fish and the pattern of runs into the river derived from fixed traps or electronic fish-counters, which are really not very useful in respect of sea trout because of the problem of distinguishing between large sea trout and salmon and also the technical

367

difficulties in counting the smaller whitling stage, we are obliged to make management decisions about the status and well-being of a fishery on the basis of the historical record of catches as obtained from the anglers and (as appropriate) the commerical fishermen. It is the catch record that forms the *sole basis* for stock management on almost all the sea-trout fisheries in the British Isles.

By comparing the catch in one year with the next, the record is used to identify trends in numbers: to judge whether the fishery is improving, declining or is relatively stable; to judge whether measures must be taken to conserve stocks by the introduction of (say) bag-limits or quotas, or whether to reduce the rate of exploitation by shortening the fishing season or restricting bait fishing or spinning; etc.

If the catch record is to be useful in any context it must be accurate. Ideally it should include every single fish caught in the fishery. This is probably a rather naïve target for many fisheries, where, for various reasons, only a proportion of the actual catch will figure in the record *but*, nevertheless, the reported catch should be as near to the true catch as possible. The greater the accuracy of the record the better.

When looking at trends over a period of years it is important to compare 'like with like' in terms of the accuracy and completeness of the record from one year to the next. It should be fairly obvious that the catch will increase if, for example, the number of anglers submitting a catch return increases from 25 to 50 per cent over the period. Unless such a change was known about, and taken into account when interpreting the catch record, the conclusion reached about the health of the fishery would be seriously awry. All it shows is a doubling of the recorded catch. It certainly does *not* show an improvement in the abundance of the stock, nor an improvement in the true catch.

The use of catch statistics as a measure of stock abundance makes the assumption that *stock* and *catch* are closely linked. This assumption when applied to sea trout and salmon must be seriously questioned. Obviously there is a link between stock and catch in that a higher catch will result from a high stock level and a lower catch will result from a low stock level. (You cannot catch fish in a fishless water!) But it is the precise relationship between the number of fish available for capture and the actual catch made that is important. It is now widely accepted that the link between stock and catch may be so tenuous and variable that it is of little practical value and that the use of catch records as an indicator of stocks may be misleading and even dangerous in practical management terms. This is well shown from an analysis of the very detailed information on stock abundance and catches at the Burrishoole fishery in Co. Mayo. The catch return from this fishery is very reliable and, as we have mentioned previously, all the fish entering Lough Feeagh are counted through the traps at the two inlet rivers. It is a fly-only boat fishery.

Data from Lough Feeagh over the period 1970–83 (Fig. 79) shows that no consistent relationship exists between stock and catch in this fishery. For example, roughly similar stock levels in 1971 and 1981 showed a 50 per cent variation in catch from 103 to 158 and a variation in the rate of exploitation from 5.5 to 12.7 per cent respectively. Similar stock levels in 1970 and 1981 yielded 400 per cent more fish in the latter year; and while the lowest stock (1983) produced the lowest catch and rate of exploitation, the best catch occurred in 1973 at a stock level that was significantly less than the maximum stock level in 1976.

Many factors can influence the rate of exploitation on the stock by angling. Weather and water conditions are clearly very important, as too are the regulations affecting fishing methods and the number of anglers fishing the water. In a drought year river fishing may be unproductive with the fly and fish may remain in the estuary or at sea and so be unavailable to the angler. In a wet year they may run through the main fisheries very quickly and so be unavailable for capture by the majority of anglers. Strong winds may make it impossible for boats to be launched on a lake fishery. In wet years, when flood follows flood, fisheries which allow spinning and worming will yield more fish than those where only fly-fishing is permitted, and the rate of exploitation will depend very much on the number of anglers fishing the water (and their individual skill). This last point is very important in determining the level of total catch. Clearly if no-one is fishing the water then no fish will be caught – no matter how many fish are present.

Data from the Burrishoole Fishery, when analysed to take into account

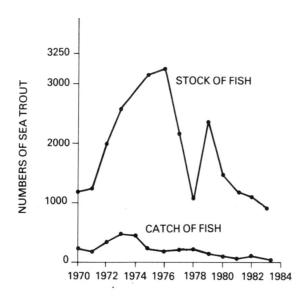

SOURCE: SALMON RESEARCH TRUST OF IRELAND INC.

Fig. 79. Relationship between the number of sea trout present and the number caught: Lough Feeagh. (Source: SRTI Inc.)

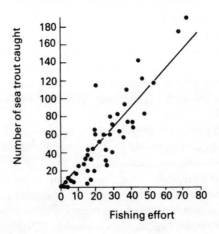

Fig. 80. Relationship between fishing effort (boat days per month) and the number of sea trout caught. (Source: Mills *et al*, 1986.)

the amount of fishing effort producing a given catch and then comparing the catch-per-unit-effort (CPUE) with the known availability of fish, has shown that the catch of fish is very dependent on fishing effort (Fig. 80). While more fish were caught in the months when stocks were higher, the relationship between stock and catch largely disappeared when fishing effort was taken into account. Curiously, the catch of sea trout was more dependent upon stock when the stock was low than when it was high (Fig. 81). The general conclusion drawn from this study was that, for practical management purposes *on this fishery*, neither catch nor catch per unit of effort are reliable indicators of stock abundance.

Another point to bear in mind is that the natural abundance of salmon and sea trout can vary enormously from year to year and over a period of years. The existence of cycles of increased and decreased abundance is well known for many fisheries, and while the reasons for this phenomenon are not fully understood, it is generally believed that it is linked with changes in the weather and climate which affect the survival of the fish and the productivity of the freshwater and marine environments.

Any angler who fished for sea trout and salmon during the early 1960s will recall the enormous runs of fish that occurred and the superlative fishing experienced at that time. Certainly the stocks of fish entering our rivers have declined markedly in recent years by comparison with that brief 'golden' period. So too has the quality of the fishing as a consequence. However, these cycles must be accepted. There is nothing that can be done about them in practical terms, other than to alter our aspirations, expectations and perspectives as anglers.

This now brings us to a further important point. What can we expect from our fishing? How do we judge the quality of our sport?

Inevitably anglers will judge the quality of the fishing on any water by what they catch as *individual anglers*. Some will have higher expectancies than others in terms of the number of fish caught on each trip or over a season. When that expectation is not fulfilled they will complain that the quality of the fishing is 'poor': and when they catch fewer fish than in previous seasons they will express the view that the fishery is in decline. It is here that we must draw attention to the distinction that should be made between the words *fishery* and *fishing*.

A common mistake is to assume that because *your* catch of fish from a particular water has decreased then the fishery itself has deteriorated; that because you caught less that the stock must be less. That may be so – but equally it may not be so. Before we expand on this point we must digress slightly to mention some of the basic principles of fisheries management. As we have said before, this is not a scientific text, but an appreciation of several factors relating to the management of the resource and the factors

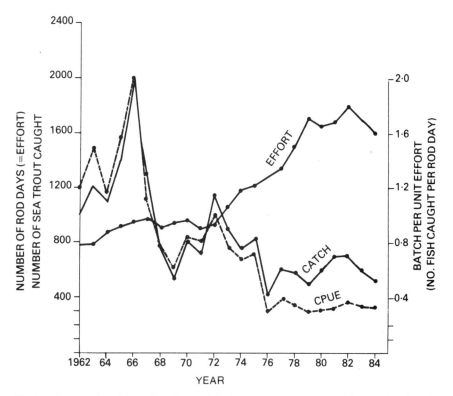

Fig. 81. An unhealthy fishery (based on real data). Despite an increase in the effort (number of rod-days) the catch per unit of effort (number of fish per rod-day) and the total catch falls steadily.

371

affecting the abundance and yield of the fisheries is of signal importance to the way in which we view our sport in the future. Thus:–

1. Fish are a renewable resource which if managed properly can support a constant and permanent level of exploitation.
2. Each river system will be capable of producing and sustaining a certain number of fish. Different rivers will have different levels of productivity and so some will produce more than others. The level of productivity will depend upon many different factors. The size of the river, the extent to which it is available to spawning fish, the quality and extent of the spawning gravels and their distribution within the river, are all fairly obvious factors affecting the number of fish produced. Productivity can also be influenced by the geology of the catchment and geographical location. Acid waters are biologically less productive than alkaline waters. Warmer southern rivers are more productive than colder, northern rivers.
3. Each river will require that a certain number of fish survive to spawn in order to regenerate the stock at its maximum level of production.
4. Where the number of spawners is below a certain critical level the stock will decline.
5. Where the number of spawners is above the number required to regenerate the stock at its maximum level the extra fish are surplus to requirements (biologically speaking) and are available for exploitation. (A large surplus of spawners may be harmful to future stocks if, for example, competition for spawning sites causes over-cutting of redds so that eggs are washed out of the gravel and wasted.)
6. The surplus stock can be exploited in different ways. To provide food, to provide recreation (= angling): or both. The exploitation of the fishery can also be manipulated to provide social and economic benefits for the community as a whole, e.g. by providing employment in the commercial fishery or in the tourist industry by promoting angling.

The crucial point to stress is that it is the surplus of spawning fish *and only this surplus that should be exploited* if the fishery is to be maintained at its maximum level of abundance. Any greater level of exploitation represents over-fishing and will reduce the number of adult fish returning to the river in subsequent years. (We have used the word 'exploited' deliberately in respect of anglers' catches. We recall a recent and 'strong' exchange of correspondence with an angler of some repute who objected to the use of this term in an article. In his view commercial fishermen *exploited* the resource whereas anglers merely *caught* fish. Since both anglers and netsmen catch and kill fish, then they both 'exploit' the resource. The fact that one group does it for profit while the other group does it for pleasure is immaterial).

Thus, the primary objective of fisheries management is to ensure that enough fish reach the spawning grounds to reproduce the stock at its highest

'Our friends from the tideway.' A seine netsman. It is a matter of fact that both anglers and netsmen are in direct competition for a 'fair share' of the available harvest of surplus fish. It is far too common for anglers to vilify the legitimate netsmen and seek to reduce their catches. In the first instance it would be far better to unite forces and attack the illegal fishermen. In some areas the illegal catch may now exceed the legal catch by rods and nets. If illegal fishing could be vanquished it might be that there would be no need for the rods and nets to vie with each other. (An unpopular statement, but true nevertheless!) (Photo: M.J. Morgan.)

possible level of natural abundance. The secondary objective is to ensure that this surplus, *and only this surplus*, is exploited as fully and effectively as possible. Any *over-fishing* is to be avoided as this will reduce the yield in terms of the available surplus in future years. If over-fishing continues the stock will continue to decrease until a point is reached when the fishery goes into total decline because too few fish survive to spawn.

This is very much an oversimplification of what, in practice, is a very complex matter. *Over-fishing* is a relative term and we have noted that stocks can fluctuate widely from year to year, and over a period of years, as a result of natural causes. It has been shown that the abundance of salmon can be significantly affected by the amount of rainfall in the autumn immediately prior to the onset of spawning. In a wet autumn the spawning fish can penetrate well into the spawning streams and so the catchment is far better utilised for the production of parr and smolts than in a dry autumn when the spawning activity is concentrated in the main river and lower sections of the tributaries. Similarly many factors can affect survival in both the river and in the sea. Eggs may be washed out of the gravel and destroyed by severe winter floods, or they may be killed by ice during severe winter freezing.

373

Tributaries may shrink to a trickle, or dry up altogether during a drought leading to a reduction in the number of smolts produced by increased competition for food and space among the parr or death from dewatering. The lack of spates during the spring may result in the smolts remaining for too long in the river with adverse effects upon their subsequent survival – and so on. Thus the management of our salmon and sea-trout fisheries is a very complex business and far from being an exact science.

The size of any stock of fish will be affected by many factors, some of which are wholly outside our control, and there is a need to allow a large margin of safety when regulating the fisheries to ensure adequate escapement of spawning fish.

That said, we can now return to our main theme which was that each individual angler will judge the quality of the fishing and the state of the fishery by his personal catch. Certainly if you catch less than before (or if you catch smaller fish – another symptom of over-fishing) then the quality of the *fishing* has certainly declined in relative terms; but that does not mean that the *fishery* has declined in any sense. What you are experiencing may be no more than a manifestation of increased fishing effort for a limited number of fish. Clearly if only so many fish are available for capture and you double the number of anglers, then *each* angler must only catch half of what he or she caught previously if over-fishing is to be avoided.

What is important as far as the fisheries manager is concerned is the *total catch* from the fishery: and whether or not this represents the optimum that the fishery can sustain. This statistic, combined with other measures of performance, such as total effort and catch per unit of effort, provides an alarm bell which may or may not ring depending on the health of the fishery and its ability to sustain increased exploitation.

The sign of a *healthy* fishery is where the total catch increases with an increase in the fishing effort over a period of years. Where this occurs the fishery was previously under-exploited. The CPUE for each angler may remain stable or increase. Ultimately a point is reached where the fishery is exploited to its maximum and any further increase in fishing effort must be compensated for by a decrease in the CPUE of each angler if the total catch is not to exceed the sustainable yield from the fishery.

By contrast, the sign of an *unhealthy* fishery is where the total catch decreases despite an increase in the fishing effort (Fig. 81). The CPUE of each angler will decrease markedly over the period, as continued over-fishing progressively reduces the spawning stock and the adult population steadily declines with each generation. *This is one of the classic symptoms of over-fishing.* It does not mean that the fishery is doomed to extinction; but warning bells should start to ring: with regulatory measures being introduced to arrest any further decline and to restore the total catch to its former level. This can only mean catching fewer fish in the short term in order to increase the escapement of fish into the spawning population.

Although the quality of our catch statistics for sea trout are generally poor at a national and regional level, some good data are locally available on individual river systems and there are clear signs that a few klaxons should be ringing loud and clear on several well-known fisheries, where not only has the total catch decreased consistently and steadily (despite the rod effort being maintained or even increased) but the average size of the fish has also declined, with far fewer large fish now figuring in the catch.

Over the last 40 years there have been several significant changes in the nature and extent of exploitation in relation to our salmon and sea trout fisheries. An awareness of these changes and how they may affect the future well-being of the fisheries and thus how they may influence our perspectives and expectations as anglers, is of crucial importance.

The nature and extent of these changes, and their impact on the fisheries, has possibly been greater in Wales than in any other region, and there are risks of over-generalisation. Nevertheless, they have occurred elsewhere, albeit to a lesser extent, and there are obvious lessons to be learnt even though immediate action may not be necessary.

Firstly, there has been a dramatic increase in the demand for salmon and sea-trout angling. Secondly, there has been an enormous increase in the amount of fishing available to the general public. Thirdly, there has been a widespread liberalisation in the angling methods now permitted on very many fisheries. All these factors have combined to increase significantly the overall catch and rate of exploitation in very many fisheries.

Wales is characterised by the vast amount of fishing controlled by angling associations. It is not an exaggeration to say that, on the many rivers to the west of the Dee in the north and the Usk in the south, virtually all of the worthwhile fishing is managed by clubs and associations on rivers. In fact with the notable exception of the Tywi and Teifi, and to a lesser extent the Glaslyn, it is very difficult to find a river where there is any quantity of prime fishing that is still exclusively private and reserved to the owner. Even on the Tywi and Teifi the amount of water owned by angling associations increases each year as new fishings are acquired at auction or by private sale. Even where the fishing is still 'private', it is likely that it is controlled by a syndicate of several rods whereas it was once only lightly fished by the owner on a fairly casual basis.

Fairly good information about the increase in fishing effort is available for Wales from the historical record of rod licences issued over the last century for salmon and sea-trout angling. These were first introduced in 1865 and sales have increased from 627 in 1868 to 2,174 in 1921, and to 30,200 in 1975. Since 1975 the number of licences issued has decreased and appears to have now stabilised at around 20,000 each year. Licence sales are in themselves a crude indicator of effort. About 50 per cent of the licences sold are for the season (as opposed to the week or the day). What must be taken into account also in calculating the overall increase in fishing effort is that people have much more leisure time today than 20 or 40 years ago. They are also more mobile and can, therefore, fish more often. Thus, whereas an angler with a season licence who 'lived away' may have fished only 10 or 20 times a year, that same angler is now likely to fish much more frequently.

The increased availability of fishing has resulted in a significant reduction in the extent of sanctuary water available to the fish. Whereas, at one time, very few people bothered to fish the minor tributaries of say, the Dyfi or the Tywi, the demand for fishing is now such that angling associations (some with large memberships) have the fishing on many of the tributaries, and these are now also heavily fished.

The reduction in sanctuary water where the fish had a fairly safe refuge from the depredations of anglers has been occasioned in major part by the improvements in fishing tackle, especially in spinning and casting reels and particularly, since the 1950s, by the dramatic improvement in nylon fishing lines. Casting a bait or spinner any reasonable distance is no longer the matter of skill that it was with the old centre-pin reels and braided lines that were previously available. The combination of the fixed-spool reel and nylon monofilament now means that every bit of available water can be fished one way or another very effectively. Thus those sections of water which were previously unattractive to the fly fisherman because they were too slow, too deep or too overgrown, are now likely to be fished by the spinner or bait.

The liberalisation of attitudes to the various methods of fishing practised on many waters has also increased the overall rate of exploitation significantly. Fly-only fishing has almost become a thing of the past on many rivers. Spinning was once only practised to any extent when the river was out-of-order

An impassable fall on an important spawning tributary. In years past very few (if any) anglers would have fished such streams for sea trout (or salmon). Today, the demand for fishing is such that these important sanctuary area are now fished by more and more anglers every year. Think on! (Photo: M.J. Morgan.)

(= in flood) and when fly fishing was impossible. Bait fishing was prohibited altogether or otherwise discouraged. Today bait fishing is widely practised at all states of the river from bank-high flood to trickling drought. Spinning is also widely practised, even on low water. Whereas the work carried out on the Burrishoole fishery has shown that the rate of exploitation on the available stock on a fly-only boat fishery can be as high as 20 per cent over the season, there is little doubt that it is *very* much higher on many river fisheries. (Investigations carried out on the Wye where spinning and bait fishing are now widely practised on many once hallowed fly-only waters has suggested that the overall rate of exploitation on the run of spring salmon for which the Wye was famous may now approach 100 per cent of the stock of .3sw and .4sw fish. If like breeds like, this has serious implications for the future!)

So we return to our provocative and seemingly complacent opening statement. You will now understand calculated use of the words *scientific*, *stocks* and *seems*, our reservations about catch as an indicator of stock, and our emphasis on the distinction between the quality of the '*fishing*' and the quality of the '*fishery*'. We hope also that you will now understand that fisheries management, while based on scientific principles, is – at the present state of our knowledge – more of an *art* than a *science*.

If our sea trout fisheries are generally healthy at present, then the future of our sport depends on keeping them that way. It is all too easy to become a prophet of doom and gloom when you are not catching fish. It is also too easy to become complacent when you are. The key to the future well-being and enjoyment of our sea-trout fishing depends on a number of things.

Conservation begins with the angler. *That means us!*

If a river can only yield 1,000 fish to the rods in a typical 'average' season, *then it can only yield 1,000 fish* regardless of whether it is lightly fished by 50 anglers using the fly or heavily fished by 500 anglers using spinner, worm and fly. In the former case the potential mean catch per angler is 20 fish per season. In the latter instance it is only 2 fish per season: irrespective of whether they each fish on average 5, 10, 50 or 100 times a season and irrespective of whether they fish fly, spinner or worm. At any time the surplus of spawning fish available for exploitation is limited and must not be exceeded if the spawning stock is not to be reduced below its optimum in respect of future yields.

So what of the future?

There is, among other things, a pressing need for a resurgence of the angling ethic in relation to sea trout and (particularly) salmon. Far too many 'anglers' are really fishmongers whose main concern is to catch enough fish to cover the cost of their fishing – and then to catch some more so that they can make a profit. Whether or not anglers should be allowed to sell fish is not a matter for discussion here. (As it stands at present, the law in the United Kingdom and in the Republic of Ireland does not preclude the sale of fish by anglers. We note with interest, however, that this is an offence in several other countries and that a change in the law to this effect has growing support in England, Wales and Scotland.)

It is quite clear that our sea-trout fisheries cannot continue to absorb ever increasing angling pressure if they are to remain healthy. There is therefore an urgent need for anglers to revise their personal aspirations as to what they want from this sport in terms of pleasure and enjoyment. Because that is what angling is really all about – *pleasure and enjoyment*. Moreover it is all things to all people. What gives *us* pleasure and satisfaction may be very different from what *you* are seeking. The one thing that is no longer acceptable is to want to catch and kill lots of fish.

We have called this book *Successful Sea Trout Angling*. 'Successful' in this context does *not* mean catching lots of fish. It means succeeding in what you have set out to achieve. Various authors have made the distinction between an 'angler' and a 'fisherman' and outlined the stages in the evolution of an 'angler'. There are various phylogenies with a different number of stages; but they can be basically reduced to a simple form:

STAGE ONE – to catch *a* fish
STAGE TWO – to catch *lots* of fish
STAGE THREE – to catch a *special* fish

Very few anglers evolve to stage three! There are many anglers of our acquaintance who catch 'lots of fish'. Most catch 50 or more in a season. Some catch 200. A few catch even more! [In order to obtain catch returns it is necessary to guarantee personal confidentiality. It does not breach that guarantee to mention that in 1981 one husband-and-wife team declared a season catch of 416 sea trout from a minor Welsh river. Bearing in mind that there are only 365 days in the year and that you would not wish to eat fish every single day, what does one do with 416 sea trout weighing an average of 2lb each?] This cannot continue! Such bags, while acceptable in the past, **must be a thing of the past**. They will certainly not be acceptable in the future. There is nothing wrong with having the occasional 'exceptional' bag: provided it *is* the exception and provided it does not jeopardise the future or the sport of others.

The future of the sport depends on all existing and would-be sea trout anglers undergoing a rapid transition to stage three and defining more acceptable targets on which to base their pleasure and enjoyment.

There is as much pleasure in actually setting your target as there is in achieving it. Catching the 'special' fish referred to in stage three can be anything in practice. The 'special' fish can be any fish that you want it to be. It is any fish that sets *you* a personal challenge. It can be your first 'specimen' fish – and then a progressively larger fish until you break the record for the fishery, the region, or whatever. It may be your first fish on the dry-fly, or the dap, or from a particularly 'difficult' section of water where nobody *ever* catches anything. It may be to do a 'treble' and catch three fish by different methods in the same day; or to catch every fish on a different fly that you

378

A catch of a lifetime – or irresponsible fishmongering? A memorable day in 1979 by two un-named anglers on an un-named river. A mixed bag of 18 salmon and sea trout before mid-afternoon (six more were caught after this shot, when a dinner engagement intervened). We leave the judgement to you! Remember: the future depends on our attitude *now*. Conservation begins first with you, and then with others like you. (Photo: Anonymous.)

have designed and tied yourself. It may be that your target is never to have a blank – to catch a fish on each and every visit, no matter how adverse the conditions, by whatever legal means *you* prefer.

It may be to become proficient in all branches of the sport or to become expert in just one branch. In fact there is no limit to the ingenuity in setting your own personal targets. It really is a matter of what appeals to you as a particular challenge. Almost anything goes provided that it is legal and provided that it does not entail going to the river with the sole purpose of filling your creel, carboot and deepfreeze! Targets can be set in advance or on the day in question. They can be long-term or short-term. Whatever they are, they must be realistic and ultimately attainable.

We have of necessity been obliged to avoid the anecdotal approach throughout this book. However, the point we are trying to make is best achieved by three short stories.

One angler we know and respect a great deal has caught an *awful lot of salmon* in his time: almost all of which he candidly admits he once sold. He made the transition from 'fisherman' to 'angler' in the late 1960s when he experienced the 'sickening' sight of a river ravaged by the disease UDN (Ulcerative Dermal Necrosis) with dead and dying fish everywhere. This experience – and it was a salutary experience for many – changed his attitude to his fishing completely. Since then he has never sold a fish and now catches very few salmon, for the simple reason that he pursues a very different objective. Instead of the *easy* fishing, his sole purpose is to take a salmon on the fly from every single pool and 'catch' on the Association water that he fishes. Since this consists of some 40 or so locations it represents some monumental target. After 20 years he is about half-way!

He admits that he may never achieve his objective because each 'step' gets progressively harder as each new location becomes more difficult. What it does mean is that instead of catching 60 or 70 salmon a season from the easiest water, he is now down to one or two (if he is lucky). The point is that while he could continue to catch 'lots', *he no longer wishes to do so*. (We once asked him what he would do if he lived to achieve his target. His reply was that he would take up dry-fly fishing and start all over again!)

One of our most enjoyable experiences in recent years was to watch an angler playing a salmon from a boat on a lough in Co. Mayo. We were in another boat on a parallel drift and were so gripped by the urgency and excitement emanating from the successful boat that we put up our rods and kept in touch with what was happening. Eventually, after much to-ing and fro-ing, the fish was boated and we moved off to another drift. At the end of the day we arrived at the jetty alongside the boat which we had been watching earlier in the afternoon. The angler concerned was still on an emotional high and visibly shaking with excitement. Eventually, after a celebratory dram and repeated photographs of angler-with-fish and fish-without-angler, we learned that he had first taken up salmon fishing seven years before on that very water and had played and lost a fish on his first outing. He could only spare a week each season for his fishing and he had returned every year to that same fishery *with one objective*: to catch, as he put it, 'the one that got away'. He had not moved a fish for the next six years – until the moment we saw him playing the 'one that got away'. The fish was not particularly large (about 6lb) but it was very 'special' to him. He had achieved a personal target which, in this case, was not to be beaten by *that* fishery. Knowing the background, the fish became 'special' to us also.

We have mentioned elsewhere that very few of our guests ever catch sea trout when they first fish with us on what is, to them, a new water. After a few visits they usually succeed, although some take longer than others.

A good friend came back year after year to fish in Wales with one single objective: to catch a sea trout weighing more than 3lb. He was an extremely skilful angler of the old-school, who had caught many salmon in Iceland, Canada, Norway, Scotland, England and Ireland. But he had never fished

Wales before, and had never caught a half-decent sea trout. Anyway, he came year after year and every time the conditions were absolutely perfect! But he just didn't catch sea trout.

Then in year 4 or 5 he arrived for a week when the river was distinctly out-of-order. Up and down like a yo-yo and dirty. No chance of fly-fishing and little chance with spinning. (He did *not* fish the worm.) Yes. You guessed! About lunchtime on the first morning he found a pocket of travelling fish and in an hour had his first, second and third largest sea trout ever – 7lb, 5lb and 4lb (or thereabouts).

He was a quiet man who never talked much unless he had something to say. He said very little at the time. But the look of contentment on his face as he carried the fish from the water was something that defied description. He had achieved *his* target: which to many Welsh sea trout anglers was modest in the extreme. Nevertheless, it clearly meant a great deal *to him*.

Apart from our general admonition for every angler to behave responsibly and set new targets which do not entail catching 'a lot of fish', there are two particular aspects of conservation relevant to the future 'quality' of our sea-trout angling that merit further discussion. These relate specifically to a) the preservation of whitling; and b) the return of large sea trout.

We do not know what constitutes the current British record for the greatest number of whitling taken by one angler in a single day – and neither do we want to! Fortunately Welsh sea-trout fisheries still have sufficient runs of larger fish to make it unnecessary for anglers to focus on the whitling

'A baker's dozen.' Thirteen sea trout in an afternoon from the Tywi, and enough in a day for any 'angler'. When fresh-run (note the sea lice on four of the fish) and when in the mood, whitling can provide wonderful sport on the dry fly or wet fly. But enough is enough! You can, of course, always catch-and-release if you wish to fish on after taking your share. (Photo: M. J. Morgan.)

as their only opportunity for some sport, and so 'whitling-bashing' is not widely practised, save on one or two notorious venues. Nevertheless it does occur, and in recent years we have heard of several bags of 50-plus fish and one bag (taken on the worm at night) of 80-plus fish from a tributary of the Tywi.

The topic of whitling conservation has been the subject of long debate in the angling literature since the turn of the century. The basic theme has been that the protection of whitling stocks by the imposition of sensible bag limits and/or size limits would result in an improvement in the fishing because of the resultant increase in the number of larger fish returning to the water.

Hamish Stuart appears to have been the first to have raised what was to become a fairly emotive subject when he advocated returning whitling to the water – unless he wished to retain '. . . one or two for the table owing to the delicate nature of the flesh'. He added: 'Protection against the indiscriminate killing of herling' even by fair angling is, in fact, as important as the regulation of the size of the mesh of nets that can be legally used to take sea trout.' (Herling is the term used for whitling in the north-west of England and in the Solway district.)

He continues: 'I hold. . . that there should be a legal size-limit for herling as far as anglers are concerned, and that the number which any angler may take in a day should be strictly limited.' He concludes: 'The indiscriminate slaughter of herling by anglers now permitted is one of the chief causes – I believe the chief cause – of the scarcity of sea trout in many waters.'

Others, writing later, echoed his views to a lesser extent, but they were restated with fullforce (and a bit more) by Henzell: 'The blunt fact is that, thanks to their numerous foes, sea trout have a difficult enough job to hold their own, let alone to increase; and their task is made more difficult, if not impossible, by selfish and inexperienced anglers, many of whom do not even know the harm that they are doing.' (We like the next bit) 'More than the anglers, I am inclined to blame some hotel keepers who do know what they are doing'. He then goes on to comment on hotel marketing strategies and the need to keep guests satisfied; but suggests that the loss of the one or two guests who are 'bad fishermen' and who would be 'annoyed' if debarred from keeping 'the wretched little fish which are all they can catch' may be necessary. He continues: '. . . but is the loss of one or two such clients of any importance at all when weighed against the certainty that, if this practice is continued, the fishing will deteriorate year by year?' He found it a '. . . sickening sight to see the trays of fish in the evening at some hotels, containing perhaps 8 or 10 sizeable fish, and forty or more finnock.' (Finnock = whitling.) His basic objection was practical. 'Every finnock killed is not only a potential sea trout of the following year, but is also a potential breeder of future sea trout. . . the destruction of small fish is. . . ruining the amenities of many of our [Scottish] waters.'

By and large most authorities have supported the views expressed by

Stuart and Henzell and a few fishery owners and Associations have taken appropriate action by fixing either a bag-limit or a size limit – or both.

Since Henzell wrote his plea for the conservation of whitling, we have learnt more – but not much more – about the biology, ecology and life history of the sea trout. Our own personal view is that whitling should be carefully preserved, but others would disagree. The basis for the disagreement is essentially one of philosophy in relation to traditional and modern concepts of management. Do we want to maximise the landings of fish flesh as a source of food or do we want to maintain and enrich the recreational benefits? Of course Henzell was right in stating that whitling are potentially larger sea trout of the next season and also a potential breeder of future sea trout; but not all whitling survive their sojourn in fresh water to return the next season; and not all whitling enter fresh water to breed anyway. Whether or not you are for or against whitling conservation much depends on where you fish and, thus, the characteristics and composition of the local stock of fish.

As we have seen (Chapter 1) there is much variation between the sea trout of various regions and districts. (Some stocks are slow growing and short-lived. Some stocks are fast-growing and long-lived. Some stocks are made up of a very high proportion of whitling. Some stocks contain only a small proportion of whitling. Some stocks contain a high proportion of previously spawned and large sea trout. Some stocks contain very few previous spawners. On some rivers the bulk of the catch is whitling. Elsewhere it is not.)

In order to make objective decisions we need to know several things: 1) the rate of exploitation by anglers on whitling; 2) the number and 3) the proportion of the whitling component in the run; 4) the survival rate of whitling to the next season; and 5) whether the stock is slow or fast-growing and short or long-lived.

There is only one fishery in the entire British Isles where this information is available: the Burrishoole Fishery, Co. Mayo (again!). The sea trout of this fishery are the slow-growing (= Atlantic feeding) and short-lived type. A 2lb fish is 'good'. A 4lb fish is 'very good indeed'. An 8lb fish has never been recorded.

The question of whitling conservation has recently been resurrected in relation to the Irish west-coast fisheries where a very large part of the stock may consist of whitling. In the Burrishoole fishery about 50 per cent of the stock consists of whitling weighing from 3 to 12oz. It is known that the survival rate of whitling to the next year is about 33 per cent and that the rate of exploitation by anglers on the available stock is about 20 per cent (= fly-only angling). It is also known that any whitling which survived to return to the river for a second time will weigh about 1lb 3oz.

Armed with these facts it is possible to come to some conclusions about the benefits and disadvantages of seeking to improve the stock of larger (and older) fish by reducing the take of whitling. Thus: for every 100 whitling returned with a total weight of 75lb, 33 will survive to the next season weighing 39lb. Of these 20 per cent will be caught. So the return of 100 whitling in one year would produce roughly 6.6 extra fish weighing 9lb 9oz the next year. Is this an attractive management option? On balance the return of whitling does not seem to do much to improve the quality of the angling. Does it do anything for the future abundance of the stock by increasing the breeding stock?

We have shown (Chapter 1) that a large proportion of the whitling run may consist of fish not destined to spawn. Precisely what proportion do mature on their first return is not known – it may vary enormously between rivers – but a figure of 25 per cent has been determined from one study. Thus only 25 of our 100 whitling are potential spawners. Assuming that half are males and the other half are females producing about 800 eggs per pound weight, then we could expect to gain 7,900 extra eggs deposited at spawning time – which is not a lot.

On the basis of this evidence it would seem that the removal of whitling by anglers is relatively unimportant in determining the overall level of sea-trout stocks or in improving the quality (= size) of the fish. However, the conclusions from this study should *not* be regarded as typical of what might apply elsewhere on a fishery characterised by a long-lived and fast-growing stock of fish. It is not possible to make a similar comparison on another river because, sadly, the necessary information on survival rates and exploitation rates does not exist for any other fishery in the British Isles. In order to test the benefits of whitling conservation on, say, the Dyfi we must use the same values as derived for the Burrishoole and, thus, make certain assumptions which may or may not be valid.

Dyfi whitling are about the same size as the Irish fish (12oz) but they are much larger (2lb 4oz) on their second return to the river. A proportion of the whitling stock survives to make up to eight spawning visits with a steady increase in weight to about 4lb on their third return, 6lb on their fourth return etc, achieving a maximum of about 16lb on their eighth return (as .8sm+ fish). Thus: 100 whitling at 12oz will weigh 75lb. If all are returned and 33 per cent survive, then 33 should return the next year weighing 74lb. Assuming an exploitation rate of 20 per cent, 6.6 fish weighing 15lb would be caught by anglers. This leaves 26 fish weighing 59lb – of which 50 per cent should be females contributing 23,600 eggs to the success of spawning (which may be useful).

In the next generation, again using the same assumptions, the 26 fish that survived to spawn should produce 9 fish weighing 36lb on their third return to freshwater, of which the yield to anglers would be 2 fish weighing 8lb, and the egg yield would be 11,200 ova. Some of these fish would survive further return visits to fresh water, albeit in decreasing proportions.

Clearly the question of whitling conservation on a river with a long-lived and fast-growing stock of fish has a very different complexion to that on rivers with short-lived and slow-growing stocks, especially if the whitling component of the stock is very high to start with. The need for further research into this important topic is evident!

Our cautious view is that whitling should be conserved to a greater or lesser degree on all fisheries with long-lived stocks. Elsewhere we would question the morality of taking an enormous bag of whitling and suggest that some form of regulation (either a bag limit or a size limit) is appropriate, if only to reinforce the angling ethic – rather than for any other reason associated with biology or management. What on earth do you do with 200 whitling, or even 50 for that matter?

The whitling has been termed the 'breakfast fish' – and very tasty it is when served with bacon or when hot-smoked and served cold as a 'starter course'. *But* – how many dinner parties does one give these days? We see no reason why anyone should want to take more than, say, six fish in any day. Having done so, they can always continue fishing, but on a 'catch-and-release' basis. The days of deriving great pride and acclaim from taking a prodigious bag of wild fish are gone forever. The fisherman who returns to the hotel to display his 40 whitling in the lobby in 'competition' with the catch of other guests does not merit acclaim: and certainly should not feel proud! It is the *angler* who had caught 40 and returned 34 that *we* wish to meet at the bar for a drink (or two).

We should add, by way of final comment on this topic, that we recognise that whitling conservation on some west-coast Irish fisheries may not be as appropriate or as necessary as on some Welsh, Scottish and English fisheries. In order to maximise the landings of fish flesh it may be appropriate to 'hammer' the whitling stocks even harder than at present on some fisheries. But the needs of conservation and management are one thing; the angling ethic is another thing which is quite different altogether. Whether or not you conserve and protect whitling by voluntary restraint, local regulation, or bye-law, depends on many factors relating to the status and well-being of the fishery and the need to conserve whitling. Whether or not you wish to catch a 'world-record' bag of whitling depends on whether you are (or wish to be seen as) an angler or a fisherman/fishmonger.

While the benefits of returning small whitling to the improvement of the fishing in later seasons may be open to question in relation to slow-growing and short-lived stocks, the conservation of large sea trout may be of far greater significance and value on many fisheries where such fish occur. There are two reasons for this: one practical and one biological.

Large sea trout are usually (but not always) old sea trout that have survived several spawning visits to fresh water and whose flesh has progressively deteriorated in colour, taste and texture after each visit. In some fish it can be off-white in colour, coarse, and almost without taste. It can still be eaten if prepared carefully, or it can be sent for smoking for the want of anything better to do with it. But it will never be the same to eat as a small maiden fish of 3–5lb in weight.

Apart from any gastronomic considerations there is the far more important

385

biological reason for considering the return of large long-lived sea trout. Such fish have proven their ability to survive longer and spawn more often than younger (smaller) sea trout, and on each return to the river they are larger in size – and it has been established that larger eggs produce bigger fry which survive better. Larger fish can also utilise larger spawning gravels than smaller fish and, in so doing, may result in a greater area of river being colonised to the benefit of increased yields in the future.

Fecundity data on sea trout are limited; but if we assume that each hen fish produces roughly 800 eggs for each one pound of body-weight we will not be far wrong. The following calculation illustrates the contribution that a 12lb sea trout may make to the success of spawning over its life-span up until the time of capture. The fish was in its ninth year of life when caught. It had spawned in the five preceding years and had gone to sea as a two-year-old smolt (scale formula = 2.1 + 5 sm+):

Sea-Age on return	.1+	.2+	.3+	.4+	.5+	(.6+)
	3	6	8	10	11	(12)
Eggs Deposited	2400	4800	6400	8000	8800	(9600)

This is fairly typical of large Welsh fish, and its flesh would be past its best. During its five previous visits to fresh water it had produced a total of 30,400 ova (equivalent to the potential egg yield from a single fish of 38lb weight!). If it were returned to spawn for a sixth time it would yield a further 9,600 eggs (assuming it survived until October/November).

Large sea trout of the long-lived type clearly have valuable genes and their conservation is of singular importance as the exploitation rate on the stock increases with greater fishing pressure. On some fisheries once famed for their large sea trout it is evident that such specimen fish are now much less common than in years past despite (or probably because of) increased fishing effort. It may be that their apparent decrease is linked in some way to changes in the weather and climate over the years, but another plausible explanation is that the probability of capture *on each return* to the river has increased as a result of greater fishing pressure so that proportionately fewer now survive long enough to reach an old age and, thus, a large size.

If the policy of the fishery is to maximise the yield of fish flesh to the rods then it is, without doubt, wasteful to return large sea trout. But who wants several pounds weight of tasteless flesh anyway? Not all large sea trout are multiple spawners. Many large sea trout in the Tweed and Coquet are short-lived and reach a large size because of very good sea feeding. Few large Tweed fish survive to make repeated visits to and from fresh water. Elsewhere, however, it is likely that any fish weighing more than 10lb will have made three, four, five or more spawning visits to the river. Such fish are usually quite easy to distinguish from a maiden fish because they tend to become more heavily spotted on each return to the river.

The quality of our sport depends upon both quantity and variety. Anyone who has fished one of the less-well-managed reservoir fisheries which is regularly stocked on a put-and-take basis will appreciate what we mean when we say that there is little pleasure in fishing when you *know* that every fish you catch will weigh almost precisely 12oz and measure almost exactly 12 inches, because that is all that the water contains. Large sea trout provide great variety and do much to enhance the appeal of the fishing to many anglers. They may be important also in terms of spawning success and stock recruitment. So pause to think before you reach for your priest to kill that double-figure specimen sea trout that represents your 'fish-of-a-lifetime'. If you can't eat it, why kill it? Its capture gave you much pleasure, and you will always have that memory. Why deny the same pleasure to others?

In addition to a change in the attitude of anglers to their sport, there is a desperate need for the fisheries themselves to be managed on a scientific basis. The basic principles of fisheries management are quite simple and have been understood for a long time. But they have yet to be applied to the way in which we manage and regulate our fisheries to ensure that they remain in a healthy condition and, where scope and need exists, that they are improved.

The crux of all management must be to ensure the optimal escapement of fish into the spawning population, and to regulate the catch so that exploitation is restricted to that component of the stock that represents the surplus of adult fish over and above the number required for spawning and regeneration of the stock.

We stated earlier that it would perhaps have been simpler and more concise to tell you *what we do not know* about sea trout rather than to refer to the scanty knowledge that is currently available. We must stress that there is still a great deal to learn in respect of the biology, ecology, behaviour, genetics and population dynamics of sea trout. If our sea trout fisheries are to have a healthy future there must be a concerted effort to fill the many gaps in our knowledge that seriously limit our ability to manage the resource effectively and efficiently.

We should add that while much has been learned from the research carried out by the Salmon Research Trust of Ireland Inc. on the Burrishoole system in Co. Mayo over the last 30 years, the sea trout of that area of the short-lived, slow-growing Irish (Atlantic) type, and, in addition, there are certain physical characteristics of the system that make it somewhat atypical. It is to be questioned whether or not the results obtained from the Burrishoole have any wider application elsewhere. Thus, with the single and notable exception of the Burrishoole, we do not have the slightest idea how many fish enter our rivers in any year – either during the fishing season or after it! While we may (or may not) know with any confidence how many sea trout are caught in any season, we do not know whether the rate of exploitation is at, above, or the maximum that the fishery can sustain because we do not know how many spawning fish are required to regenerate the stock at its existing level. Neither do we know whether the 'existing' level of stock in any fishery is at or below its maximum. Thus, in short, not only do we not know what it is that we are managing, but we would be unable to manage it properly even if we did! There is almost a complete void in our knowledge about the juvenile stage throughout the period of freshwater residence from the fry to smolt stage and there is still much to be learnt about the marine stage in the life history of the fish.

While there is probably a genetic difference between sea trout and brown trout, the management implications of the question 'What is a sea trout?' are still just as important as when it was first asked some 70 years ago.

The characteristics of Scottish sea trout have been described by the prodigious scale reading investigations of Nall, Went, and others have similarly characterised Irish sea trout stocks, but there are still gaps in those regions and an obvious need to characterise Welsh and English sea trout stocks in much greater detail. (Many of Nall's characterisations are more than 50 years old. They bear repetition. A great deal can change in half a century!)

What we do know about Scottish, Irish and Welsh sea trout fisheries serves to suggest that there is an enormous range of variation in the characteristics of the stocks between and (sometimes) within different geographical areas. Work on the Atlantic salmon has shown that many of these differences have a genetic basis (e.g. fecundity, smolt age, homing ability, extent of marine migrations, growth rate, longevity, sea-age, time of return, etc). It is now widely recognised that future management must seek to maintain the genetic integrity of different local stocks. These differences may have an adaptive value for the rivers where they occur. Their recognition and preservation may be vitally important for the future management and survival of the resource.

Considerable importance is now being given worldwide to maintaining the genetic integrity of Atlantic salmon stocks (and sub-stocks). If this is important for salmon, *then it is equally as important for sea trout.*

There are many other gaps in our knowledge which have direct or indirect implications for our future ability to manage the resource: the relevance of conserving whitling and large sea trout, and the practical merits of catch-and-release (do released fish survive to spawn and/or return the next year?), are patently obvious future research 'areas'. So too is research into the seaward migration of autumn smolts and parr; the competitive relationships between salmon and sea trout and between sea trout and brown trout is another. The shopping list of 'research needs' could be endless and it would be gratuitously confusing to go any further. Nevertheless, we sincerely hope we have made our point (which for those who missed it was that we know very little that is relevant to the future management of the resource). 'Ignorance may be bliss': but there is too much at stake to be complacent!

20 · ADVICE FOR BEGINNERS

We are frequently asked 'Where can I find good sea trout fishing?' Our first response is invariably to ask a whole series of related questions. Where do you live? How much can you afford? Is your fishing limited to just annual vacations, or can you fish on a regular basis over the season? Do you want night fishing or day fishing? River fishing or lake fishing? Fly-only or spinning and worming? Big fish or lots of fish? Do you want exclusive fishing or will you share the water with others? Hotel or club fishing? And so on. Eventually we are usually able to provide the requested information.

'Good' is a very subjective term when applied to sea-trout angling. Every angler has different perspectives, aspirations and opportunities. Good fishing is *not*, and never should be, catching a lot of fish. It is the circumstances of their capture that are important. The personal targets set, and achieved. The how, where, when and why of the catch for each individual fish. The quality of the total experience; both at the time and in retrospect.

We both consider ourselves fortunate to live within a short drive of some of the finest sea-trout fishing in the world in terms of the quality and quantity of the fisheries and their availability at a very cheap cost. In fact we are spoilt for choice! For an outlay of some £300–400 a year we could readily join angling clubs on some five or six different rivers no more than an hour by car from our homes with access to, perhaps, 100 miles of river. Few are as lucky. [We calculate that the worst place to live in terms of its distance from worthwhile season or day-ticket fishing is probably Suffolk on the east coast of England].

Earlier we declared that this is not an 'Angling Guide' and that all we could do here was to point you in the right direction. Once you have decided what it is you want of your sea-trout fishing in terms of frequency of visit, type, cost, quantity and quality, etc, you can start to home in on specifies such as regions, districts, venues.

Many angling guides are available from various publishing houses, fishery authorities and tourist agencies. But there are other sources of information. Several country-sport magazines contain adverts for fishing. Perhaps the best source of information is the monthly publication *Trout and Salmon*, available from newsagents. This contains many inserts by estates, hotels and private owners advertising salmon and sea-trout fishing. Angling Associations, however, rarely advertise (they do not need to do so!). Another way of obtaining information for the novice is to join the local branch of the Salmon and Trout Association (see p. 395). Inevitably, you will encounter someone who fishes for sea trout and who will be only too happy to help you. In England and Wales you could telephone the appropriate Water Authority; in Scotland, the appropriate District Fisheries Board; or in the Republic of Ireland the appropriate Regional Fisheries Board.

Having decided what you want (and where and when) then *don't delay – book today*. We mean that seriously. Many of the better-known fisheries are heavily booked in advance. Do not expect to arrive at your chosen venue and purchase your fishing that same day. Many of the best-known hotel waters are pre-booked during the peak periods (July/August/September) for several years ahead. Many of the better-known Association waters have limited season membership with a waiting list of up to ten years or more. Weekly permits are often reserved at least a year in advance, maybe more, and day tickets are often limited in number and availability. Some of the best sea-trout fishing in Scotland and the 'Islands' is so renowned that it does not *need* to be included in angling guides, or to advertise at all! Some of the most enjoyable (and, therefore, some of the 'best') sea-trout fishing we have experienced has been on small waters unknown to all but a few. If you are disposed towards club fishing then get your name on the waiting list of three or four associations as soon as possible. You can always refuse the 'offer' of a season rod if you have already accepted a previous offer that appeals to you more.

Anyway, having chosen and gained access to your fishing then *stick to it* for at least three or (more likely) five seasons if it has potential. *Do not* expect to catch fish immediately. Getting the best out of a fishery takes time, effort and commitment. In our experience the common mistake is to change venue each season because *you* did not catch fish, many fish, or do as well as the other rods on your last visit. *Give the fishery – and yourself – a reasonable chance.*

Between us we take many guests to our favourite fisheries each season; and we were once very concerned if they did not catch fish – particularly when *we* did. We are now wiser! We are *'happy'* if they see fish; *'pleased'* if they move a fish; *'delighted'* if they play a fish and *'ecstatic'* if they actually land one! Very few of our guests give us cause to be ecstatic the first time that they fish with us. Our combined experience is that it is unusual for an angler to catch fish the first time out on a completely new and strange water; no matter how skilled and versatile he or she might be. This applies particularly at night! Rivers, and lakes, must be learnt. Each is different, and the learning curve can be short or long depending on the individual angler.

Thus, having selected your fishing; and having resolved to stick to it for a few seasons at least, what next? Assuming that it is a reasonable length of river, then our best advice is to focus your attention on perhaps no more than three or four different pools or glides *and to learn them like the back of your hand*. Learn every inch of water so that you know where the fish lie, where they take; *and where they don't.* Get to know *every* rock and over-hanging branch, *every* swirl and eddy. Become so familiar *with every characteristic of the water* that you could fish it wearing a blindfold – because that is, more or less, what you will have to do at night. Night fishing requires an intimate feel, an empathy (almost an affinity) for the section of water being fished.

Having learnt your favoured sections of water, then learn them again at *all* stages of river flow from drought conditions to a bank high flood. We cannot stress too strongly the importance of river level in determining when, where, how (and whether or not) you fish any water. The difference between success and failure may be no more than fishing in the right place at the right time; and a yard or two one way or another as the river level fluctuates may be crucial!

You may choose to concentrate on learning the same sections of water for use with all methods or to select different sections for the fly, the spinner, and the bait. Not all sections will be suitable for all methods. A good fly pool on normal flows may not be a good worming pool on floodwater: while a good low water worming pool may be impossible to fish with the fly.

A useful tip if you fish Association waters is to find one or two sections of water that are not popular with the other anglers sharing the fishing. Club fishing can sometimes get overcrowded during the peak weeks of the season so that all the best water is usually occupied before sunset. (Most *good* Associations prohibit the 'booking' of pools for night fishing: but it is almost impossible to prevent it happening just the same.) Rather than share an *overcrowded pool* we try to fish elsewhere, if we can; and so we have identified one or two places where it is very unlikely that we will find another angler. Inevitably these are not the better pools, but, provided there is at least a chance of a fish, it is usually better to fish in comfort than to feel crowded. Such places may be hard to find but we now know of several on all our favourite rivers. They may be unpopular with other anglers because, for example, they are long flat glides with no flow to move the fly around properly. They may be small 'pots' with difficult back-eddies; they may be over-grown or have high banks behind the angler to make casting difficult. They may necessitate wearing chest-waders and fishing upstream. And they usually entail a long walk from the nearest access point. If you are a regular angler on club fisheries, then try to find such places in advance so that if the need arises you can fish in peace and tranquillity. There is nothing more galling than trudging along the river bank at night looking for somewhere (anywhere) to fish. It wastes valuable fishing time – and you will never feel comfortable if you finish up on a completely unknown and strange piece of water that you have never fished before.

Many anglers tend to view Association fishing with disdain, mainly because they object to sharing the water with a large number of other anglers and partly because some club fishing has a very bad reputation.

It is true that there are some badly managed club waters where almost

391

anything is condoned and where some remarkably bad behaviour may be encountered on the river bank; but there are also many very good clubs with an exemplary record of forward-looking and conservation-orientated management. Several of the larger clubs in Wales, for example, now regulate and restrict spinning and bait fishing to certain sections of river or to floodwater. Membership is frequently limited to prevent overcrowding and over-fishing, and some employ their own keepers. Yes, Association water can get overcrowded at times when the fishing is at its peak and a larger than normal proportion of members turn out, but at most times there is no real problem. We normally choose to fish club waters as the disadvantages of having to share are far outweighed by the advantages of low-cost and the extent of water available. Moreover, it is often not unusual to find a higher standard of bankside courtesy and manners on an Association water than on some of the high cost, limited length, 'exclusive' fisheries. Visiting rods are usually made to feel welcome by the local and regular anglers who will often invite you to 'fish through' in front of them or, if night fishing, to 'join' them on a section of water. Provided *your* approach is correct in the first place, you need have little concern about your reception. Of course you may encounter someone who is less than civil or courteous; but that is just as likely to occur on any other water that you do not have for your exclusive use. There seems to be an inverse relationship between cost and manners in our experience: the higher the price the lower the standard of bankside courtesy!

Association fishing provides many opportunities for the angler of more modest means. It is by no means second-rate in respect of the quality of the fishing available and it can result in many pleasurable and long-lasting friendships being formed over the years.

The learning curve for any new water can be much shortened if you make friends with a local angler who fishes the water regularly. Good local contacts are very important for any fishery if you live some distance away. It is very useful indeed to have one, or two, local anglers that you can telephone before you set off from home in order to find out what state the river is in and how it is fishing; to find out who has been catching what, where and how; to ascertain the pattern and strength of the runs and their distribution within the river; and other relevant intelligence that may even make you decide to extend the trip – or postpone it. Even better than finding someone local that you can telephone is to find someone local *who will telephone you* whenever the river is in good order and fishing well so that you can drop everything for a quick, unscheduled visit.

If you can find an Association with fishing spread along a particular river to embrace sections in the lower, middle and upper reaches, then join it. If you can't, then consider joining two clubs – one with water near the tideway and one with water on the upper reaches. This is so that you stand a chance of finding fish in a wet year (when they may run straight through the lower sections) and in a drought year (when they accumulate above the tidal reaches and do not penetrate far upriver). Most sea-trout rivers are relatively short and the distribution of the fish can vary considerably from year to year with the strength of the runs and the rainfall. Usually the lower sections are most productive and provide the best fishing; but this is not always so. In some years the middle reaches or, occasionally, the upper reaches can fish as well or even better.

Certain aspects of the above advice apply equally to lake fishing. Local knowledge is very important and it is much more difficult in our experience to become familiar with a large loch or lough than it is with a section of river.

But while local advice and guidance is invaluable, do not let it blinker your vision and prevent you from trying out your own ideas and initiatives or developing your own particular styles and preferences. Just because everyone else fishes with small wet flies on a sink-tip line, do not let that stop you trying a dry fly or a large lure on a sunk line if that is what *you* really want to do. Our main theme throughout this book has been to stress the need for flexibility, versatility, and a degree of competence with a range of styles and techniques. That message is fundamental to our approach.

Night fishing can be very tiring, especially if you have been unable to rest up during the day. We all need sleep. Think carefully about driving more than a few miles as dawn approaches. The second author has twice fallen asleep at the wheel driving no more than 40 miles back home after a day's work followed by an all-night fishing session, and luckily survived two fairly major car crashes as a result. He now always dozes off for an hour or so in his car before setting off from the river.

If you are on a fishing trip or holiday for several days, try to pace yourself so that you get the best out of the fishing. Every season we encounter visiting anglers on weekly permits who are 'fished out' by the third or fourth day because they could not resist the temptation to fish all day and then continue through the night. You cannot fish properly if you are tired, listless, and short-tempered through lack of sleep. It is, therefore, · necessary to decide whether your preference or best option is to fish by day or by night and to sacrifice one to benefit your success with the other.

If you have been fishing through the night we suggest that the best strategy is to go to bed and sleep for as long as you can (not always easy in daylight). You can fish for a few hours around lunch time if you must as this can double as your daytime reconnaisance (page 202), but then force yourself to bed in the afternoon for two or three hours and only go out again an hour or so before sunset refreshed and ready for the next session of night fishing. If the best of the fishing is to be had in daylight – say just after a summer spate – then fish until dusk and forget about night fishing until the daylight fishing wanes.

If you reserve accommodation at a guest-house or a non-fishing hotel check: a) that they do not mind you returning at 4 am; b) that they will serve you a late breakfast at 10 or 11 am; c) that they do not mind you going to bed at 2 pm; d) that they can deepfreeze your fish; e) that they will serve dinner at 6 pm; and f) that they will keep refilling flasks with coffee, tea, or whatever, at a *sensible* price! (If you explain that you are coming for the fishing they *may* understand!)

Always make sure that you read (and understand) the local fishery bye-laws and the rules and regulations relating to the fishing. Do not assume that they are the same from one region to another or even from one river, or section of river, to another. The use of floats, maggots, worms, prawns, shrimps and spinners may be tightly controlled or even prohibited altogether. Above all, DO NOT FORGET TO SUBMIT YOUR CATCH RETURN by the required date, in the required format, and with *complete* details of your catch. This information is vitally important to the statutory agencies and to the owner of the fishing. It is used in many different contexts to define various policies for the maintenance, improvement and regulation of the fishery. Do not include just your better fish and leave out the 20 or 30 small whitling that you also took over the season. Their inclusion in the catch record is equally important. We suggest that anyone who fishes regularly over the season should make a habit of completing the catch return form *after each visit*. It may be impossible to remember in November what you caught in terms of number of fish, individual sizes, and methods of capture in May or June.

Remember also that public interest in all things relating to the protection of the environment and the conservation of wildlife has increased dramatically in recent years. The future of our sport may well depend on how others see us. Recent reports on the damage caused to swans by discarded lead fishing weights and the miles of nylon line left mindlessly around our waterways have severely tarnished the anglers' historical claim to be the protector of the aquatic environment. Many people see angling as being cruel and no different to any other blood sport. There are many who would abolish blood sports tomorrow, and there is already one militant animal rights group targeted directly against angling. Respect your fish and kill it cleanly. Dispose of your nylon properly, and do not fish with ultra-fine lines that will snap if you hook the slightest snag or get stuck into a half-decent fish. Never fish from a position where you cannot follow your fish if it decides to run for any distance downstream or upstream or where it would be impossible to land it. We may never vanquish the opposition but we need not give them the ammunition to fire at us!

Finally, do not just a 'taker' be. Try to give something back to the sport that will give you so much pleasure and enjoyment: or which has already done so. Think of those anglers of the next generation and try to ensure that the fisheries of the future are at least as good as they are now. How you do this is really up to you. You may decide to join the Anglers Co-operative Association – a private charity that takes legal action on behalf of fisheries owners and angling clubs against polluters to obtain financial reparation following fishkill incidents. Or you may take out a covenant with the Atlantic Salmon Trust Ltd – another private charity (whose remit includes sea trout also) that acts as a catalyst to bring about improvements in the legislation and

Anglers of the future being taught the 'Gentle Art'. Hopefully there will be fish for them to catch. Much depends on us! (Photo: S. Oliver.)

basis for scientific management relating to the fisheries resource at a national and international level. Both organisations have achieved a great deal; but could do much more if they were properly funded. The Salmon & Trout Association is another important organisation worthy of membership. It publishes a twice-yearly journal *The Salmon and Trout Magazine*, and has done a great deal over the last 83 years to further the interests of game fishing.

If you are a member of an angling club then you should certainly attend its Annual General Meeting and contribute to its current and future well-being and strength. Do not leave everything to the dedication of the secretary and a few other members of the 'executive'. *Their efforts on your behalf* deserve your interest and support at the very least. Far too many anglers are apathetic. They will complain bitterly about the decline in the fishing: but do nothing *positive* to help. If *you* see a poaching incident or encounter a pollution, then do not write in about it and complain that it ruined your day's fishing. The correct procedure is to get to the nearest telephone as quickly as possible (*i.e. immediately*) and inform the local bailiff, the fishery owner/club secretary or the police. The keyword is immediately – the next day will be too late to do anything about it.

Finally, whatever you do *never, ever, take your fishing for granted.* That you can enjoy it today is a consequence of the efforts of your predecessors: and their predecessors. That others may enjoy it in the future is down to *you* and others like you.

* * *

Tight Lines!

INDEX